Atlantic
Ocean

Pacific
Ocean

Pacific
Ocean

Indian
Ocean

HABITAT Gray wolves live throughout a large part of North America.

BEHAVIOR Wolves live in family groups called packs. The pack hunts together.

COVERING Wolves have two coats of fur that keep them warm in winter. They can stay warm in temperatures as cold as –40° C.

GROOMING Wolves sometimes bathe in rivers or streams to wash mud from their fur.

New York City Edition
Science

Gray Wolf

Harcourt

SCHOOL PUBLISHERS

Visit the Learning Site!
www.harcourtschool.com

Gray Wolf

ISBN 13: 978-0-15-374543-0
ISBN 10: 0-15-374543-6

1 2 3 4 5 6 7 8 9 10 032 16 15 14 13 12 11 10 09 08 07

Consulting Authors

Michael J. Bell
Assistant Professor of Early Childhood Education
College of Education
West Chester University of Pennsylvania

Michael A. DiSpezio
Curriculum Architect
JASON Academy
Cape Cod, Massachusetts

Marjorie Frank
Former Adjunct, Science Education
Hunter College
New York, New York

Gerald H. Krockover
Professor of Earth and Atmospheric Science Education
Purdue University
West Lafayette, Indiana

Joyce C. McLeod
Adjunct Professor
Rollins College
Winter Park, Florida

Barbara ten Brink
Science Specialist
Austin Independent School District
Austin, Texas

Carol J. Valenta
Senior Vice President
St. Louis Science Center
St. Louis, Missouri

Barry A. Van Deman
President and CEO
Museum of Life and Science
Durham, North Carolina

Dear Students,

What's special about this Science textbook? It has been printed just for students in New York City. Inside you will find exciting hands-on science investigations and engaging minds-on science content. You will also discover features like Science Spin from Weekly Reader and lots of links to online explorations.

Using this book will ensure that you gain the Major Understandings in the New York State Science Core Curriculum and New York City Scope and Sequence. The contents have been arranged around the chapters you will be studying. A special Table of Contents has also been provided just for students in New York City.

This book was changed to match the New York City Scope and Sequence. The extra chapters were removed. This will help you and your classmates focus on those science topics that are required on your grade level.

We hope that you have a successful and exciting year in SCIENCE!
Sincerely,
Harcourt School Publishers

UNIT 1 Animals and Plants in Their Environment

What roles do plants and animals play in their environments?

▼ HARCOURT SCIENCE CHAPTERS AND LESSONS

UNIT 2 Electricity and Magnetism

What are the properties of electricity and magnetism?

▼ HARCOURT SCIENCE CHAPTERS AND LESSONS

UNIT 3 Properties of Water
What makes water so special?

▼ HARCOURT SCIENCE CHAPTERS AND LESSONS

UNIT 4 Interactions of Air, Water, & Land
How do natural events affect our world?

▼ HARCOURT SCIENCE CHAPTERS AND LESSONS

Enrichment Chapter

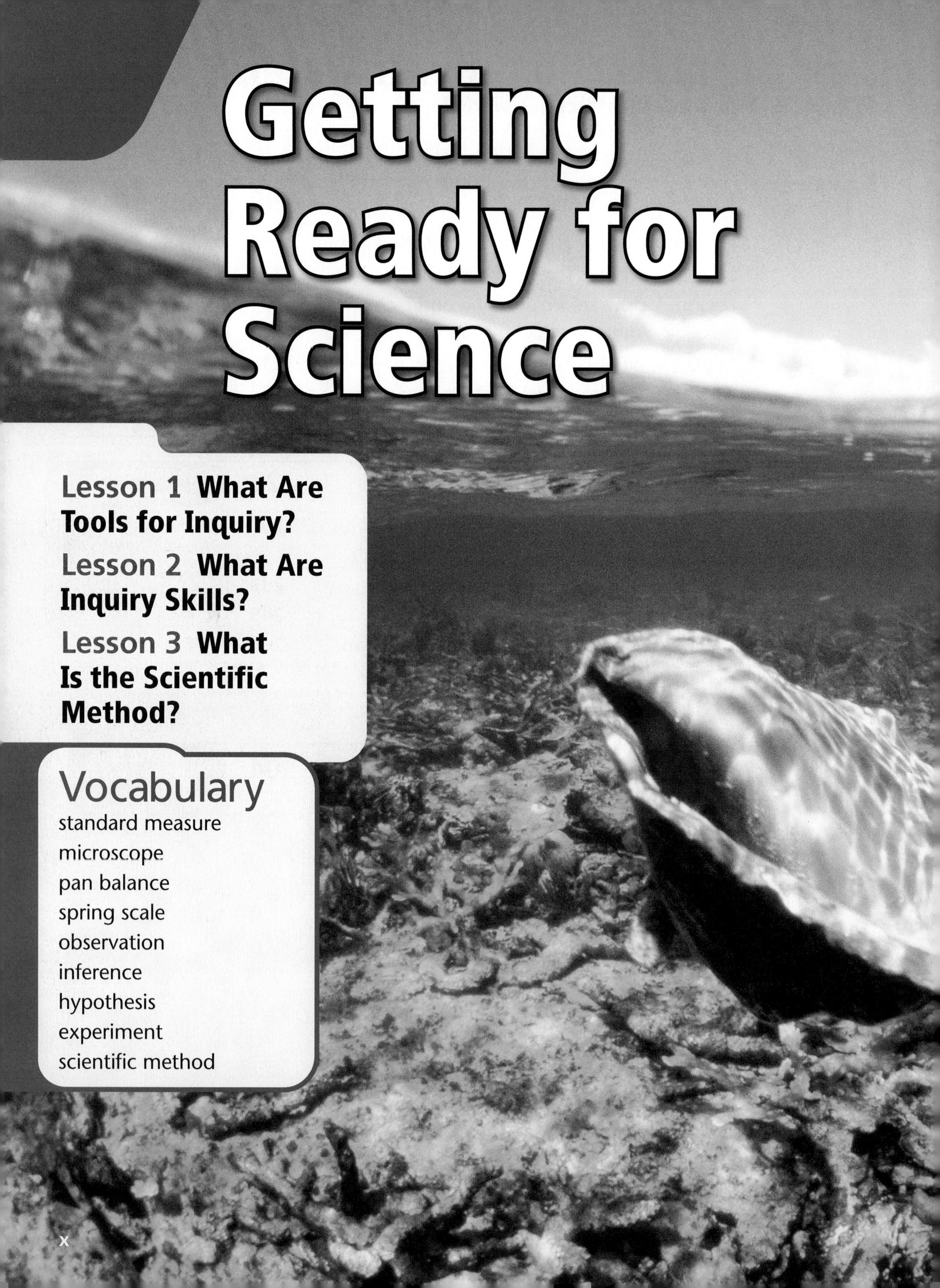

Getting Ready for Science

Lesson 1 What Are Tools for Inquiry?

Lesson 2 What Are Inquiry Skills?

Lesson 3 What Is the Scientific Method?

Vocabulary

standard measure
microscope
pan balance
spring scale
observation
inference
hypothesis
experiment
scientific method

What do YOU wonder?

Does "doing science" require special skills? Which science skills is this young snorkeler using?

What Are Tools for Inquiry?

Fast Fact

Out-of-This-World Tools The wheels of the Mars Rovers were tools for exploration. They exposed layers of soil. Scientists used the soil data to draw conclusions about Mars. In the Investigate, you will draw conclusions about ways to measure.

Measuring with Straws

Materials
- plastic straws
- 2 cups
- classroom objects
- water
- marker

Procedure

1 Use straws to measure length and width (distance). For example, you might measure this textbook or another flat object. Record your measurements.

2 Now use straws to measure the distance around a round object (its circumference). Hint: Flatten the straws before you start. Record your measurements.

3 Next, work with a partner to find a way to use straws to measure the amount of water in a cup (its volume). Record your measurements.

Draw Conclusions

1. Compare your measurements with those of other students. What can you conclude?

2. **Inquiry Skill** Scientists measure carefully so they can record changes accurately. Why do all scientists need to use the same unit of measurement when working on the same problems?

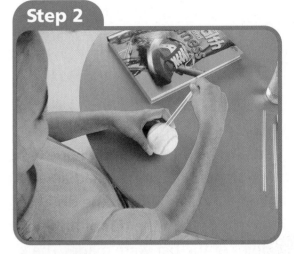

Step 2

Step 3

Investigate Further

How could you mark a straw to divide it into smaller units? How would this change the way you collect data? What might be a reason to do this?

Reading in Science

VOCABULARY
standard measure p. 4
microscope p. 6
pan balance p. 8
spring scale p. 8

SCIENCE CONCEPTS
▶ how scientists use tools to measure, observe, and manipulate
▶ how to use tools properly and safely

 READING FOCUS SKILL
MAIN IDEA AND DETAILS
Look for tools that scientists use.

```
          Main Idea
    ┌─────────┼─────────┐
  detail    detail    detail
```

Tools for Measuring Distance

Long ago, people sometimes used body parts to measure distance. For example, King Henry I of England had an iron bar made. It was as long as the distance from his nose to the tips of his fingers. Copies of the bar were made. The king told everyone to use the bars to measure things. This bar became the standard length for one yard. A **standard measure** is an accepted measurement.

When it was introduced, the meter, another unit of length, was not based on a body part. It was defined as 1/10,000,000 of the distance from the North Pole to the equator. Imagine measuring that distance!

These units of measurement may seem strange. Yet they helped people agree on the lengths of objects and the distances between places.

 MAIN IDEA AND DETAILS Why do we have standard units of measure?

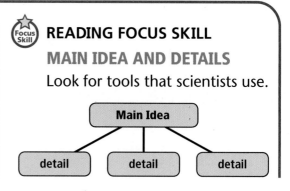

▼ A flexible measuring tape can measure circumference.

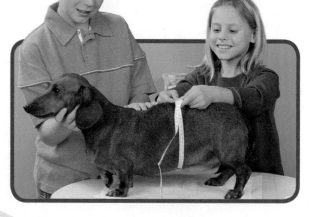

Geologists and surveyors use this tool to measure large distances.

◀ A ruler measures length. Place the first line of the ruler at one end of the object. The point on the ruler where the object ends is its length.

Tools for Measuring Volume

Cooks use cups and spoons to measure ingredients for a recipe. Scientists measure volume with tools, too. To find the volume of a liquid, you put it into a container such as a measuring cup, a beaker, or a graduate. The numbers on the side of the container show the volume of the liquid. Never use tools from your science lab for measuring food or medicine!

To measure the volume of a solid, multiply its length by its width by its height. For example, one box has a length of 4 centimeters and a width of 2 centimeters. Its height is 2 centimeters. The volume is 4 cm x 2 cm x 2 cm = 16 cubic centimeters.

MAIN IDEA AND DETAILS How do you measure the volume of a solid? Of a liquid?

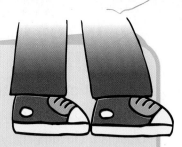

Insta-Lab

Personal Measuring Tools

Think of other ways that you could measure distance or volume, using items you have at home or in the classroom. Test your new measuring tools, and exchange ideas with other students.

To measure a liquid, place the graduate on a flat surface. Your eyes should be even with the top of the liquid. The volume is the marking that is closest to the top of the liquid.

◀ Droppers are used to measure small amounts of liquids.

Tools for Observing and Handling

Sometimes scientists need to observe an object closely. Certain tools can help them observe details they might not be able to see using just their eyes.

A hand lens makes things look larger than they are. It magnifies them. Hold the lens a few centimeters in front of your eye. Then move the object closer to the lens until you can see it clearly. Never let the lens touch your eye. Never use it to look at the sun!

Forceps let you pick up a sharp or prickly object without getting hurt. They can also protect a delicate object from too much handling. However, you must squeeze the forceps gently.

A magnifying box is sometimes called a bug box. Students often use it to observe live insects. An insect can move around in the box while you watch.

A **microscope** makes an object look several times bigger than it is. The microscope on the next page has several lenses that can magnify a little or a lot. Two knobs help you adjust the image until you can see it clearly.

 MAIN IDEA AND DETAILS How do the tools on these pages help scientists?

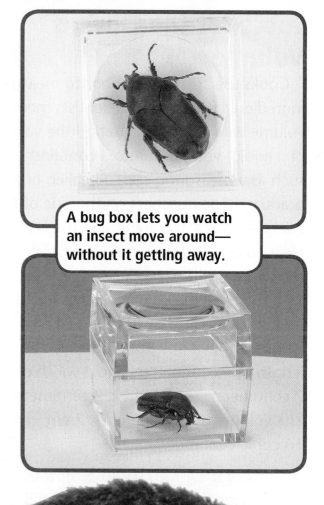

A bug box lets you watch an insect move around— without it getting away.

A hand lens allows you to see many details. When you use forceps to hold an object, you can observe it without your fingers getting in the way.

As you look through the eyepiece with one eye, close your other eye.

Use the coarse-adjustment knob to get the image nearly in focus.

Use the fine-adjustment knob to bring the image into clear focus.

The arm supports the lenses.

The stage holds the object you are studying.

The base supports the microscope.

Other Tools

Many other tools can help you measure. A thermometer can measure the temperature of the air or of a liquid. Be sure to touch the thermometer as little as possible. Otherwise, it will just measure the warmth of your fingers. Be careful! Glass thermometers break easily.

A **pan balance** measures mass. Mass is the amount of matter in an object. It is measured in grams (g). A **spring scale** measures forces, such as weight. The pull is measured in newtons (N).

 MAIN IDEA AND DETAILS What do a pan balance and a spring scale each measure?

The number closest to the top of the liquid is the temperature.

▼ Before you use a pan balance, make sure the pointer is at the middle mark. Place the object in one pan, and add standard masses to the other pan. When the pointer is at the middle mark again, add the numbers on the standard masses. The total is the mass of the object.

This girl is using a spring scale to measure the rabbit's weight. ▶

pans

middle mark

standard masses

8

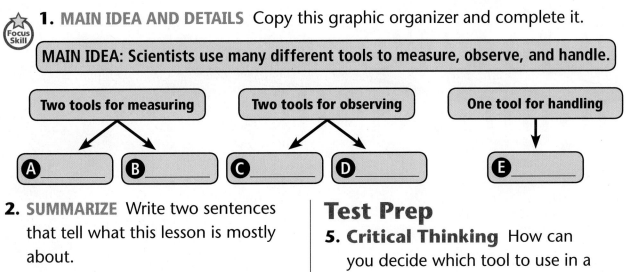

1. MAIN IDEA AND DETAILS Copy this graphic organizer and complete it.

MAIN IDEA: Scientists use many different tools to measure, observe, and handle.

Two tools for measuring

Two tools for observing

One tool for handling

Ⓐ_____ Ⓑ_____ Ⓒ_____ Ⓓ_____ Ⓔ_____

2. SUMMARIZE Write two sentences that tell what this lesson is mostly about.

3. DRAW CONCLUSIONS How would scientific experiments change if scientists had no tools to use?

4. VOCABULARY Write a fill-in-the-blank sentence for each vocabulary word. Trade sentences with a partner.

Test Prep

5. Critical Thinking How can you decide which tool to use in a certain experiment?

6. Which tool would help you measure how different colors absorb the energy in sunlight?
 A. beaker **C.** pan balance
 B. meterstick **D.** thermometer

Links

Writing

Persuasive Writing

You are a scientist, but you can afford only two of the tools described in this lesson. Choose two tools, and write a persuasive **paragraph** about why they are the most important.

Math 9÷3

Solve a Problem

You are using a measuring wheel to determine the width of a street. A rotation of the wheel is one meter (3.3 ft). The wheel rotates $9\frac{1}{2}$ times. About how wide is the street?

Art

Looking Closer

Draw an object as you would see it with your eyes. Then draw the same object as you think it would look under a hand lens. Now draw it as it looks under the highest-power microscope lens.

For more links and activities, go to www.hspscience.com

2

What Are Inquiry Skills?

Fast Fact

Windows in the Roof The clear, curving roof of Telstra Stadium in Sydney, Australia, lets in light but keeps out rain. Engineers built and tested many models before the final stadium was built. In the Investigate, you'll make a model building.

Build a Straw Model

Materials • 16 plastic straws • 30 paper clips • 30 cm masking tape

Procedure

1 You will work with a group to construct a model of a building. First, discuss questions such as these: What should the building look like? What are some ways to use the paper clips and the tape with the straws? What will keep the building from falling down?

2 Have one group member record all the ideas. Be sure to communicate well and respect each other's suggestions.

3 Predict which techniques will work best, and try them out. Observe what works, draw conclusions, and record them.

4 Plan how to construct a model building, and then carry out the plan.

Draw Conclusions

1. Why was it important to share ideas before you began construction?

2. Inquiry Skill Scientists and engineers often use models to better understand how parts work together. Models help find problems before building. What did you learn about constructing a building by making the model?

Step 3

Step 4

Investigate Further

Choose one additional material or tool to use in constructing your model. Explain how it will improve your model.

Reading in Science

VOCABULARY
observation p. 12
inference p. 12
hypothesis p. 15
experiment p. 15

SCIENCE CONCEPTS
▶ how scientists think
▶ how asking questions helps scientists learn and understand

READING FOCUS SKILL
MAIN IDEA AND DETAILS
Look for inquiry skills scientists use.

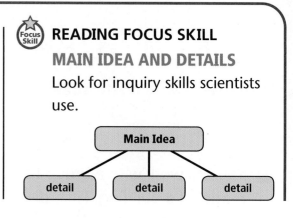

Scientists practice certain ways of thinking, or *inquiry skills.* You use these skills, too. Keep reading to learn more about inquiry skills.

Observe Did you notice the clouds when you woke up today? If so, you made an observation. An **observation** is information from your senses. You can observe how tall or smooth an object is.

Infer Did you ever try to explain why something is a certain color or why it smells like old socks? You were not observing. You were inferring. An **inference** is an untested conclusion based on your observations.

Scientists might observe that one star looks brighter than others. They could infer that the brighter star is bigger, hotter, or closer to Earth.

Predict You often use your knowledge to guess what will happen next. You are predicting. You figure out patterns of events. Then you say what will happen next. For example, scientists might observe a series of small earthquakes. Then they use that information to predict a nearby volcano eruption.

MAIN IDEA AND DETAILS Why do scientists observe, infer, and predict?

◀ You use inquiry skills to infer when a flower's buds will open. You might even predict what color the flowers will be.

▲ How are these plants different and the same? What words and numbers can be used to describe them?

Compare Scientists—and you— often compare things. You describe how the things are different and the same. For example, you learn about two rocks by comparing the minerals in them.

Classify/Order Is your music collection sorted in some way, such as by performer or type of music? Then you've classified it. You sorted it based on an observation. Scientists classify, or sort, things, too. For example, they might group rocks by color or texture.

You might also put objects or events in order. You could put planets in order by their size or their distance from the sun. You might put sounds in order by their pitch or their loudness. Putting things in order helps you see patterns.

Use Numbers Where would scientists be without numbers? They use exact numbers to show the mass of a seed. They use estimates to show the mass of a planet. Scientists—and you— use numbers to experiment and learn.

MAIN IDEA AND DETAILS Name a way you use each skill on this page in your daily life.

13

Use Time and Space Relationships How do the orbits of planets relate to one another? What are the steps in the water cycle? How does a pulley work? To answer these questions, you need to understand time and space relationships. Scientists—and you—need to understand how objects and events affect each other. You also need to know the order in which events happen.

Measure You often need to measure the results of your experiments. How tall did each plant grow? How far did the block slide on sandpaper and on waxed paper? Measuring allows you to compare your results to those of others anywhere. Scientists use the International System (SI) of measurements. It is also called the *metric system.*

Formulate or Use Models Have you ever used a little ball and a big ball to show Earth orbiting the sun? Have you ever drawn the parts of a cell? You were making models. Models help you understand how something works. For example, a globe is a model of Earth.

Scientists often formulate, or make, models. Models help them understand things that are too big, small, fast, slow, or dangerous to observe in person.

 MAIN IDEA AND DETAILS How would you use these three skills to make a diorama of an ecosystem?

▼ These students are measuring how fast loaded and unloaded toys move. Which variables are they controlling? Which variable changes?

◀ What is a possible hypothesis for an investigation using these materials?

Plan and Conduct a Simple Investigation Your CD player will not work. You think of several possible causes, such as dead batteries. Then you plan and conduct a simple investigation. You find and fix the problem. Scientists also use this approach.

Hypothesize Suppose you have a more complex problem. Your class is making sandwiches to sell at a school fair. You must decide how to keep the sandwiches fresh.

A **hypothesis** is a statement of what you think will happen and why. You hypothesize that small, resealable bags work best because they keep air out. Next, you test your hypothesis.

You set up an **experiment** to test your hypothesis. You put different sandwiches in different wrappings. A day later, the meat and cheese sandwich in the resealable bag is freshest. However, maybe it was the cheese, and not the bag, that kept the sandwich fresh. You can't be sure!

Identify and Control Variables To make a fair test, you must identify the variables—the things that can change—in an experiment. Then you need to control—keep the same—all the variables except the one you change and the one you observe. So, only the kind of sandwich wrapping should change.

MAIN IDEA AND DETAILS Why is it important to control variables?

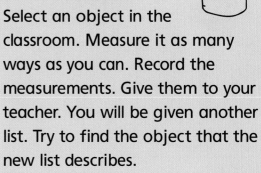

Insta-Lab

Full Measure
Select an object in the classroom. Measure it as many ways as you can. Record the measurements. Give them to your teacher. You will be given another list. Try to find the object that the new list describes.

Draw Conclusions For the sandwich experiment, suppose the results support your hypothesis. You can draw a conclusion based on the data you collected. Small, resealable bags do keep sandwiches fresher than other wrappings. You are ready for the school fair!

Gather/Record/Interpret/ Display Data In this experiment, you gathered data by checking the freshness of each sandwich. You recorded the results for each wrapping so you would not mix them up. Then you interpreted the data by drawing a conclusion.

If this investigation were for a science class, you would display the results. You might organize the results into a graph, table, or map.

Communicate You would probably tell your friends which sandwich wrapping works best. If this experiment were for a science fair, you would use other tools to share information— writing, pictures, and graphs. You might even display some sandwiches. They would help communicate how well each kind of wrapping worked.

⭐ **Focus Skill** **MAIN IDEA AND DETAILS** Why is communication an important skill?

▼ These students are using words, objects, and pictures to communicate. They are sharing how they conducted their experiment with toys and what conclusions they drew.

1. MAIN IDEA AND DETAILS Write details to complete this organizer.

MAIN IDEA: Scientists use many different inquiry skills.

Ⓐ _____   Ⓑ _____   Ⓒ _____

2. SUMMARIZE Write a sentence that tells the most important information in this lesson.

3. DRAW CONCLUSIONS You cannot understand a friend's science project. What inquiry skill or skills does your friend need to strengthen?

4. VOCABULARY Create a word puzzle with the vocabulary words.

Test Prep

5. Critical Thinking Which skills could help you find out what kind of muscle tissue is on a slide?

6. Which inquiry skill helps you notice a change?
   A. communicate   **C.** observe
   B. hypothesize   **D.** predict

Links

Writing

Narrative Writing

Write a **story** about how you or an imaginary person your age uses several inquiry skills to solve a problem. At the end of the story, name the skills used.

Math   9÷3

SI Units

Find out more about the International System (SI) of units. What SI units are most like these common units: inches, yards, miles, quarts?

Health

Get Moving

What do you believe is the main reason some people do not like to exercise? Now think of a way to find out whether your reason (hypothesis) is accurate. Write the steps you would take.

For more links and activities, go to www.hspscience.com

What Is the Scientific Method?

Fast Fact

Olympic Wind Tunnels Wind tunnels help scientists study how drag affects athletes. Smooth airflow means skiers can go faster. In the Investigate, you will study building strength by testing the straw models you made in Lesson 2.

Testing a Straw Model

Materials
- straw models from Lesson 2
- paper cups
- large paper clips
- pennies

Procedure

1. Bend a paper clip to make a handle for a paper cup, as shown.

2. With your group, predict how many pennies your straw model can support. Then hang the cup on your model and add one penny at a time. Was your prediction accurate?

3. Now work together to think of ways to strengthen your model. You might also look for other places on your model to hang the cup. Record your ideas.

4. Form a hypothesis about what will make the model stronger. Then experiment to see if the results support the hypothesis.

5. Discuss what made your straw model stronger, and draw conclusions.

6. Communicate your findings to the class.

Step 1

Step 2

Draw Conclusions

1. Were you able to increase the strength of your model? How?

2. **Inquiry Skill** Scientists experiment to test their hypotheses. What did you learn from your experiments in this activity?

Investigate Further

Will your model support more pennies if their weight is spread across the structure? Plan and conduct an experiment to find out.

Reading in Science

SCIENCE CONCEPTS
▶ how to explain the steps in the scientific method
▶ how the scientific method helps scientists gain knowledge

 READING FOCUS SKILL

MAIN IDEA AND DETAILS
Look for the steps in the scientific method.

```
          Main Idea
       ┌──────┼──────┐
    detail   detail   detail
```

Using the Scientific Method

The **scientific method** is a way that scientists find out how things work and affect each other. The five steps of this method help test ideas. You learned the terms used in this method in Lesson 2. Now you will see how scientists—and you—can put these terms to work.

❶ Observe and Ask Questions

After observing the straw models your class built, you might ask:

• Is a cube stronger than a triangle?

• Are straws more likely to bend if they are placed at an angle?
• Is a shorter straw stronger?
• Why do buildings use triangles?

 MAIN IDEA AND DETAILS What is the scientific method?

▼ You can find triangle shapes in bridges and other structures. Why is that?

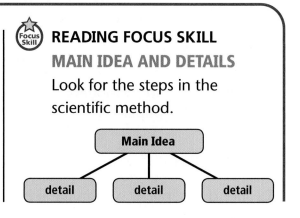

② Form a Hypothesis

Maybe you wonder whether a pyramid or a cube is stronger. Now form a hypothesis. A hypothesis is a statement that tells what will happen and why. A hypothesis must be testable. Here is a possible hypothesis: *Pyramids hold more weight than cubes because triangles are stronger than squares.*

③ Plan an Experiment

How can you test your hypothesis? You think of a plan and then write it as steps. For example, you might hang a cup on each model, and then add one penny at a time to each cup.

Next, you need to think about all the variables. Make sure that you are changing only one each time you do the experiment.

In this experiment, both models are made of straws. Both are made the same way. The cups will be the same. Only one variable will be tested—the shape of the structures. The complete plan should list all the materials. After that, it should list what to do in order.

④ Conduct an Experiment

Now it's time to conduct, or carry out, your experiment. You follow the steps in the correct order. At each step, you record everything you observe, especially any results you didn't expect.

MAIN IDEA AND DETAILS How do you plan an experiment?

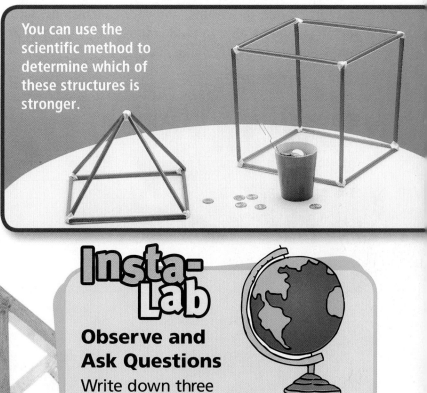

You can use the scientific method to determine which of these structures is stronger.

Insta-Lab

Observe and Ask Questions

Write down three questions about anything you can see while seated at your desk. Discuss the questions with two classmates. Choose one question none of you could answer. Plan a way to find the answer.

5 Draw Conclusions and Communicate Results

The final step is drawing conclusions. You look at the hypothesis again. Then you look at the observations you recorded. Do the results support your hypothesis? Was the pyramid able to support more pennies than the cube?

In this experiment, you could give the results in numbers. Other times, you might describe the results in other ways. For example, you might explain that a liquid turned blue or a plant wilted.

Scientists share the results of their investigations. That allows others to double-check the results. Then scientists can build new ideas on knowledge they are sure is reliable.

You can share your findings in a written or oral report. Charts, graphs, and diagrams help explain your results and conclusions. A written procedure allows others to repeat what you did.

Focus Skill **MAIN IDEA AND DETAILS** Why should a report on an investigation be clear and detailed?

▼ Your report should describe your hypothesis, the steps you carried out, the results, and your conclusions. Another person should be able to read your report, repeat your investigation, and get similar results.

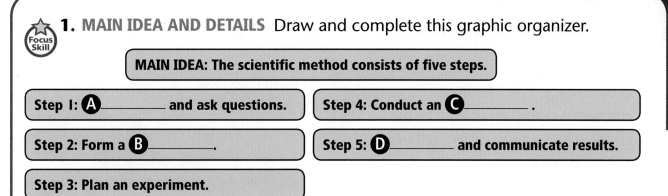

1. MAIN IDEA AND DETAILS Draw and complete this graphic organizer.

MAIN IDEA: The scientific method consists of five steps.

Step 1: **A**_____ and ask questions.

Step 2: Form a **B**_____.

Step 3: Plan an experiment.

Step 4: Conduct an **C**_____.

Step 5: **D**_____ and communicate results.

2. SUMMARIZE Write a summary of this lesson, beginning with this sentence: *The scientific method helps us gain new knowledge.*

3. DRAW CONCLUSIONS Will the scientific method be different 100 years from now? Why or why not?

4. VOCABULARY Write a fill-in-the-blank sentence for the vocabulary term.

Test Prep

5. Critical Thinking Name a problem in a young person's life that could be solved using the scientific method.

6. When you use the scientific method, what are you testing?

A. conclusions
B. experiment
C. hypothesis
D. observations

Links

Writing

Expository Writing

Choose an investigation you conducted or observed. Write a **report** on it. Describe how each step of the scientific method was completed—or how it should have been.

Math

Solve a Problem

A penny weighs 2.8 grams (0.1 oz). Let's say a pyramid supports 10 pennies, and a cube supports 6. How much more weight will the pyramid support than the cube?

Social Studies

Super Scientists

Choose a scientist who interests you, and research his or her life, challenges, and successes. Then make a poster to share interesting facts about this scientist with others.

For more links and activities, go to **www.hspscience.com**

Review and Test Preparation

Vocabulary Review

Use the terms below to complete the sentences. The page numbers tell you where to look in the chapter if you need help.

microscope p. 6
spring scale p. 8
inference p. 12
hypothesis p. 15
experiment p. 15
scientific method p. 20

1. Forces are measured by a _____.

2. A _____ is a testable explanation of an observation.

3. When you make an observation and then draw a conclusion, you make an _____.

4. To observe very small details, you might use a _____.

5. Scientists find out how things work and affect each other by using the _____.

6. A scientific test in which variables are carefully controlled is an _____.

Check Understanding

Write the letter of the best choice.

7. Which tool measures distance?
  A. forceps   **C.** meterstick
  B. graduate   **D.** microscope

8. Which of these is a hypothesis?
  F. I wonder how long a cactus can live without water here on a sunny windowsill.
  G. How long can a desert cactus live without water on a sunny windowsill?
  H. This experiment will test how long a desert cactus can live without water on a sunny windowsill.
  J. A cactus will live without water for a month on a sunny windowsill, since it can live in a desert.

9. **MAIN IDEA AND DETAILS** What is the main purpose of the scientific method?
  A. to ask questions
  B. to share information
  C. to test ideas
  D. to plan an experiment

10. In the scientific method, which of these do you do first?
  F. draw conclusions
  G. ask questions
  H. communicate
  J. hypothesize

11. Which of these is an observation?
  A. The plant needs more water.
  B. The plant wilted on the third day.
  C. The plant will need water daily.
  D. The plant will not live in a desert.

12. Which prediction for recycling in 2010 is based on the graph?

Waste Recycled

F. The rate will increase a little.
G. The rate will decrease a little.
H. The rate will level off.
J. The rate will decrease a lot.

13. Which tool measures volume?
   A. hand lens   C. scale
   B. measuring cup   D. ruler

14. Which inquiry skill is based on identifying common features?
   F. classify   H. predict
   G. infer   J. use numbers

15. Which of these is a possible inference based on seeing a bird eat seeds?
   A. The bird ate only the seeds.
   B. The bird has a thick beak.
   C. The bird doesn't eat meat.
   D. The males are quieter.

16. **MAIN IDEA AND DETAILS** Which of these is not an inquiry skill?
   F. infer
   G. communicate
   H. scale
   J. classify/order

Inquiry Skills

17. A model is not the real thing, so why do scientists **use a model**?

18. Which tool or tools would you use to **measure** and **compare** the mass of a cup of fresh water and a cup of salt water?

Critical Thinking

19. A scientist repeats another scientist's experiment but gets different results. What are possible causes?

20. You want to find out how water temperature affects the movement of goldfish.
Part A Write a hypothesis for your investigation.
Part B Identify the variables you will control in your experiment and the variable you will change.

A World of Living Things

LIFE SCIENCE

Bronx Zoo

TO: sydney@hspscience.com

FROM: julia@hspscience.com

RE: Bronx, New York

Dear Sydney,

My family and I visited the Bronx Zoo. It is the largest city zoo in the United States. The animals' habitats look like their natural homes. The tiger habitat has hot and cold rocks. They help to keep the tigers warm in the winter and cool in the summer.

Julia

TO: tia@hspscience.com

FROM: andre@hspscience.com

RE: Alaska

Dear Tia,

I saw a humpback whale leap out of the water. It was 50 feet long! What an amazing sight. In the summer, about 20 humpback whales feed in the waters of Glacier Bay National Park. They migrate to Alaska from Hawai'i. Sadly, these beautiful animals are endangered. For now, I'm glad we can see them each summer at Glacier Bay National Park.

Your friend,

Andre

Experiment!

Lung Capacity In this unit you will learn about living things. No two living things are exactly the same. People look different on the outside, but we also have differences inside. One difference inside our bodies is how much air our lungs can hold. Are males' lungs the same size as females' lungs? Do your lungs get larger as you get taller? Plan and conduct an experiment to find out.

Classifying Living Things

Lesson 1 **How Are Living Things Classified?**

Lesson 2 **How Are Plants and Fungi Classified?**

Lesson 3 **How Are Animals Classified?**

Vocabulary

organism	nonvascular
microscopic	fungi
bacteria	vertebrate
protist	invertebrate
vascular	

Which Is It? You might think that these sea anemones (uh•NEM•uh•neez) look like beautiful flowers, but they are really meat-eating animals. How do you think they get their food?

How Are Living Things Classified?

Fast Fact

Cute But Smelly Don't bother this mother skunk and her young! If you do, you'll be covered with an oily liquid whose bad smell will stay with you for a long time. These animals are made up of cells. In the Investigate, you will make a model of a cell.

Make a Model Cell

Materials
- marker
- malted-milk ball
- raisins
- plastic cup
- plastic knife and plastic spoon
- liquid gelatin
- paper plate
- small jelly beans

Procedure

1. Write your name on a plastic cup. Pour liquid gelatin into the cup until it is two-thirds full. Allow the gelatin to set.

2. Carefully remove the gelatin. Use the plastic knife to slice the set gelatin in half. Place the halves on a paper plate.

3. Use a spoon to make a small hole in the center of one of the gelatin halves. Place the malted-milk ball in the hole.

4. Scatter a few raisins and jelly beans on the gelatin that has the malted-milk ball.

5. Place the plain gelatin half on top of the half that has the candy and raisins.

6. Compare your model to the pictures of animal cells in this lesson, which show a cell's parts.

Step 3

Step 4

Draw Conclusions

1. Draw conclusions about what the gelatin, raisins, jelly beans, and malted-milk ball each represent.

2. **Inquiry Skill** Scientists often use models to understand complex structures. How does the model help you understand some parts of an animal cell?

Investigate Further

Find out what a bacteria cell looks like. Then make a model of it. How does this cell compare to the animal cell you made?

Reading in Science

VOCABULARY
organism p. 32
microscopic p. 33
bacteria p. 33
protist p. 33

SCIENCE CONCEPTS
▶ how living things are grouped
▶ what the characteristics are of bacteria and protists

READING FOCUS SKILL

MAIN IDEA AND DETAILS
Look for how living things are classified.

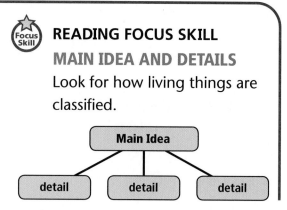

Classifying Living Things

How many kinds of animals and plants would you see in a park? How many kinds of living things are found in the ocean? There are millions of different kinds of organisms in the world. An **organism** is a living thing. Scientists study organisms to find out how they live. Scientists classify organisms so they can study them. When you classify, you group things that are alike.

There are many ways to group organisms. Organisms that live in the ocean may be grouped together. You might group living things by how they move. Or you could group organisms that have the same kinds of body parts.

At first, scientists classified organisms by how they got their food. They put

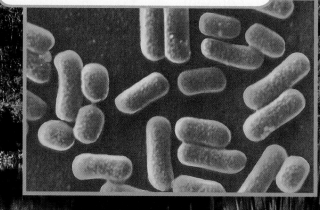

A stentor is a protist, a one-celled organism. It lives in ponds.

Streptobacillus (strep•tuh•buh•SIL•uhs) bacteria consist of rod-shaped cells that are chained together.

Organisms from every kingdom are found in every habitat.

all living things into either the animal kingdom or the plant kingdom. Animals need to eat. Most of them move to get their food. Plants make their own food, but they cannot move around. This way to classify worked for most living things, but not for all. For example, fungi (FUN•jy) can't move, but they also can't make food. So they became their own kingdom, the fungi kingdom.

When microscopes were invented, scientists found organisms that had never been seen before. Organisms that cannot be seen with the eyes alone are **microscopic**. Most microscopic organisms have one cell. Scientists compared one-celled organisms to animal cells and to plant cells. One-celled organisms were different. These organisms are in the **bacteria** and **protist** kingdoms.

Organisms are no longer classified by how they get food or move. Now organisms are also classified by what their cells look like.

MAIN IDEA AND DETAILS Why are plants and fungi in separate kingdoms?

Tree ferns are a type of plant that has been around for a long time. Ancient ferns could be 15 meters tall.

A chipmunk is in the animal kingdom. It holds food in its cheeks until it can store it in a burrow.

This bracket fungus is part of the fungi kingdom. Some brackets can mass 90 kilograms.

Cells

Every part of you is made of cells. An elephant's body is made of cells, too. Big or small, every organism is made of at least one cell.

Most cells have the same parts that you put in the model you made. All cells have a cell membrane. Materials needed by the cell pass into the cell through the cell membrane. Cells must also get rid of waste products. Waste products also pass through the cell membrane. In the mitochondria, activities are carried out that release energy for the cell. The nucleus controls all functions of an organism. It is surrounded by a nuclear membrane.

Cells make new cells by dividing. All the material in a cell is split between two new cells. Multicelled organisms grow as their cells divide. When the cells of some one-celled organisms divide, they make new organisms.

Plant cells have all the same parts as animal cells. They take in materials, get rid of wastes, and divide, just as

▼ This is an animal cell photographed through a microscope. It is greatly magnified.

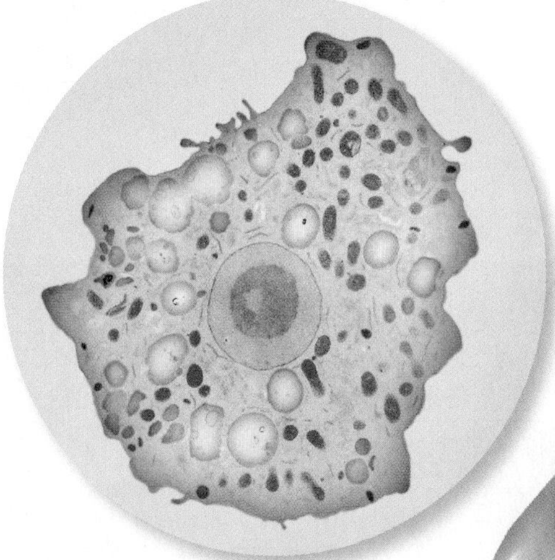

▼ This diagram shows an animal cell. Almost every cell in an animal has these parts.

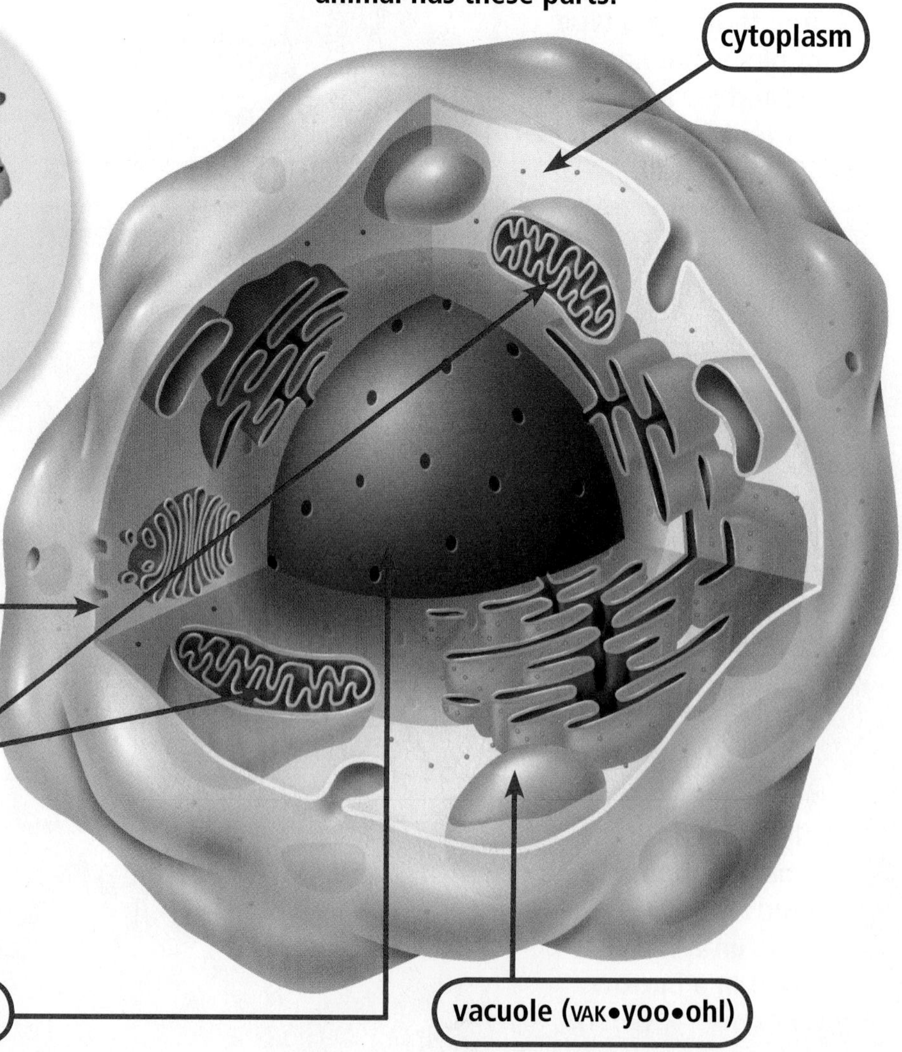

cytoplasm

cell membrane

mitochondria
(myt•oh•KAHN•dree•uh)

nucleus

vacuole (VAK•yoo•ohl)

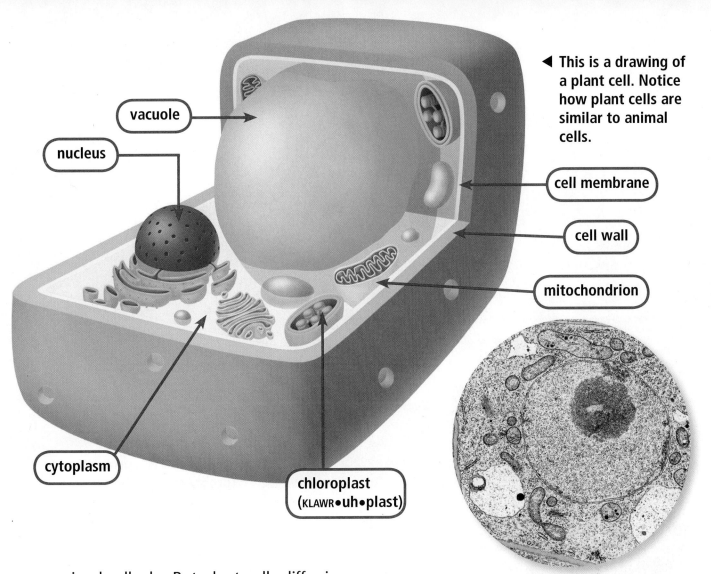

vacuole

nucleus

▣ This is a drawing of a plant cell. Notice how plant cells are similar to animal cells.

cell membrane

cell wall

mitochondrion

cytoplasm

chloroplast
(KLAWR•uh•plast)

▲ This is a plant cell photographed through a microscope. It is greatly magnified.

animal cells do. But plant cells differ in some ways. Plant cells are surrounded by a stiff cell wall. Plant cells also have chloroplasts, where food is made. Look at the pictures of plant cells to notice other parts that are different from those of animal cells.

Bacteria cells have cell walls, as do plant cells. But, bacteria cells are different from all other cells because they do not have a nucleus.

 MAIN IDEA AND DETAILS How are plant and animal cells alike?

Make a Simple Animal Shape

Use paper clips to make the shape of a simple multicelled animal. How do the paper clips represent cells?

◄ A diatom is an alga with a hard shell made out of silica, or glass.

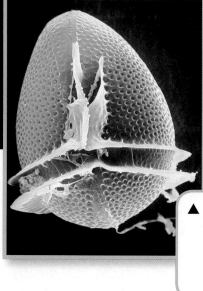

▲ A dinoflagellate (dy•noh•FLAJ•uh•lit) is an alga. This dinoflagellate produces poisonous materials that kill fish.

▲ An amoeba is a protozoan (proht•uh•ZOH•uhn). It surrounds its food, then digests it.

One-Celled Organisms

One-celled organisms need food, water, and oxygen, as do animals and plants. They need to get rid of wastes. They grow and reproduce.

Some one-celled organisms, such as most algae, make their own food. Like plant cells, algae have chloroplasts. Some algae do not have stiff cell walls. Other one-celled organisms, such as amoebas, have no cell walls and no chloroplasts.

All one-celled organisms have a cell membrane. Most also have a nucleus that has its own membrane. Bacteria have no nucleus. They have the same material found in a nucleus, but the material is not inside its own membrane.

 MAIN IDEA AND DETAILS What do all one-celled organisms have?

Bacteria

Bacteria are the most numerous organisms on Earth. Billions of them can be found in just one handful of soil. Bacteria are commonly grouped by their shape. Some are rod-shaped. Some are shaped like balls. Others are spiral-shaped. Some bacteria live as individuals. Others cluster together in pairs or chains. Some colonies are large enough to be seen.

Bacteria have been found in $3\frac{1}{2}$-billion-year-old rock. They are probably the oldest living organisms.

Bacteria live in every part of the world. They live in ice at the North Pole and in hot springs. They live at the bottom of the oceans. And they live in your stomach and on your skin, too.

Some bacteria cause disease. When you scrape your knee, bacteria may cause infection. But not all bacteria are bad. Most of them are useful. They help digest food and are used to clean up oil spills.

Focus Skill **MAIN IDEA AND DETAILS How are bacteria commonly grouped?**

Cyanobacteria (sy•uh•noh•bak•TIR•ee•uh) live in water and make their own food. They grow in ponds in colonies that are easy to see. ▶

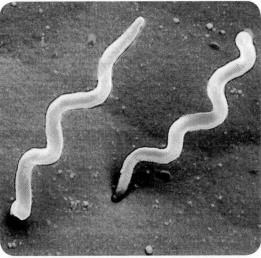

▲ **These spirochetes (SPY•roh•keets), or spiral-shaped bacteria, cause Lyme disease.**

◀ *Diplococci* **(dih•ploh•KAHK•sy) are spherical—or ball-shaped—bacteria that grow in chains.**

37

Protists

There are more than 80,000 kinds of protists. Algae and protozoans (proh•tuh•ZOH•unz) make up the protists.

Algae are found in fresh and salt water everywhere in the world. Algae also grow on rocks and trees and in moist soil. Most algae make food and put oxygen into the air. One type of alga that does not make food is the dinoflagellate. Instead, it stuns fish and then eats the fish's fluids.

▼ *Chlamydomonas* (kluh•MID•uh•moh•nuhs) is an alga. It has a cell wall, one chloroplast, and an "eye" that "sees" light.

▼ This *chromatium* (kroh•MAT•ee•uhm) lives in the pools of boiling water in Yellowstone National Park. It takes sulfur from the water for energy.

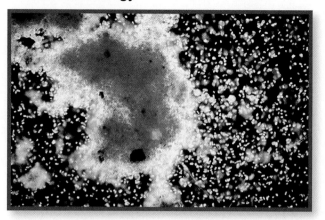

We use the shells of some algae, the diatoms, to make the grit in toothpaste and for the shiny paint used on roads. Diatoms come in all shapes. Some look like leaves, and some look like pinwheels.

Protozoans, like animals, hunt and gather food. They eat other protists and bacteria. The amoeba is a type of protozoan.

Focus Skill **MAIN IDEA AND DETAILS** Which two groups make up the protists?

Look at a drop of this pond water through a microscope, and you can see protists moving about.

Focus Skill

1. MAIN IDEA AND DETAILS Copy and complete this table.

Kingdom	Food Source	Movement	Cell Traits
Animals	**A** _____	move around	have a nucleus
Plants	make food	**B** _____	have a cell **C** _____
Protists	**D** _____	most move about	one-celled organisms
Fungi	can't make own food	**E** _____	have a cell wall
Bacteria	some make food, some don't	some move about	**F** _____

2. SUMMARIZE Use the chart to help you write a short description for each group of organisms.

3. DRAW CONCLUSIONS What would happen to animals if there were no more plants?

4. VOCABULARY Use vocabulary words and other science words to describe a diatom.

Test Prep

5. Critical Thinking How might you protect yourself if your friend had an infection caused by bacteria?

6. Which statement is not true?
   A. All cells need food.
   B. Organisms are made of one or more cells.
   C. All cells are alike.
   D. All plant cells have stiff cell walls.

Links

Writing

Write to Describe
Write a **letter** to a biologist to tell her about an organism you found and how you classified it. Explain why you classified the organism the way you did.

Math

Solve a Problem
A protozoan is $\frac{1}{50}$ of an inch long. How long would 25 protozoans in a row be?

Health

Bacteria Facts
Research bacteria to find the names of some bacteria that make people ill. Make a list of the bacteria and the illnesses they cause.

For more links and activities, go to www.hspscience.com

How Are Plants and Fungi Classified?

Fast Fact

Big and Little Duckweed is covering this frog. It is the smallest flowering plant in the world. It floats on the water in ponds. The redwood tree is the tallest living plant. How do leaves at the top of a tall tree get water? In the Investigate, you will find out.

Plant Stems

Materials
- plastic knife
- paper towel
- white carnation with stem
- two containers
- hand lens
- blue and red food coloring
- water
- two clothespins

Procedure

Step 3

1. Use the plastic knife to trim the end off the carnation stem. Split the stem from the middle to the bottom. Do not cut the stem completely in half.

2. Half-fill each container with water. Add 15 drops of blue food coloring to one container. Add 15 drops of red food coloring to the other container.

3. With the containers side by side, place one part of the stem in each container. Hold the stem parts in place with clothespins.

4. Observe the carnation every 15 minutes for an hour. Record your observations in a chart like the one here.

Time	Observations

5. Put a paper towel on your desk. Cut 2 cm off the bottom of each stem part. Use the hand lens to observe the cut ends of the stem.

Draw Conclusions

1. What do you observe about the flower? What do you observe about the stem?

2. **Inquiry Skill** Scientists can use space relationships to better understand what happens in a process. Based on your observations, what can you conclude about the movement of water in a stem?

Investigate Further

Use tincture of iodine to test for starch in a carrot. Where there is starch, the carrot will turn dark. What can you conclude?

SCIENCE CONCEPTS
▶ how vascular and nonvascular plants are structured
▶ how fungi are structured

READING FOCUS SKILL
MAIN IDEA AND DETAILS
Look for how plants and fungi are classified.

Main Idea
detail   detail   detail

Vascular Plants

How many plants can you name? There are about 270,000 kinds of plants in the world. That's too many to study in one group. The plant kingdom is divided into two groups.

One of the two large groups of the plant kingdom is made up of vascular plants. **Vascular** means "having tubes." Vascular plants have tubes that carry water and food to all their parts. In the Investigate, could you see the colored tubes? You were looking at the tubes that carry water through the plant.

Vascular plants are made up of three systems—roots, stems, and leaves. The roots help anchor the plant in the ground. They absorb water and nutrients from the soil. The plant needs both of these to live.

Stems connect the roots and the leaves. They carry water and food. Water in the stem helps keep the plant standing up straight.

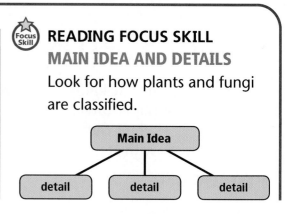

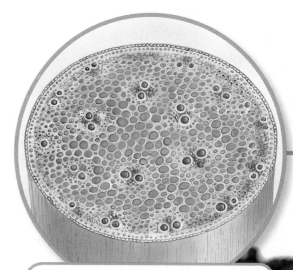

Tubes in the stem bring water up from the roots to the leaves. Food made in the leaves travels through tubes to the plant.

Roots have tiny root hairs that absorb water and nutrients.

The veins of a leaf are made up of small tubes. A leaf is covered with a waxy coating to keep in moisture.

This coleus plant is a typical vascular plant. It has leaves, stems, and roots.

Leaves are like a factory. They make food and give off oxygen. The chloroplasts in plant cells contain *chlorophyll* (KLAWR•uh•fil). Chlorophyll is a green substance that absorbs sunlight. Chloroplasts use carbon dioxide, water, and light energy from the sun to make sugar. The sugar is food for the plant. This process is called *photosynthesis* (foht•oh•SIN•thuh•sis). In this process, plants take carbon dioxide from the air. They give off oxygen. Food made in the leaves is carried to all parts of the plant. Some food is also stored as starch in the roots.

Vascular plants are divided into three smaller groups. One group is the flowering plants, which make seeds in fruits. Another group is the cone-bearing plants, which make seeds in cones. The third group is the ferns, which do not make seeds.

 MAIN IDEA AND DETAILS What are the three systems that make up vascular plants?

▲ Moss looks like a green carpet on decaying logs. It is really made up of many tiny plants.

▲ You can see tiny moss plants with a hand lens. These plants make spores, but do not make seeds.

Nonvascular Plants

The second of the two large groups of the plant kingdom is made up of nonvascular plants. **Nonvascular** means "without tubes." Nonvascular plants do not have any tubes to carry water and food to parts of the plant. They absorb water directly, like a sponge. In fact, if you put water on a dried moss plant, a nonvascular plant, you would see it swell up and become green.

Nonvascular plants are very small. Plants in this group are called *bryophytes* (BRY•oh•fyts). Bryophytes grow in damp, shady places. They grow close to the ground, where they can absorb water and nutrients from their surroundings. Water moves from cell to cell in the tiny plant. Bryophytes don't have real roots, either. Instead, they have rootlike parts that anchor them to the ground. Their leaflike parts make food, which moves from cell to cell.

All bryophytes reproduce by spores and sex cells. The sex cells must travel in water to make new plants.

The hornwort gets its name from the hornlike part rising off the low, leafy plant. It splits open to spread spores. ▼

▲ The leaflike part of the liverwort plant is said to look like liver. The cuplike parts are full of spores.

The three groups of bryophytes include mosses, liverworts, and hornworts. Different groups have different ways of producing spores.

Mosses are the bryophytes that you probably know best. They grow where it is moist. You can find them growing on buildings, on brick walls, and on damp pavements. Liverworts and hornworts grow in damp forests and along rivers.

 MAIN IDEA AND DETAILS How do nonvascular plants get water and nutrients?

Insta-Lab

Soak It Up

Put some water in a dish. Take a dry sponge, and stand it on its edge in the dish. Observe how it absorbs water. How does this compare to a moss plant?

Fungi

Fungi are organisms that absorb food and can't move about. They were once classified in the plant kingdom. They look a little like plants and have stiff cell walls that let them grow upright. But in one important way, fungi are not at all like plants—fungi cannot make food. Their cells lack chloroplasts. Instead, fungi absorb nutrients from living things and from the remains of living things. They break down parts of these materials. This releases nutrients. The cells of the fungi take in the nutrients.

Fungi are divided into several groups. These include molds, mushrooms, and sac fungi.

⭐ **Focus Skill** **MAIN IDEA AND DETAILS** **How do fungi get their food?**

Some puffballs crack open to send spores into the wind.

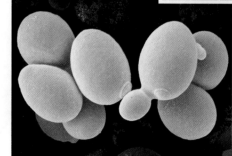

Yeast is a sac fungus used to help make bread rise.

Pilobolus (py•LAHB•uh•luhs), a sac fungus, lives in cow dung and helps decompose it.

This amanita mushroom is very poisonous. Never touch or eat a wild mushroom!

Oyster mushrooms grow in clusters on dead wood. They look, taste, and smell somewhat like oysters.

If you leave bread in a dark place, mold will grow.

Focus Skill

1. MAIN IDEA AND DETAILS Copy and complete this graphic organizer.

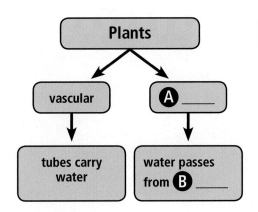

Plants
- vascular → tubes carry water
- A _____ → water passes from B _____

Fungi → absorb nutrients

2. SUMMARIZE Use the graphic organizer to summarize the characteristics of plants and fungi.

3. DRAW CONCLUSIONS What are some good reasons to plant trees?

4. VOCABULARY Write a paragraph that uses the vocabulary words.

Test Prep

5. Critical Thinking What would you do if you saw a potted plant looking limp?

6. Which do all groups of plants have?
- **A.** chloroplasts
- **C.** spores
- **B.** roots
- **D.** tubes

Links

Writing

Narrative Writing
Write a **story** for a school newspaper about a strange fungus you have found. Describe what it looks like, where it's growing, and why you think it's a fungus.

Math

Make a Bar Graph
Show the following in a bar graph. Nutrients in an edible mushroom: water 90%, proteins 3%, carbohydrates 5%, fats 1%, vitamins and minerals 1%.

Art

Draw Plants
Draw pictures of several kinds of plants to illustrate a children's book about plants. Choose at least one flowering plant.

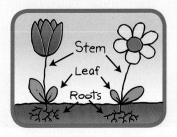

For more links and activities, go to www.hspscience.com

How Are Animals Classified?

A Sticky Subject Banana slugs are animals without a backbone. They creep along on a cushion of slimy mucus. In the Investigate, you will compare models of an animal with a backbone and one without a backbone.

Backbones

Materials • newspaper • ruler • modeling clay
• straight drinking straw

Procedure

1. Cover your desk with newspaper. Work in pairs to make models to compare animals with and without a backbone.

2. Make a base 5 cm in diameter and 3 cm high, using modeling clay.

3. Next, cover a straight drinking straw with modeling clay. The clay should have a diameter of 3 cm to represent the body. The straw represents the backbone.

4. Poke the body into the base. You can build the base up around it to support it. The base represents legs. You can add arms and a head, too.

5. Repeat Steps 2–4 without the straw.

6. Compare the way the models stand.

Draw Conclusions

1. What do you observe when you compare the two models?

2. **Inquiry Skill** Scientists plan simple investigations to test ideas. What steps would you follow to find out if the thickness of the backbone is important?

Step 3

Step 5

Investigate Further

Find a garden snail. Observe it. Record how it moves. What can you infer about whether this animal has a backbone?

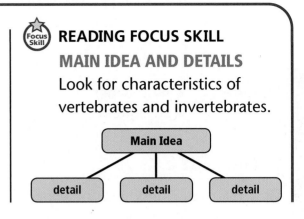

Vertebrates

How many animal pets can you name? What about wild animals? The animal kingdom is a large and diverse group of organisms. There are many different kinds of animals. The animal kingdom is divided into two groups—animals with a backbone and animals without a backbone.

Animals with a backbone belong to a group called **vertebrates**. You are a vertebrate. All vertebrates have bones inside their bodies that make up a skeleton.

Vertebrates are the most complex of all the animals. They have a system of nerves that carry messages to and from the brain. They have a system that brings nutrients, water, and oxygen in the blood to every cell of the body. The respiratory system brings oxygen to the blood and removes carbon dioxide. There is a system for digesting food and a system of muscles to move the body. There is a reproductive system.

A kangaroo is a mammal. A kangaroo mother nurses her baby while it's inside her pouch. ▶

▲ A fish is a vertebrate, too. Its backbone supports it as it swims.

An iguana is a reptile. It suns itself to keep its body warm. ▶

▲ Like all birds, a hummingbird has light, strong bones for flying.

▲ A salamander is an amphibian. Amphibians can live out of the water but must return to water to lay their eggs.

There are five groups of vertebrates—mammals, birds, reptiles, amphibians, and fish. Fish live in water. Their gills take oxygen from the water.

Amphibians have two lives—one in water and one on land. Most amphibians begin life in water. They grow lungs and legs and often lose their tails before they can live on land. They have smooth skin and lay eggs in water. Frogs, toads, and salamanders are amphibians.

Reptiles live on land. They don't have gills. Their bodies are the same temperature as what is around them. This is also true of fish and amphibians.

Reptiles lay eggs on land. Lizards, turtles, and snakes are reptiles.

Most birds can fly. They're covered with feathers, which keep them warm and dry and help them fly. Birds are warm-blooded. This means that their bodies stay at the same temperature no matter what the temperature around them is. All birds lay eggs.

You are a mammal. Female mammals nurse their young. All mammals are warm-blooded and have hair or fur. Their young are born live.

Focus Skill **MAIN IDEA AND DETAILS** **How are vertebrates complex?**

◄ A snail is a mollusk. It uses its shell for protection.

A tarantula is an arachnid (uh•RAK•nid). It has eight legs and no antennae. ►

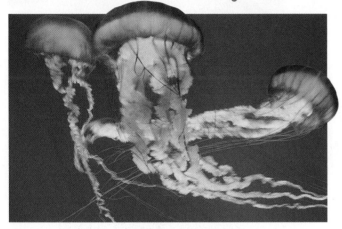

▲ A jellyfish stings its prey with tiny poison darts from its tentacles.

▲ A Christmas tree worm lives in a tube it builds on coral reefs. It filters food into its body with its tentacles.

Invertebrates

Animals without a backbone belong to a group called **invertebrates**. There are more than a million kinds of invertebrates, but scientists think that many more are yet to be found.

Many invertebrates live in the oceans. Water supports the bodies of underwater invertebrates.

Invertebrates have been divided into groups based on their body structures. Many groups have very simple body plans. Sponges are simple organisms with only a few types of cells. Members of the group that includes jellyfish and sea anemones are saclike organisms with

a place for digesting food. Some corals are communities of tiny animals.

Mollusks are more complex. They include snails, slugs, mussels, and clams. A mollusk has a soft body and a muscular foot. It also has nerves that send messages through the body.

There are several groups of worms. Earthworms and fan worms have a brain and a system of nerves. An earthworm has five "hearts" that pump blood to all its parts.

Arthropods are the largest group of invertebrates. They live almost everywhere on land and in water. All arthropods have jointed legs. They

A grasshopper is a typical insect because it has six legs and three main body parts. ▶

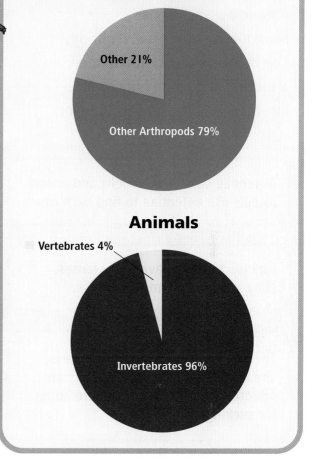

Crabs, which are crustaceans, walk on jointed legs and shed their shells as they grow. ▼

Math in Science
Interpret Data

Based on these circle graphs, what statement could you make about insects?

Invertebrates

Other 21%

Other Arthropods 79%

Animals

Vertebrates 4%

Invertebrates 96%

have a rigid body covering, called an *exoskeleton*, that covers the outside of their bodies. The exoskeleton doesn't grow. So when an arthropod grows, it molts, or sheds the old exoskeleton and grows a new one.

Insects are the largest group of arthropods. Crustaceans (kruhs•TAY•shuhnz), such as crabs and shrimps, are also arthropods. Spiders and scorpions are arthropods that belong to a subgroup called arachnids.

MAIN IDEA AND DETAILS What supports the bodies of ocean invertebrates?

Insta-Lab

What Kinds of Animals?

Make a list of as many different kinds of animals in your community as you can. Then classify the animals. You can make up your own groups.

A Typical Insect

A typical insect has an exoskeleton to protect its body. The body is divided into a head, a thorax, and an abdomen. An insect has six legs and antennae.

Antennae can detect smells and sounds. Insects use antennae to find each other.

An insect's eyes have many lenses. They are called compound eyes.

The head has eyes and mouth parts. The mouth parts of some insects are adapted for chewing. Some are adapted for sucking.

The thorax is divided into three parts. A pair of legs is attached to each part of the thorax. If the insect has wings, the wings are also attached to the thorax.

The six legs are jointed.

The abdomen contains most of the insect's body systems. An insect breathes through the sides of its abdomen.

Focus Skill

1. MAIN IDEA AND DETAILS Copy this chart, and fill in the boxes.

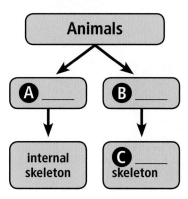

Animals

→ **A** ____   **B** ____

↓   ↓

internal skeleton   **C** ____ skeleton

2. SUMMARIZE Write a summary of this lesson by using the lesson vocabulary words in a paragraph.

3. DRAW CONCLUSIONS Why do you think a snake can move faster and in more directions than a slug?

4. VOCABULARY Use the vocabulary words as headings for a table. List at least three animals under each heading.

Test Prep

5. Critical Thinking If you found a newborn squirrel and took it to a vet, what would the vet feed it? Why would the vet choose that food?

6. Which animal has an exoskeleton?
A. fish   **C.** jellyfish
B. grasshopper   **D.** snail

Links

Writing ✏

Expository Writing
Write a **description** of an animal you learned about in this chapter. Without naming the animal, see if a classmate can identify it.

Math 9÷3

Using Fractions
There were 100 arthropods in a garden. If 75 percent of them were insects, how many insects were there? How many other arthropods were in the garden?

Social Studies 🌐

Useful Insects
Research an insect that is used by farmers to control insect pests. Write a report about this insect.

For more links and activities, go to www.hspscience.com

Where the Wild Things Are

Don't bother looking for the yellow-billed cuckoo in a tropical forest. You won't find the bird there. But you might spot a rare creature like it in a city near you.

Recently, scientists discovered a yellow-billed cuckoo in a city park in Connecticut. The scientists were at the park to take part in BioBlitz, a 24-hour race to count every species, or type, of plant and animal in sight. By the end of the long day, they had found nearly 2,000 different species.

A Range of Life

BioBlitz is held in cities across the country. The program teaches people about the biodiversity of wildlife at their doorsteps. Biodiversity refers to the number and variety of life forms in a certain area. According to one BioBlitz organizer, you don't have to travel to a tropical forest to find a variety of life. "What we're saying is that there's biodiversity in our very own backyard."

Species Search

BioBlitz combines education with round-the-clock fun. The participants compete to collect the most—and the most unusual—species. Hundreds of people come to watch.

Teams use insect nets and special lights in their search. One volunteer brought a recording of a screeching owl. The noise attracted other owls for the team to count. Teams use microscopes and wildlife guides to help identify the species they find.

In many cases, computers play an important role in keeping track of the information gathered by scientists and students. For example, in Vermont a running total of BioBlitz data was kept in a spreadsheet that had all the major classification groups, such as butterflies, worms, and lichens, that might be found in the area. In New York City, the BioBlitz

Divers search a lake in New York City during a recent BioBlitz.

Health Check

One of the goals of BioBlitz is to measure the health of city parks. Healthy parks should contain a variety of mammals, insects, fish, and reptiles. BioBlitz volunteers log every species that they locate in a park. Over time, scientists can compare current species counts with those from previous years to see whether some park creatures are in danger of dying out.

data was input into a special software program created just for the event.

Perhaps the best part of BioBlitz is that everyone who participates sees something new. "We hope this event helps people pay closer attention to the world around them," another program organizer said.

THINK ABOUT IT

1. Are projects like BioBlitz important to the environment? Why or why not?
2. In what other ways could computers be used to help the environment?

Find out more! Log on to
www.hspscience.com

BUGS ARE COOL!

Madeline Holzhauer loves collecting bugs. Madeline especially likes to collect ladybugs, inchworms, caterpillars, fireflies, moths, and butterflies.

Before she collects an insect, she gets books from the library to find out what it eats. Madeline is careful not to put in her box an insect that will eat the other insects.

Madeline uses a net to catch flying insects, but picks up the inchworms and caterpillars with her fingers. She puts flowers, leaves, twigs, and water in the box for the insects to eat and drink. Madeline sets the bugs free after a day or two.

SCIENCE Projects
for Home or School

You Can Do It!

Colors in Leaves

Materials
- leaves
- paper towel
- coin

Procedure

1. Gather leaves from several trees or ferns.
2. Lay the leaves on a plastic surface, and cover them with a paper towel.
3. Rub the paper towel over the leaves with a coin. Press down firmly to break down the cell membranes.
4. **Observe** and **compare** the leaf prints.

Draw Conclusions

What made the green color on the paper towel? Are there other colors on the paper towel? If there are, what might have made the other colors?

Design Your Own Investigation

How Do Molds Grow?

Use bread and sealable plastic bags to design an experiment that shows how molds grow. Place slices of bread in the bags. Leave the bags sealed, and discard them when the experiment is complete. Write up your results, including what the molds looked like, where the molds grew, and how long it took them to grow. Be sure to dispose of your materials properly.

Review and Test Preparation

Vocabulary Review

Use the terms below to complete the sentences. Some terms may be used twice. The page numbers tell you where to look in the chapter if you need help.

organism p. 32   **nonvascular** p. 44
microscopic p. 33   **fungi** p. 46
bacteria p. 33   **vertebrate** p. 50
protist p. 33   **invertebrate** p. 52
vascular p. 42

1. Organisms that grow on plant materials and absorb food from them are _____.

2. A plant with conducting tubes is called _____.

3. Anything that is too small to be seen with the eye alone is _____.

4. A one-celled organism that has a nucleus is a _____.

5. A multicelled animal without a backbone is an _____.

6. A living thing is an _____.

7. One-celled organisms without a nucleus are _____.

8. A multicelled animal with a backbone is a _____.

9. A plant that does not have conducting tubes is called _____.

10. A skunk is a _____.

Check Understanding

Write the letter of the best choice.

11. **MAIN IDEA AND DETAILS** Which statement is true of nonvascular plants?
    A. They absorb water that surrounds them.
    B. They have conducting tubes.
    C. They have stems and roots.
    D. They reproduce by seeds.

12. What kind of cell does this picture show?
    F. animal cell
    G. bacteria
    H. protist
    J. plant cell

13. **MAIN IDEA AND DETAILS** Which statement is true of arthropods?
    A. They can live only in water.
    B. They can't see or hear.
    C. They have an internal skeleton.
    D. They have an exoskeleton.

14. Which is **not** true of flowering plants?

   F. They are vascular plants.

   G. They produce oxygen.

   H. They produce seeds.

   J. They make cones.

15. What does this circle graph show?

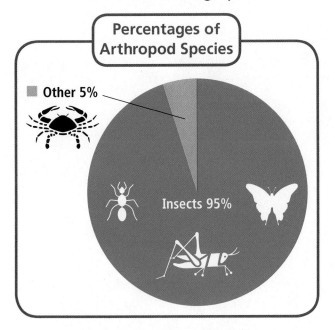

Percentages of Arthropod Species

Other 5%

Insects 95%

   A. Almost all arthropods are insects.

   B. Insects are more important than arthropods.

   C. Most insects must live on land.

   D. There are more insects than any other kind of animal.

16. Which would you plant on a hillside to stop soil from washing away?

   F. trees   **H.** liverworts

   G. mosses   **J.** fungi

Inquiry Skills

17. How can you **use models** to compare fungus cells and plant cells?

18. You observe a brown carpet of moss turn green after a rain. What are two things you might **infer**, based on this observation?

Critical Thinking

19. Why do you think amphibians return to the water to lay their eggs?

20. You are walking through your neighborhood when you find a plant you have never seen before. It is very short and has flowers.

Part A What are some other characteristics you should look for in order to classify this plant?

Part B Based on how you classify the new plant, what can you infer about its root system?

Life Cycles

Lesson 1 **What Is Heredity?**

Lesson 2 **What Are Some Life Cycles of Plants?**

Lesson 3 **What Are Some Life Cycles of Animals?**

Vocabulary

trait
heredity
gene
life cycle
direct development
metamorphosis

Travel to the Sea It took these sea turtle hatchlings several days to dig out of the sandy hole where their mother laid her eggs. The hatchlings are on a journey to find their way to the sea. How do you think they know the way?

What Is Heredity?

All Sizes and Shapes All dogs belong to the same species. Fossils and genetic evidence show that all are descended from wolves. So why do dogs vary in size and shape? In the Investigate, you'll explore an answer—inherited traits.

Inherited Characteristics

Materials • **hand mirror**

Procedure

1. Make a two-column table.

2. Make a fist with your thumb extended. Can you bend your thumb into the "hitchhiker position" as shown on the right? Record the results.

3. Use the mirror to observe your earlobes. Are they attached at the neck as shown on the left? Do they hang free as shown on the right? Record your observations.

4. Your teacher will ask members of the class to report their observations. Tally the results as your classmates report them.

5. Total the number of students who have each trait. Then use the numbers to find the fraction of the class that has each trait.

Draw Conclusions

1. Why would you infer that not all persons could learn to bend their thumbs into the hitchhiker position?

2. **Inquiry Skill** Based on your observations and inferences, what can you conclude about hitchhiker thumbs and attached earlobes?

Step 2

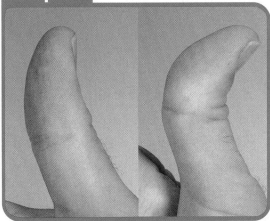

Step 3

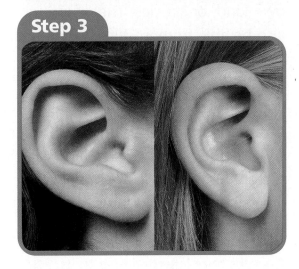

Investigate Further

Predict traits your family members will prove to have. Gather data from your family. Use it to make a chart.

Reading in Science

VOCABULARY
trait p. 66
heredity p. 66
gene p. 67

SCIENCE CONCEPTS
▶ how traits are inherited
▶ how traits develop

READING FOCUS SKILL
MAIN IDEA AND DETAILS
Look for ways you get your traits.

Main Idea

detail   detail   detail

Parents and Offspring

Look around the room at your classmates. Notice ways you are all like one another. Notice the differences, too.

When living things breed, or *reproduce,* they make more of their own kind, or species. The offspring will also be able to reproduce. When bears reproduce, they produce bear cubs. Maple seeds grow into maple trees, and oak seeds grow into oak trees. But offspring also differ from one another. The members of the Asian family in the picture look like one another, but they are still unique individuals.

Children look more like their parents and grandparents than like people in other families. Do you have your mother's eyes or your grandfather's nose? Do your aunts and uncles look like your grandparents? Offspring look like parents because of similar traits.

A **trait** is a form of a characteristic that not all organisms have in common. All people have thumbs, but having a hitchhiker thumb is a trait. Where do our traits come from? Traits are passed on through heredity. **Heredity** is the process by which traits are passed from parents to offspring.

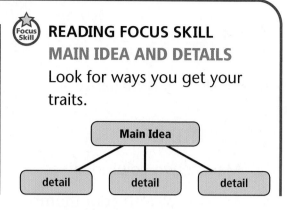

The cubs have inherited their traits from their mother and father. ▶

66

All the members of this Asian family have many similar traits.

This son looks very much like his father. ▶

A **gene** is a basic unit of heredity. Genes carry instructions for how a living thing will grow and develop. The genes in each cell determine what kind of cell it will become. Every human has the same number and type of genes, but the instructions on the genes vary. Different forms of genes cause people to have different traits. For example, everyone has genes for earlobe type. One form makes earlobes attached. Another form makes earlobes hang free.

Where did you get your gene set with all of its instructions? Genes are transferred from parents to offspring during *reproduction*. This is when a sperm cell and an egg cell join. Genes work in pairs. A sperm cell from the father carries only half of each pair. An egg cell from the mother also has only half of each pair. When the sperm and egg join, a new cell with a full set of genes forms. Half of the set comes from the mother, and half comes from the father. In the same way, the gene sets of the mother and father came from their parents.

So your genes came from your parents. But your combination of forms of genes differs from those of anyone else.

⭐ **Focus Skill** **MAIN IDEA AND DETAILS** Why might a girl look like her mother's father?

Traits

Thousands of different traits make you who you are. Some traits, such as those determining eye color, are affected only by genes. Most traits, however, develop through a combination of heredity and nurture. *Nurture* is everything in your life—where you live, the people you know, and the activities you do.

The traits you studied in the Investigate are determined by heredity alone. No matter where you live, those traits will not change. The traits shown here are also determined by heredity.

Nurture influences many traits. A hydrangea (hy•DRAYN•juh) plant may have genes for colored flowers. But soil nutrients control whether its flowers are pink or blue. The environment affects the trait. The gene for the trait does not change. The gene passed to the offspring will still be for white flowers. In a similar way, people may dye their hair. Their genes for hair color do not change.

The people around you influence your behavior and traits, too. For example, you can learn to speak because of certain genes. However, the language

Eye color, hair color, the shape of the nose, and the shape of the lips are inherited traits.

A toucan (top) has a big beak for eating large fruit. A hawk (middle) tears at prey with its beak. A heron's beak (bottom) is suited for fishing.

You can identify a tree by its leaves. These leaves are from different trees: maple (top), oak (left), and palm (right).

you speak and the words you use are learned from the people in your life. You inherit the taste buds on your tongue, but many things influence the foods you like.

Some behaviors are not learned. Many animals hatch from eggs and never see their parents. They are born with a full set of instructions on how to survive. Animals with more-developed brains have more to learn. When they're young, they depend on their parents. They inherit traits for survival, but they have to learn how to use the traits. They learn from their parents or other adults.

 MAIN IDEA AND DETAILS How does dyeing the hair influence the genes for hair color?

Insta-Lab

A Family Tree

Draw your family tree or that of a friend. Start with the grandparents, and show their children. Then show the children's children. Ask family members for help. Do the people in the family tree look like one another?

Variations

Genes affect characteristics such as height, shape, and color. Some characteristics are affected by several genes. For instance, several genes control eye color. When a human sperm and egg cell join, many kinds of eye color are possible. Look at the variations of eye colors of students in your classroom. Eyes are usually not just blue or brown. They can be green or something different. This is because of the many possible gene combinations.

You can't change your eye color. But you can change some characteristics by the way you live. For example, genes carry information for how tall you can be. However, what you eat and how you take care of your body also influence your height. Eating healthful food and getting proper exercise enable your body to grow as tall as possible.

Focus Skill **MAIN IDEA AND DETAILS** Why are there many different skin colors?

▼ When seeds from different colors of tulips are mixed, many colorful tulips result.

▲ Many dogs are bred so that they have certain traits. These three Labrador retrievers all have different mixes of genes.

1. MAIN IDEA AND DETAILS Draw and complete the graphic organizer.

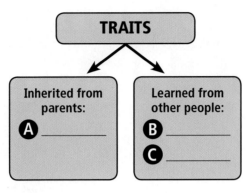

TRAITS

Inherited from parents:

A _____

Learned from other people:

B _____

C _____

2. SUMMARIZE Summarize the process of heredity.

3. DRAW CONCLUSIONS What is wrong with the statement "You look exactly like your mother"?

4. VOCABULARY Complete the following sentence by using the lesson vocabulary words. By ____, a child's parents pass on their ____, which carry instructions for some ____ the child will have.

Test Prep

5. Critical Thinking Why can't bears breed and produce monkeys?

6. Which trait is affected by behavior?

A. eye color   **C.** leaf shape

B. height   **D.** attached ear lobes

Links

Writing

Expository Writing

Write a **description** of how the dogs in the picture on the previous page are alike and different. Write why you think the dogs are the same.

Math

Make a Bar Graph

Review the data that you gathered during the Investigate. Use it to make a bar graph about your class's thumbs and ear lobes. What does the data tell you?

Health

Healthy Bodies

Write a paragraph explaining how you could affect development of your inherited traits by your health habits.

For more links and activities, go to www.hspscience.com

What Are Some Life Cycles of Plants?

Blowing in the Wind When you blow on a head of dandelion seeds, the seeds sail through the air. They can travel on the wind across great distances. In the Investigate, you'll find out what seeds need to grow after they're in the ground.

Sprouting Seeds

Materials
- radish seeds
- cup
- water
- 2 sponges
- 2 aluminum pie pans
- cardboard box

Procedure

1. Work in a group. Soak some radish seeds in a cup of water overnight. Write a hypothesis about whether seeds need light to sprout.

2. Place a wet sponge on a pie pan. Pour about 1 cm of water in the pan.

3. Poke some of the radish seeds into the holes of the sponge.

4. Place the pie pan in a warm, sunny place, and observe the sponge for the next 3 to 5 days. Be sure the sponge stays moist.

5. Repeat Steps 2 and 3 with the second pie pan. However, place the pan and sponge on a table, and cover them with a box so that no light gets in. Be sure the sponge stays wet, but keep it in the dark as much as possible.

6. Compare the growth on the two sponges, and record your observations.

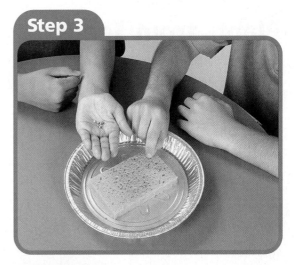
Step 3

Step 5

Draw Conclusions

1. What do you conclude about light and the sprouting of seeds?

2. **Inquiry Skill** How did the experiment support or reject your hypothesis?

Investigate Further

Form a hypothesis about whether plants need soil to grow. For a test, use a radish seed on a moist sponge and a radish seed in soil in a pot.

VOCABULARY
life cycle p. 74

SCIENCE CONCEPTS
▶ the stages in a plant's life cycle
▶ how plants reproduce

(Focus Skill) **READING FOCUS SKILL**
SEQUENCE Look for stages in the life cycles of plants.

Plants from Seeds

Flowering plants grow from seeds. A seed forms when an egg is fertilized. Each seed holds a tiny plant called an *embryo*. The tiny plant stays inside the seed until conditions are right for it to grow. When the soil is warm and there is enough moisture, the plant will *germinate* (JER•muh•nayt), or begin to grow.

Germination (jer•muh•NAY•shuhn) is one stage in a plant's life cycle. A **life cycle** is all of the stages a living thing goes through, from the beginning of one generation to the next.

When there is enough moisture, a seed swells and cracks open. Tiny roots begin to grow down into the soil. Inside the seed, the embryo is surrounded by food. This food gives the plant energy to grow until it can make its own food. After the roots begin to take up water, a tiny stem pushes up out of the soil. Leaves begin to grow, and the plant can now make its own food. A new plant, or seedling, is formed. The *seedling stage* is the next stage of a plant's life cycle.

Next, the plant grows and develops flowers. The *flowering stage* is the next stage of the life cycle. Flowers produce

◀ In pine trees, wind spreads pollen from the male cones to the female cones, where seeds develop.

A coconut is the biggest seed. It can float in the ocean to a new island, where it will grow into a tree. ▶

▲ In orange trees, the flowers and fruit grow at the same time.

Tomato-Plant Life Cycle

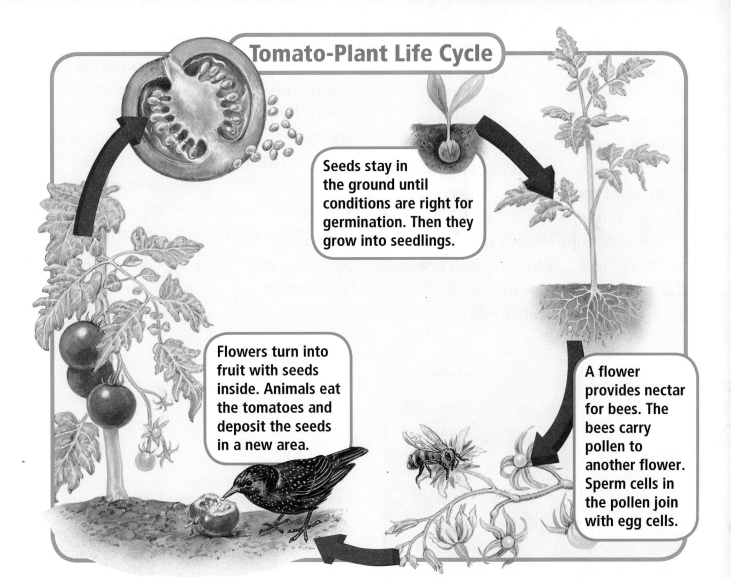

Seeds stay in the ground until conditions are right for germination. Then they grow into seedlings.

A flower provides nectar for bees. The bees carry pollen to another flower. Sperm cells in the pollen join with egg cells.

Flowers turn into fruit with seeds inside. Animals eat the tomatoes and deposit the seeds in a new area.

pollen. It contains the male sex cells, or sperm cells, of the plant. The colors and scents of flowers attract birds and insects. As the birds and insects move from flower to flower, they *pollinate* (PAHL•uh•nayt), or bring pollen to, the flowers. Wind also carries pollen to other flowers and plants. A flower is pollinated when pollen grains are deposited onto the female part of the flower. Then sperm cells from the pollen grains join with egg cells inside the flower. New seeds develop, beginning a new life cycle.

A pollinated flower grows into a fruit that surrounds the seeds. When animals eat the fruit, the seeds go through their digestive systems. The seeds may be deposited far away from the parent plant. Other seeds are spread by wind. Still others are carried away in and drop from an animal's fur. When conditions are right, the seeds will grow into new plants.

SEQUENCE After germination, which comes first—the flowers or the leaves?

Plants from Spores

Ferns, plants related to ferns, and other plants without roots reproduce by *spores* and don't make seeds. The Science Up Close shows a fern life cycle. Plants that use only spores to reproduce need moist environments. This enables the sperm to move to the eggs.

Mosses are nonvascular plants that also make spores. Mosses grow close to the ground in wet environments. The life cycle of a moss is much like a fern's.

First, fertilized eggs, or eggs that have joined with sperm, develop into small plants. When those plants become adult plants, they release spores. The spores are released into the moist environment. They develop into new plants. During this stage, the tiny plants develop sperm and eggs. The sperm are released and swim to the eggs. The cycle starts over.

Focus Skill **SEQUENCE** **After a spore-producing plant grows, which happens first— spore release or egg fertilization?**

◀ Many tiny individual moss plants are in the moss you see growing on logs and trees.

▼ A takakia (tah•KAH•kee•uh) plant grows parts that produce sperm and eggs.

Insta-Lab

Spores on Leaves

Use a hand lens to look at the spore clusters on the back of a fern frond. Then rub the clusters over white paper, and look at the individual spores. How are spores different from seeds?

Fern Life Cycle

Ferns reproduce without seeds.

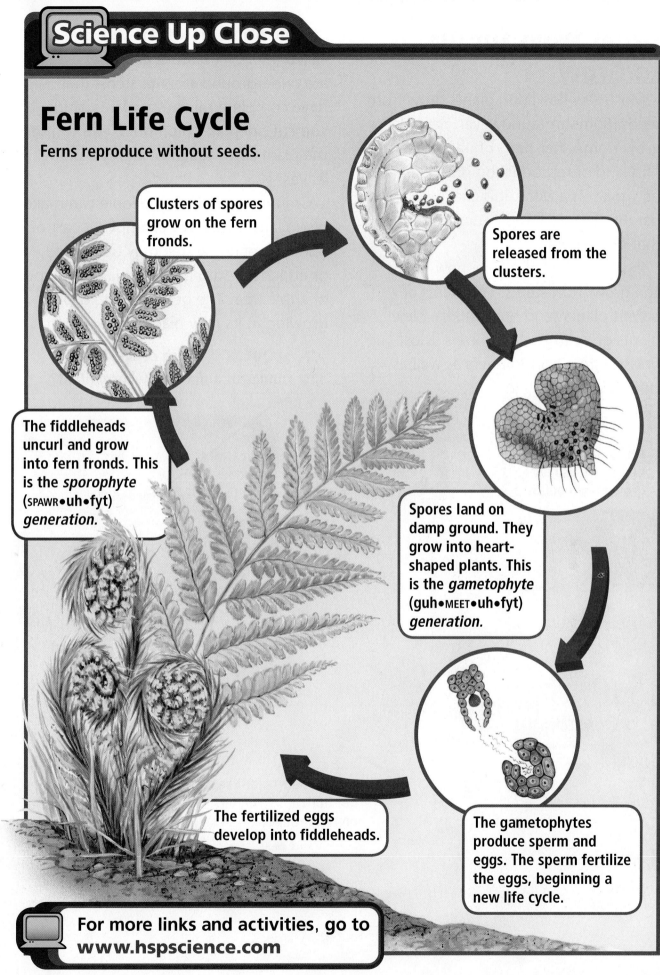

Clusters of spores grow on the fern fronds.

Spores are released from the clusters.

Spores land on damp ground. They grow into heart-shaped plants. This is the *gametophyte* (guh•MEET•uh•fyt) *generation*.

The fiddleheads uncurl and grow into fern fronds. This is the *sporophyte* (SPAWR•uh•fyt) *generation*.

The gametophytes produce sperm and eggs. The sperm fertilize the eggs, beginning a new life cycle.

The fertilized eggs develop into fiddleheads.

For more links and activities, go to www.hspscience.com

Other Ways for Plants to Grow

Most new flowering plants grow from seeds. Sometimes, however, new plants grow from other parts of parent plants. This kind of reproduction is *asexual*. The new plant is a *clone.* It is exactly like the parent because it has genes from only that one parent.

In some types of plants, new plants can grow from stems. The stems of parent plants send out runners. New plants grow from the runners. Most grasses grow from runners as well as from seeds.

Some plants grow from a storage stem called a *tuber.* Potatoes are tubers. Bulbs are underground storage stems that have complete miniature plants inside. If you cut open an onion bulb, you can see the plant surrounded by fleshy storage leaves.

Grafting is a way that people can make new plants grow. For example, a part of one type of apple tree may be grafted, or attached, onto part of a different type of apple tree. The grafted part keeps growing in its new place.

Focus Skill

SEQUENCE Which comes first—a runner or a new strawberry plant?

A daffodil flower has seeds, but daffodil plants are usually grown from bulbs.

A potato plant grows from the "eyes" on a potato.

A strawberry plant sends out horizontal runners on the ground.

1. SEQUENCE Draw and complete these two plant life cycle sequences.

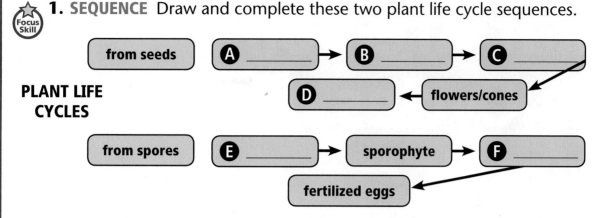

PLANT LIFE CYCLES

from seeds → **A** ___ → **B** ___ → **C** ___

D ___ ← flowers/cones

from spores → **E** ___ → sporophyte → **F** ___

fertilized eggs

2. SUMMARIZE Use the graphic organizer to describe the stages in the life cycles of flowering plants and ferns.

3. DRAW CONCLUSIONS Each kernel of corn is a seed inside a fruit. Seeds form from pollinated flowers. What can you conclude about the kernels on an ear of corn?

4. VOCABULARY Write definitions for *life* and *cycle,* and tell how they relate to the compound term *life cycle*.

Test Prep

5. Critical Thinking How could you start a new grass plant?

6. Which of the following grows from a fern spore?

A. seed   **C.** fern clone

B. flower   **D.** a tiny heart-shaped plant

Links

Writing

Narrative Writing

Write a **story** about a seed as it "wakes up." Tell what happens to it as it grows and has offspring.

Math 9÷3

Estimate

Potato plants grow from the eyes of potatoes. Count the eyes of a potato. Then estimate how many potatoes you would need to grow 100 potato plants.

Language Arts

Word Parts

Look up the meaning of the word part *-phyte*. Write a definition of it. Look up other word parts related to plants. Share them with the class.

For more links and activities, go to www.hspscience.com

What Are Some Life Cycles of Animals?

Fast Fact

A "Comet" in the Forest This comet moth from Madagascar did all its eating when it was a larva. Adult comet moths have no mouths and die in about 10 days. In the Investigate, you'll find out more about the life cycles of animals.

Animal Life Cycles

Materials • pictures of animal life cycles   • paper bag for whole class
• scissors

Procedure

1 Work in a group to understand the life cycle of the animal that is assigned to you.

2 First, study the pictures of the animal's life cycle. Then, draw the stages of the life cycle on separate sections of paper that you've cut apart.

3 Put the pieces of paper into the bag, together with your classmates' pieces.

4 Pick a piece from the bag. Then find the students who have other pieces showing stages of the same animal's life cycle.

5 Put the stages of the cycle in order.

6 Compare your finished life cycle with the other life cycles.

Draw Conclusions

1. How would you describe animal life cycles in general?

2. **Inquiry Skill** How did ordering stages in life cycles and comparing them help you describe life cycles?

Step 2

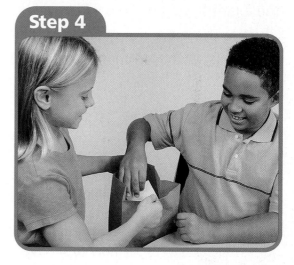

Step 4

Investigate Further

How does your animal's life cycle compare to the human life cycle?

VOCABULARY
direct
    development p. 84
metamorphosis p. 86

SCIENCE CONCEPTS
▶ the stages of an animal's life cycle
▶ how some animals grow and develop

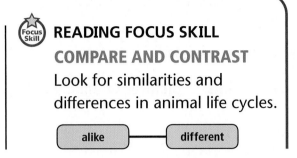 **READING FOCUS SKILL**
COMPARE AND CONTRAST
Look for similarities and differences in animal life cycles.

| alike |————| different |

Animal Life Cycles

Have you ever seen a litter of newborn kittens? In this stage of their life cycle, cats need to be taken care of. This is the *infant stage*. The mother cat feeds her kittens and keeps them warm. Soon the kittens can run about and become playful. Before long, they're fully grown and can have kittens of their own. This is one example of an animal life cycle.

Just as there are many different kinds of animals, there are many kinds of life cycles. Many animals change as they grow, but their basic body plans stay the same. Almost all animals come from fertilized eggs—eggs that have joined with sperm cells. Kittens grow from fertilized eggs that develop inside the mother's body.

Mammals, such as kittens and humans, begin life inside a mother. Marsupials (mar•soo•pee•uhlz) are mammals that don't develop fully inside

Some young sea animals stay close to their mothers as they grow and learn how to survive. ▼

The young kangaroo is blind and only the size of a honeybee when it is born. It crawls through the mother's fur and into her pouch. ▶

The corn snake lays up to 30 eggs once a year. The mother snake does not take care of her young. ▶

Animal and Plant Life Spans

Each kind of animal and plant has a different life span, or amount of time to live. How does the average human life span compare to the life spans shown in the chart? Why do you think there is a big difference in life spans?

Fruit fly	37 days
Hummingbird	9 years
Galápagos Island land tortoise	150 years
Bristlecone pine	5000 years
Mouse	2 years
Sugar maple	300 years

◄ Bristlecone pines are the oldest living trees.

Galápagos Island land tortoises have the longest life span of any animal. ▶

the mothers' bodies. They need to stay in the mother's pouch until they get bigger. The kangaroo is an example of a marsupial.

A kangaroo's offspring first develops for only about 33 days. Then the mother gives birth. In only about three minutes, the baby moves to its mother's pouch. It begins to drink its mother's milk as soon as it gets there. Inside the pouch, the tiny kangaroo continues to grow.

Another animal that grows in a pouch is a sea horse. The female sea horse deposits eggs in the male's pouch. There, the eggs are fertilized. After several weeks, young sea horses pop out of the pouch and swim away.

Many birds lay eggs in nests. The eggs have shells that protect the growing

embryos inside. When many young birds hatch, they have no feathers. They need to be fed and kept warm.

Like birds, most reptiles also lay eggs. But when reptiles hatch, they are ready to survive on their own.

Fish and amphibians lay their eggs in water. When fish hatch, they look just like their parents. They are ready to survive on their own. Amphibians usually go through changes in their bodies after they hatch. You'll read more about those changes later in the lesson. Many insects also go through complete body changes before they become adults.

COMPARE AND CONTRAST How is a bird's life cycle similar to a reptile's life cycle? How is it different?

Growth and Development

Animals grow and develop in different ways. The bodies of many animals change as they grow older. Cats and dogs are born with very little fur. Their legs are wobbly, they have baby teeth, and their eyes are closed. They are tiny and cute. As they grow, their bodies lengthen and their faces change. However, their basic body plan is the same as an adult animal's.

Spiders also are very tiny when they hatch, but they are otherwise like their parents. They get larger, but they don't go through other major changes. The same is true of fish and other animals. This kind of growth is called **direct development**.

Shedding an outer covering is *molting*. A horseshoe crab sheds its shell 16 or 17 times in its lifetime. Each time it molts, the crab grows a little bigger. Then it grows a new and larger shell. Spiders, insects, and similar animals molt. Reptiles also shed their skins.

Animals grow at different rates. A fruit fly grows to be an adult in about 10 days. An elephant nurses for three years. An elephant is an adolescent at about 12 years. A dog develops about seven times faster than a human. A dog, depending on the breed, is an adult at about three years.

The stages in the human life cycle are infancy, childhood, adolescence, and adulthood. You began as a fertilized egg inside your mother. When you were

◀ Bald eagle young have dark brown feathers all over.

◀ Young deer are born with spots that help them hide in bushes and tall grass.

Snakes shed their skin as they grow.

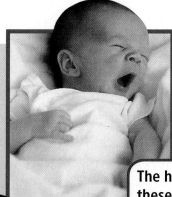

The human life cycle includes these stages: infant, child, adolescent, adult, senior.

born, you were completely dependent on your parents. You were an infant from birth to two years. In those two years, you learned to walk and talk, and the size of your body changed.

Right now, you're in the childhood stage. During childhood, you grow a lot, but not quite as fast as during infancy. You lose some teeth and get some new ones. Your body changes, and you learn many new things.

Next you'll become an adolescent. Adolescents go through many changes in their bodies as they move toward adulthood. Not everyone reaches adolescence at the same time.

When you reach adulthood, your body will be fully developed. You will have reached your full height. A person over the age of 50 is considered a senior.

Focus Skill **COMPARE AND CONTRAST** **List similarities and differences between human adult and child stages.**

Insta-Lab

What Will You Look Like as an Adult?

Draw a picture of yourself as you think you will look when you're about 50 years old. How tall will you be, and what might you be doing in life?

Metamorphosis

Did you know that a caterpillar is an insect? Look at the pictures showing the life cycle of a sphinx (SFINGKS) moth. Notice the caterpillar and other stages of the life cycle. Major changes in the body form of an animal during its life cycle are called **metamorphosis** (met•uh•MAWR•fuh•sis). Butterflies, moths, bees, and flies undergo metamorphosis. An insect that changes completely from one stage to the next undergoes *complete metamorphosis.*

There are four stages in complete metamorphosis. First, an insect lays fertilized eggs. A tiny caterpillar, or larva, hatches from each egg. The larva eats, grows, and then rolls up and becomes a pupa (PYOO•puh) in a chrysalis (KRIS•uh•lis) or a cocoon. The pupa changes to become the adult insect.

Some animals look like the adults when they hatch but don't have all the adults' parts. For example, young grasshoppers don't have wings. They are *nymphs* (NIMFS). Once a nymph grows wings, it is an adult. This kind of change is called *incomplete metamorphosis.*

Most amphibians, such as frogs, show complete metamorphosis. When a tadpole, or young frog, hatches, it has a tail and lives in water, breathing with gills. Later it grows legs and loses its tail. When its legs and lungs are fully grown, it hops onto land as an adult frog.

 COMPARE AND CONTRAST Compare the life cycle stages of a moth with those of a grasshopper.

Life Cycle of a Moth

1 The first stage in the life of a sphinx moth is the fertilized egg.

2 In the second stage, the egg hatches. The caterpillar, or larva, begins eating and growing.

3 In the third stage, the caterpillar spins threads around itself to make a cocoon, in which it becomes a pupa.

4 In the fourth stage, the adult sphinx moth breaks out of the cocoon.

1. COMPARE AND CONTRAST Draw and complete the graphic organizer.

complete metamorphosis — four stages: **A** _____

direct development — definition: **B** _____

human life cycle — four stages: **C** _____

2. SUMMARIZE Use the graphic organizer to compare animal life cycles.

3. DRAW CONCLUSIONS What kind of habitat does a tadpole need in order to survive?

4. VOCABULARY Use the vocabulary terms to describe the way a fish develops and the way a fly develops.

Test Prep

5. Critical Thinking Why would your parents want you to be a good helper if there were a new baby in your family?

6. Which animal goes through the most body shape changes in its life cycle?

A. grasshopper   **C.** moth

B. kitten   **D.** spider

Links

Writing

Narrative Writing
Write a **biography** (life story) of a pet. The pet can belong to you or to someone you know. Start with how it was born.

Math

Calculate Stages
One year in the life of a human is like seven years in a dog's life. What stage is a dog in at the age of two? At age nine, is it an adult or an older adult?

Art

Make a Mobile
Research the life cycle of a monarch butterfly. Then make a mobile illustrating the four stages of its life cycle. Share your mobile with the class.

For more links and activities, go to www.hspscience.com

Butterfly Tag

Keeping Track

A group of Canadian scientists began tagging monarchs in the 1930s. Today, dozens of organizations and groups help to track the migration of monarchs by tagging or simply counting the monarchs they observe.

Catching monarch butterflies is no easy task. "You have to sneak up behind them and then slip your net on them," said 8-year-old Evan Shauer from Wisconsin.

Before releasing the butterflies, Evan had a job to do. He placed a tiny numbered sticker on the back of each monarch. Those black-and-orange butterflies were among thousands that kids across the country tagged.

Flying South for Winter

Monarch butterflies do something very unusual for an insect. They migrate, or travel to a new location when the season changes. Each fall, millions of monarchs from North America head south. Most fly more than 2,000 miles to forests in Mexico.

Volunteers in Mexico look for the monarchs wearing tags. The tiny sticky tags tell scientists when and where the butterfly was caught and tagged. As a result, scientists can figure out which butterflies reached Mexico and how far they flew.

Monarchs in Danger

Scientists fear that monarchs may become endangered, or at risk of dying out. People are cutting down trees in Mexico where the butterflies spend the winter. "Our goal is to save the monarch migration," said butterfly expert Chip Taylor. "To do this, we have to learn as much as we can about how the number of monarchs changes from year to year." Kids like Evan are helping scientists do just that!

THINK ABOUT IT

1. Why are volunteers important to keeping track of the monarch population?

2. Why is it important to protect the trees in Mexico where monarch butterflies roost in the winter time?

Find out more! Log on to
www.hspscience.com

Dian Fossey

Dian Fossey was a scientist who did not work in a lab. Instead, she worked in the mountain forests of Rwanda, a country in Africa. Fossey went to Africa to study mountain gorillas. These animals live in forests about 10,000 feet above sea level.

Much of what is known about mountain gorillas comes from Fossey's work. For example, Fossey showed that the gorillas have a complex family structure. Fossey also worked to stop the illegal hunting of gorillas.

When Fossey later returned to the United States, she wrote a book. *Gorillas in the Mist* tells about her life in the jungle. She died in 1985 in Africa.

Career   Zoo Veterinarian

Animals in zoos have doctors that care for them when they are sick or injured. These doctors also care for them when they are healthy by providing them with regular vaccinations and checkups. Veterinarians use special equipment to check animals, just as medical doctors use special equipment to keep people healthy. Zoo veterinarians must understand how to keep many different animals healthy and to treat many exotic diseases.

Feeding a pangolin

Quick and Easy Project

Fruit Fly Life Cycle

Materials
- 2-L plastic bottle
- scissors
- tape
- film canister
- plastic butter tub
- fruit

Procedure

1. Make a hole in the top of the bottle. Cut off the top, and tape the top upside down inside the bottle. Cut the bottom off the bottle. **CAUTION: Be careful when using sharp instruments**.

2. Tape the film canister to the bottom of the butter tub. Fill the canister with pieces of fruit, such as bananas, berries, and apples. Push the bottle over the butter tub, and tape it in place.

3. Set the fruit fly trap anywhere, and watch it for two weeks. Try to identify each stage of the fruit fly life cycle.

Draw Conclusions

Describe the life cycle of a fruit fly. What kind of cycle does a fruit fly have? Why does it have such a short cycle?

Design Your Own Investigation

Are Some Traits Linked?

Design an experiment to test whether right-handedness and right-footedness are connected. Before you begin, make a prediction about what you will find. After you finish your experiment, draw a conclusion about your findings. Make a chart or graph to show the results. Explain your conclusion.

Review and Test Preparation

Vocabulary Review

Use the terms below to complete the sentences. The page numbers tell you where to look in the chapter if you need help.

trait p. 66   **genes** p. 67
heredity p. 66   **life cycle** p. 74
direct development p. 84
metamorphosis p. 86

1. The stages a plant or an animal goes through from the beginning of one generation to the beginning of a new generation is a _____.

2. The passing on of characteristics from parents to offspring is _____.

3. The change from a larva stage to a nymph stage is a kind of _____.

4. The basic units of heredity are _____.

5. Fish grow and develop in a process known as _____.

6. A characteristic that is passed from parent to child is a _____.

Check Understanding

Write the letter of the best choice.

7. How many complete sets of genes did you receive from your father?
   A. $\frac{1}{4}$ of a set   **C.** one full set
   B. $\frac{1}{2}$ of a set   **D.** two full sets

8. Which of the following plant structures are on a moss plant?
   F. leaves   **H.** seeds
   G. roots   **J.** spores

9. How can you **best** explain the resemblance between offspring and parents?
   A. eating habits   **C.** daily activity
   B. heredity   **D.** behavior

10. Which of this girl's characteristics is **not** controlled by genes?

   F. the color of her hair
   G. her dimples
   H. the shape of her earlobes
   J. her hairstyle

11. In which stage of the human life cycle is the body completely developed?
   A. adolescent   **C.** child
   B. adult   **D.** infant

12. What makes Grant such a fast runner?

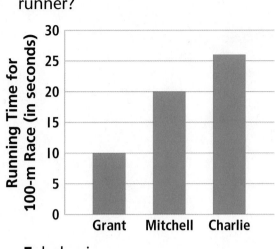

F. behavior

G. behavior and inherited traits

H. direct development

J. inherited traits

13. COMPARE AND CONTRAST Sexual and asexual production both result in more plants. What makes the product of asexual reproduction different?

A. The new plant is a different species.

B. The new plant is a clone.

C. The new plant cannot reproduce.

D. The new plant is a different color.

14. SEQUENCE Which stage is missing from this plant life cycle?

F. embryo   **H.** leaves

G. flower   **J.** roots

15. Which stage of a moss plant's life cycle produces sperm and eggs?

A. gametophyte   **C.** seed

B. plant   **D.** sporophyte

16. Which is the first stage of incomplete metamorphosis?

F. adult   **H.** larva

G. egg   **J.** nymph

Inquiry Skills

17. Describe an **experiment** that would help you **conclude** whether or not a plant needs water to grow.

18. Suppose you **observe** a tadpole grow into a frog. What can you **infer** about its life cycle?

Critical Thinking

19. How can you explain why the eyes of different humans can be many different colors?

20. Humans need to be cared for until they can care for themselves.

Part A Why do you think humans need to be taken care of much longer than all other animals?

Part B List some of the things you need to learn before you can take care of yourself completely.

Chapter 3

Adaptations

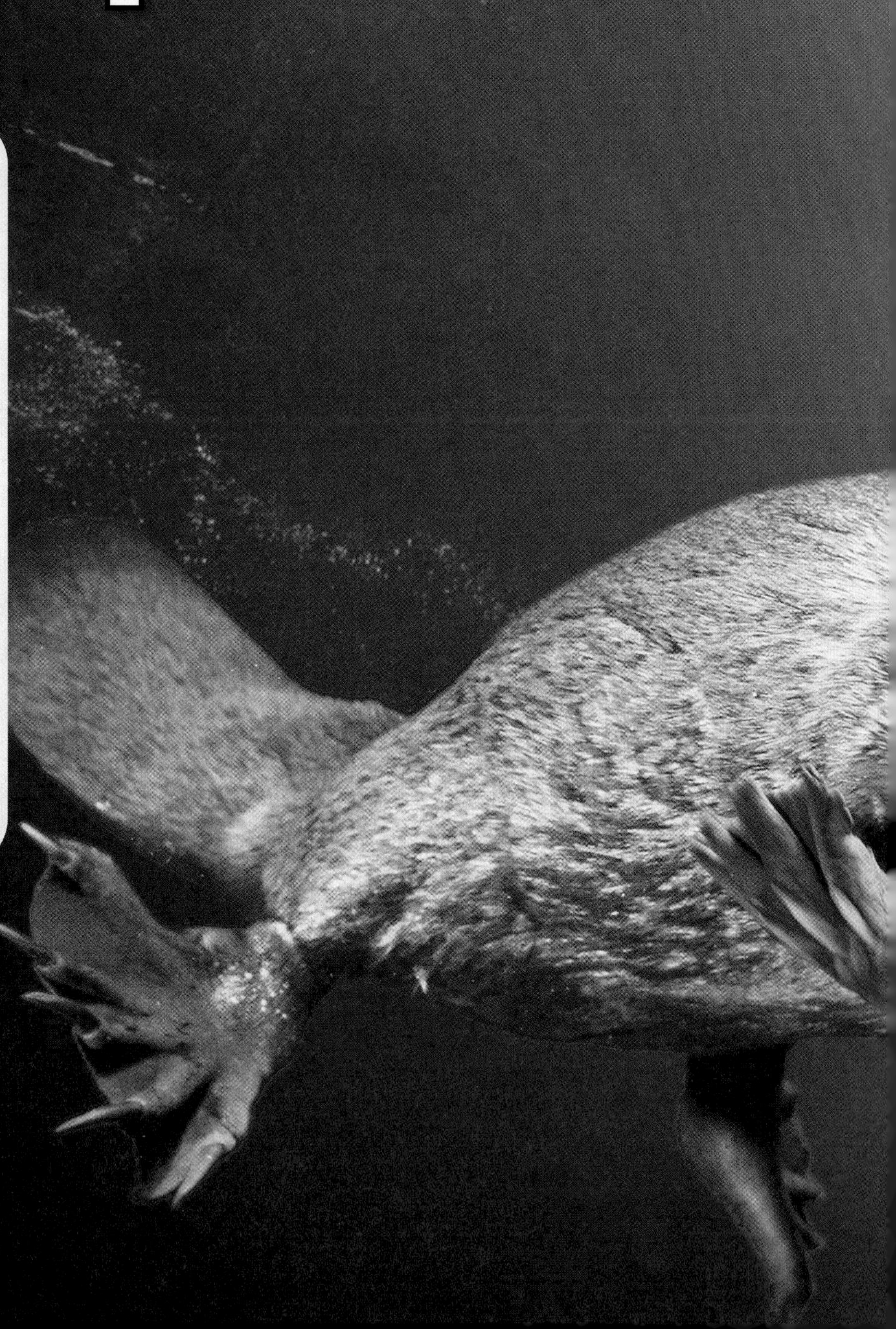

Lesson 1 How Do the Bodies of Animals Help Them Meet Their Needs?

Lesson 2 How Do the Behaviors of Animals Help Them Meet Their Needs?

Lesson 3 How Do Living Things of the Past Compare with Those of Today?

Vocabulary

basic needs
adaptation
instinct
hibernation
migration
learned behavior
fossil
extinction

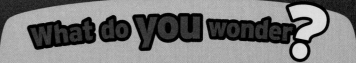

The platypus (PLAT•uh•puhs) is a mammal that lays eggs. It has specialized body parts for swimming and for eating in water. Why do you think it has webbed feet?

How Do the Bodies of Animals Help Them Meet Their Needs?

Fast Fact

Big Beak! This toucan is an eye-catching sight! Its long, colorful beak looks heavy, but it's really very light. The long beak helps the toucan reach fruit at the ends of branches. In the Investigate, you will explore characteristics that help birds survive in their ecosystems.

Eating Like a Bird

Materials tools—
- 2 chopsticks or unsharpened pencils
- clothespin
- spoon
- pliers
- forceps

food—
- plastic worms
- cooked rice
- cooked spaghetti
- raisins
- birdseed
- peanuts in shells
- water in a cup
- small paper plates

Food	Best Tool (Beak)	Observations

Procedure

1. Make a table like the one shown here.

2. Put the tools on one side of your desk, and think of them as bird beaks. Put each kind of food on a paper plate.

3. Place one type of food in the middle of your desk. Try picking up the food with each tool (beak), and decide which kind of beak works best.

4. Test all the beaks with all the foods and with the water. Use the table to record your observations and conclusions.

Step 3

Draw Conclusions

1. Which kind of beak is best for picking up small seeds? Which kind is best for crushing large seeds?

2. **Inquiry Skill** Scientists experiment and then draw conclusions about what they have learned. After experimenting, what conclusions can you draw about why bird beaks are different shapes?

Investigate Further

Use a reference book about birds. Match the tools you used with real bird beaks. Make a hypothesis about how beak shape relates to food. Then read your book to find out if you are correct.

VOCABULARY
basic needs p. 98
adaptation p. 100

SCIENCE CONCEPTS
▶ what basic needs are shared by all living things
▶ how adaptations allow living things to meet their needs

 READING FOCUS SKILL

MAIN IDEA AND DETAILS
Look for different kinds of basic needs.

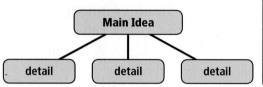

Basic Needs

What do you need to survive? You might want jeans in the latest style. You might want pizza for dinner every night. But you do not really need these things to survive.

All living things, from ants to tigers to you, have the same basic needs. These **basic needs** are food, water, air, and shelter.

Living things meet their needs in a variety of ways. Plants can make their own food, but they must have sunlight to do it. Most other living things depend on plants—or on animals that eat plants—for food.

Many animals, such as frogs and wolves, get their food by catching it. Some animals, such as vultures, wait until another animal has killed something. Then they eat the leftovers. Humans get most of their food by growing and raising plants and animals.

Plants get water from rain and from moist soil. Many animals drink water from streams and puddles, but some desert

Like every other living thing, a tiger needs water.

animals obtain enough water to survive from the foods they eat.

All animals must take in oxygen. Animals that live on land and some animals that live in water get oxygen from air. Other animals that live in water get oxygen from the water.

Shelter can take many forms. Some insects live under rocks, while foxes make dens in hollow logs. Prairie dogs dig burrows in the ground, and eels hide in coral reefs. Delicate plants grow in protected places. People build homes of many sizes and shapes.

Hunger and thirst signal the need to eat and drink. Rain and cold tell many animals to find shelter. Meeting basic needs isn't always easy, but living things must do it to survive.

 MAIN IDEA AND DETAILS How do you meet your basic needs?

After beavers cut sticks and twigs from trees, they eat the leaves and bark. Then they use the sticks to build shelters. ▶

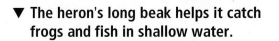

▼ The heron's long beak helps it catch frogs and fish in shallow water.

▲ Like other living things, this alligator needs air. It keeps its nostrils above water while it watches for food.

Adaptations

Plants and animals have adaptations that help them meet their needs. An **adaptation** is a body part or a behavior that a living thing gets from its parents, and that helps it to survive.

One adaptation is fur color. For example, during the summer, the snowshoe hare is rusty brown. This helps it blend with the ground. In the winter, the rabbit's fur turns white. This helps it blend with the snow. The color change helps the rabbit hide from enemies.

Instead of fur, fish and reptiles have scales. Their scales help protect them from injury and from drying out. Often, the color and pattern of their scales help them hide from enemies. A snake's scales help it slide along the ground to find food, water, and shelter.

Many frogs and lizards have long tongues that help them catch insects. Imagine how such a long tongue would look on a lion. Lions have other adaptations that help them catch their food, such as speed, strength, long claws, and sharp teeth.

You have explored differences in bird beaks. Different kinds of feet also help birds meet their needs. A robin's feet allow it to perch on a branch. An eagle's claws help it snatch up food, while a penguin's feet help it swim.

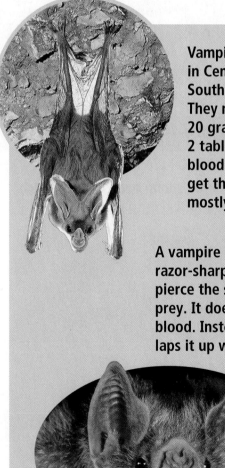

Vampire bats live in Central and South America. They need about 20 grams (about 2 tablespoons) of blood a day. They get their food mostly from cattle.

A vampire bat's tiny, razor-sharp teeth easily pierce the skin of its prey. It doesn't suck the blood. Instead, the bat laps it up with its tongue.

◀ A goat's teeth are adapted for the food it eats. Large and flat, these teeth are just right for grinding up grasses.

▼ Most goats eat grasses during the summer. During the winter, they eat hay, which is a dried grass. All these grasses require a lot of chewing.

No one is sure how birds find their way from a summer home to a winter home. They might have an inner compass that guides them.

Birds often fly in a V formation. This adaptation helps them move through the air more easily. A group can fly farther in this formation than one bird can fly alone.

During a long, cold winter, food and water can be scarce. Animals need more shelter. Many have adapted to winter by migrating or hibernating.

Migration means "moving from a summer home to a winter home and back again." Gray whales' bodies allow them to swim 16,000 to 23,000 kilometers (10,000 to 14,000 mi) a year. They spend summer in the Arctic. In the fall, they swim to warmer waters. There, they give birth to their young.

Monarch butterflies migrate up to 4,800 kilometers (3,000 mi). As the weather cools, monarchs west of the Rocky Mountains fly to the west coast. Monarchs east of the Rockies fly to Mexico. There, they rest for the winter.

During *hibernation,* an animal's heart and breathing rates slow almost to a stop. Bats, ground squirrels, and woodchucks hibernate. Their bodies are adapted to survive for long periods on a tiny amount of food and oxygen.

Bears, skunks, and chipmunks sleep a lot. This helps them survive the cold winter months. Yet their body systems are still active. They are not hibernating.

 MAIN IDEA AND DETAILS What are three examples of adaptations?

Insta-Lab

All Thumbs
Use masking tape to tape your partner's thumb to his or her hand. Then ask your partner to write, pick up a pencil, eat, and so on. How is a thumb an adaptation?

Growth and Decay

All plants and animals follow a cycle of life. It begins with a fertilized egg. Sprouting, being born, or hatching come next. Then the seedling or baby grows into an adult. Adult living things reproduce in many ways. Some make seeds, some give birth to babies, and some lay eggs.

Living things are being born all the time. They are also dying and decaying. Fungi, insects, bacteria, and other plants help to decay, or decompose, dead organisms. The nutrients in a dead organism often become part of the soil.

This makes the soil richer, which helps new plants to grow.

Living things can complete their life cycles only if they are able to meet all their basic needs. Adaptations help living things meet their basic needs.

If a plant or an animal can't meet its needs, it might die before it can reproduce. If this continues for every member of the species, this kind of living thing will no longer survive on Earth.

 MAIN IDEA AND DETAILS What parts make up the cycle of life?

◀ This tree fell years ago in the rain forest. As the log decayed, seeds blew onto it and sprouted. Now the dead tree is a "nurse log" for new trees. The new trees will grow in a row.

Adult trees stretch their roots around the nurse log and into the soil.

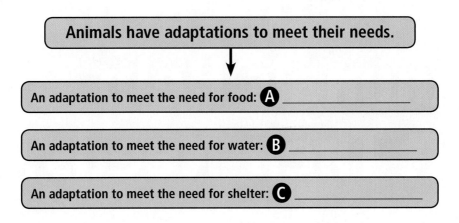

Focus Skill

1. MAIN IDEA AND DETAILS Draw and complete this graphic organizer.

Animals have adaptations to meet their needs.

An adaptation to meet the need for food: **A** _____

An adaptation to meet the need for water: **B** _____

An adaptation to meet the need for shelter: **C** _____

2. SUMMARIZE Write a summary of this lesson. Begin with the sentence *All living things have basic needs.*

3. DRAW CONCLUSIONS Name three adaptations in behavior that some animals show during winter.

4. VOCABULARY Write a paragraph that includes a blank for each vocabulary term. Have a partner fill in the terms.

Test Prep

5. Critical Thinking Explain two ways that a body covering can help an animal meet its basic needs.

6. Which adaptation helps a robin catch a worm?
A. sharp eyesight   **C.** perching feet
B. feather coloring **D.** nest building

Links

Writing ✏

Narrative Writing
Write a **story** about how a real animal in a forest uses an adaptation to meet its needs in some way. Make your story exciting!

Math 9÷3

Solve a Problem
A deer must have about 20 acres of land to meet its need for food, water, and shelter. One square mile has 640 acres. How many deer could live on 2 square miles of land?

Art ✏

Collage
Cut out magazine pictures, or use your own drawings, to make a collage of the basic needs of a person or a specific animal. Then display your work.

For more links and activities, go to www.hspscience.com

How Do the Behaviors of Animals Help Them Meet Their Needs?

Fast Fact

Whale Song Some people call beluga whales the canaries of the sea. Beluga song can be heard above the water! Young belugas learn how to survive by watching adult belugas. In the Investigate, you will see if a goldfish has the ability to learn.

Train a Fish

Materials ● **goldfish in a bowl** ● **goldfish food**

Procedure

① Work in a group of three or four classmates to train a goldfish. On the first day, observe the behavior of the fish when you hold your hand above the bowl. Then feed the fish by dropping some food into the bowl. Record the fish's behavior.

② The next day, hold your hand a little closer above the bowl. Then drop the pellet. Record the fish's behavior.

③ Each day, repeat Step 2, moving your hand nearer the water.

④ Use your observations to plan how to continue the experiment.

Draw Conclusions

1. From your observations, what can you infer about a fish's ability to learn?

2. **Inquiry Skill** When scientists experiment, they design procedures to gather data. How did observing the fish help you plan the experiment?

Step 1

Step 2

Investigate Further

Observe a pet's behavior. List things that the pet does that no one taught it to do. Also list things it may have learned.

Reading in Science

VOCABULARY
instinct p. 106
hibernation p. 107
migration p. 108
learned behavior
    p. 110

SCIENCE CONCEPTS

how instinctive
    behaviors help
    animals meet their
    needs

how learned behaviors
    help animals meet
    their needs

READING FOCUS SKILL

MAIN IDEA AND DETAILS
Look for ways animals fill their
basic needs.

Instincts

When you were born, you already
knew how to suck to get milk. You
knew how to cry. Animals already know
things, too. A spider knows how to spin
a web to catch food. Some animals,
like zebras, know that living together
in herds helps protect them from
predators. Some animals know how to
protect themselves from the weather.
All of these behaviors are **instincts**—
behaviors that animals begin life with
that help them meet their needs.

MAIN IDEA AND DETAILS What are
some instinctive behaviors?

▼ Orb-weaver spiders spin new webs every
    night. Each kind of spider begins life
    knowing the pattern for its own kind of web.

▲ Weaverbirds build
complex nests from
grasses and other
materials. They hatch
knowing how to
weave their nests.

Hibernation

Some animals live where winters are very cold. Many of them know by instinct how to get ready for winter. First, they eat more food than normal, so they can gain fat. Then, they find dens or build shelters. When the days become short and cold, the animals move to shelters. They enter a dormant, inactive state called **hibernation** (hy•ber•NAY•shuhn). Normal body activities slow. The heart barely beats, and breathing almost stops. The body temperature drops to just above freezing.

Since the body is barely working, a hibernating animal doesn't use much energy and doesn't need to eat. There is enough fat stored in the animal's body to keep it alive through the winter. By springtime, hibernating animals are thin. They are very hungry!

MAIN IDEA AND DETAILS Why do some animals hibernate?

Some turtles hibernate in winter. They don't breathe, but they get oxygen from special cells inside their tail openings. ▶

◀ When the weather is cold, koi fish hibernate at the bottom of a pond.

A bat's normal heartbeat rate is 400 beats per minute. When the bat hibernates, its heart beats 11 to 25 times per minute. ▶

▼ A woodchuck digs a winter burrow. Its body temperature drops from 36°C (97°F) to less than 8°C (47°F).

Some male frogs hibernate at the bottom of ponds. The female frogs and their young stay in holes or dens on land. ▶

Migration

Every year, people gather to watch whales. People also like to watch caribou travel. It's possible to predict when to watch whales and caribou. These animals travel every year at about the same time.

Migrate means "to move from one region to another." When animals regularly move as a group from one region to another and back, it's a **migration**. Animal migrations can depend on seasons or on other factors.

Migration is an instinctive behavior. Generally, animals migrate to a place that has more food and a better climate. Some migrations are puzzling. For example, young salmon go out to sea. They return to lay eggs in the mountain stream where they were hatched.

 MAIN IDEA AND DETAILS How do animals know when to migrate?

Math in Science
Interpret Data

Which Animal Migrates the Farthest?

Migration Distances (in kilometers)

Animal Migration Routes

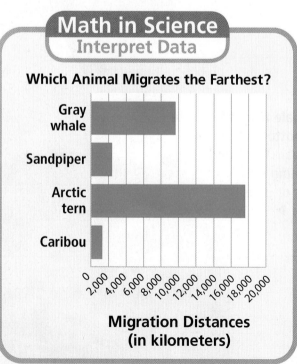

Gray whales feed in cold northern waters in winter and travel south in summer to look for mates and to give birth.

108

Caribou spend the winter in forests in northern Canada. Then, in early spring, they move north.

The sandpiper spends summers in eastern Canada. In winter, it flies nonstop over the Atlantic to South America.

The arctic tern travels farther than any other animal. It breeds in the summer, north of the Arctic Circle. In fall, it migrates to the Antarctic ice packs.

For more links and activities, go to www.hspscience.com

Learned Behaviors

Many animals have only instinctive behaviors to help them meet their needs. But some animals also have **learned behaviors**. What instincts did you have when you were born? Did you have to learn how to eat, drink, and sleep? What other behaviors have you learned? You learned to walk and feed yourself. Now you can write and play sports. Most of your behaviors are learned. Who helped you learn these things? Older animals usually teach young animals learned behaviors.

Most mammals raise their young. Mammal mothers usually teach their young how to get food and how to protect themselves. Among some animals, both parents care for and teach their young.

Some animals can be trained to change their behaviors. Dogs often instinctively bark at strangers, but people can train them not to do so. Horses are trained to respond to their riders. These are learned behaviors.

 MAIN IDEA AND DETAILS What are some behaviors bears learn?

Bear cubs learn to climb trees when they are about six months old. The mother sends them up a tree for safety. ▶

Robins are ready to leave the nest two weeks after hatching. Then the parents teach them how to fly. ▶

▼ Tiger cubs imitate their mother's every move while she hunts. They learn from her example.

Insta-Lab

Learn How

Make a list of behaviors you have learned in order to meet your basic needs. Compare your list with a classmate's. Why do you think humans have many more learned behaviors than most other animals?

110

Focus Skill

1. MAIN IDEA AND DETAILS Copy and complete this graphic organizer.

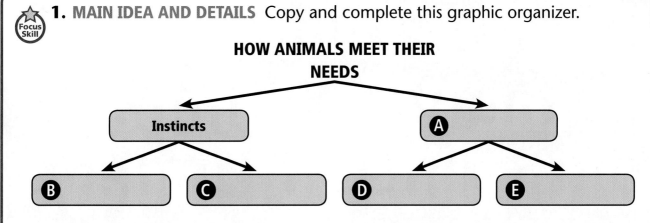

HOW ANIMALS MEET THEIR NEEDS

- Instincts
  - **B**
  - **C**
- **A**
  - **D**
  - **E**

2. SUMMARIZE Use the graphic organizer to write a paragraph in which you summarize how animals meet their basic needs.

3. DRAW CONCLUSIONS Does a butterfly meet its basic needs by instinct or by learned behavior? What leads you to your conclusion?

4. VOCABULARY Write a paragraph, using all the vocabulary terms from this lesson.

Test Prep

5. Critical Thinking Why would you **not** feed koi in a pond in winter?

6. Why does a hibernating animal's temperature drop?

A. to gain energy   **C.** to protect its young

B. to provide food   **D.** to conserve energy

Links

Writing

Narrative Writing
Choose an animal that migrates. Research its migration path. Then write a **story** about its migration.

Math   9÷3

Multiply Whole Numbers
A gray whale eats for only four months of the year. Then it eats 300 kilograms (660 lb) of food each day. How many pounds of food does it eat in one week?

Health

Basic Needs
Make a list of behaviors you have learned to keep yourself healthy and meet your basic needs.

For more links and activities, go to **www.hspscience.com**

How Do Living Things of the Past Compare with Those of Today?

Fast Fact

Step Back in Time Thousands of fossils have been found at Thomas Farm in central Florida. More are still being discovered. In the Investigate, you will learn more about fossils.

Make a Fossil

Materials
- **white glue**
- **8 sugar cubes**
- **strainer**
- **sink or large bowl**
- **warm water**

Procedure

1. Use the glue to put together 4 sugar cubes, making a 2 x 2 layer.

2. Glue the other 4 cubes together to make a second layer. Let both layers dry separately for 5 minutes.

3. Spread glue in the shape of a shell on one layer, and place the other layer on top. Let them dry overnight.

4. Put the two-layer structure in the strainer. Hold the strainer over a sink or bowl.

5. Pour warm water over the structure. Observe what happens to the sugar and the glue. Record your observations.

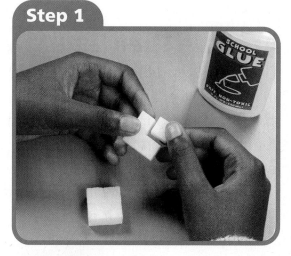

Step 1

Draw Conclusions

1. You made a model of a fossil. What parts of a plant or an animal did the sugar cubes stand for? What parts did the dried glue stand for?

2. **Inquiry Skill** Scientists infer, or explain, based on what they observe. Based on your observations, what can you infer about how fossils form?

Step 5

Investigate Further

Why might fossil skeletons break apart? Hypothesize what will happen if you put your fossil in a bag with rocks and shake it. Try it. Record your results.

Reading in Science

VOCABULARY
fossil p. 114
extinction p. 118

SCIENCE CONCEPTS
▶ how living things of long ago compare with those of today

 READING FOCUS SKILL
COMPARE AND CONTRAST
Look for ways animals of long ago are like those of today.

| alike | — | different |

Animals Then and Now

A **fossil** is evidence of a plant or an animal that lived long ago. Footprints that formed when an animal stepped in mud are one kind of fossil. Over a long time, the mud hardened into rock. Footprints tell us about an animal's size. They also can tell how it moved.

Many fossils are bones that became buried before they could decay. Minerals replaced the bones, but the shapes remain.

Scientists compare these fossils with the footprints and bones of animals that are alive today. Using the comparisons, they can infer how animals have changed.

Although they are completely unrelated, fossils show that the triceratops (try•SAIR•uh•tahps) and today's rhinoceros (ry•NAHS•er•uhs) share the same body shape and a horned nose. Dinosaurs were reptiles, while rhinos are mammals.

Triceratops fossil skeleton

Modern-day rhinoceros

Triceratops

114

Camels lived in North America many years ago. Fossils tell us that some ancient camels were about the size of a rabbit. Others were about 4.5 meters (15 ft) tall at their shoulders!

Modern-day camel

Florida camel

Florida camel fossil

A few animals, such as turtles, are much like ones from long ago. Others are very different now. By a careful study of their fossils, scientists can link animals of long ago with those of today. However, many ancient animals are now gone.

 COMPARE AND CONTRAST How is the study of ancient animals different from the study of animals that live today?

Modern-day coelacanth

By the early part of the twentieth century, the coelacanth (SEE•luh•kanth) fish shown in this fossil was thought to exist no longer. But a live coelacanth was caught near South Africa in 1938. ▶

Plants Then and Now

You might have found a plant fossil on a flat rock in a park or in your own back yard. Some of these fossils were formed when plant leaves fell on muddy ground millions of years ago. The leaves made an impression in the mud. When the mud dried, the imprint of the leaf was still there. This imprint shows the size, shape, and details of the leaf.

Have you ever held a piece of wood that felt like a rock? Petrified wood is another kind of plant fossil. It formed when a tree fell on the ground and was buried in mud before it could decay.

Minerals slowly replaced the wood. In time, the wood became rock.

Like some animals of long ago, many plants of long ago disappeared. Scientists know about them only because of fossils. You can also find fossils that look much like some plants that still grow today.

Many other plants have survived, but they have changed over time. In fact, plants are still changing. For example, farmers are now growing new kinds of corn that resist insects.

COMPARE AND CONTRAST **How are plants of long ago like animals of long ago?**

About 300 million years ago, most of the plants on Earth were ferns. These plants and others died and were buried under many layers of soil. ▼

Fern fossil

Insta-Lab

Fossil Quiz

Flatten some clay, and lightly press an object into it. Don't let anyone see the object you used. Then challenge others to identify the object you used by looking only at the imprint. How is your imprint like a fossil imprint?

Modern-day fern

Ginkgo trees are often called living fossils because they have not changed much in 100 million years. Some types of ginkgo trees growing in China have existed more than 3000 years.

Ginkgo leaf fossil

Ginkgo leaves

Modern-day ginkgo tree

Bristlecone pine trees were growing 100 million years ago. The oldest tree living today is almost 5000 years old! Fossils show that these trees have changed very little.

Bristlecone pine

Pine cones

Fossilized pine cones

Extinction

Many plants and animals are now extinct (ek•STINGKT). **Extinction** means that all the members of a certain kind of living thing have died. Extinction can happen when a habitat changes. For example, a habitat may become drier. Then the habitat may no longer meet the needs of some living things. Plants in these places die. Animals must find new places to live or they will die, too.

Extinction can also happen for other reasons. One reason is an increase in predators. Another is a decrease in the food supply. About 65 million years ago, 70 percent of all living things became extinct. It is possible that an asteroid hit Earth, changing the environment and reducing the food supply.

Extinction is still happening. People may cause extinction when they cut forests or fill in wetlands. This change in the environment can cause living things to lose their habitats.

COMPARE AND CONTRAST How might a change in the environment affect plants differently than it would animals?

The last woolly mammoth died about 30,000 years ago. ▼

◀ **The last great auk died in 1844. These birds, which could not fly, were killed for food and to be used as bait.**

Fossils of saber-toothed cats have been found in California's La Brea (BRAY•uh) tar pits. The last saber-toothed cat died about 10,000 years ago.

1. **COMPARE AND CONTRAST** Copy and complete this graphic organizer. Show how a rhinoceros and a triceratops are the same and different.

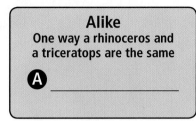

Alike
One way a rhinoceros and a triceratops are the same

A _____

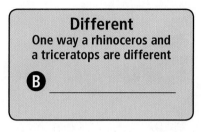

Different
One way a rhinoceros and a triceratops are different

B _____

2. **SUMMARIZE** Write two sentences to tell the most important information in this lesson.

3. **DRAW CONCLUSIONS** Suppose you have found a fossil. Why should you be careful with it?

4. **VOCABULARY** Write a paragraph, leaving spaces for this lesson's two vocabulary words. Have a partner fill in the words.

Test Prep

5. **Critical Thinking** Why are fossils important?

6. Which of these could be called a living fossil?
   A. woolly mammoth   **C.** camel
   B. rhinoceros   **D.** bristlecone pine

Links

Writing

Persuasive Writing

Suppose you find an unusual fossil. Write a **letter** to a scientist, describing your fossil. Try to persuade him or her to come to see it. Explain why the fossil might be important.

Math 9÷3

Make a Bar Graph

Make a bar graph to show how many plants and animals are close to extinction in these states: Hawai'i, 317; California, 299; Florida, 111; Tennessee, 96; Texas, 91.

Social Studies

Then and Now

Research what your region may have looked like 65 million years ago. What kinds of plants and animals lived in your neighborhood then?

For more links and activities, go to www.hspscience.com

Slithering
Through the Air

Look, up in the sky. It's a bird. It's a plane. No, it's a snake. That's right, a snake. The paradise tree snake can soar through the air, even though it doesn't have wings.

The paradise tree snake can glide through the air to move from one tree to another, to chase prey, or to avoid being eaten by a predator. Until recently, scientists were not sure how the snake managed to move through the air.

A Soaring Serpent

Scientist Jake Socha has been studying this "flying snake" for several years. He has tried to learn how it performs its aerial feats. Socha traveled to Southeast Asia, where he built a *scaffold,* or support structure. He attached a branch to the top of the scaffold and placed still cameras and video cameras around the branch. He also used a *theodolite* to set up the platform. A theodolite is a tool used by engineers to determine the horizontal or vertical angle of a structure being built.

After his "tree" was complete, Socha placed a paradise tree snake on the branch and waited for it to take off. "Occasionally, when the snake wouldn't move, I'd give it a prod," he said, "and sit there and wait and hope it would jump off."

As soon as the snake began to move, the cameras started snapping photos. The photos show that as the snake soars through the air, it flattens itself out and forms an S shape. The snake then begins twisting back and forth and from top to bottom. The motion helps it control its path through the air and glide to a smooth landing.

Not Really a Flier

The paradise tree snake is one of several kinds of flying snakes.

According to Socha, the snake is more of a parachuter than a flier, which means that it can only glide downward.

But you shouldn't worry too much about a paradise tree snake falling on you from the sky. Not only has Socha never heard of that happening, but the paradise tree snake can only be found in a remote part of Southeast Asia.

THINK ABOUT IT

1. Do you know of any other animals, other than birds, that fly from tree to tree?
2. In what other ways can cameras be used in doing scientific research?

Find out more! Log on to
www.hspscience.com

Lydia Villa-Komaroff

Lydia Villa-Komaroff grew up in a big family in New Mexico. When Villa-Komaroff was five, her father brought home a set of encyclopedias. He told her that all she needed to know was in those books.

She must have listened to her dad because Villa-Komaroff grew up to be one of the top scientists in her field. She has made many important discoveries in the field of biology.

Her most important discovery was in 1978 when she proved that bacterial cells could be changed to make **insulin.** Insulin is important in treating diabetes. People with diabetes need insulin to live. Villa-Komaroff's discovery made it easier and cheaper to get insulin.

Career | Biologist

When a drug company develops a new drug, biologists usually take part in the important first steps. Biologists study living things and how those things interact with their environments. These scientists work on a wide range of projects, including developing new drugs, increasing crop yields, and protecting the environment.

You Can Do It!

Observe Decomposition

Materials
- 1-gallon plastic bag
- vegetable scraps
- dried leaves
- green leaves
- dirt

Procedure

1. Fill the plastic bag one-fourth full of dried leaves. Add two handfuls of dirt.
2. Add green leaves and vegetable scraps until the bag is one-half full. Don't add any grease, oil, or meat or dairy products.
3. Add a little water. Seal the bag and shake it well. Then partially open the bag. Place the bag in sunlight.
4. Observe the bag for two weeks. Shake it or mix it every day or two.

Draw Conclusions

What caused the plant materials to decompose? Would the material in the bag be good for a garden? Which basic need would decomposing plant matter provide for earthworms?

Design Your Own Investigation

Earthworm Behavior

Design an experiment to see how earthworms react to changes in their environment. What do they do when they're uncovered? How do they respond to the light and heat of a flashlight? What do they do when it rains? Be sure to return the worms to a garden.

Review and Test Preparation

Vocabulary Review

Use the terms below to complete the sentences. The page numbers tell where to look in the chapter if you need help.

basic needs p. 98
adaptation p. 100
instincts p. 106
hibernation p. 107
migration p. 108
learned
behavior p. 110
fossil p. 114
extinction
p. 118

1. Both breathing rate and body temperature change during _____.

2. The development of a thick beak for grinding seeds is an _____.

3. Behaviors that you begin life with are _____.

4. Air and water are _____.

5. When all the members of a species have died out completely, the result is called _____.

6. Speaking is a _____.

7. When you see a flock of geese fly south in the fall, you are watching a _____.

8. An imprint of an ancient fern in rock is a type of _____.

Check Understanding

Write the letter of the best choice.

9. Why does a whale surface?
   A. for fun   **C.** for air
   B. for food   **D.** to see

10. **MAIN IDEA AND DETAILS** Which detail relates to learned behavior?
    F. A mother feeds her baby.
    G. A fish swims in a pond.
    H. You yawn.
    J. A kitten watches its mother hunt.

11. Which animal on this bar graph has the shortest migration route?

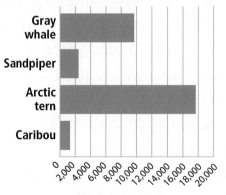

**Migration Distances
(in kilometers)**

    A. arctic tern
    B. caribou
    C. sandpiper
    D. gray whale

12. COMPARE AND CONTRAST Which statement compares the camels of long ago with camels of today?

F. Camels that live in Africa have hooves.

G. Skeletons of camels of long ago are similar to those of camels today.

H. Ancient camels ate grass.

J. The bones of ancient camels are fossils.

13. Notice the beak pictured here. What is it an adaptation for?

A. eating fruit

B. eating leaves

C. grinding seeds

D. spearing fish

14. Why don't you see any ground squirrels in winter?

F. They are migrating.

G. They don't like the cold.

H. They are hiding.

J. They are hibernating.

15. What can you learn by studying fossils of an organism?

A. how long it lived

B. how well-adapted it was

C. its color

D. how it compares with modern-day organisms

16. What will probably happen to a tiger that isn't raised with other tigers?

F. It will become friendly.

G. It will never learn to hunt.

H. It will live longer.

J. It will lose its instincts.

Inquiry Skills

17. Explain how your **observations** of the goldfish's behavior helped you plan how to train it.

18. What tool would you use for a **model** of a beak of a bird that eats seeds?

Critical Thinking

19. Why do you think caribou grow hair on the bottom of each foot in winter and lose it in summer?

20. Suppose you want to help save a bird that is threatened with extinction.

Part A What things should you study about its habitat?

Part B Why would it be a good idea to find out if the birds are laying eggs and how many chicks are hatching?

Looking at Ecosystems

LIFE SCIENCE

Coyne Center Elementary Theme Gardens

TO: maria@hspscience.com

FROM: steven@hspscience.com

RE: Milan, Illinois

Dear Maria,

You asked me where I learned how to be a gardener. Believe it or not, I learned at school! My school has a schoolyard habitat that has 12 outdoor garden areas. We even have a pizza garden! We grow all of the toppings to make a delicious pizza!

Your pen pal friend,

Steven

Colorado's Ocean Journey

TO: jalen@hspscience.com

FROM: destiny@hspscience.com

RE: Colorado

Dear Jalen,

At Colorado's Ocean Journey, you can see a model of the long route a fish has to swim to get from the Colorado River to the sea. Lots of plants and animals rely on the water to survive. You get to see those up close as you travel along the way. That is quite a journey!

Your pen pal,

Destiny

Experiment!

Counting Species When people develop land and build new houses, the environment that was already there is changed. The animals living in the habitat must find new places to live. Is there a difference between natural habitats and habitats that humans have developed? Are there more types of living things in one of the two kinds of environments? Plan and conduct an experiment to find out.

Chapter

4

Understanding Ecosystems

Lesson 1 What Are the Parts of an Ecosystem?

Lesson 2 What Factors Influence Ecosystems?

Lesson 3 How Do Humans Affect Ecosystems?

Vocabulary

environment
ecosystem
population
community
biotic
abiotic
diversity
pollution
habitat restoration

This hawk has very sharp claws, called talons. Why don't birds such as sparrows have talons?

1

What Are the Parts of an Ecosystem?

Fast Fact

Silver Kings The tarpon in this photograph are not yet full-grown! These fish don't become adults until they are between 7 and 13 years old, when they can weigh more than 91 kilograms (200 lb). Tarpon live in salt water, but they can survive in a variety of ecosystems. In the Investigate, you will observe how sunlight affects plants in another ecosystem.

Modeling an Ecosystem

Materials
- gravel
- 6 small plants
- 2 empty 2-L soda bottles with tops cut off
- sand
- water in a spray bottle
- soil
- clear plastic wrap
- 2 rubber bands

Procedure

1. Pour a layer of gravel, a layer of sand, and then a layer of soil into the bottom of each bottle.

2. Plant three plants in each bottle.

3. Spray the plants and the soil with water. Cover the top of each bottle with plastic wrap. If necessary, hold the wrap in place with a rubber band.

4. Put one of the terrariums you just made in a sunny spot. Put the other one in a dark closet or cabinet.

5. After three days, observe each terrarium and record what you see.

Draw Conclusions

1. What did you observe about each of your ecosystems after three days? What part was missing from one ecosystem?

2. **Inquiry Skill** Scientists often learn more about how things affect one another by making a model. What did you learn by making a model and observing how its parts interact?

Step 2

Step 3

Investigate Further

What effect does sunlight have on seeds that have just been planted? First, write your hypothesis. Then plan an experiment to see if your hypothesis is supported.

VOCABULARY
environment p. 132
ecosystem p. 132
population p. 134
community p. 136

SCIENCE CONCEPTS
▶ how living and nonliving parts of an ecosystem interact
▶ what populations and communities are

READING FOCUS SKILL

MAIN IDEA AND DETAILS
Look for the parts that make up an ecosystem.

```
                    Main Idea

      detail         detail         detail
```

Ecosystems

Where do you live? You might name your street and town. You also live in an environment. An **environment** is all the living and nonliving things that surround you. The living things in your environment are people, other animals, and plants. The nonliving things around you include water, air, soil, and weather.

The parts of an environment affect one another in many ways. For example, animals eat plants. The soil affects which plants can live in a place. Clean air and clean water help keep both plants and animals healthy. All the living and nonliving things in an area form an **ecosystem** (EE•koh•sis•tuhm).

An ecosystem can be very small. It might be the space under a rock. That space might be home to insects and tiny plants. You might need a microscope to see some of the things living there.

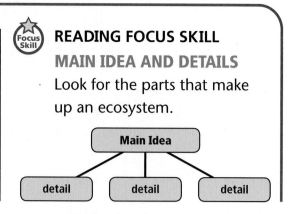

This prairie smoke plant grows well in the hot, dry climate of prairies and grasslands. ▼

Prairie dogs also live on the prairies and grasslands. ▼

Moose thrive in a coniferous, or evergreen, forest ecosystem.

The small ecosystem found under a rock has nonliving parts, too. They include pockets of air and the soil under the rock. You might find a few drops of water or maybe just damp soil. All ecosystems must have at least a little water.

The ecosystem under this rock has a climate. The *climate* in an area is the average weather over many years. Climate includes temperature and rainfall. The climate of an ecosystem depends on where the ecosystem is. If this rock is in Florida, its climate is warm and wet. If the rock is in Maine, its winters are icy.

An ecosystem can also be as large as a forest. A forest can provide many kinds of food and shelter. This ecosystem may include hundreds of kinds of plants and animals. Each organism finds what it needs in the forest.

Like all ecosystems, a forest has nonliving parts. They include water, air, soil, and climate. Later, you will read more about ways living and nonliving parts of an ecosystem affect one another.

 MAIN IDEA AND DETAILS Name the two parts of an ecosystem, and give two examples of each part.

133

This individual waterlily is part of a large population of waterlilies.

Individuals and Populations

One plant or animal is an *individual.* For example, one blueberry bush is an individual. One honeybee is an individual. One blue jay is an individual. You are an individual.

A group made up of the same kind of individuals living in the same ecosystem is a **population**. A group of blueberry bushes is a population. So is a hive of bees. So are all the blue jays living in one forest. So are all the people living in one city.

Robins might live in the same forest as the blue jays. Robins are a different kind of bird. That makes them a different population.

The members of a population might not live in a group. For example, frogs don't live in families. Still, a number of green tree frogs may live near the same pond. They belong to the same population. Bullfrogs might also live near that pond. They are a different population.

Many animals live in groups. People live in families. How many people are in your family? Wolves live in packs. A pack can have from 3 to 20 wolves. A wolf population may have several packs. The wolf population in Yellowstone National Park includes 19 packs.

Some populations can live in more than one kind of ecosystem. For instance, red-winged blackbirds often live in wetlands, but they are also found in other areas. Red-winged blackbirds can live in different ecosystems. If one ecosystem no longer meets the needs of these birds, they fly to another one.

Some populations can live in only one kind of ecosystem. One such animal is the Hine's emerald dragonfly. This insect can live only in certain wetlands. It can't survive in other places. Because this dragonfly can live only in specific places, its total number is very small.

Ecosystems are often named for the main population that lives there. For example, one kind of ecosystem forms where a river flows into the ocean. There, fresh water mixes with salt water. Many trees can't live in salty water. But mangrove trees have roots that allow them to get rid of the salt in the water.

When many mangrove trees live in a salty ecosystem, the area is called a *mangrove swamp.*

Focus Skill **MAIN IDEA AND DETAILS** **Name an individual and a population that are not mentioned on these two pages.**

Insta-Lab

Eeek! Oh System!

Work with a partner to list some of the populations in your school ecosystem. Think about the building and the land around it. Then compare lists with other students. Did you list the same populations?

This individual male red-winged blackbird is part of a large population of blackbirds.

A population of red-winged blackbirds can include several million birds. Some of the birds fly 80 kilometers (50 mi) to find food.

Communities

You live in a community. Other animals and plants do, too. A **community** is all the populations that live in the same place.

Have you visited the Everglades National Park? Many different populations make up this community. The plants include mangrove trees, cypress trees, and saw grass. If you have been to the Everglades, you may know about the mosquitoes from getting bitten! The area has 43 kinds. And 50 kinds of butterflies live there.

Animals found in the Everglades community include alligators, bobcats, and raccoons. Bird-watchers like to visit the Everglades. They try to see some of the 350 kinds of land birds and 16 kinds of wading birds that live there.

In some ways, the Everglades is like all communities. The plants and animals there depend on one another. Some animals eat the plants. Other animals eat the plant eaters. The animals help spread the plants' seeds. The plants provide shelter for the animals.

MAIN IDEA AND DETAILS **Name three populations that might be found in a forest community.**

▼ Many populations make up the communities in this cold taiga ecosystem. They include evergreen trees, moose, and many kinds of birds.

Focus Skill

1. MAIN IDEA AND DETAILS Draw and complete this graphic organizer.

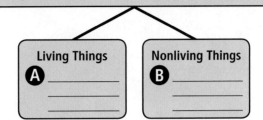

A pond ecosystem is made up of living and nonliving things.

Living Things
A _____
_____
_____

Nonliving Things
B _____
_____
_____

2. SUMMARIZE Write a summary of this lesson by using the lesson vocabulary words in a paragraph.

3. DRAW CONCLUSIONS Why do some ecosystems include more living things than other ecosystems?

4. VOCABULARY Use the lesson vocabulary words to create a matching quiz.

Test Prep

5. Critical Thinking How is a population different from a community?

6. Which word describes a group of cows standing together?
A. community   **C.** individual
B. ecosystem   **D.** population

Links

Writing

Expository Writing
You are a scientist planning an ecosystem on the moon. Write **two paragraphs** explaining what this ecosystem should include.

Math 9÷3

Solve a Problem
The Everglades includes many "rivers of grass." The water in these rivers moves slowly, only 30 meters (100 ft) a day. How many meters would the water move in June? In February?

Social Studies

Ecosystems and People
Choose a group of people who live in an ecosystem different from yours. Find out how that ecosystem affects the people. Share what you learn in an oral or written report.

For more links and activities, go to www.hspscience.com

2
What Factors Influence Ecosystems?

Fast Fact

That's Dry! This photograph shows the Atacama Desert in Chile. It's the driest place on Earth. Less than 0.01 centimeter (0.004 in.) of rain falls there every year. It hasn't rained in some parts of this desert for 400 years! In the Investigate, you will explore what happens when there is no rain.

Observing the Effects of Water

Materials
- **4 small identical plants in clay pots**
- **water**
- **large labels**

Procedure

	Day 1	Day 4	Day 7	Day 10
Plant 1 (watered)				
Plant 2 (watered)				
Plant 3 (not watered)				
Plant 4 (not watered)				

1. Use the labels to number the pots 1, 2, 3, and 4. Label pots 1 and 2 *watered*. Label pots 3 and 4 *not watered*.

2. Make a table like the one shown here. Draw a picture of each plant under Day 1.

3. Place all four pots in a sunny window.

4. Water all four pots until the soil is a little moist. Keep the soil of pots 1 and 2 moist during the whole experiment. Don't water pots 3 and 4 again.

5. Wait three days. Then observe and record how each plant looks. Draw a picture of each one under Day 4.

6. Repeat Step 5 twice. Draw pictures of the plants on Days 7 and 10.

Step 4

Draw Conclusions

1. What changes did you observe during this Investigate? What do they tell you?

2. **Inquiry Skill** Scientists compare changes to determine how one thing affects another. How could you compare how fast the soil dries out in a clay pot with how fast it dries out in a plastic pot?

Investigate Further

How does covering a plant with plastic wrap affect the plant's need for water? Write your hypothesis. Then design and carry out an experiment to check your hypothesis.

VOCABULARY
biotic p. 140
abiotic p. 142
diversity p. 146

SCIENCE CONCEPTS
▶ how biotic and abiotic factors affect ecosystems
▶ how climate influences an ecosystem

READING FOCUS SKILL
CAUSE AND EFFECT
Look for ways in which factors affect ecosystems.

| cause | → | effect |

Living Things Affect Ecosystems

Do plants and animals need each other? Yes, they do! Plants and animals are living parts of an ecosystem. These living parts are **biotic** factors. *Bio* means "life." Biotic factors affect the ecosystem and one another in many ways.

For example, plants provide food for caterpillars, birds, sheep, and other animals. People eat plants every day—at least they should.

Plants also provide shelter for animals. For instance, many insects live in grasses. Squirrels make dens in trees. Your home likely contains wood from trees.

Animals help plants, too. When animals eat one kind of plant, it can't spread and take over all the available space. This gives other kinds of plants room to grow.

A gypsy moth can lay 1000 eggs or more. Most of the eggs hatch into hungry caterpillars like this one. ▶

A healthy tree isn't hurt when a few insects nibble on it.

Gypsy moth caterpillars can eat all the leaves on a tree. Bad weather or an attack by other insects may kill trees.

Animals help plants in other ways. Animal droppings make the soil richer. Earthworms help loosen the soil. Rich, loose soil helps plants grow.

At the same time, too many plant eaters can be harmful. A herd of hungry deer can eat enough leaves to kill a tree. A huge swarm of locusts can leave a field bare of plants.

You know that animals affect one another. For example, wolves eat rabbits. If the wolf population becomes too large, wolves can wipe out the rabbits. Then the wolves go hungry. Without the rabbits to eat them, the grasses spread.

In this case, an increase in wolves causes a decrease in rabbits. Fewer rabbits causes an increase in plants.

A change in plants can also cause a change in animals. If dry weather or disease kills the grasses, the rabbits starve. Then the wolves go hungry, too. Disease can also kill animals in an ecosystem.

Sometimes, a new kind of plant or animal changes an ecosystem. For example, people brought the skunk vine to the United States from Asia in 1897. For a time, they planted it as a crop. Now it grows wild. This smelly vine can grow 9 meters (30 ft) long! It crowds out other plants, and it can even grow underwater.

 CAUSE AND EFFECT
Explain how an increase in plants could affect an ecosystem.

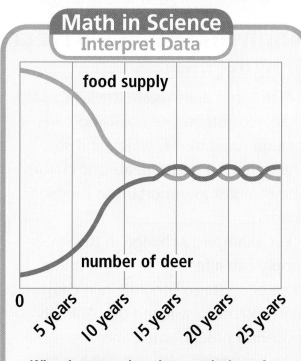

Math in Science
Interpret Data

food supply

number of deer

0 | 5 years | 10 years | 15 years | 20 years | 25 years

What happened to the population of deer as the food supply got smaller?

Tree leaves are a main source of food for deer. It takes 15 to 30 acres of land to provide enough food for one deer.

Nonliving Things Affect Ecosystems

Plants and animals are the living parts of an ecosystem. The nonliving parts include sunlight, air, water, and soil. The nonliving parts are **abiotic** factors. They are just as important as the biotic factors.

For example, a change in the water supply can affect all the living things in an ecosystem. Too little rain causes many plants to wilt and die. Animals must find other homes. Some may die.

An ecosystem with rich soil has many plants. Where the soil is poor, few plants grow. Few plants mean few animals in the ecosystem.

Air, water, and soil can contain harmful substances. They can affect all living things. You will learn more about this problem later in the chapter.

CAUSE AND EFFECT How might a change in the water supply affect a rabbit?

Super Soil!
With a partner or a group, compare two different soil samples. How might each soil affect its ecosystem?

Nonliving Factors
Without the nonliving parts of an ecosystem, there would be no living parts.

Sunlight

Plants need sunlight to produce food. Where trees shade the ground, not many other plants can grow.

Water

Almost all living things need water. Plant roots absorb water, and animals drink it.

Soil

Most plants need soil to grow. The kind of soil in an ecosystem is one of the factors that determines which plants grow there.

For more links and activities, go to www.hspscience.com

Climate Affects Ecosystems

What is the climate like where you live? Is it warm and sunny, or is it cool and rainy? Maybe it's something in between.

Climate is an abiotic factor. It's a combination of other abiotic factors. Climate includes the amount of rainfall and sunlight in a region. It also includes the repeating patterns of the temperature of the air during the year.

Climate affects the soil. Some climates allow many plants to grow and help dead plants decay. Animals that eat the plants leave behind their droppings. The decaying plants and droppings make the soil richer.

Climate affects the kinds of plants and animals in an ecosystem. For example, warm, wet climates support tropical rain forests. Hot summers and cold winters result in temperate forests.

The frozen tundra suits the hardy caribou. The mosses they eat thrive there. Zebras could not survive in the tundra. They need the mild climate and tender grasses of the savanna.

Focus Skill **CAUSE AND EFFECT** **What would happen to an ecosystem if its climate changed?**

World Climate Zones

This map shows six climate zones around the world.

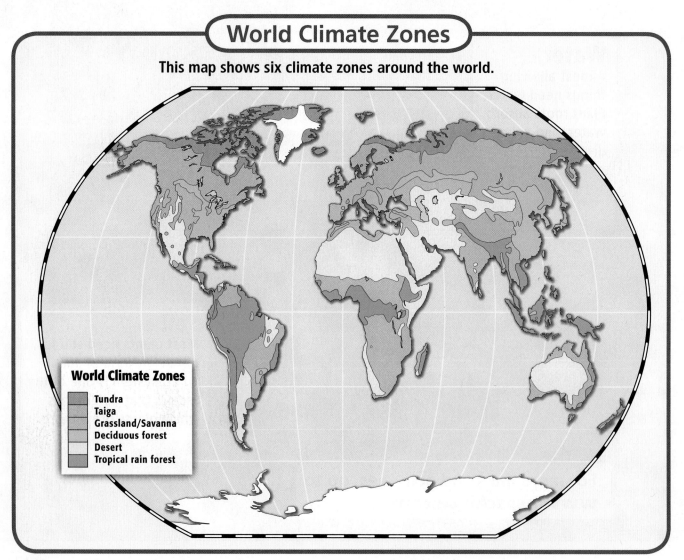

World Climate Zones
- Tundra
- Taiga
- Grassland/Savanna
- Deciduous forest
- Desert
- Tropical rain forest

Deciduous forests have four seasons. The trees, such as oaks and maples, lose their leaves in the fall. This helps them survive the cold winters.

Rain forests receive 2000 to 10,000 millimeters (7 to 33 ft) of rain each year! Tropical rain forests are near the equator.

The climate in the grassy savanna is nearly the same all year. The temperature stays between 18°C and 22°C (64°F and 72°F).

Deserts get only about 250 millimeters (10 in.) of rain a year. Plants there grow very quickly after a rain. Their seeds can survive for years as they wait for more rain.

The taiga covers more of Earth than any other kind of plant community. The taiga is mostly just south of the tundra and is very cold in winter. Most of its trees are evergreens.

The tundra has the coldest climate: −40°C to 18°C (−40°F to 64°F). *Tundra* means "treeless plain."

There are layers in a rain forest.

The *canopy* is the upper part of the trees. It is home to most rain-forest animals.

Diversity

A rain-forest ecosystem provides many sources of food and shelter. That's why it has the most diversity of all of Earth's ecosystems. **Diversity** refers to the number of different kinds of living things.

In a rain forest, a wide range of plants and animals can find what they need to survive. Many kinds of monkeys live in the treetops. Snakes slip from branch to branch. Bright butterflies flit among the flowers. Frogs of many colors cling to tree trunks. Mushrooms and earthworms hide under decaying leaves. Some rain-forest plants have giant leaves. Other plants can't be seen without using a microscope.

Some ecosystems don't have much diversity. The tundra, for example, is very cold and dry. Much of its soil is frozen. Few living things can survive there.

How much diversity does the ecosystem where you live have?

Focus Skill **CAUSE AND EFFECT** What leads to a diversity of living things in an ecosystem?

The next layer is the cool, dark *understory*. This layer is just right for plants that grow well in shade.

The bottom layer is the *forest floor*, where decaying matter provides food for plants.

146

Focus Skill

1. CAUSE AND EFFECT Draw and complete the graphic organizer.

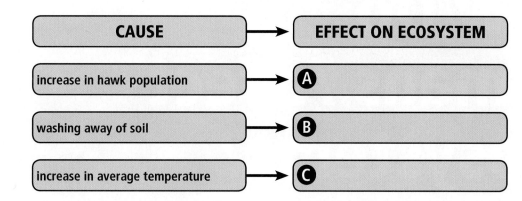

CAUSE	→	EFFECT ON ECOSYSTEM
increase in hawk population	→	A
washing away of soil	→	B
increase in average temperature	→	C

2. SUMMARIZE Use your completed graphic organizer to write a lesson summary.

3. DRAW CONCLUSIONS Which can exist without the other—biotic factors or abiotic factors? Explain your answer.

4. VOCABULARY Write a quiz-show-type question for each of the vocabulary words.

Test Prep

5. Critical Thinking How might flooding in their ecosystem affect some robins?

6. Which of these is an abiotic factor in an ecosystem?

   A. ant   **C.** earthworm

   B. decaying plant   **D.** sand

Links

Writing

Persuasive Writing

Write a **travel brochure** for a climate zone where few people vacation, such as the tundra or taiga. Tell your readers what interesting things they can see and experience there.

Math

Make a Graph

Find the average rainfall in five of the six world climate zones, including your own region. Then make a bar graph that compares the rainfalls.

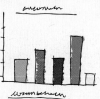

Literature

Learn More

Read a current nonfiction book about one of the world climate zones, such as the desert. After learning more about that climate zone, share what you know by making a display or a written report.

For more links and activities, go to www.hspscience.com

How Do Humans Affect Ecosystems?

Fast Fact

Saving Soil Contour-plowing slopes helps keep rain from washing away the soil. It can reduce erosion by as much as 75 percent! In the Investigate, you will experiment with "rain" and erosion.

Losing It: Observing Erosion

Materials
- marker
- soil and small rocks
- 2 paper cups
- water
- 2 clean plastic foam trays
- sharpened pencil
- measuring cup

Procedure

1. Use the marker to write *A* on one tray and on one paper cup. Write *B* on the second tray and on the second paper cup.

2. In each tray, make an identical slope out of soil and rocks.

3. Carefully use the pencil to make three small holes in the bottom of cup A. Make six larger holes in the bottom of cup B.

4. Record how the two slopes look now. Label your drawings *A* and *B*.

5. Hold cup A over the slope in tray A. Slowly pour 1 cup of water into the paper cup, and let it run down the slope. Record how the slope looks now.

6. Repeat Step 5, using cup B and tray B. Then record how the slope looks.

Draw Conclusions

1. At the end of the activity, compare the slopes. What did each cup represent?

2. **Inquiry Skill** An experiment is a careful, controlled test. What were you testing and what did you control in the activity?

Step 2

Step 5

Investigate Further

Try the same activity, using only rocks, using level soil, or using plants growing in the soil. Make a prediction about what will happen, and then do the activity to see if your prediction was accurate.

149

VOCABULARY
pollution p. 152
habitat restoration
p. 153

SCIENCE CONCEPTS
▶ how humans use the resources in ecosystems
▶ the positive and negative ways humans affect ecosystems

READING FOCUS SKILL
COMPARE AND CONTRAST
Compare positive and negative effects that humans have on ecosystems.

| alike | | different |

Humans Within Ecosystems

Do you use any natural resources? You do if you breathe! Natural resources are the parts of ecosystems that humans use, including air.

What other natural resources do you use? Do you ever go to the seashore or a park? Those are natural resources. When you turn on a light, you use natural resources. Most electricity is produced by burning coal. Coal is a natural resource that is taken from under the ground.

Do you ride a bus to school? The fuel that makes the bus run is made from oil. Oil is a natural resource that is also taken from under the ground.

Minerals are natural resources, too. Iron, copper, and aluminum are examples of mineral resources.

Some natural resources can be replaced. Sunlight, air, and water are renewable resources. People can grow more trees and plant more crops.

▼ **Natural resources include lakes, fresh air, and sunlight.**

Fish and other living things are also natural resources.

More than 2000 years ago, people drank tea made from the bark of the white willow tree to help ease pain. In 1829, scientists discovered the chemical in the willow that reduces pain. They used it to make aspirin tablets.

Aspirin can be bought without a prescription. However, it is a powerful and valuable drug.

People have been growing wheat for 10,000 years.

Making bread is just one way wheat is used. This grain is also used in cakes, cookies, cereals, and pastas. Parts of the wheat plant are fed to cattle.

Some natural resources can't be replaced. They include coal, gas, and oil. After the supplies buried underground are used, these resources will be gone.

Humans use natural resources in many ways. People build homes and furniture from wood. They make bricks from clay, and glass from sand. They use iron to make steel, which they then use to make cars and many other things.

People raise crops to feed themselves and their animals. They use plants as medicines, too. Humans learned long ago that plants could help treat or cure some illnesses. More than 40 percent of the medicines used today originally came from plants.

For example, a medicine made from a plant called foxglove can help treat heart disease. Scientists use the bark of the Pacific yew tree to make a medicine to treat cancer.

Scientists have tested only 2 percent of all plants to see if they can be used as medicines. Who knows how many more medicines plants may provide?

Focus Skill **COMPARE AND CONTRAST** Compare the supply of crops with the supply of coal.

Negative and Positive Changes

Humans make many negative changes in ecosystems. When people clear land for houses and shopping malls, they destroy habitats. As a result, the animals that lived there can no longer meet all their basic needs. They must move or die.

Farmers plow land to plant crops. Plowing loosens soil. That makes it easier for rain and wind to carry away the soil. Humans also cause some kinds of pollution. **Pollution** happens when harmful substances mix with water, air, or soil.

Storms washing chemicals off fields can cause water pollution. These chemicals flow into streams and rivers. Trash and waste from homes and businesses can also enter the water supply.

Much air pollution comes from burning gasoline. Fumes from car engines carry chemicals into the air. Factory smokestacks release more chemicals. Some of these chemicals form acid rain. Acid rain can burn trees and other plants. It can poison lakes and rivers.

Soil pollution can come from fertilizers and trash. Wastes, such as old paint and drain cleaners, can poison the soil.

Cars and other vehicles are a major source of air pollution in cities. This pollution causes smog and breathing problems.

Bicycles don't release pollution. They also provide a good way to get exercise.

Many laws are designed to prevent water pollution, but it still happens.

Water treatment plants remove harmful substances from water before it reaches people's homes. ▶

Without plant roots to hold soil in place, much of the soil can wash away.

These people are helping prevent beach erosion by planting dune grasses.

Humans also make positive changes. Many groups are working to repair damage to ecosystems. They plant new trees and create new wetlands. They build parks over closed landfills. This process is **habitat restoration**.

People are also polluting less. For example, cars now have special devices on their tailpipes. These devices reduce the harmful gases that escape into the air. Factories now release fewer chemicals. They don't dump wastes into rivers and streams.

Many people now use natural ways to get rid of weeds and insects. They spread fewer chemicals on fields and lawns.

People also recycle paper, glass, metal, and plastic. Recycling uses less energy than making new products. That means less coal is burned. Burning less coal means less pollution.

People are learning other ways to help reduce pollution. Science is one way of finding solutions to the problems caused by pollution.

Focus Skill **COMPARE AND CONTRAST** Which kind of pollution is most harmful—water, air, or soil? Why?

Insta-Lab

Acid or Not?

Use pH paper to measure the acidity in rainwater or in water from a stream or lake. The redder the strip turns, the more acid the water contains. What might be the source of this acid?

Planning for Change

Earth's human population keeps growing. People need more space for places to work and live. But before we build, we have to consider both abiotic and biotic factors. Some abiotic factors include the type of soil, the amount of rain, and the climate. A building set on soft soil will not stand. A home must be able to withstand the weather of the area where it is built.

Biotic factors can affect more than humans. Building new structures often means destroying wildlife habitats. Builders should plan new projects in ways that protect ecosystems. A building near a river must not pollute the water.

Even working close to a river can cause problems. Soil can wash into the water. Too much soil in the water can harm fish and plants.

Wetlands near the river must not be filled in. Wetlands help keep the water clean and provide homes for many plants and animals. Builders often leave or create ponds or pockets of forest. These habitats provide homes for some wildlife. Every ecosystem has a delicate balance. People must do their part to protect that balance.

COMPARE AND CONTRAST **Compare a human and an animal seeking a new habitat. How are they the same?**

Construction must be carefully planned to protect natural ecosystems. ▶

◀ **Land-use planners must consider the biotic and abiotic factors in an ecosystem.**

Focus Skill **1. COMPARE AND CONTRAST** Draw and complete this graphic organizer.

Human Effects on Ecosystems

Negative Change: destruction of habitats

Positive Change: **A**

Negative Change: **B**

Positive Change: devices to reduce air pollution from cars

2. SUMMARIZE Write two sentences that tell what this lesson is mainly about.

3. DRAW CONCLUSIONS Why do humans affect natural ecosystems in negative ways?

4. VOCABULARY Make an acrostic for *pollution*. Each letter begins a sentence about that term.

Test Prep

5. Critical Thinking How can a weedkiller used on a cornfield pollute a lake miles away?

6. Which of these is soil pollution likely to cause?
   A. air pollution   **C.** abiotic factors
   B. biotic factors   **D.** water pollution

Links

Writing

Persuasive Writing
Think of a way your community has had a negative effect on an ecosystem. Write a **letter** you might send to the editor of a local newspaper describing the problem.

Math   9÷3

Comparing Gas Use
An older, larger car gets 10 miles per gallon of gasoline. A newer, smaller car gets 35 miles per gallon. How many fewer gallons would the newer car use on a 70-mile trip?

Health

Pollution and You
With a small group, research the health effects of water, air, or soil pollution. Then share what you learn in a written report, an oral presentation, or a poster.

For more links and activities, go to **www.hspscience.com**

AQUARIUS
An Underwater Lab with a View

Many U.S. kids share their bedrooms with a brother or sister. Sharing a room can be a pain. Six scientists know it! They squeezed into a small underwater laboratory to study a coral reef. They worked and slept in the tiny space for ten days.

"I've been on missions where people snored," said Celia Smith, who led the mission in October. "You just kind of kick their bunk and try to get to sleep before they do."

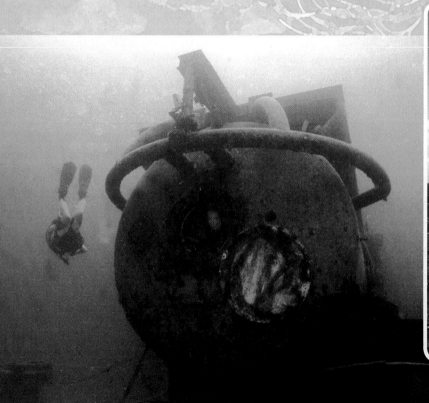

This buoy supplies the *Aquarius* with fresh air and electricity.

▲ An aquanaut peers through a window in the *Aquarius* as another aquanaut swims around the laboratory.

The underwater lab is called *Aquarius*. It looks like a little yellow submarine.

The *Aquarius* was placed near the Florida Keys National Marine Sanctuary, a protected area of the ocean. Each year, several teams of scientists have lived in *Aquarius* for up to ten days at a time. The scientists who live and work in *Aquarius* are called aquanauts (AH•kwuh•nawts). The aquanauts study the nearby coral reef and the creatures that live in it.

A Room with a View

The latest team to visit *Aquarius* says the best part of living there is the view. They can see colorful fish swimming in the nearby reef. Smith said it's hard to tell, though, whether the aquanauts are watching the fish or the fish are watching the aquanauts.

The aquanauts spend as much time as they can on the reef studying sea life.

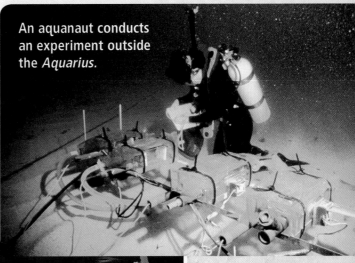
An aquanaut conducts an experiment outside the *Aquarius*.

◀ Inside, an aquanaut rests on his bunk. He doesn't have much room.

They can spend up to nine hours at one time outside the laboratory.

Smith likes to remind people that humans have barely begun to explore the oceans and need to learn more about life in the deep. "The really important thing for us to realize is how much we don't know about the oceans," she said.

THINK ABOUT IT

1. How might living underwater help scientists learn more about a coral reef ecosystem?
2. What might be the best thing about living underwater? What might be the worst thing?

IN THE DEEP

Aquarius is located about 19 meters (63 ft) deep in the ocean. It has sleeping space for six, a bathroom, a trash compactor, and computer stations.

Electrical cables and tubes connect the *Aquarius* to a buoy on the ocean's surface. The tubes carry fresh air to the *Aquarius*, and the cables supply electricity.

The work the aquanauts are doing is expected to help NASA. NASA scientists say that living and working on the *Aquarius* is similar to what it will be like to live and work in a space station. They hope to better prepare astronauts for space by studying how the aquanauts live and work underwater.

Spin-In Find out more! Log on to www.hspscience.com

Meet a Young CONSERVATIONIST

Fourth grader Blake Wichtowski told people at last year's Kids' Summit that wild blue lupine flowers would help the endangered Karner blue butterfly. Officials from New York are turning this idea into a reality.

Blue lupine is the only food that Karner caterpillars will eat.

With the help of the Seneca Park Zoo in Rochester and other officials, Blake's fourth-grade class and a class at another elementary school will plant seeds for a blue lupine garden near the local airport.

You Can Do It!

Materials
- plastic funnel
- gravel
- sand
- bowl
- water with some soil and leaves in it

Getting Out the Dirt

Procedure

1. Fill the bottom of a funnel with gravel. Then add a thick layer of sand.

2. Hold the funnel over a bowl. Pour the "dirty" water into it. The water will run out the bottom of the funnel, into the bowl.

3. Observe the water in the bowl. See if you can find the soil and leaves.

Draw Conclusions

How did your funnel filter affect the dirty water? Where might you find this kind of natural filter? How might soil and other substances get into a water supply?

Checking for Air Pollution

Is the air in your school or neighborhood polluted? Air pollution often includes bits of ash and dust. If you smear petroleum jelly on the inside of baby-food jars and put them somewhere for several days, bits of pollution may stick to the jelly. Which areas of your school or neighborhood do you think might have this kind of pollution? Write a hypothesis. Then design an experiment, and carry it out to see whether your hypothesis is supported.

Review and Test Preparation

Vocabulary Review

Use the terms below to complete the sentences. The page numbers tell you where to look in the chapter if you need help.

environment p. 132
ecosystem p. 132
population p. 134
community p. 136
biotic p. 140
abiotic p. 142
diversity p. 146
pollution p. 152

1. A group of maple trees is an example of a _____.

2. The living parts of an ecosystem are _____.

3. All the living and nonliving things in an area interact to form an _____.

4. An ecosystem that includes many kinds of living things has _____.

5. Several kinds of plants and animals living in the same place form a _____.

6. Trash in a stream is one kind of _____.

7. Nonliving factors in an ecosystem are _____ factors.

8. An _____ includes all the living things and nonliving things in an area.

Check Understanding

Write the letter of the best choice.

9. Which of these is an abiotic factor?
   A. lack of food
   B. disease
   C. cold temperatures
   D. introduction of a new plant

10. Which of these is **not** an abiotic factor?
    F. air   H. mushrooms
    G. soil   J. water

11. **MAIN IDEA AND DETAILS** What is the main idea behind planting trees in an area that has been logged?
    A. pollution
    B. habitat restoration
    C. harvesting natural resources
    D. preserving an ecosystem

12. **CAUSE AND EFFECT** Which statement is true about an ecosystem?
    F. Biotic factors are the climate.
    G. The climate affects biotic factors.
    H. Biotic factors cause abiotic factors.
    J. Biotic factors never change.

13. What does the picture show?

   A. abiotic factors   **C.** habitat restoration

   B. diversity   **D.** pollution

14. Which of these has the greatest effect on an ecosystem?

   F. communities   **H.** climate

   G. biotic factors   **J.** population

15. Which of these is **never** a result of human actions?

   A. population increases

   B. changes in abiotic factors

   C. natural increase in diversity

   D. pollution

16. Which climate zone is probably shown in the photo?

   F. savanna   **H.** temperate forest

   G. taiga   **J.** tundra

Inquiry Skills

17. Compare an environment and an ecosystem.

18. A scientist has tracked the migration route of a Yellowstone elk herd every winter for 10 years. The table shows how far south the elk herd has traveled each year. **Draw conclusions** about the elk herd's migration pattern over the 10-year period.

Year	Kilometers Migrated
1990	122
1991	122
1992	130
1993	126
1994	130
1995	133
1996	132
1997	133
1998	133
1999	136

Critical Thinking

19. Imagine that a new kind of animal has suddenly appeared. How might it affect the local ecosystem?

20. A builder has bought land that includes a forest. The builder is planning to put in a housing development.

Part A Name two possible negative effects the builder and other humans might have on this forest.

Part B Now name two possible positive effects the builder and other humans might have on this ecosystem.

Chapter

5 Energy Transfer in Ecosystems

Lesson 1 What Are the Roles of Living Things?

Lesson 2 How Do Living Things Get Energy?

Vocabulary

producer

consumer

herbivore

carnivore

omnivore

decomposer

habitat

niche

food chain

prey

predator

food web

energy pyramid

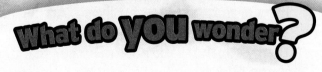

What do YOU wonder?

This lynx must catch and eat hares and many other small animals in order to live. This hare may provide energy for the lynx. Where do hares get the energy they need to live?

What Are the Roles of Living Things?

Fast Fact

Nothing Fishy About Eating This archer fish is leaping for its prey. It eats insects to get energy for living. Archer fish also hunt by spitting at insects to knock them into the water. Some archer fish are eaten by other animals or die and then decay in the water. In the Investigate, you will find out how decomposers (dee•kuhm•POHZ•erz) help once-living matter decay.

Decomposing Bananas

Materials
- 2 slices of banana
- 2 zip-top plastic bags
- spoon
- package of dry yeast
- marker

Procedure

1. Put a banana slice in each bag.

2. Sprinkle $\frac{2}{3}$ spoonful of dry yeast on one banana slice. Yeast is a decomposer, so use the marker to label this bag *D*.

3. Close both bags. Put the bags in the same place.

4. Check both bags every day for a week. Observe and record the changes you see in each bag.

Draw Conclusions

1. Which banana slice shows more changes? What is the cause of these changes?

2. **Inquiry Skill** Scientists use time relationships to measure progress. How long did it take for your banana slices to begin showing signs of decomposition? How long do you think it would take for your banana slices to completely decompose?

Step 2

Step 4

Investigate Further

What will happen if you put flour, instead of yeast, on one banana slice? Write down your prediction, and then try it.

Reading in Science

VOCABULARY
producer p. 166
consumer p. 166
herbivore p. 168
carnivore p. 168
omnivore p. 168
decomposer p. 170

SCIENCE CONCEPTS
▶ how living things use the energy from sunlight
▶ how living things get energy from other living things

READING FOCUS SKILL
MAIN IDEA AND DETAILS
Look for details about the movement of energy among living things.

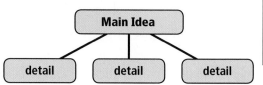

Producers and Consumers

Most living things on Earth get the energy to live from sunlight. Green plants and algae (AL•jee) use energy in sunlight, plus water and carbon dioxide, to make their own food. Any living thing that can make its own food is called a **producer**. Producers can be as small as a tiny moss or as large as a huge redwood tree.

Some animals, such as deer and cattle, get the energy they need to live by eating plants. When these animals eat, the energy stored in the plants moves into the animals' bodies.

Not all animals eat plants. Lions and hawks, for example, get the energy they need by eating other animals.

An animal that eats plants or other animals is called a **consumer**. Consumers can't make their own food, so they must eat other living things.

These plants are using energy in sunlight to produce food. Without sunlight, the plants would die.

Horse

Which animal gets its energy directly from producers? Which one gets its energy from other consumers? Which one gets its energy from both?

Florida panther

Some consumers eat the same kind of food all year. Horses, for example, eat grass during warm weather. During winter, they eat hay, a kind of dried grass.

Other consumers eat different things in different seasons. For example, black bears eat grass in spring. Later on, they might eat birds' eggs. Bears might also dig up tasty roots or eat fish from streams. In fall, bears eat ripe berries.

Florida panthers eat other consumers, but their diet varies. Mostly, panthers consume wild hogs, which are easy for them to catch. Another favorite meal is deer. Panthers also eat rabbits, raccoons, rats, birds, and sometimes even alligators.

 MAIN IDEA AND DETAILS What is a producer? What is a consumer? Give two examples of each.

Black bear

Kinds of Consumers

Consumers are not all the same. In fact, there are three kinds—herbivores, carnivores, and omnivores.

A **herbivore** is an animal that eats only plants, or producers. Horses are herbivores. So are giraffes, squirrels, and rabbits.

A **carnivore** is an animal that eats only other animals. The Florida panther and the lion are carnivores. A carnivore can be as large as a whale or as small as a frog.

An **omnivore** is an animal that eats both plants and other animals. That is, omnivores eat both producers and other consumers. Bears and hyenas are omnivores. Do any omnivores live in your home?

Producers and all three kinds of consumers can be found living in water. Algae are producers that live in water. They use sunlight to make their own food. Tadpoles, small fish, and other small herbivores eat algae. Larger fish that are carnivores eat the tadpoles. Some animals, including green sea turtles, are omnivores. Green sea turtles eat seaweed, algae, and fish. In fact, algae make the flesh of the green sea turtle green!

MAIN IDEA AND DETAILS Name the three kinds of consumers. Give two examples of each.

This diagram shows how kinds of consumers get energy to live. The arrows show the direction of energy flow.

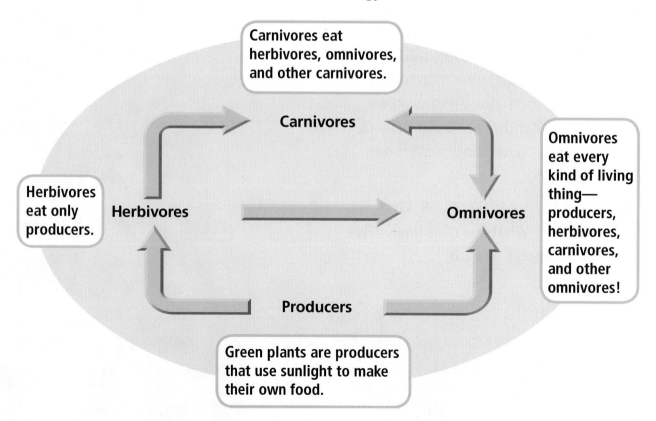

Carnivores eat herbivores, omnivores, and other carnivores.

Herbivores eat only producers.

Omnivores eat every kind of living thing—producers, herbivores, carnivores, and other omnivores!

Green plants are producers that use sunlight to make their own food.

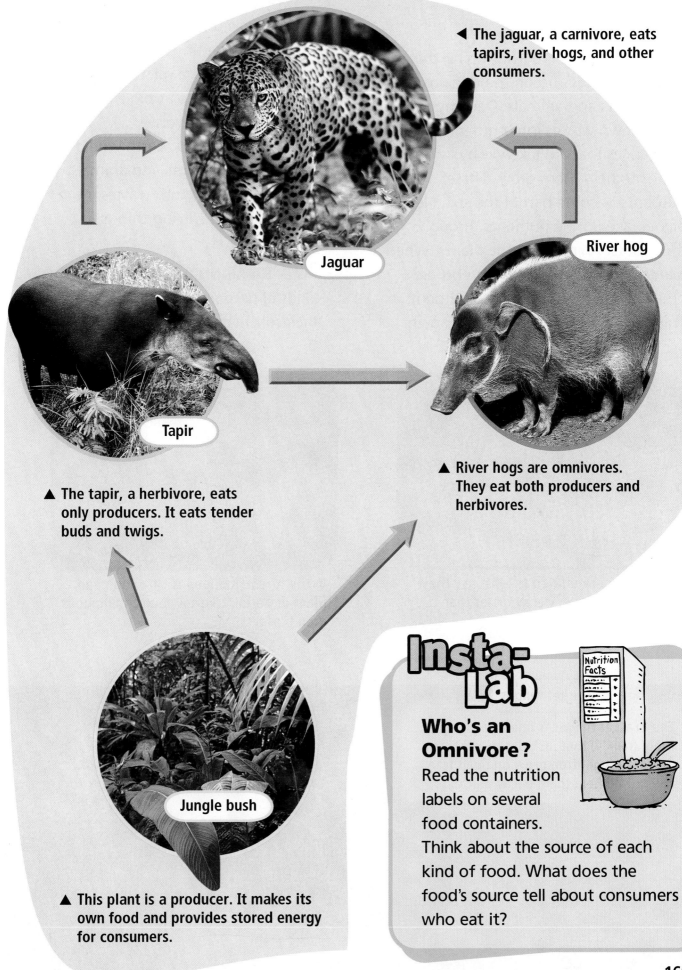

◄ The jaguar, a carnivore, eats tapirs, river hogs, and other consumers.

Jaguar

River hog

Tapir

▲ River hogs are omnivores. They eat both producers and herbivores.

▲ The tapir, a herbivore, eats only producers. It eats tender buds and twigs.

Jungle bush

▲ This plant is a producer. It makes its own food and provides stored energy for consumers.

Insta-Lab

Who's an Omnivore?

Read the nutrition labels on several food containers. Think about the source of each kind of food. What does the food's source tell about consumers who eat it?

Decomposers

A **decomposer** is a living thing that feeds on wastes and on the remains of dead plants and animals. Decomposers break down wastes into nutrients, substances that are taken in by living things to help them grow. These nutrients become part of the soil. Next, plants take up the nutrients through their roots. Animals eat the plants. When plants and animals die, decomposers break down their bodies into nutrients. This cycle is repeated again and again.

Decomposers come in many shapes and sizes. Some are tiny bacteria that you can see only with a microscope. Other decomposers are as big as mushrooms and earthworms.

Without decomposers, Earth would be covered with dead plants and animals. Instead, decomposers turn wastes into nutrients. They allow living things to recycle nutrients.

 MAIN IDEA AND DETAILS Name two kinds of decomposers, and describe their role in nature.

Sow bugs

Sow bugs are related to lobsters. They help plant matter decay faster than it would without them.

Millipede

In the forest, millipedes chew up dead plant material. Like sow bugs, millipedes aren't insects.

Bracket fungus

The bracket fungus is one of a group of fungi (FUN•jy) that includes mushrooms. Bracket fungi often grow on dead tree trunks and help them decay quickly.

1. MAIN IDEA AND DETAILS Copy and complete this graphic organizer.

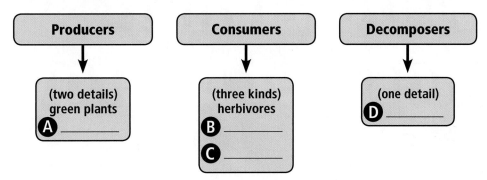

Producers	Consumers	Decomposers
(two details) green plants **A** _____	(three kinds) herbivores **B** _____ **C** _____	(one detail) **D** _____

2. SUMMARIZE Write two sentences that tell what this lesson is mainly about.

3. DRAW CONCLUSIONS How are decomposers consumers?

4. VOCABULARY Construct a crossword puzzle, using this lesson's vocabulary words.

Test Prep

5. Critical Thinking How do eagles depend on sunlight for their energy?

6. Which term describes a hyena?
A. carnivore   **C.** omnivore
B. herbivore   **D.** producer

Links

Writing

Narrative Writing
Write a **science fiction story**. Tell about a time when all the producers on Earth disappear. Describe what happens to the consumers.

Math 9÷3

Solve a Problem
A shrew eats about $\frac{2}{3}$ of its body weight daily. Suppose a child who weighed 30 kilograms (66 lb) could eat $\frac{2}{3}$ of his or her body weight. How many kilograms of food is that?

Health

Eating Decomposers
Find out what vitamins and minerals are in mushrooms. Find healthful recipes that have mushrooms as one of the ingredients.

For more links and activities, go to www.hspscience.com

171

How Do Living Things Get Energy?

Fast Fact

Ouch! Only female mosquitoes bite people and other animals. They need the blood to produce eggs. In the Investigate, you will make food chains. You might include a mosquito in yours!

Make a Food Chain

Materials • 8 to 10 blank index cards   • reference books about animals
• colored pencils or markers

Procedure

1. Choose a place where animals live. Some examples are pine forest, rain forest, desert, wetland, and ocean.

2. On an index card, draw a living thing that lives in the place you have chosen. Draw more living things, one kind on each card. Include large animals, small animals, and producers. Look up information about plants and animals if you need help.

3. Put your cards in an order that shows what eats what. You might have more than one set of cards. If one of your animals doesn't fit anywhere, trade cards with someone. You can also draw another animal to link two of your cards. For example, you could draw a rabbit to link a grass card and a hawk card.

Draw Conclusions

1. Could the same animal fit into more than one set of cards? Explain your answer.

2. **Inquiry Skill** Scientists communicate their ideas in many ways. What do your cards communicate about the relationships of these living things to one another?

Step 2

Step 3

Investigate Further

Draw a series of cards in order, with yourself as the last consumer. Compare your role with the roles of other consumers.

Reading in Science

VOCABULARY
habitat p. 174
niche p. 175
food chain p. 176
prey p. 176
predator p. 176
food web p. 178
energy pyramid p. 180

SCIENCE CONCEPTS
▶ how consumers depend on other living things
▶ how energy moves through food chains and food webs

★ Focus Skill **READING FOCUS SKILL**

SEQUENCE Look for the order in which things happen.

☐ → ☐ → ☐

Habitats

You probably wouldn't see a heron in a desert or a penguin in a swamp. Animals must live in places that meet their needs. A **habitat** is an environment that meets the needs of a living thing. An insect's habitat can be as small as the space under a rock. A migrating bird's habitat can cross a continent.

Many habitats can overlap. For example, the three living things pictured on this page all live in a desert habitat. This desert habitat meets all their needs. Sagebrush grows well here. Sidewinders and tarantulas find many small consumers to eat.

> These living things thrive in the desert habitat, even though it's hot and has little water.

The venomous sidewinder eats mice, rats, lizards, and birds. ▶

Sidewinder

◀ Tarantulas are venomous, too. They eat insects, other spiders, and small lizards.

Tarantula

Sagebrush can grow where other plants can't. Sheep and cattle often eat sagebrush in the winter. ▶

Sagebrush

Each living thing in a habitat has a role, or **niche** (NICH). The term *niche* describes how a living thing interacts with its habitat. Part of a living thing's niche is how it gets food and shelter. Its niche also includes how it reproduces, cares for its young, and avoids danger. Each animal has body parts that help it carry out its role. For example, a cat's pointed claws and sharp eyes help it catch its food.

Part of the sidewinder's niche is to eat small animals in its habitat. If all these snakes died, the desert would have too many mice, birds, and lizards. These small animals would eat all the available food and would soon starve. The sidewinder's niche helps keep the number of small desert animals in balance.

⭐ **Focus Skill** **SEQUENCE** **What would happen next if all the sagebrush disappeared from a desert?**

Crab

Lion-fish

Anemone

This coral reef habitat has a balance of producers and consumers. Everything in this picture is a consumer.

175

Food Chains

Living things depend on one another to live. A **food chain** is the movement of food energy in a sequence of living things. Every food chain starts with producers. Some consumers, such as deer, eat these producers. Then the deer are eaten by other consumers, such as mountain lions. Consumers that are eaten are called **prey**. A consumer that eats prey is a **predator**. Prey are what is hunted. Predators are the hunters.

Some animals in a habitat are prey, while other animals are predators. Predators limit the number of prey animals in a habitat. Wolves are predators of antelope. They keep the population of antelope from increasing too much, so the antelope don't eat all of the producers. Predators often compete for the same prey. This limits the number of predators in a habitat.

Focus Skill **SEQUENCE** What would happen next if the number of predators in a habitat increased too much?

A mangrove swamp is one kind of habitat. Special prop roots hold mangrove trees in the muddy soil. Fresh water and salt water mix in this habitat.

Many organisms live in and around the mangrove roots.

Mullets are fish that can live in fresh water or salt water.

Without hawks, the chipmunk population would get very large. The chipmunks would eat all the acorns and then starve.

Acorns provide energy for the chipmunk, which in turn provides energy for the hawk.

An alligator is just one of the predators in a mangrove swamp. Alligators dig burrows for themselves that also provide shelter for other animals during dry times.

Insta-Lab

Chain of Life

Cut white paper into strips that are 2.5 cm (1 in.) by 12.5 cm (5 in.) On each strip, write the name of a producer or a consumer. Then use glue or tape to combine the strips into paper food chains. Which food chains end with you?

Food Webs

A food chain shows how an animal gets energy from one food source. But food chains can overlap. One kind of producer may be food for different kinds of consumers. Some consumers may eat different kinds of food. For example, hawks eat sparrows, mice, and snakes.

Several food chains that overlap form a **food web**. There are food webs in water habitats, too. For example, herons eat snails, fish, and other birds.

On the next page, you can see an ocean food web. It shows that energy moves from plankton, small producers in the ocean, to small shrimp. These shrimp are called *first-level consumers.*

These shrimp then become prey for fish and other *second-level consumers.* They, in turn, are eaten by the biggest fish and mammals in the ocean, called *top-level consumers.*

⭐ **SEQUENCE** What happens after a first-level consumer eats a producer?

Follow several paths in this food web. Begin at the bottom, with a producer, and trace the movement of energy through the web.

Antarctic Ocean Food Web

This food web begins with energy from the sun. The producers are tiny plants called phytoplankton (FYT•oh•plangk•tuhn). They float near the water's surface because sunlight can't reach deep underwater. No plants grow at the bottom of the ocean. Where would decomposers fit in this food web?

For more links and activities, go to www.hspscience.com

Energy Pyramids

An **energy pyramid** shows how much energy is passed from one living thing to another along a food chain. Producers form the base of the pyramid. They use about 90 percent of the energy they get from the sun to grow. They store the other 10 percent in their stems, leaves, and other parts.

Next, consumers eat the producers. They get only the 10 percent of energy that the plants stored. These consumers use about 90 percent of the energy they get from the producers to grow and then store the other 10 percent in their bodies. That 10 percent is passed on to the consumers that eat them.

You can see how little energy is passed from one level to the next. That's why consumers must eat many living things in order to live.

SEQUENCE What happens next to the energy that plants get from the sun?

Math in Science
Interpret Data

Only 10 percent of the food energy, measured in calories, passes up to the next level in an energy pyramid. Suppose the bottom level contains 10,000,000 calories. How many would be passed up to each level?

The fox and the owl must eat many smaller animals to get enough energy to live. ▶

Birds, mice, and other small animals must eat many producers to get the energy they need to live. ▶

The bottom of an energy pyramid can include thousands of producers. ▶

◀ A wolf must eat many smaller animals, such as foxes and owls, to get the energy it needs to live.

180

1. SEQUENCE Copy and complete this graphic organizer. Put the living things in order to create a food chain.

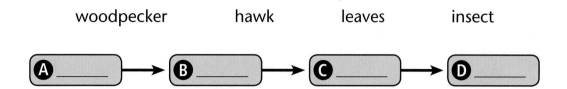

woodpecker   hawk   leaves   insect

A _____ → B _____ → C _____ → D _____

2. SUMMARIZE Write a summary of this lesson by using the lesson vocabulary terms in a paragraph.

3. DRAW CONCLUSIONS How are predators good for prey?

4. VOCABULARY Use the vocabulary terms to make a quiz. Then trade quizzes with a partner.

Test Prep

5. Critical Thinking How would the deaths of all of one kind of consumer affect a food web?

6. Which of these best shows why deer must eat grass all day long?

A. diagram   **C.** food chain

B. energy pyramid   **D.** food web

Links

Writing

Expository Writing

Write a **description** of ways humans might affect a food web and what would then change. For example, people might clear trees for a housing development or feed the deer in a park.

Math 9÷3

Solve a Problem

Producers in a field have stored 20,000 calories. Herbivores get 2000 calories by eating the producers. How much energy is available to the next level of the energy pyramid?

Art

Food Chains

Choose any art medium, such as watercolor, charcoal, collage, or torn paper, and show the living things in a food web. (You don't have to show them eating one another!)

For more links and activities, go to www.hspscience.com

On the Prowl

Cameras are helping scientists count jaguars.

A sleek, spotted jaguar sneaks along the thick forest floor. As it passes a fig tree, there is a whirring noise. A flashing light and click follow. A camera has just snapped the cat's photograph.

No person was behind the camera's lens. The camera was triggered by motion and heat from the passing cat.

A Narrowing Range

Scientists from the Wildlife Conservation Society in New York have placed about 30 such cameras in trees throughout the tropical forest of Belize (beh•LEEZ). That is a country in Central America.

The forest is also the site of the world's first jaguar reserve. A reserve is an area set apart for a special purpose. At the reserve in Belize, jaguars are protected and can safely roam.

Belize has a healthy number of jaguars. The wildlife group estimates that about 14 jaguars live within a 143-square-km (55-square-mile) area there. The cameras are helping researchers count the jaguars within certain areas of Belize and in other places where jaguars roam.

"Camera trapping" will help scientists because jaguars are hard to study. Despite the cats' hefty size, their mysterious nature and the thick jungle where they live make them difficult to spot.

A camera snaps a photograph of a passing jaguar.

UNITED STATES

ATLANTIC OCEAN

MEXICO

PACIFIC OCEAN

CENTRAL AMERICA

SOUTH AMERICA

KEY
Where jaguars live now
Where jaguars used to live

The map shows how the range of jaguars has changed.

"The cameras help researchers determine how many cats are out there and where they make their homes," jaguar expert Kathleen Conforti told WR.

The researchers will use that information to help protect the endangered animals. They want to conserve, or save, the jaguars' habitat. A habitat is the area where the animal naturally lives.

The actions of people have caused a decline in the animal's range. The cutting down of trees has destroyed some of the jaguar's habitat.

THINK ABOUT IT

1. How might the loss of trees affect how jaguars live?
2. How might equipment such as cameras help protect endangered animals around the world?

What a Roar

- Jaguars, which are carnivorous, can grow up to 1.8 meters (6 ft) long and weigh up to 136 kilograms (300 pounds).
- Jaguars are the third-largest cats, after tigers and lions.
- The cats usually live alone and are very territorial. That means they protect their habitat from other jaguars.
- In Spanish, this cat's name is *el tigre,* which means "the tiger."

Find out more! Log on to
www.hspscience.com

WORKING WITH ELEPHANTS

In India, adult Asian elephants have no natural enemies. However, humans have killed many elephants. Now elephants are close to dying out. Raman Sukumar wants to save them.

Sukumar studied how building changes elephant habitats. New dams, roads, and railways force elephants closer to towns. He also studied elephant deaths. He found that illegal hunting has killed many elephants.

Sukumar has found ways to help humans and elephants live together. Areas of the wild are being linked. Elephants can move safely from one area to the next. They don't have to go through farms or towns. Farmers now use different types of fences so that elephants will not eat crops.

Career Paleontologist

If you like digging, then you may want to become a paleontologist. These scientists study the fossils of ancient animals and plants. As a result, paleontologists can figure out why some species disappeared long ago while other species still exist today.

You Can Do It!

Quick and Easy Project

Energy Pyramid

Procedure

1. Identify producers, herbivores, carnivores, and omnivores that live in your area. List them on scrap paper.

2. Use the ruler to draw a large pyramid on the white paper. Divide the pyramid into three or four levels, depending on the kinds of living things you have identified.

3. Arrange some or all of these living things on your energy pyramid. Draw only one animal at the top level, ten at the next level, and so on.

Materials

- scrap paper
- ruler
- large sheet of white paper
- colored pencils

Draw Conclusions

Do all the things from your list fit into your pyramid? If not, why not? If you lived in a different kind of habitat—for example, a desert or a seashore—how would your energy pyramid change?

Design Your Own Investigation

Carnivore or Herbivore?

Identify several insects of the same kind, such as caterpillars or ants, from your area. Design an experiment to determine if this kind of insect is a herbivore, a carnivore, or an omnivore. For example, you might give the insects a choice of foods and see which foods they eat. Be sure to use safety precautions. Release the insects when the experiment is over.

Review and Test Preparation

Vocabulary Review

Use the terms below to complete the sentences. The page numbers tell you where to look in the chapter if you need help.

producers p. 166   **niche** p. 175
consumer p. 166   **predators** p. 176
omnivores p. 168   **food chain** p. 176
decomposers p. 170   **energy pyramid** p. 180

1. An animal that eats other living things is a _____.

2. Nutrients would be lost without _____.

3. The animals at the top of a food chain are always _____.

4. The kind of food that an animal eats is part of its _____.

5. Animals that eat both producers and other consumers are _____ .

6. Herbivores and omnivores both eat _____.

7. A food web shows relationships among living things more accurately than a _____.

8. The loss of energy along a food chain is shown in an _____.

Check Understanding

Write the letter of the best choice.

9. Which of these must a pond food chain have?
   A. algae   **C.** tiny fish
   B. sunlight   **D.** whales

10. **MAIN IDEA AND DETAILS** Which term includes herbivores, carnivores, and omnivores?
   F. consumers   **H.** prey
   G. predators   **J.** producers

11. How much energy is used at each level of the energy pyramid and not passed on?
   A. 10 percent   **C.** 80 percent
   B. 20 percent   **D.** 90 percent

12. Which of the following do herbivores eat?
   F. consumers   **H.** predators
   G. omnivores   **J.** producers

13. What is shown below?

   A. niche   **C.** habitat
   B. food chain   **D.** food web

14. What are robins, which eat worms and insects?

    F. carnivores   **H.** omnivores

    G. herbivores   **J.** prey

15. Antelopes are herbivores. What other term describes them?

    A. omnivores   **C.** prey

    B. predators   **D.** producers

16. SEQUENCE What is the first organism on a food chain?

    F. a consumer

    G. a decomposer

    H. a producer

    J. a predator

Inquiry Skills

17. Compare a carnivore and a predator. How are these living things the same? How are they different?

18. While hiking with your family, you follow a trail that leads past many dead plants. Even the trees seem to be dying. The soil is very dry. What can you **infer** is happening to the consumers in this area?

Critical Thinking

19. Which of these could survive without being part of a food chain— a strawberry plant, a chicken, or a dog? Explain your answer.

20. Different types of diagrams are used to show the relationships among living things. Study the diagram below.

Part A Would this diagram be correct if there were two snakes at the top? Explain your answer.

Part B How is this diagram different from a food chain?

Earth's Changing Surface

EARTH SCIENCE

Bandera Crater and Ice Cave

TO: jake@hspscience.com

FROM: riley@hspscience.com

RE: Grants, New Mexico

Dear Jake,

My family and I hiked out to the Bandera Crater. We went to Look Out Point. The crater is 1200 feet wide and over 750 feet deep. Nearby, you can hike over to the Ice Cave. It's very cold in there. It never gets above 31 degrees Fahrenheit. The ice floor is 20 feet deep! It's amazing that Earth's changes have formed these beautiful sights.

Riley

Elephant Rocks State Park

TO: luke@hspscience.com
FROM: tory@hspscience.com
RE: Missouri

Dear Luke,

Can you imagine a circus train of elephants made out of rocks? That's exactly what you will see if you go to Elephant Rocks State Park and use your imagination! These giant granite rocks have become rounded boulders that look like elephants. The biggest is known as Dumbo. It weighs 680 tons! I wonder how much the 'real' Dumbo weighed. Write back soon.

Tory

Experiment!

Earthquake-Resistant Buildings

Many people find beauty in the formations that make up Earth's surface. But a calm scene can quickly become frightening during events like earthquakes and volcanoes. Scientists and engineers work together to design buildings that can withstand the forces of an earthquake. What types of structures and materials are more likely to fall over during an earthquake? Plan and conduct an experiment to find out.

Chapter 6

The Rock Cycle

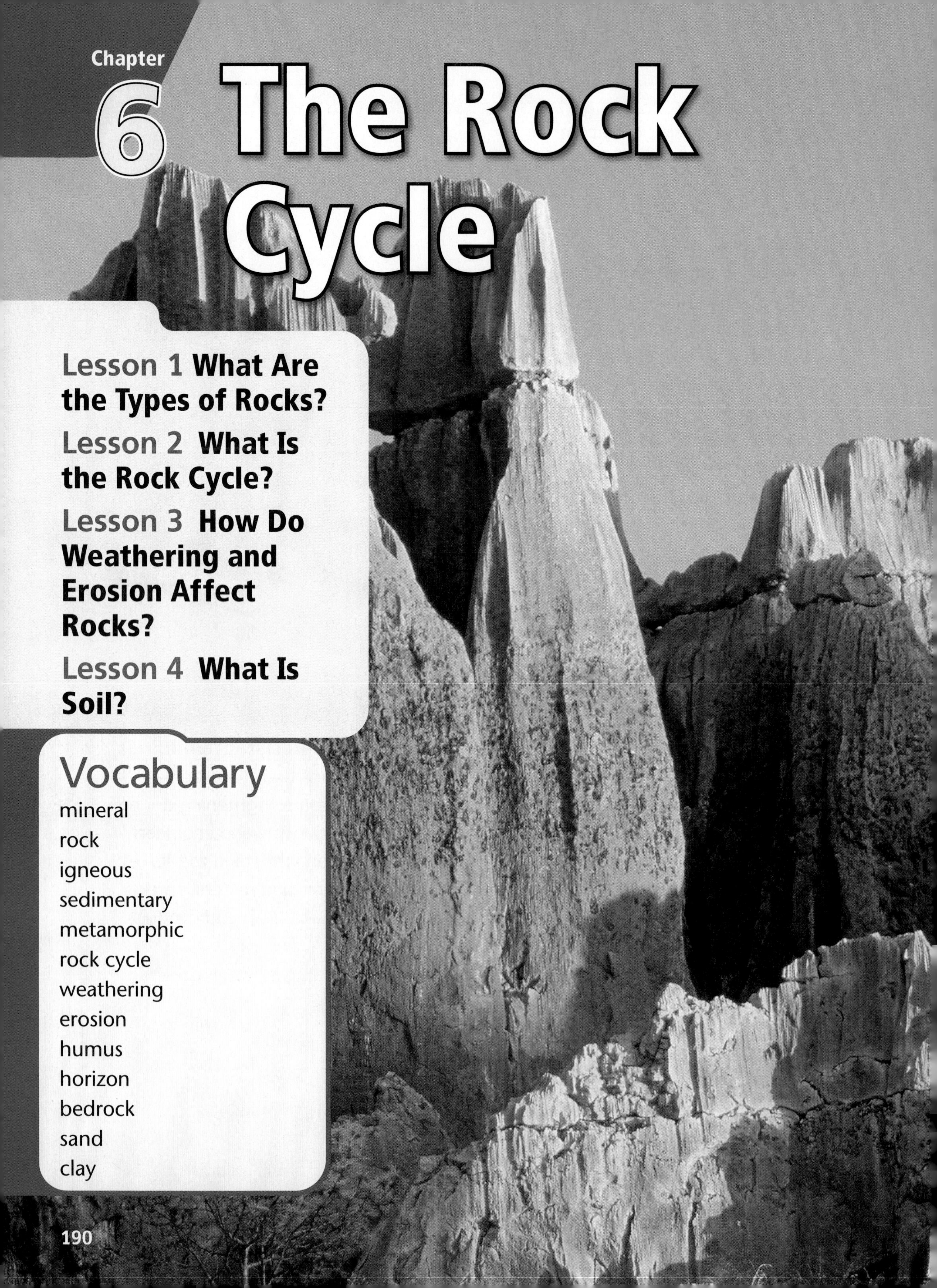

Vocabulary

mineral
rock
igneous
sedimentary
metamorphic
rock cycle
weathering
erosion
humus
horizon
bedrock
sand
clay

What do YOU wonder?

Rocky Forest These formations are part of the Stone Forest near Kunming, China. How do you think such landscapes might form?

191

Lesson 1

What Are the Types of Rocks?

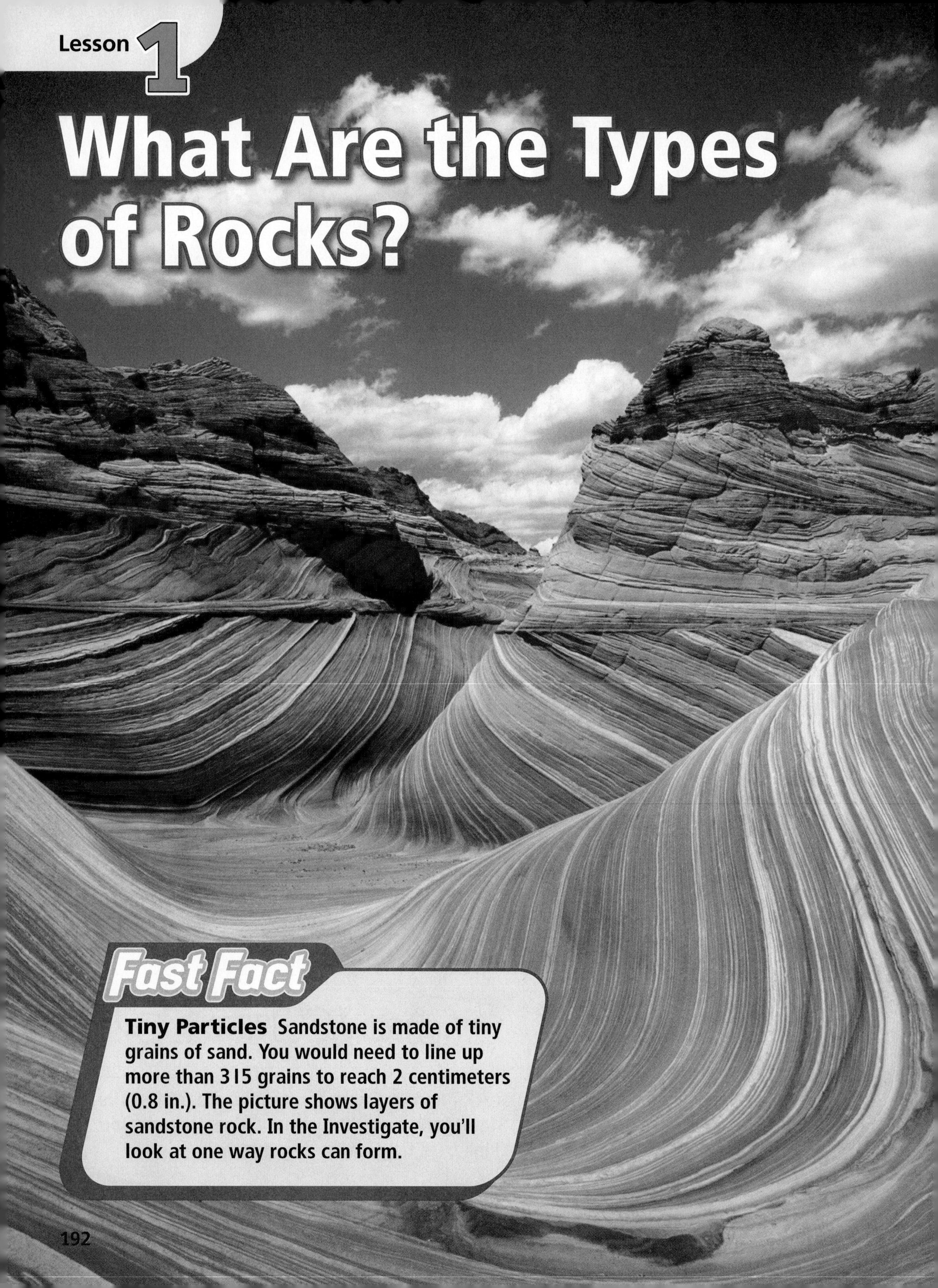

Fast Fact

Tiny Particles Sandstone is made of tiny grains of sand. You would need to line up more than 315 grains to reach 2 centimeters (0.8 in.). The picture shows layers of sandstone rock. In the Investigate, you'll look at one way rocks can form.

Making Sedimentary Rock

Materials
- 2 small plastic cups
- sand
- measuring cup
- white glue
- water
- plastic stirrer for mixing
- pushpin
- ring stand
- hand lens
- aluminum pan
- scissors

Procedure

Step 1

1. Use the pushpin to make a small hole in the bottom of one cup. The hole should be big enough to let water out but not sand.

2. Place 60 mL water and 60 mL white glue in the other cup. Mix and set aside.

3. Fill the first cup with sand.

4. Using a ring stand, suspend the cup holding sand over the pan.

5. Pour the glue mixture into the sand. Let the liquid drain into the pan. Let the glue dry. This could take two or three days.

6. When the liquid stops draining, remove the cup with the sand in it. Cut away the plastic cup with the scissors.

Step 4

Draw Conclusions

1. **Observe** and describe the structure that has formed in the cup. Use a hand lens.

2. **Inquiry Skills** Scientists often use models to study real-world processes. Compare the way you made your rock with the way you think an actual rock would form. Check your answer when you finish the lesson.

Investigate Further

Make a sandstone rock with several layers. Plan the investigation so you can easily observe each layer in the rock.

VOCABULARY
mineral p. 194
rock p. 194
igneous p. 196
sedimentary p. 197
metamorphic p. 198

SCIENCE CONCEPTS
▶ what minerals are
▶ what the three types of rocks are

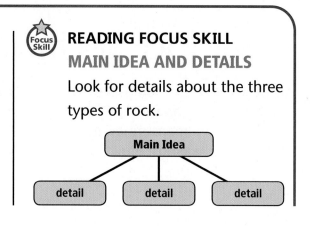

READING FOCUS SKILL
MAIN IDEA AND DETAILS
Look for details about the three types of rock.

Minerals

Do you remember the last time you picked up a pebble? Maybe it had sparkling specks or wavy lines. Maybe it was as clear as glass.

Minerals formed the colors and patterns in the pebble. A **mineral** (MIN•er•uhl) is a solid, nonliving substance that occurs naturally in rocks or in the ground. Every mineral has unique properties. Earth's surface is **rock**, a solid substance made of minerals. Rock can be made of many minerals or of one mineral with different-sized grains. Look at the granite. Each of its colors is a different mineral.

There are more than 4000 minerals. Many of them look alike. Scientists use the minerals' physical properties to tell them apart. For example, scientists can compare the hardness of two minerals by how easily they can be scratched. Gypsum and calcite can look alike, but gypsum is easier to scratch than calcite.

Fluorite often forms cube-shaped crystals of blue, purple, green, yellow, and white.

Calcite is a soft mineral. It can be white or perfectly clear, as this sample is. It makes up most limestone and marble rocks.

Agate is a type of quartz. It forms in cracks and holes in other rocks. The colored bands take the shape of the hole in which it formed.

▼ Silvery galena is a common mineral from which we get lead.

These two minerals are types of mica. The darker one is biotite. The yellowish one is muscovite.

▲ Hornblende is one of a group of hard green, black, and brown minerals.

▼ Copper is produced from the mineral chalcopyrite (kal•koh•PY•ryt).

The way a mineral reflects light is its *luster.* Two minerals may be the same color, but one may have a shiny luster and the other a dull luster.

When you rub a mineral across a surface, the mineral leaves a *streak* of powder. This colored streak can help scientists identify two minerals that look alike.

Minerals have other properties, too. Is the mineral magnetic? What shape are its crystals?

Two minerals might look alike and share some properties, but they don't share all properties. Gold and pyrite are both shiny and gold in color. Pyrite is sometimes called "fool's gold," because people have mistaken it for gold. Gold is much softer than pyrite. Gold leaves a golden streak. Pyrite's streak is greenish black.

MAIN IDEA AND DETAILS What properties can scientists use to identify minerals?

195

Igneous Rocks

Scientists classify rocks into three groups, based on how they form. One group is **igneous** (IG•nee•uhs) rocks. Igneous rocks form when melted rock cools and hardens.

The idea of melted rock might seem strange. Deep inside Earth, it is so hot that some rock is liquid, like syrup. This melted rock is *magma*. Inside Earth's crust, magma cools slowly. Volcanic eruptions release magma. Magma on Earth's surface is *lava*. Lava cools quickly.

 MAIN IDEA AND DETAILS **How does igneous rock form?**

Sometimes two igneous rocks form from the same magma, so they have the same chemical makeup. How they look depends on how deep in Earth they form. On Earth's surface lava cools quickly and grains don't have time to grow big. Inside Earth's surface magma cools slowly, giving grains time to grow big.

▼ Basalt

▼ Rhyolite

Gabbro ▶

◀ Diorite

Granite ▶

▼ Conglomerate forms from very large sediments. Notice the grains have rounded edges.

Shale is Earth's most common sedimentary rock. It forms from very fine sediments of silt and clay.

▼ Sandstone rock forms from sand-sized sediment.

▲ Scientists group sedimentary rocks by how they form and the size of the sediment grains that form them. This picture shows grains of sand, silt, and clay.

Sedimentary Rocks

Another type of rock is very common on Earth's surface. **Sedimentary** (sed•uh•MEN•ter•ee) rock forms from sediment. *Sediment* is pieces of rock that have been broken down and moved. Water, wind, and ice break down rock and then carry the sediment. When the wind or water slows down, the sediment falls to the surface. It piles up in layers. The layers get pressed together. Water, carrying minerals, moves through the sediment. Over time, the minerals cause the sediment to stick together. This is what you modeled in the Investigate.

(Focus Skill) **MAIN IDEA AND DETAILS** How does sedimentary rock form?

Insta-Lab

Making Layered Rock

Use small round pieces of clay to make a model of a sedimentary rock. How are these layers like the layers of real sedimentary rocks? How are they different?

Metamorphic Rocks

Another group of rock is metamorphic (met•uh•MAWR•fik) rock. **Metamorphic** rock is rock that has changed from another type of rock. High temperature and pressure form this type of rock.

Mountain building often causes metamorphic rock to form. Mountains form when plates that make up Earth's surface push together. Rock near the surface can get pushed down. Pressure on the rock squeezes it. Mineral grains in the rock get pressed more tightly together. If pressure is great enough, minerals in the rock change.

As natural forces push the rock deeper into Earth's crust, the temperature around it rises. High temperatures can change the minerals in rock. But the rock must not melt if it is to become metamorphic rock. If the rock melts, it becomes magma and eventually igneous rock.

Metamorphic rock can form from any type of rock. This includes other metamorphic rock.

MAIN IDEA AND DETAILS What two processes form metamorphic rock?

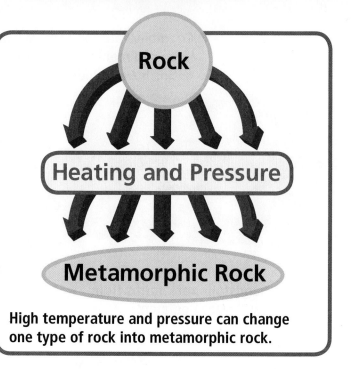

High temperature and pressure can change one type of rock into metamorphic rock.

Metamorphic slate forms from shale or mudstone.

Gneiss (NYS) is a metamorphic rock that forms from schist or granite.

Under high temperature and pressure, sedimentary limestone becomes metamorphic marble.

The grains in the rock show the effect of pressure on this metaconglomerate rock.

Focus Skill

1. MAIN IDEA AND DETAILS Fill in the graphic organizer below.

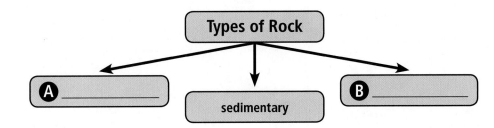

Types of Rock

A _____

sedimentary

B _____

2. SUMMARIE Write two sentences that summarize this lesson.

3. DRAW CONCLUSIONS Igneous rocks are the most common type of rocks in Earth's crust. Why do you think this is so?

4. VOCABULARY In your own words, write definitions of the three types of rock.

Test Prep

5. Critical Thinking You find a mineral that is shiny and a golden color. How can you tell if it is gold?

6. Under which of these conditions would igneous rock form?
  A. water breaks down rock
  B. pressure builds
  C. magma cools
  D. sediment collects

Links

Writing

Expository Writing
Choose a type of mineral or rock. Write a **description** of how it forms, where it is found, and what it is used for.

Math 9÷3

Make a Circle Graph
About 75 percent of rock on Earth's surface is sedimentary. Together, what percent are the other two types? Draw a circle graph to show the relationship.

Art

Rock Art
Draw a picture of the type of rock or mineral you wrote about in your description. Include details that would help someone else identify it.

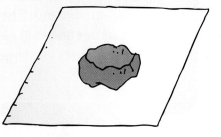

For more links and activities, go to www.hspscience.com

What Is the Rock Cycle?

Hot Rock Basalt rock doesn't melt easily. It can stay solid at 1000°C (1832°F). This basalt lava flowed from a Hawaiian volcano. The Hawaiians call this pāhoehoe (pah•ʜoʜ•ee•hoh•ee) lava. In the Investigate, you'll model how rocks change over time.

Model a Rock Cycle

Materials
- small plastic pencil sharpener
- crayons of three colors
- metal cookie sheet
- wax paper
- iron
- aluminum pie pan
- toaster oven

Procedure

1. Use the sharpener to make three piles of crayon shavings, each a different color.

2. Place the crayon shavings in three layers, on a cookie sheet. Press down the layers with your hand.

3. Place wax paper over the shavings. Your teacher will press down on the shavings lightly with a warm iron. The teacher will leave the iron for a few seconds, until the shavings soften. They should not melt completely. Let the shavings cool for a few minutes.

4. Place the block of shavings into the pie pan. **CAUTION: Your teacher will put the pan in the toaster oven. Let the shavings melt. Your teacher will remove the shavings and let them cool.**

Step 2

Step 3

Draw Conclusions

1. What type of rock does Step 2 represent? What type of rock does Step 3 represent? How about Step 4?

2. **Inquiry Skill** How would you plan and conduct a simple investigation that uses the "rock" from Step 4 to model how sedimentary rock forms?

Investigate Further

Design a similar investigation that models the same cycle but with the events in a different sequence.

VOCABULARY
rock cycle p. 202

SCIENCE CONCEPTS
▶ what the rock cycle is
▶ what processes take place during the rock cycle

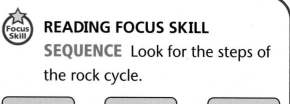

READING FOCUS SKILL

SEQUENCE Look for the steps of the rock cycle.

The Rock Cycle

Earth's surface is always changing. Forces inside Earth push mountains upward. Rain and wind wear down the rocks in those mountains. Rivers, winds, and oceans carry sediment. They deposit it in different places. New layers of rock form. Volcanoes erupt lava onto Earth's surface. Lava cools and hardens into rock. This rock wears away, too.

Often you can't see these changes. Many of them take thousands of years. They can even take millions of years. All of these changes are part of the rock cycle. The **rock cycle** is the sequence of processes that change rocks over long periods. In the rock cycle, the materials in rocks change again and again.

The rock cycle can follow many paths. There is a close-up look at one of them later in the lesson.

SEQUENCE Is there a first and last step in the rock cycle?

The Rock Cycle

During the rock cycle, each type of rock can be changed into any of the others. Notice that there is more than one path to each type of rock.

Igneous rock

■ = Melting and cooling
■ = Being broken down and carried by water, wind, and ice
■ = Pressure and heat

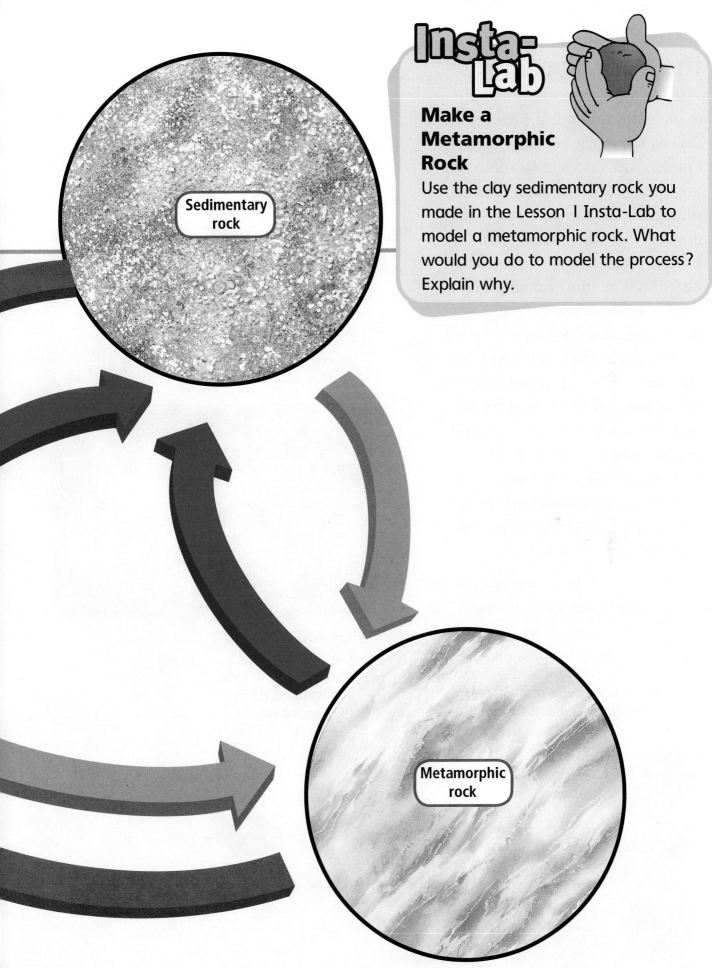

Sedimentary rock

Metamorphic rock

Insta-Lab

Make a Metamorphic Rock

Use the clay sedimentary rock you made in the Lesson 1 Insta-Lab to model a metamorphic rock. What would you do to model the process? Explain why.

One Path Through the Rock Cycle

These three rocks show one of many paths through the rock cycle. During mountain building, the igneous rock andesite (AN•duh•zyt) might be pushed upward to Earth's surface. There it could be broken down into smaller pieces, and this sediment could be deposited in water. In time, the sediment might form a sedimentary rock such as sandstone. This sandstone may get pushed deep into Earth's crust. With high temperature and pressure, the sandstone may become quartzite (KWAWRT•syt). Suppose even higher temperature acts on quartzite. The rock would melt, and eventually it would cool. It could harden as an igneous rock. Then the rock cycle continues.

 SEQUENCE What new type of rock can form after quartzite melts?

▲ Andesite is a common rock that forms from volcanic lava.

▲ Although sandstone can be made of any small sediment, most sandstone is made of rounded quartz sediment.

▼ The grains in sandstone are pressed together tightly. The new metamorphic rock, quartzite, is much harder than sandstone and has different properties.

1. SEQUENCE Copy and add processes to complete the graphic organizer.

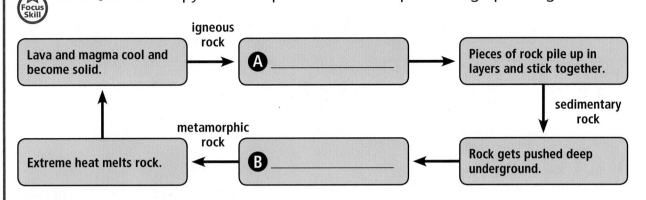

2. SUMMARIZE Write a paragraph that summarizes this lesson. Begin with the sentence *The rock cycle works slowly and never stops.*

3. DRAW CONCLUSIONS How might igneous rock become metamorphic?

4. VOCABULARY Define the term *rock cycle* in your own words without using the word *cycle.*

Test Prep

5. Critical Thinking Identify a part of the rock cycle that you might see.

6. Which of these isn't produced by the rock cycle?

A. lava   **C.** sediment

B. minerals   **D.** fungi

Links

Writing

Expository Writing

Choose one path through the rock cycle. Write a step-by-step **explanation** of the way one rock changes into another. Don't choose the path explained on the opposite page.

Math

Solve Problems

A layer of sedimentary rock is 5 meters thick. The layer was deposited at a rate of 1 centimeter per year. How many years did it take to form?

Language Arts

Word Origins

Research the origins of the words *igneous, sedimentary,* and *metamorphic.* Write a short explanation about each one.

For more links and activities, go to www.hspscience.com

205

How Do Weathering and Erosion Affect Rocks?

Fast Fact

Rising Seas The Giant's Causeway in Ireland is made of basalt, which can form five- or six-sided columns as it cools and shrinks. The sea is wearing away these cliffs. In the Investigate, you'll get an up-close look at one way rock breaks down.

Shake Things Up

Materials
- **6 medium-size rocks**
- **2 pieces of chalk**
- **empty clear plastic juice container with lid (2 qts)**

Procedure

1. Make a model of the way rocks break down in nature. Add two pieces of chalk to the container.

2. Place six rocks in the container.

3. Put the lid on the container.

4. Shake the container so that the rocks and chalk rub against each other. Do this for several minutes. You can take turns with your lab partner.

Draw Conclusions

1. Compare the way the rocks and chalk looked at the start and at the end of the investigation.

2. **Inquiry Skill** Scientists often infer the reasons for an investigation's results. Why do you think some of the materials in the cup broke down faster than other materials? How do you think this relates to rocks in nature?

Step 2

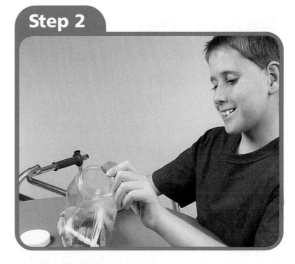

Step 4

Investigate Further

First, weigh the chalk that is left after the investigation. Then, add water to the container and repeat the test. Compare the mass of the chalk before and after the water. What conclusion can you draw?

VOCABULARY
weathering p. 208
erosion p. 212

SCIENCE CONCEPTS
▶ how weathering affects rock
▶ how erosion affects rock

READING FOCUS SKILL
CAUSE AND EFFECT Look for the causes of weathering.

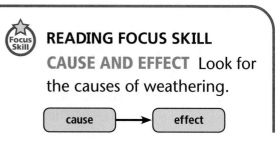

cause ➝ effect

Weathering

Have you ever seen a weed growing through a crack in a sidewalk? Maybe you've seen a statue with its features worn away. These are examples of weathering. **Weathering** is the breaking down of rock on Earth's surface into smaller pieces. Weathering helps shape landforms. It also helps make soil.

There are two types of weathering. One type of weathering physically breaks rock into smaller pieces.

The other type of weathering is different. It changes the chemical makeup of rock. This softens and weakens the rock, helping water wear it away. Water causes most weathering. It can break down some rock by itself. For example, water can wear away rock salt, calcite, and limestone.

Sinkholes are the result of weathering. They form when water slowly dissolves underground rock.

▼ Water can help wear away bits of surface rock.

A chemical change has turned the surface of this rock brown. Iron oxide, or rust, breaks down the outer layer of some kinds of rock.

Some rocks break down when oxygen combines with minerals in them. This often happens in rocks that have iron. When iron mixes with oxygen, iron oxide, or rust, forms. Rust makes it easier for other processes to weather the rock.

 CAUSE AND EFFECT **What is the effect of weathering?**

Science Up Close

Formation of a Sinkhole

1 Rain soaks into the ground. The rainwater eats away limestone rock under the surface. Water carries away the dissolved rock. A small opening forms.

2 The opening in the rock becomes larger as time passes.

3 Rock and soil that covered the underground opening cave in. A sinkhole forms on the surface. Do you think this process happens quickly or slowly? Explain.

This 15-story-deep sinkhole formed in Florida in 1994. It formed in an area where large amounts of minerals were taken out of the ground.

For more links and activities, go to www.hspscience.com

209

Weathering by Other Processes

The other type of weathering doesn't change the rock chemically. It breaks rock down through physical processes. Water, ice, living things, and wind are causes of this type of weathering.

You see the results of this weathering around you each day. It can cause cracks in sidewalks and potholes in streets. Rain enters cracks in rock and cement. If the water freezes into ice, it expands. The ice cracks and breaks rock around it. Stones in streams are also a sign of weathering. These stones were broken from larger pieces of rock. As they tumble against each other, they break down even more.

Large ocean waves weather coastlines. Waves smash into the bottom of a cliff. The rock that the waves hit cracks and breaks. In time, rock at the top of the cliff falls into the sea.

Even temperature changes can weather rock. Rock expands when it heats up. It contracts when it cools. Repeated heating and cooling can

Pounding waves force air into cracks. This helps split the rock. Water also carries sediment. This scrapes rock like sandpaper.

▼ Waves hit cliffs like this with great force. Thousands of tons of water smash into coastal rocks during storms.

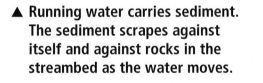

▲ Running water carries sediment. The sediment scrapes against itself and against rocks in the streambed as the water moves.

Scraping and bumping against each other in a moving stream gives these rocks rounded edges.

weaken some rock. The rock can then crack or break.

Living things can cause weathering. You have probably seen plants grow through cracks in rocks. The roots wedge into the rocks, splitting the rock around them as they grow. Animals can cause weathering, too. When animals dig in soil, they move rocks closer to Earth's surface. Then rainwater can reach them more easily.

Wind also causes weathering. Wind picks up bits of rock and soil and throws them against other rocks. This chips away the rocks' surface bit by bit.

(Focus Skill) **CAUSE AND EFFECT** How does ice cause weathering?

Insta-Lab

Observe Weathering

Use a large rock or brick to press down on a handful of rock salt. What happens to the rock salt? What kind of weathering does this model?

Erosion

What happens after weathering breaks down rock into sediment? Erosion takes over. **Erosion** is the process of moving sediment.

Water can cause erosion. Rivers carry sediment downstream. They drop it on their banks or at their mouths. Ocean waves pick up sediment and leave it on the shore as sand.

Wind erosion is most common in deserts. With few plants to hold sediment in place, wind picks it up easily. Wind stacks sand into huge mounds called sand dunes.

Glaciers are important causes of erosion. As these giant sheets of ice move, they scrape the ground. They pick up rocks and soil. During the last Ice Age, huge glaciers covered large parts of what is now the northern United States. They eroded and helped shape the plains and other landforms we see today. As glaciers moved over land, they also formed lakes. When the glaciers melted, they left behind huge ridges of sediment and large amounts of water.

CAUSE AND EFFECT **What are the main causes of erosion?**

What is the largest type of sediment? What is the smallest? Which would erosion affect more, boulders and cobbles or silt and clay? Why is that?

SEDIMENT COMES IN ALL SIZES		
256 mm and up	BOULDERS	GRAVEL
64-256 mm	COBBLES	GRAVEL
2-64 mm	PEBBLES	GRAVEL
0.0625-2 mm	SAND	
0.002-0.0625 mm	SILT	
0.002 mm and under	CLAY	

This photo shows one river flowing into another. Soil washes into rivers from areas along its banks. One of these rivers is carrying much more sediment than the other. The sediment has turned parts of the water brown.

Water that washes over areas of bare soil can create gullies. Planting vegetation can help prevent this type of soil erosion.

Focus Skill

1. CAUSE AND EFFECT Copy and complete the graphic organizer below.

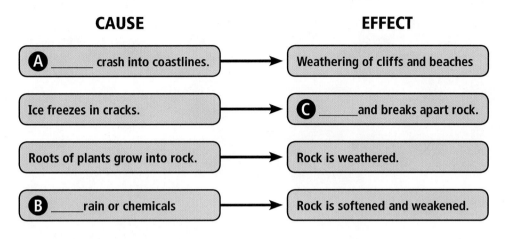

CAUSE

EFFECT

A _____ crash into coastlines. → Weathering of cliffs and beaches

Ice freezes in cracks. → **C** _____ and breaks apart rock.

Roots of plants grow into rock. → Rock is weathered.

B _____ rain or chemicals → Rock is softened and weakened.

2. SUMMARIZE Summarize the lesson section on physical weathering.

3. DRAW CONCLUSIONS The Colorado River flows through the bottom of the Grand Canyon. Does the river cause weathering or erosion? Explain.

4. VOCABULARY Make a crossword puzzle using the vocabulary for the first three lessons in this chapter.

Test Prep

5. Critical Thinking You see a marble sign. Its letters are too worn to read. What caused this?

6. Which of these doesn't cause weathering?
  A. wind   **C.** water
  B. magma   **D.** plants

Links

Writing

Narrative Writing

Write the **story** of a grain of sediment that has been weathered from a mountain, carried to the sea by a river, and left on a beach. Write from the sediment's point of view.

Math 9÷3

Solve Problems

A farmer plants $\frac{1}{5}$ of his land with trees to stop erosion. If he plants trees on 525 hectares, how much land does he have? Show your work.

Social Studies

Famous Features

Research a famous natural feature, such as a canyon, mountain, or rock formation. Explain how it formed. Draw a map that shows where the feature is located. Share with the class what you find.

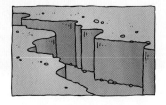

For more links and activities, go to **www.hspscience.com**

What Is Soil?

Forming Soil This tree is starting soil formation by weathering rock. Over a long time, the rock will be broken down into soil. It can take up to 1000 years for 2 centimeters ($\frac{3}{4}$ in.) of topsoil to form!

Testing Soil

Materials
- measuring scoop
- sand
- 2 large jars with wide mouths
- potting soil
- 250 mL measuring cup
- water

Procedure

1. Place several scoops of sand in a jar. Place an equal amount of potting soil in another jar.

2. Put 200 mL of water in the measuring cup.

3. Slowly pour the water into the sand. Stop when water starts to puddle on top.

4. Record how much water you used.

5. Repeat steps 2, 3, and 4 for the potting soil.

Draw Conclusions

1. Compare the amounts of water the two types of soil absorbed. Infer where the water you poured into them went.

2. **Inquiry Skill** When scientists do an experiment, they often do it in more than one way and compare results. What do your results tell you about how the size of particles and the spaces between them compare in sand and potting soil?

Step 2

Step 3

Investigate Further

Repeat the investigation, using a different type of soil. Predict how the new results will compare with the results of the Investigate. Is your prediction correct?

215

Reading in Science

VOCABULARY
humus p. 216
horizon p. 217
bedrock p. 217
sand p. 218
clay p. 218

SCIENCE CONCEPTS
▶ what soil is
▶ how soil forms and how soils differ

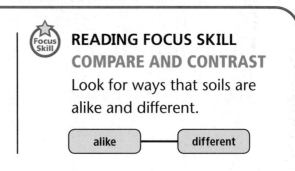

READING FOCUS SKILL
COMPARE AND CONTRAST
Look for ways that soils are alike and different.

| alike | different |

Soil Formation

If you walk in the woods, you are walking on soil. If you grow flowers on a windowsill, you use soil. Soil is one of the most important things on Earth. Plants can't grow without soil. Without plants, animals could not exist.

So what is soil? The largest part of soil is weathered rock. Sediment makes up almost 50 percent of soil.

Soil has living and nonliving parts. It contains **humus** (HYOO•muhs), or the remains of decayed plants and animals. Soil is crawling with living organisms. There are worms and insects as well as bacteria, fungi, and roots that you can't see with just your eyes.

Water and air make up about half the volume of a soil sample. Water and air are in the spaces between soil particles.

▼ These three pictures show steps of soil formation.

Bedrock is broken down into smaller pieces.

Subsoil is partly weathered rock.

Topsoil is a mix of humus, minerals, and small sediment.

Most soil has **horizons**, or layers. Some soils have several horizons that are easy to see. Other soils have few horizons.

Because horizons form differently, each has particles of different sizes. Horizons also may have different minerals. Horizons all share some properties. The upper layer is topsoil. It includes humus. The lower horizons have partly weathered rock. The lower horizons also contain minerals that rain has carried from upper layers. The bottom horizon is **bedrock**, or the solid rock that forms Earth's surface.

Soil is always forming, but it takes a long time. Some soils take thousands of years to form. That is one reason why soil is such an important resource.

 **COMPARE AND CONTRAST How are the top and bottom horizons of soil different?**

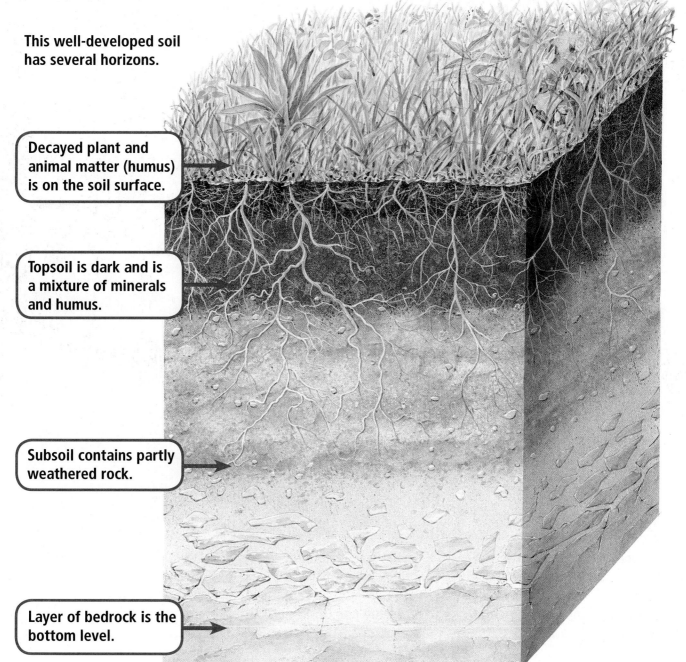

This well-developed soil has several horizons.

Decayed plant and animal matter (humus) is on the soil surface.

Topsoil is dark and is a mixture of minerals and humus.

Subsoil contains partly weathered rock.

Layer of bedrock is the bottom level.

Types of Soil

You might think that one type of soil is very much like another, but there are many types of soil. Soils are classified by their physical properties. The size of soil particles is one property. Each type of soil is a mix of particles of different sizes. The largest particles are **sand**. A sand particle might be 1 to 2 millimeters (0.04 to 0.08 in.) across. The smallest soil particles are **clay**. Clay particles might be $\frac{1}{1000}$ the size of sand particles. The size of silt is between sand and clay.

Different amounts of sand, silt, and clay in soil give it texture. Texture is how the soil feels in your hands. Soil with more sand feels rough, while soil with more clay feels smooth. Soils differ in other ways, also. They have different compositions. Soil under a desert has less humus than grassland soil. Some soils hold water well, while others don't. Soil horizons can be just a few centimeters thick, or they can reach several meters underground.

Soil type depends on the area where it forms. Bedrock breaks down to form

Sandy soils have large particles. Water passes through quickly. They can be good for growing crops.

Fertile soils often have a thick layer of topsoil. Large amounts of humus make the soil dark.

Clay soils have tiny particles. They hold nutrients and water so well it's hard for plants to grow.

Soil Horizons in Three Different Places

Soils of grasslands often have a thick top horizon that is full of humus. They are loose, soft, and fertile.

Desert soils don't have much humus. They are pale gray to red in color and high in salts. Horizons are not well developed.

This typical Florida soil is sandy, with a thin layer of humus. It forms from limestone bedrock.

the soil above it. Granite bedrock forms coarse soil. Soil formed by basalt bedrock is fine-grained.

A soil's color is also dependent on where the soil forms. A dark soil may have formed in a place with a lot of humus, such as a forest. A light-colored soil may have little organic matter, such as in a desert.

 COMPARE AND CONTRAST How might desert soil and forest soil be alike? Different?

Insta-Lab

How Much Water?

With a dropper, drop water onto a tablespoon of soil and onto a small sponge. Compare how much water soaks in and how much runs off in each case. What property of soil are you modeling?

Soil and Plants

Most plants need soil. Their roots draw nutrients, water, and oxygen from soil.

Some soils are fertile. They are good for growing plants. Other soils lack nutrients. To make the soil better for growing plants, many farmers and gardeners add nutrients to soil. The nutrients they add are fertilizer (FERT•uhl•eye•zer).

There are natural fertilizers and artificial fertilizers. Artificial fertilizers are human-made mixtures of chemicals. They add to the soil nutrients that plants need. Natural fertilizers include compost and animal waste. People make compost by putting food and plant scraps in a pile. The scraps decay to make fertilizer.

Some soils hold more moisture than other soils. Humus helps soil hold water. Soils with small particles hold water better than soils with large particles. When soil is too dry for plants, people add water. They pump water from wells and other sources and sprinkle it on soil.

COMPARE AND CONTRAST Compare and contrast the two types of fertilizers.

Soils can lose nutrients because of erosion or heavy use. Fertilizers put back important nutrients, such as phosphorus, nitrogen, and potassium.

Many farmers use fertilizers on their soil.

FEEDS 5,000 SQ. FT.
NET WT. 2.5 LBS.

FALL FERTILIZER 10-18-10

Many farmers and gardeners use compost to give soil nutrients. Compost is a natural fertilizer that adds humus to soil.

Focus Skill

1. COMPARE AND CONTRAST Fill in the graphic organizer below.

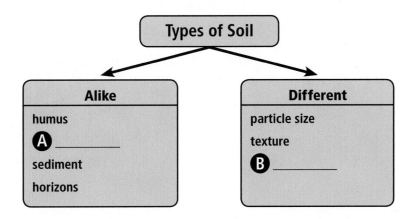

Types of Soil

Alike	**Different**
humus	particle size
A _____	texture
sediment	**B** _____
horizons	

2. SUMMARIZE Write one sentence to summarize each section in the lesson.

3. DRAW CONCLUSIONS Erosion can wash away soil. Why is it important to control this type of erosion?

4. VOCABULARY Make a page for a picture dictionary, using the five lesson vocabulary words.

Test Prep

5. Critical Thinking Why is understanding soil and how it forms useful to all people?

6. Which of these makes up the largest part of soil?

    A. water   **C.** air

    B. humus   **D.** sediment

Links

Writing

Persuasive Writing

Write a short **e-mail** to the editor of a newspaper. Persuade gardeners to use compost instead of other fertilizers in their gardens. Explain why you think compost is a better choice.

Math 9÷3

Solving a Problem

Soil in a certain area erodes at a rate of 3.2 centimeters per month. How much soil erodes over a period of 5 years?

Social Studies

Report

Write a **report** about the problems of drought and soil erosion that led to the "Dust Bowl." If possible, interview someone who was affected by the "Dust Bowl." Include a map.

For more links and activities, go to **www.hspscience.com**

Crumbling HISTORY | WILL THE GREAT SPHINX CRUMBLE LIKE A COOKIE?

The Great Sphinx in Egypt has stood the test of time. For at least 4,500 years, the sphinx has towered over a desert in Egypt. Now, however, rising groundwater may cause the ancient statue to crumble.

The Mysterious Sphinx

A sphinx is a figure with the head of a person and the body of a lion. No one knows for sure why the Great Sphinx was built. Some say it honors an ancient king named Khafre. Others say the sphinx was made to represent an ancient Egyptian god.

The sphinx was built at about the same time that the Great Pyramid was built. Even though scientists know little about the sphinx, they do know something about the Great Pyramid and the other nearby pyramids.

The ancient Egyptians built the pyramids as tombs for their kings. When an Egyptian king died, his body was mummified. The body was then placed in the tomb. Many of the king's belongings were also placed in the tomb.

Wind has blown desert sand into the Great Sphinx, wearing away the monument.

Damaging History

The sphinx and pyramids have suffered damage over time. For example, wind has blown the desert sand into the monuments, causing them to wear away. Some of the blocks that make up the monuments have come loose and fallen.

Now the ancient monuments are facing the most serious threat ever—water. A dam built near the monuments traps water. That water is used to irrigate farm crops grown nearby. Irrigation has caused the level of groundwater to increase. The water is filled with salts. The salts and water react with the stone that makes up the monuments. The chemical reaction causes the stones to crumble and turn into dust.

Two scientists are now trying to protect the ancient monuments. They want to find ways to keep groundwater from flowing under the monuments. If the water isn't stopped, the Great Sphinx and pyramids may one day crumble into dust blown by the desert wind.

THINK ABOUT IT

1. Why did the ancient Egyptians build the pyramids?

2. Can you think of any monuments in the United States that need protecting?

THE GREAT SPHINX

20 meters (66 ft) high
73 meters (240 ft) long
4-meter-wide (13-ft-wide) face
2-meter-high (7-ft-high) eyes

Find out more! Log on to
www.hspscience.com

223

The Color of Dirt

What's the color of dirt? Brown right? Not always!

In the early 1900s a scientist named Dorothy Nickerson helped scientists who test soil. Nickerson helped to make standards that scientists can use when they study dirt and rocks.

As part of her work, Nickerson worked with Albert H. Munsell. Munsell had invented a color chart system. Nickerson worked with Munsell so that the chart could be used for describing soil color.

Why is studying dirt important? Experts use the Munsell color chart and color names when surveying soil. The surveys show scientists what kind of soil exists in our country. Then scientists can decide the best way to use the soil.

Career Landscaper

Where to plant that Japanese maple? What kind of grass would grow best in this yard? These are questions a landscaper can answer. Landscapers study how plants live in different soils and in different climates. They know which soil is good for which plants and how to help soil that is not good for planting.

You Can Do It!

Quick and Easy Project

Deep Freeze

Materials
- drinking straw
- glass of water
- clay
- freezer

Procedure

1. Put a straw into a glass of water.
2. Suck on one end of the straw to fill it completely with water.
3. Keep your tongue over the top end of the straw to stop water from running out. Then pull the straw from the water. Plug the bottom end with a small piece of clay.
4. After removing your tongue, plug the other end of the straw with clay.
5. Put the straw into a freezer. Leave it for about 3 hours.
6. Take out the straw. Observe the ends.

Draw Conclusions
Describe what happened to the straw. Draw conclusions about why this happened. What Earth process does this model?

Design Your Own Investigation

Signs of the Rock Cycle

Look for evidence of a stage of the rock cycle in the area where you live. Explain the change that is going on. Take photos or draw sketches of what you see. How would you design a way to observe changes over time? Which stages of the rock cycle are you most likely to see? Which are you not likely to see? Share what you find with other students.

Review and Test Preparation

Vocabulary Review

Use the terms below to complete the sentences. The page numbers tell where to look in the chapter if you need help.

mineral p. 194
igneous p. 196
sedimentary p. 197
metamorphic p. 198
rock cycle p. 202

weathering p. 208
erosion p. 212
humus p. 216
horizon p. 217
bedrock p. 217

1. Rock that formed from other weathered rock is _____.

2. The process of moving sediment from one place to another is _____.

3. Rock that forms when melted rock cools and hardens is _____.

4. A group of processes that change rocks over a long time is the _____.

5. A soil layer is a _____.

6. A solid substance that occurs naturally in rocks or in the ground is a _____.

7. The breaking down of rock on Earth's surface into smaller pieces is _____.

8. The solid rock that forms Earth's surface is _____.

9. Rock that has changed from another type of rock is _____.

10. The remains of dead plants and animals is _____.

Check Understanding

Write the letter of the best choice.

11. Of which substance are rocks made?
    A. clay
    B. horizons
    C. humus
    D. minerals

12. Identify the rock below.

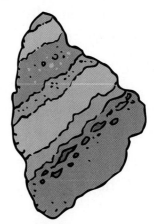

    F. igneous granite
    G. metamorphic quartzite
    H. sedimentary conglomerate
    J. sedimentary sandstone

13. **MAIN IDEA AND DETAILS** Which of these is **not** a part of the rock cycle?
    A. Metamorphic rock melts.
    B. Lava hardens into rock.
    C. Nitrogen enters soil.
    D. Plants weather rock.

14. COMPARE AND CONTRAST Which describes how some igneous rock forms?

   F. Water freezes in cracks in rock.

   G. Magma cools underground.

   H. Pressure changes minerals in rock.

   J. Water erodes sediment.

15. What is the name of the lowest soil horizon?

   A. bedrock

   B. magma

   C. subsoil

   D. topsoil

16. What makes up humus?

   F. decayed plants and animals

   G. fertilizer

   H. minerals

   J. sediment

Inquiry Skills

17. Why is the ability to **use models** important when studying processes that are part of the rock cycle?

18. What are you looking for when you **compare** rocks?

Critical Thinking

19. Why is most metamorphic rock harder than the sedimentary rock from which it formed?

20. Jameer is on vacation with his family in Hawai'i. He sees rock formations all around the Kīlauea volcano. Some of these look like the diagram below. Help Jameer identify the part of the rock cycle shown in the diagram.

   Part A What happened just before this step?

   Part B List two possible steps in the cycle after this one.

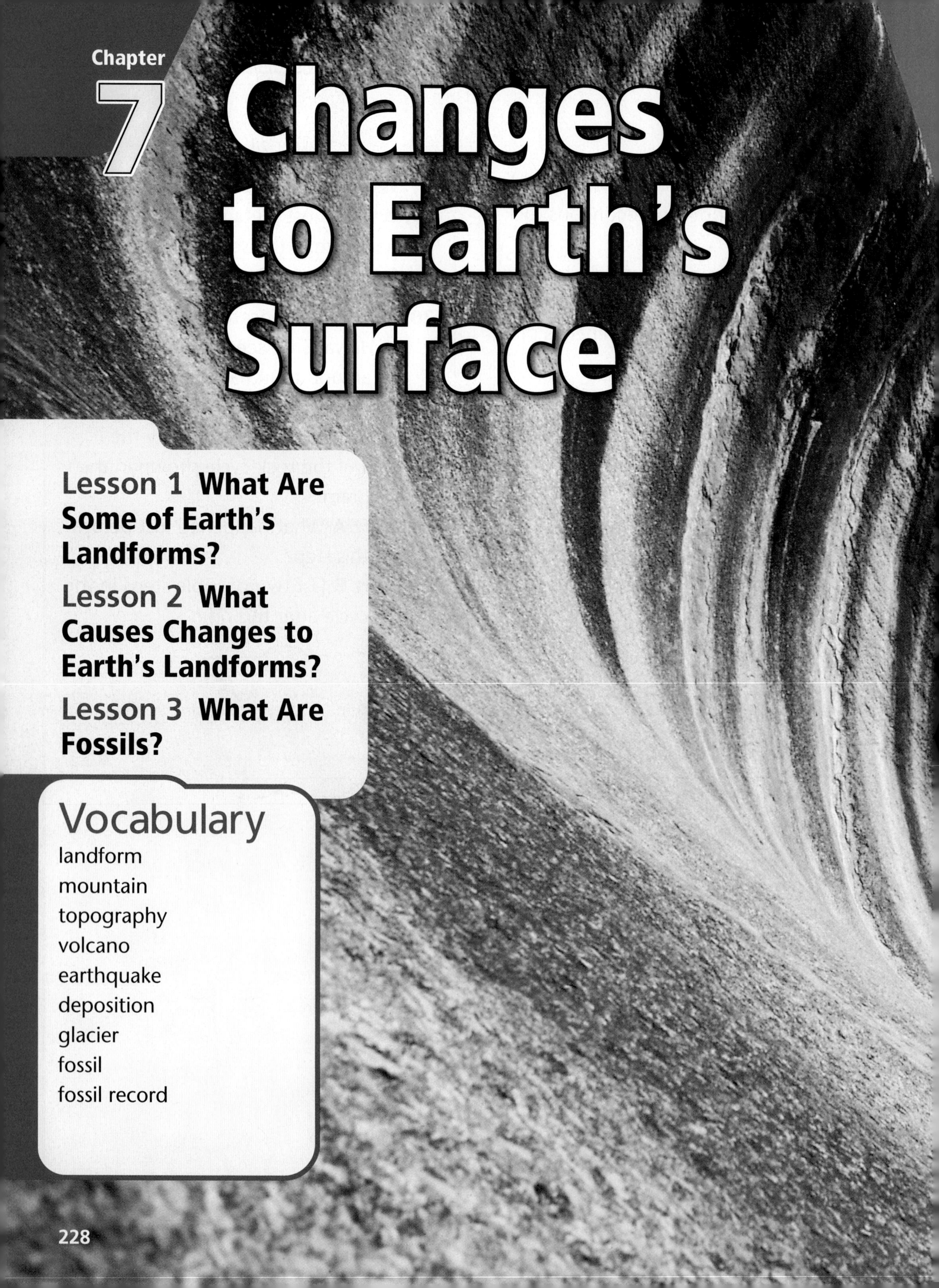

Chapter 7

Changes to Earth's Surface

Vocabulary

landform
mountain
topography
volcano
earthquake
deposition
glacier
fossil
fossil record

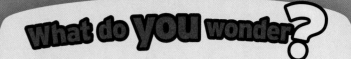

This formation, near Hyden, Australia, looks like a tumbling wave. But what is it? From what material do you think it is made? How do you think it formed?

What Are Some of Earth's Landforms?

Fast Fact

Deep Valley Water from melting glaciers cut through Earth's crust to form the Upper St. Croix River gorge in Wisconsin about 10,000 years ago. In the Investigate, you will choose a natural landform and make a model of it.

Make a Landform Model

Materials
- paper
- pencil
- modeling clay
- heavy cardboard

Procedure

1. Look for a landform in your area. It might be a mountain, hill, dune, valley, plateau, canyon, or cliff.

2. Observe the landform's shape and size. Sketch the landform on a sheet of paper.

3. Get a piece of modeling clay from your teacher. Place it on a sheet of cardboard.

4. Use clay and your sketch of the landform to make a model.

Draw Conclusions

1. Which type of landform did you make a model of with the clay?

2. Predict how the landform might change in the future. What might cause the change?

3. **Inquiry Skill** Scientists often observe objects in nature and then use models to understand them better. How did observing the model help you understand the landform you chose?

Step 2

Step 4

Investigate Further

Use the information on a topographic map to make a model of one of the landforms shown on the map.

Reading in Science

VOCABULARY
landform p. 232
mountain p. 232
topography p. 234

SCIENCE CONCEPTS
▶ what major landforms are
▶ how some landforms form

 READING FOCUS SKILL
COMPARE AND CONTRAST
Look for ways that landforms differ.

| alike | | different |

Mountains and Hills

Earth's surface looks flat from space. However, it is wrinkled, cracked, and folded into many landforms. A **landform** is a natural feature on Earth's surface.

Mountains are some of Earth's most spectacular landforms. A **mountain** is an area that is higher than the land around it. Mountains are usually at least 500 meters (1,600 ft) tall. Hills look like mountains, but they are smaller.

Mountains form in many ways. Some mountains are volcanoes. Other mountains form when forces bend and fold Earth's crust. Blocks of Earth's crust can also get pushed upward to form mountains. It can take millions of years for a chain, or group, of mountains to form.

COMPARE AND CONTRAST How are mountains and hills different?

▼ The temperature of the air decreases as you move up a mountain. Snow and ice always cover the tops of the highest mountains.

▼ These hills are green because of plentiful rainfall. Hills in dry areas can be bare and rocky.

This wide, green valley is in Scotland. Its wide floor and gently sloping sides are different from those of a canyon.

Palo Duro Canyon in Texas is 193 kilometers (120 mi) long, as much as 32 kilometers (20 mi) wide, and more than 240 meters (790 ft) deep.

Valleys and Canyons

You have learned that mountains are highlands. There are also lowland areas called valleys. A *valley* is an area with higher land around it. Valleys stretch between mountains and between hills.

The bottom of a valley is its floor, and its sides are its walls. There are different kinds of valleys. A canyon is a valley with steep walls. Some canyons are so deep and narrow that sunlight barely reaches the floor. Other canyons, like the one shown here, are wide and open.

Rivers or glaciers form most valleys. The moving water or ice cuts through rock and soil. Erosion from rainfall moves soil and rock from valley walls. Some of this rock and soil settles on valley floors. The floors of many valleys have fertile soil that is excellent for farming.

COMPARE AND CONTRAST How are a valley and a canyon alike?

Focus Skill

Plains and Plateaus

Some parts of Earth's surface are mostly flat. These large, flat landforms are called plains. A plain can have a gently rolling surface. It can even have a slight slope. Plains don't have highlands or deep valleys.

Some plains are inland and others are along coasts. A plain that slopes toward the sea along a coast is a coastal plain.

Some plains extend along rivers. Sometimes rivers overflow their banks, causing floods. When the floods go down, soil and sediment are left behind. This soil helps form plains called floodplains.

A *plateau* (pla•TOH) is also a flat area, but it is higher than the land around it. The edges of plateaus can form steep cliffs. As plateaus erode, they can become other landforms. A much smaller landform with the shape of a plateau is a mesa (MAY•suh). A smaller mesa is a butte (BYOOT). These landforms sometimes make unusual topography (tuh•PAHG•ruh•fee). **Topography** is the shape of landforms in an area.

COMPARE AND CONTRAST **How are plateaus and plains alike?**

▼ **Many farms are located on plains. This wide plain in Asia has rich soil.**

This plateau is in Australia. Weathering and erosion are wearing away parts of it.

Deltas can look like different things from space. Some deltas resemble fans or triangles, while another delta might resemble a bird's foot.

Deltas and Dunes

Deltas and dunes look very different, but both are formed by the movement of sand and sediment.

Deltas form at the ends of rivers. Fast-moving rivers carry away bits of soil and rock. When a river enters a lake or an ocean, it slows down. When this happens, the water can't carry as much material. It drops most of the rock and soil where it meets the lake or ocean, forming a delta.

Dunes form in dry areas or along sandy coasts. They form where wind carries sand. As the wind flows over rocks or other barriers, its speed slows. The wind drops the sand around the object. Over time, a dune forms.

 COMPARE AND CONTRAST What is different about the way deltas and dunes form?

The dunes of White Sands, New Mexico, are made of the mineral gypsum. The highest dunes are about 18 meters (60 ft) tall.

Islands

Every *island* is a body of land surrounded by water. Islands differ in the way they form. Some were once linked to a mainland. When the sea level rose thousands of years ago, water covered the land that formed the link. The British Isles formed this way.

Other islands are the tops of volcanoes that have been built up from the sea floor. Alaska's Aleutian Islands formed this way. Barrier islands are thin, sandy islands that build up along coasts. Barrier islands form where waves deposit sand near the shore.

Coral islands form from the remains of tiny sea animals. The remains form huge structures of limestone in the sea. There are many coral islands in the Pacific Ocean.

 COMPARE AND CONTRAST How are coral islands different from all other types of islands?

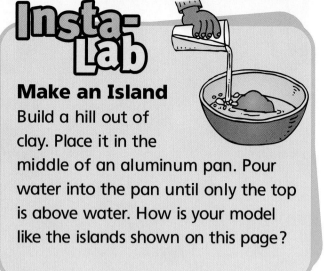

Insta-Lab

Make an Island
Build a hill out of clay. Place it in the middle of an aluminum pan. Pour water into the pan until only the top is above water. How is your model like the islands shown on this page?

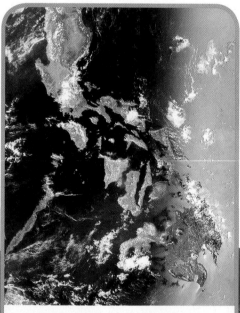

This view from the air shows a chain, or group, of islands.

This is the tiny island of Mokoli`i in Hawai`i. All the islands of Hawai`i are the result of volcanic eruptions from the ocean floor.

236

1. COMPARE AND CONTRAST Copy and fill in the graphic organizer below.

VALLEY   CANYON

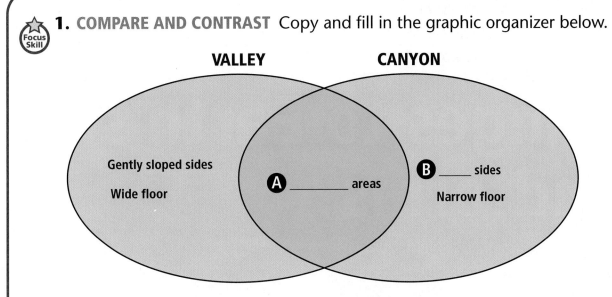

Gently sloped sides

Wide floor

A _____ areas

B _____ sides

Narrow floor

2. SUMMARIZE Write one or two sentences to summarize the lesson.

3. DRAW CONCLUSIONS How might a mountain become a plain over a long time?

4. VOCABULARY Write a definition of one of the vocabulary terms. Use your own words.

Test Prep

5. Critical Thinking You want to start a farm. Should you choose land on a mountain or in a valley? Explain your answer.

6. Which of these landforms is all or partly flat?
   A. hill   **C.** dune
   B. plateau   **D.** mountain

Links

Writing

Expository Writing
Choose an important landform outside the United States. Write an **explanation** of how it formed. Share your explanation with classmates.

Math

Organize Data
Look in an encyclopedia to find the world's five largest islands. Arrange them in a table in order from the largest to the smallest.

Social Studies

Use a Map
Locate two major landforms on a map of the United States. They can be a mountain, valley, canyon, plateau, plain, delta, or island. Write a one-sentence caption to identify each landform.

For more links and activities, go to www.hspscience.com

What Causes Changes to Earth's Landforms?

Fast Fact

Rocky Coast These tall rocks along the Australian coast are sea stacks. They are all that is left of a rocky cliff that was pounded to pieces by ocean waves. In the Investigate, you will find out about the forces that shape volcanoes.

Volcanic Eruptions

Materials
- 2-liter plastic bottle
- small piece of modeling clay
- aluminum pie plate
- puffed rice cereal
- funnel
- air pump

Procedure

1. Ask your teacher to make a hole near the bottom of a bottle. Stick the bottom of the bottle to a pie plate with clay.

2. Use a funnel to add cereal to the bottle until it is one-fourth full.

3. Attach an air pump to the hole in the bottle. Make sure the nozzle points down. Put a piece of clay around the hole to make it airtight.

4. Pump air into the bottle. Observe what happens.

Draw Conclusions

1. What happened to the cereal when you pumped air into the bottle?

2. Predict how you could model a very large eruption.

3. **Inquiry Skill** Scientists often make models to help them understand things that happen in nature. How does the bottle model an erupting volcano?

Step 2

Step 3

Investigate Further

Make models using fine sand and gravel to test this hypothesis: A volcano that forms from thick lava is steeper.

239

VOCABULARY
volcano p. 242
earthquake p. 242
deposition p. 244
glacier p. 245

SCIENCE CONCEPTS
▶ characteristics of Earth's structure
▶ what forces change Earth's surface

READING FOCUS SKILL
CAUSE AND EFFECT Look for causes of changes to Earth's surface.

cause	→	effect

Layers of Earth

Every minute of every day, you are on Earth's surface. If you could cut open Earth and look inside, you would find the four layers shown in the diagram below.

Earth's thin outer layer is the crust. The crust includes the land that makes up the continents as well as the land under the oceans.

The mantle is the rock layer below the crust. Deep below Earth's surface, the temperature rises. The upper parts of the mantle are so hot that the rock can flow. In some places the rock is melted to form *magma*.

At Earth's center is the core. The core is made mostly of iron and nickel. The outer core is liquid. The inner core is solid. The inner core is almost as hot as the surface of the sun. It is solid because there is so much pressure on it.

Earth's crust and upper mantle are broken into large slabs of rock called plates. The plates move on a layer of the mantle that can flow like taffy.

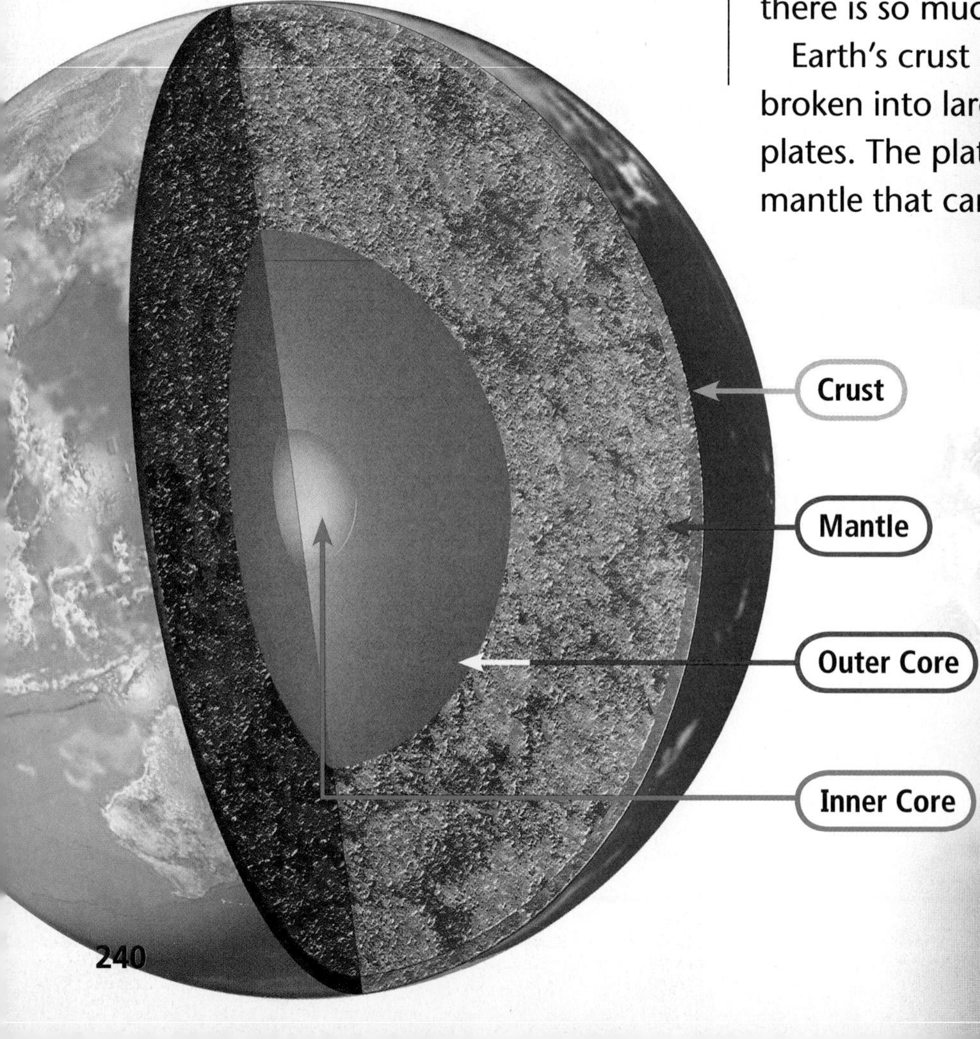

Crust

Mantle

Outer Core

Inner Core

◀ The crust is Earth's thinnest layer. It is solid rock. The crust sits on top of the mantle, which is Earth's thickest layer. Earth's core is mostly metal, and it's very hot. Temperatures in the core reach as high as 5000°C (9000°F).

You can't see the movement of these plates. The plates move only a few centimeters per year. Over a long time, this movement leads to the formation of different landforms.

Plates move in several ways. Some move toward each other. When two land plates meet, the edges crush and fold as one is pushed down under the other, forming mountain chains. Where a land plate and an ocean plate or two ocean plates meet, islands made of volcanic mountains can result.

Some plates travel away from each other. Large cracks can form where the two plates are moving apart. Magma from the mantle oozes up through these cracks. It hardens and makes new crust. Often this happens in the oceans.

Plates can also slide past each other. Where this happens, huge cracks appear at Earth's surface.

CAUSE AND EFFECT What landform can form where two land plates collide?

Insta-Lab

How Mountains Grow

Place both hands flat on a table, with the fingertips facing each other. Keep moving your hands toward each other until your fingertips are pushing against each other. What happens to your fingers? How does this model mountain formation?

▼ The Himalayas are Earth's highest mountain chain.

Indian Plate

Asian Plate

The Himalayas began to form when the Indian plate and the Asian plate pushed into each other.

Volcanoes and Earthquakes

On the morning of May 18, 1980, the volcano Mount St. Helens, in the state of Washington, erupted. A **volcano** is a mountain that forms as lava flows through a crack onto Earth's surface. This major eruption threw ash 19 kilometers (12 miles) into the air. The lava, ash, rock, and hot gases that shoot out of volcanoes change the land. Hot rock and gas from Mount St. Helens covered the land, filled in streams, and destroyed forests around the volcano. Since 1980 there have been many small eruptions of Mount St. Helens.

There are different types of volcanoes. One type is *composite volcanoes*. They are made of layers of lava, rock, and ash. They can have steep peaks and are usually explosive when they erupt. Hawai`i has *shield volcanoes*. These huge mountains erupt slowly, and lava flows steadily down their gently sloping sides. *Cinder cone volcanoes* are small and have steep sides. They shoot chunks of rock into the air and down their slopes.

Movement between two plates can cause earthquakes. An **earthquake** is the shaking of Earth's surface caused by movement of rock in the crust.

The base of this Indonesian volcano is on the sea floor.

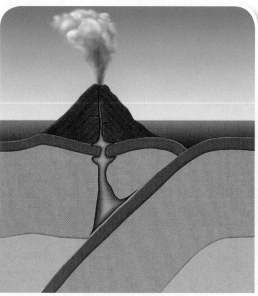

When two ocean plates push together, one plate is forced under the other. In the process, the upper plate melts and forms magma. This magma rises and forms volcanoes.

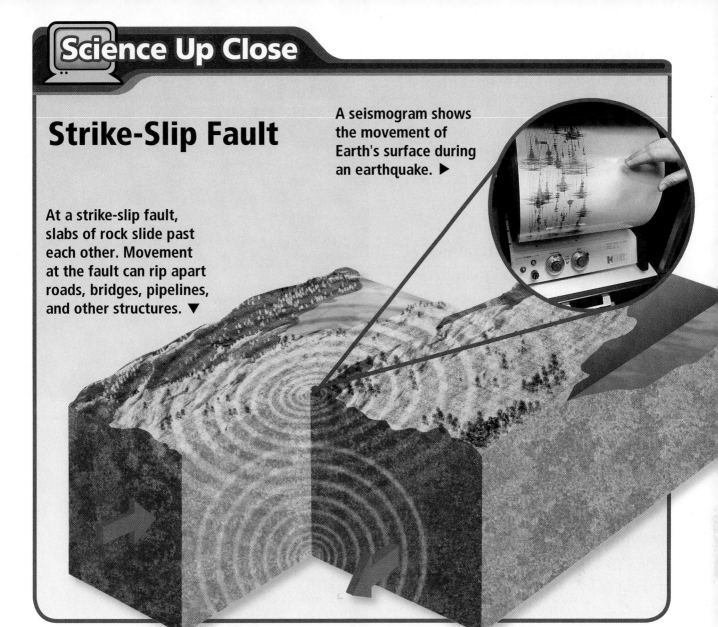

Strike-Slip Fault

At a strike-slip fault, slabs of rock slide past each other. Movement at the fault can rip apart roads, bridges, pipelines, and other structures. ▼

A seismogram shows the movement of Earth's surface during an earthquake. ▶

Most earthquakes occur along faults. A *fault* is a break in the crust, where rock moves. Sometimes this rock sticks. After some time, it may move forward suddenly. The movement sends out waves of energy that move through the crust. This energy causes shaking, rolling, and cracking in the crust and Earth's surface.

Focus Skill **CAUSE AND EFFECT** What is the cause of most earthquakes?

▲ The motion of an earthquake tore this Californian highway into several pieces.

Rivers

Rivers are found all over Earth. Although they aren't as dramatic as volcanoes or earthquakes, rivers can cause big changes to Earth's surface. Rivers just take longer to affect the land around them.

Rivers flow through valleys. The shape of a valley depends on the way the river runs through it. In steep areas, rivers move quickly. The rushing water cuts into the soil and rock. These valleys are narrow and V-shaped.

As a river gets older, its valley becomes less steep. The floor of the river becomes more level. The valley walls become farther apart. As a result, older rivers often have wide valleys with flat floors. They flow through the valleys in wide curves.

As rivers flow, they carry soil and rock. As a river moves, deposition occurs. In **deposition** (dep•uh•ZISH•uhn), rivers drop bits of rock and soil along the way. The slower a river moves, the more deposition occurs. River deposition builds landforms such as deltas and floodplains.

 CAUSE AND EFFECT What causes deposition to increase?

> Rivers on wide plains flow in large curves like these.

> Rivers that flow down steep slopes can cut deep valleys.

Math in Science
Interpret Data

Longest Rivers in the World

In the United States, the longest river is the Missouri, which is 4087 km (2540 mi) long. There are other rivers in the world that are longer. How much longer are each of these rivers than the Missouri?

River	Location	Length
Nile	Africa	6700 km (4163 mi)
Amazon	South America	6430 km (4000 mi)
Yangtze	China	6300 km (3900 mi)
Huang He	China	5464 km (3395 mi)
Amur	Asia	4413 km (2742 mi)

Cracks appear in this glacier as it flows slowly down a mountain valley. Glaciers may move as little as a few centimeters or as much as several meters per day.

Fiords form where the sea has flooded valleys formed by glaciers.

Glaciers

In some places, snowfall is high and temperature is low. Sometimes more snow falls in winter than melts in summer. The snow piles up year after year. As it thickens, it turns to ice. If the mass of ice starts to move downhill, it becomes a glacier. A **glacier** (GLAY•sher) is a large, moving mass of ice.

There are two main types of glaciers—alpine glaciers and ice sheets. Alpine glaciers flow down mountain valleys. The ice scrapes the floor and sides of the valley as it moves. The glacier widens the valley, giving it a U shape. *Fiords* (FYAWRDZ) form where these valleys reach the coast. Ice sheets are huge glaciers that cover large areas, such as Antarctica and Greenland.

Thousands of years ago, ice sheets covered much of Earth. As these ice sheets moved over the land, they shaped many landforms people see today.

CAUSE AND EFFECT What causes glaciers to form?

Wind and Waves

You have seen trees bend and move on a windy day. Wind can affect the way Earth's surface looks. In dry areas and along sandy coasts, soil is dry and loose. There aren't many plants. Wind lifts particles and carries them.

Wind slams sand into rocky surfaces. The wind-blown sand makes pits and grooves in rock. Wind also carries sand and deposits it in dunes, as you learned in Lesson 1.

Waves break down rocky cliffs. As the cliffs crumble, they move farther inland. Structures such as stone arches and pillars are left behind. As the sea moves inland, the structures are left offshore.

Waves also change the shape of sandy coastlines. They remove sand from some areas and deposit it in other places. This erosion and deposition of sand creates beaches, sand bars, and barrier islands along the shore.

Focus Skill **CAUSE AND EFFECT** **What conditions are needed for wind erosion?**

▼ The pounding of waves carved this sea arch. The hole formed when water wore away rock at the center of a solid formation sticking out into the sea.

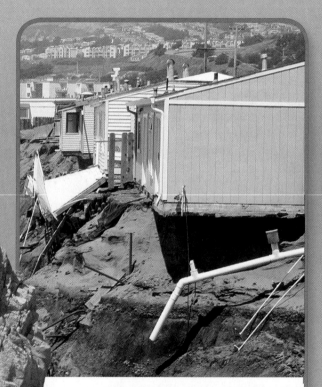

Erosion from waves has washed away the cliff under this house. It will soon topple onto the shore below.

Focus Skill

1. CAUSE AND EFFECT Copy and fill in the graphic organizer below.

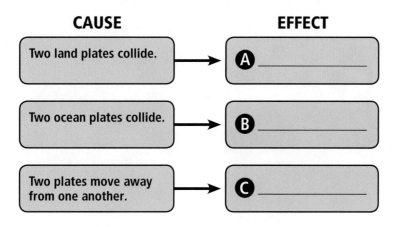

CAUSE → **EFFECT**

- Two land plates collide. → **A** _____
- Two ocean plates collide. → **B** _____
- Two plates move away from one another. → **C** _____

2. SUMMARIZE Briefly describe the cause and effect of an earthquake.

3. DRAW CONCLUSIONS Which do you think has a greater effect on landforms—wind or water? Why?

4. VOCABULARY Make a crossword puzzle, using the vocabulary terms from Lessons 1 and 2.

Test Prep

5. Critical Thinking What evidence of wave erosion might be seen in landforms along the shore?

6. What is magma?
- **A.** hot gases
- **B.** hard rock
- **C.** melted rock
- **D.** hot metals

Links

Writing

Descriptive Writing

Write a **report** that describes the journey of a piece of rock that erupts from a volcano. Follow the rock from the mantle until it shoots out of the volcano onto Earth's surface.

Math 9÷3

Make a Bar Graph

Use an encyclopedia to identify the world's five most deadly earthquakes during the past 100 years. Use the number of people who died as the measure. Make a bar graph to compare the earthquakes.

Art

Illustration

Read in a science book or an encyclopedia about a major earthquake or volcanic eruption. Make a drawing that shows some part of what happened. Write a caption to describe it.

For more links and activities, go to
www.hspscience.com

What Are Fossils?

Fast Fact

Big Shell Ammonites (AM•uh•nyts) were animals similar to squids with shells. They lived millions of years ago. The largest ammonite fossil found so far has a shell almost 2 meters ($6\frac{1}{2}$ ft) across. In the Investigate, you will model another type of fossil.

Sets of Animal Tracks

Materials
- poster board
- animal footprint stamps
- ink pad
- markers, crayons, or colored pencils

Procedure

1. Old animal tracks, or fossil footprints, are one thing that helps scientists learn about animals from the past. On the poster board, draw a picture of an area where you might find animal tracks, such as a riverbank or a sandy beach.

2. Each person in your group should choose a different animal. Using an ink pad and stamps or other materials, mark the animal's tracks on the poster board. Keep a record of which animal made tracks first, second, third, and so on.

3. Trade finished poster boards with another group. Figure out the order in which the other group's tracks were made. Record your conclusions in an ordered list. Give reasons for the order you choose.

Draw Conclusions

1. Did all the animals move in the same way? How could you tell what kind of animal made the tracks?

2. **Inquiry Skill** Scientists often observe an ecosystem at different times of day to see animals that are out at different times. Predict which tracks you might see if the picture showed tracks of night animals.

Step 1

Step 2

Investigate Further

Make animal tracks on a sheet of paper. Have a classmate infer from the tracks how the animal moves. Does it slither, walk, or jump?

VOCABULARY
fossil p. 250
fossil record p. 252

SCIENCE CONCEPTS
▶ what fossils are and how they form
▶ what the fossil record is

READING FOCUS SKILL

SEQUENCE Look for the steps in the formation of fossils.

☐ → ☐ → ☐

Fossils

Have you ever seen a movie about dinosaurs? The movie probably showed how dinosaurs looked, how they moved, and what they ate. Dinosaurs became extinct millions of years ago. That was long before there were people on Earth. So, how do people today know so much about dinosaurs?

People today know about many plants and animals of the past because of fossils. A **fossil** is the remains or traces of an organism that lived long ago.

Most fossils form in sedimentary rock. First, sediment covers an organism. Then, the sediment hardens into rock, preserving the fossil shape. The soft parts of organisms break down quickly and decay. Because of this, most fossils

Molds and casts, like those of this trilobite, are common fossil types.

Mold and Cast Formation

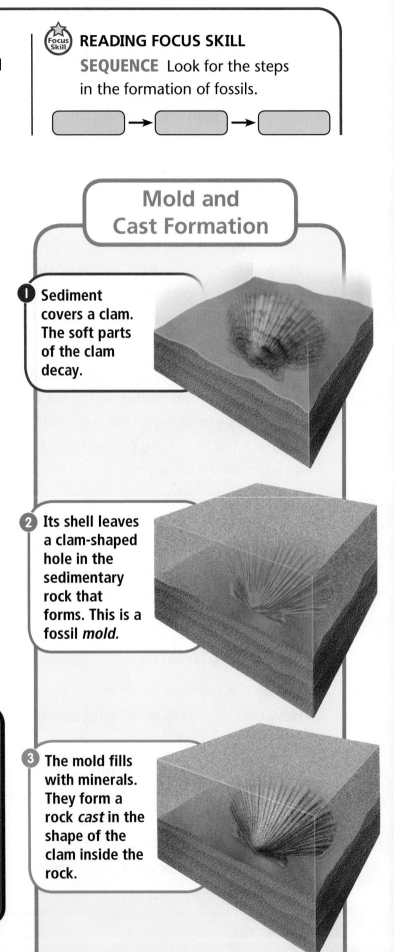

❶ Sediment covers a clam. The soft parts of the clam decay.

❷ Its shell leaves a clam-shaped hole in the sedimentary rock that forms. This is a fossil *mold.*

❸ The mold fills with minerals. They form a rock *cast* in the shape of the clam inside the rock.

▲ Minerals have seeped into these dinosaur eggs and turned them into stone.

▲ Amber has encased this insect. Amber is sticky tree sap that trapped a living insect and then hardened around it.

A fossilized dinosaur track gives clues about the animal's size. ▶

are formed from only the hard parts of living things, such as shells, bones, and teeth. The numbered diagram shows the steps of forming a mold and cast fossil.

There are other kinds of fossils. When minerals fill the cells of once-living things, a different kind of fossil forms. Petrified wood is an example. It is the wood of a tree that has been replaced by rock. The Petrified Forest, in Arizona, has thousands of stone logs that were trees millions of years ago.

Another type of fossil is a trace fossil. It doesn't show how a whole plant or

animal looked, but it tells something about it. A fossil footprint is a trace fossil that helps tell about an animal's size or how it moved. Fossils of animal droppings show what an animal ate.

Some fossils are the remains of whole animals. They were trapped in ice or tree sap that hardened. Scientists have found woolly mammoths preserved in ice in Siberia. These animals died long ago. People know about them because of fossil evidence.

Focus Skill **SEQUENCE How do a mold and a cast form?**

Fossil Record

Earth is about 4.5 billion years old. People have lived on Earth for a very small part of that time. Scientists have found clues about Earth's past by using fossils as a record of ancient times. The **fossil record** is the information about Earth's history that is contained in fossils. It's the main source of clues about Earth's past life and environment.

Because of the fossil record, we know about animals that lived and died long, long ago. Dinosaurs and trilobites are examples of such animals. No one has ever seen a living one. We know about them because people have found and studied their fossils.

The fossil record also shows how some species changed over time. Mammoths lived during the last Ice Age. At that time, ice sheets covered much of Earth. The Ice Age ended, and the mammoths died out. Other animals much like them continued to live. It is likely that the elephants of today are related to some of these animals.

▼ Sediment covered the reef, and it became fossilized over millions of years.

Millions of years ago, this reef was home to corals and many other sea animals. ▶

Scientists study reef fossils to find out about animals that lived in oceans and on reefs long ago.

▲ A dinosaur laid these eggs millions of years ago.

The eggs have become part of the fossil record. The size and number of eggs tell scientists about the dinosaur that laid them. ▶

The fossil record helps scientists learn how Earth's environment has changed over time. Today, palm trees live in warm areas. Scientists have found fossils of palm trees in Wyoming, where it's too cold for palms to grow today. From this evidence, scientists infer that the climate there must have been much warmer in the past.

Scientists have also found fossils of sea animals in Kansas. Today, Kansas is far from any ocean. Scientists have inferred that a shallow sea covered parts of Kansas long ago.

SEQUENCE What does the fossil record tell us about climate change in Wyoming?

Insta-Lab

Fossil Hunt

Get a cupful of soil from outside. Examine it closely with a hand lens. Describe what you see. Can you see any evidence of fossils? Why or why not?

Geologic Time Scale

Many living things have lived and died out during Earth's long history. Scientists use the *geologic time scale* to understand better what was living during each part of this history.

The scale has several divisions. The table here shows the four eras of the time scale. Each era is millions of years long. In the middle of the Paleozoic (pay•lee•uh•ZOH•ik) Era, there were more fish than any other life form. In the next era, the dinosaurs became the most common vertebrate.

Why is the geologic time scale divided the way it is? The scale shows the way life has changed over time. The fossil record shows that animals died out at certain times during Earth's history. Scientists use these times to mark when eras start and end. For example, trilobites were common at the start of the Paleozoic Era. They died out about 248 million years ago. That marks the end of the Paleozoic Era and the start of the next era. Dinosaurs became extinct about 65 million years ago. That time marks the end of the Mesozoic Era and the start of the present era.

Focus Skill **SEQUENCE** **What are the four main eras of the geologic time scale, from earliest to the present?**

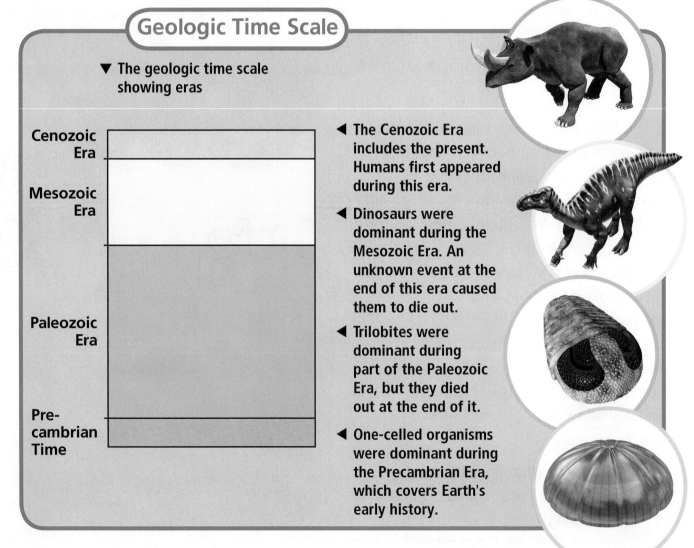

Geologic Time Scale

▼ The geologic time scale showing eras

Cenozoic Era	
Mesozoic Era	
Paleozoic Era	
Pre-cambrian Time	

◄ The Cenozoic Era includes the present. Humans first appeared during this era.

◄ Dinosaurs were dominant during the Mesozoic Era. An unknown event at the end of this era caused them to die out.

◄ Trilobites were dominant during part of the Paleozoic Era, but they died out at the end of it.

◄ One-celled organisms were dominant during the Precambrian Era, which covers Earth's early history.

1. SEQUENCE Copy and fill in the graphic organizer below.

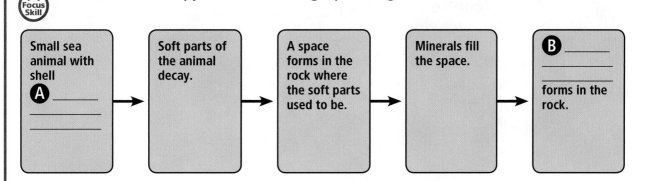

Small sea animal with shell **A** _____ _____ → Soft parts of the animal decay. → A space forms in the rock where the soft parts used to be. → Minerals fill the space. → **B** _____ _____ forms in the rock.

2. SUMMARIZE Write a brief summary of this lesson. Begin with the sentence *Fossils hold clues to Earth's past.*

3. DRAW CONCLUSIONS Are fossils being formed today? Explain.

4. VOCABULARY Use each of the lesson's vocabulary terms in a sentence.

Test Prep

5. Critical Thinking In which type of rock are you most likely to find a fossil? Why?

6. Which kind of fossil is a dinosaur footprint?

A. tar pit fossil   **C.** petrified fossil

B. cast fossil   **D.** trace fossil

Links

Writing

Narrative Writing

Suppose you are hiking near a cliff. You see a large bone trapped in rock. Write a **story** that describes the animal whose fossil you found. Tell how you think it lived and how the fossil formed.

Math 9÷3

Compare Two Whole Numbers

Ammonites were like squids with shells. Use an encyclopedia to find the size of squids today. Compare their size with the size of the largest ammonite.

Social Studies

Make a Brochure

Research a place in the United States where people can see fossils. It could be a national park, a museum, or another type of area. Design a brochure that encourages people to visit it. Share it with the class.

For more links and activities, go to www.hspscience.com

WIPEOUT!
Splash

Research by Simon Day, of University College London, United Kingdom, indicates history's biggest tsunami (tsoo•NAH•mee) might be caused by a future eruption of the Cumbre Vieja (KOOM•bray vee•AY•ha) volcano. Cumbre Vieja is on the island of La Palma in the Canary Islands, a group of islands in the Atlantic Ocean off the northwest coast of Africa.

Day predicts that a volcanic eruption could cause a giant landslide on the unstable western side of the volcano, plopping a trillion tons of rock into the Atlantic. A tsunami caused by such a big landslide would travel a long distance at great speed.

Coastal Terrors

The landslide's impact would produce swells, large waves that radiate from their source until they hit land. Out at sea, the swells are harmless and virtually undetectable. As they approach land, however, they become monstrous. In shallow water the swells bunch up and gain height. Coming ashore, a tsunami pummels coastal cities and shores with destructive force.

Danger, Danger

Simon Day and wave expert Steven Ward, of the University of California, recently used a computer model to calculate the possible impact of a Cumbre Vieja tsunami. Their calculations indicate the danger zones lie north, west, and south of the Canaries.

After 6 hours

After 3 hours

NORTH AMERICA

EUROPE

AFRICA
Epicenter of tsunami (La Palma)

ATLANTIC OCEAN

SOUTH AMERICA

Danger Zones

A tsunami triggered by a giant Cumbre Vieja landslide would travel north, west, and south of the Canaries and pummel coastal areas in Africa, South America, and North America.

On Africa's Western Sahara shore, waves would reach heights of 100 meters (328 feet)—higher than a 30-story building!

The scientists calculate that waves on the north coast of Brazil would be more than 40 meters (131 feet) high. Florida and the Caribbean would be walloped with waves 50 meters (164 feet) high, hours after a powerful landslide from Cumbre Vieja.

THINK ABOUT IT

1. What changes to Earth's surface may cause tsunamis?
2. How is technology used to study tsunamis?

TSUNAMI OF 2004

- On December 26, 2004, an earthquake at the bottom of the Indian Ocean triggered a tsunami. The wave destroyed coastal areas from Thailand in Asia to Somalia in Africa.
- More than 250,000 people died from the tsunami and earthquake, and millions were left homeless.
- This tsunami was one of the deadliest natural disasters in history.

Find out more! Log on to
www.hspscience.com

WATCHING A VOLCANO

People use telescopes most often to study the planets or stars. But Michael Ballard is using a telescope to look at Earth. He is looking at a special type of Earth landform—a volcano. A volcano is an opening in the crust of the Earth from which hot lava and steam erupt.

Michael is studying a volcano named Mount St. Helens in Washington. He is watching the volcano as steam erupts from its top. In 1980, the top of Mount St. Helens blew off in a huge eruption.

Since then the volcano has had a few small eruptions, but nothing like in 1980. Recently, Mount St. Helens became active again, sending smoke and steam many kilometers up into the sky. Michael continues to watch the volcano for activity like this with his telescope.

You Can Do It!

Quick and Easy Project

Making Seismic Waves

Materials
- goggles
- apron
- 9" × 13" cake pan
- water
- food coloring
- spoon
- 2 foam blocks
- sandpaper
- masking tape

Procedure

1. **CAUTION: Put on goggles and an apron.** Pour about 1 cm of water into the cake pan. Add a few drops of food coloring. Mix with the spoon.

2. Tape sandpaper to one long, thin side of each foam block. Put the blocks in the water. Push them together so the sandpaper sides touch.

3. Quickly slide the two blocks along each other in opposite directions. Observe what happens to the water.

Draw Conclusions

What happens if you move the blocks more slowly? Describe how this model is similar to moving plates in an earthquake.

Design Your Own Investigation

How Do Rivers Change the Land?

You know that rivers can change Earth's surface. Some rivers flow down steep slopes. Other rivers flow over flat land. Design an investigation to see how the slope of the land determines how a river changes Earth's surface. Decide what materials to use to model the river and its banks. How will you change the slope of your model? How does the slope of a river affect the way it changes Earth's surface?

Review and Test Preparation

Vocabulary Review

Use the terms below to complete the sentences. The page numbers tell you where to look in the chapter if you need help.

landform p. 232   earthquake
                                    p. 242

mountain p. 232   deposition p. 244

topography p. 234   glacier p. 245

volcano p. 242   fossils p. 250

1. A mountain that forms as lava flows through a crack onto Earth's surface is a _____.

2. When rivers slow down, they drop sediment in a process called _____.

3. Any natural shape on Earth's surface is a _____.

4. The traces or remains of an organism that lived long ago are _____.

5. The shape of the landforms in an area is _____.

6. The shaking of Earth's surface caused by movement of rock in the crust is an _____.

7. An area that is higher than the land around it is a _____.

8. A huge, moving mass of ice is a _____.

Check Understanding

Write the letter of the best choice.

9. **COMPARE AND CONTRAST** In which pair are the landforms most alike?
   A. plain/plateau   **C.** valley/fault
   B. canyon/mesa   **D.** butte/mountain

10. **CAUSE AND EFFECT** Which kind of landform is formed by deposition?
    F. mountain   **H.** delta
    G. valley   **J.** plateau

11. Which is the name of the layer of Earth indicated by X?

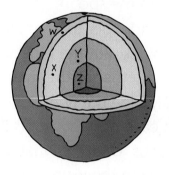

    A. inner core   **C.** outer core
    B. crust   **D.** mantle

12. What happens where two land plates push against each other?
    F. valleys form
    G. mountains form
    H. islands form
    J. new sea floor forms

13. What is happening where these two plates meet?

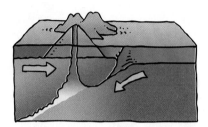

A. The sea floor is spreading apart.
B. An undersea canyon is forming.
C. Volcanic islands are forming.
D. The coast is eroding.

14. Which of these does **not** come from an erupting volcano?

F. ice   **H.** lava
G. gases   **J.** ashes

15. Which of these changes to land does an earthquake cause?

A. Soil is deposited.
B. River valleys become wider.
C. Rocks split in Earth's crust.
D. Lava covers the surface.

16. Which kind of fossil is illustrated by this picture?

F. amber fossil   **H.** fossil cast
G. trace fossil   **J.** petrified wood

Inquiry Skills

17. Why is it useful to **use a model** to study processes such as stream and river deposition?

18. What would be the importance of being able to **predict** when a volcano will erupt?

Critical Thinking

19. You discover a fossil in the bottom layer of a canyon wall. You identify the fossil as an animal that lived between 250 and 230 million years ago. What information can this fossil give you about the area where the canyon is located?

20.

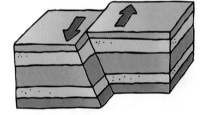

A. Describe what is happening in the diagram. How is the event changing Earth's surface in the area right around it?
B. How could this affect Earth's surface several kilometers away?

Weather and Space

EARTH SCIENCE

Ice Box Days

TO: TO: nicole@hspscience.com

FROM: FROM: ely@hspscience.com

RE: RE: International Falls, Minnesota

Dear Nicole,

Have you ever gone bowling with a frozen turkey? I doubt that happens much where you live! My town is nicknamed the "Icebox of the Nation." Each year people come here to join in on the fun of Ice Box Days. My favorite part is the smoosh race. One year the wind chill factor was 70 degrees below zero! No thanks!

Come and visit sometime...in the summer.

"Warm" regards,

Ely

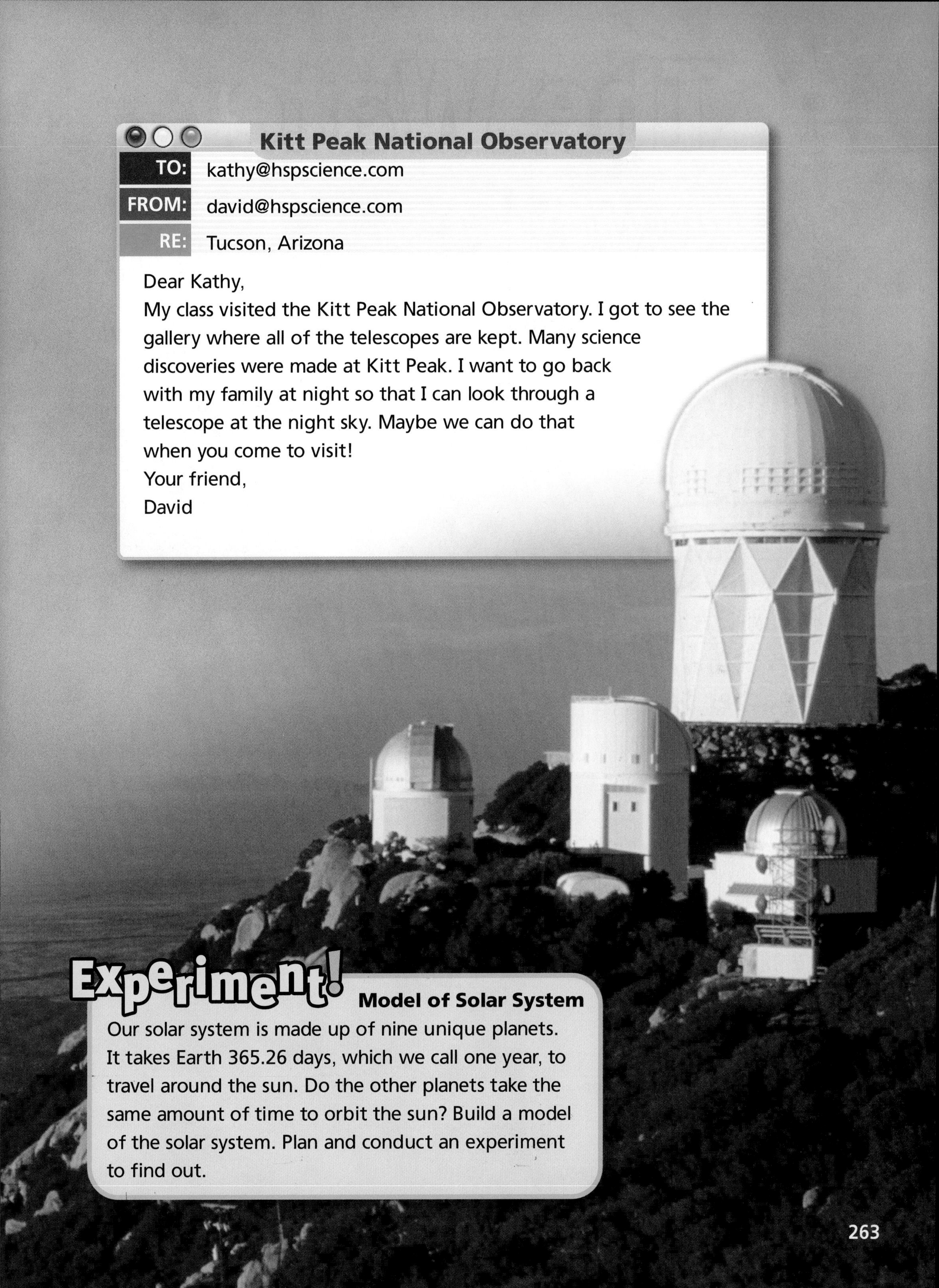

Kitt Peak National Observatory

TO: kathy@hspscience.com

FROM: david@hspscience.com

RE: Tucson, Arizona

Dear Kathy,

My class visited the Kitt Peak National Observatory. I got to see the gallery where all of the telescopes are kept. Many science discoveries were made at Kitt Peak. I want to go back with my family at night so that I can look through a telescope at the night sky. Maybe we can do that when you come to visit!

Your friend,

David

Experiment!

Model of Solar System

Our solar system is made up of nine unique planets. It takes Earth 365.26 days, which we call one year, to travel around the sun. Do the other planets take the same amount of time to orbit the sun? Build a model of the solar system. Plan and conduct an experiment to find out.

The Water Cycle

Vocabulary

water cycle	hurricane
precipitation	sea breeze
evaporation	land breeze
condensation	rain shadow
rain	air mass
sleet	cold front
snow	warm front
hail	barometer
tornado	anemometer

What do YOU wonder?

Each spring as the weather warms, snow and ice in the Yukon begin to melt. The snow and ice turn into millions of gallons of moving water. Where do you think this water goes?

1

What Is the Water Cycle?

Fast Fact

Got Water? Almost all of Earth's water is in the oceans. In fact, more than 97 percent of Earth's water is ocean water! In the Investigate, you will find out what ocean water is like.

From Salt Water to Fresh Water

Materials
- 500 mL of warm water
- cotton swabs
- plastic wrap
- salt
- large bowl
- large rubber band
- masking tape
- spoon
- small glass jar
- small ball

Procedure

1. Stir two spoonfuls of salt into the warm water. Dip a cotton swab into the mixture. Touch the swab to your tongue. Record what you observe. **CAUTION: Do not share swabs. Throw the swab away.**

2. Put the jar in the center of the bowl. Pour the salt water into the bowl. Be careful not to get any salt water in the jar.

3. Put plastic wrap over the bowl. The wrap should not touch the jar. Use the rubber band to hold the wrap in place.

4. Put the ball on the wrap over the jar. Make sure the wrap doesn't touch the jar.

5. Mark the level of the salt water with a piece of tape on the outside of the bowl. Put the bowl in a sunny spot for one day.

6. Remove the wrap and the ball. Use clean swabs to taste the water in the jar and in the bowl. Record what you observe.

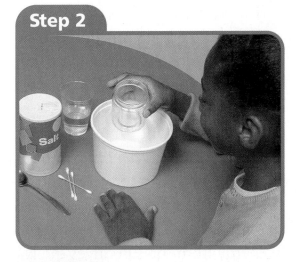

Step 2

Step 4

Draw Conclusions

1. What did you observe during the investigation?

2. **Inquiry Skill** Scientists infer based on what they observe. What can you infer is a source of fresh water for Earth?

Investigate Further

What would happen if you left the bowl and jar in the sun for several days? Write a hypothesis. Try it!

Reading in Science

VOCABULARY
water cycle p. 268
precipitation p. 268
evaporation p. 270
condensation p. 271

SCIENCE CONCEPTS
► what processes make up the water cycle
► how a raindrop is formed

Focus Skill **READING FOCUS SKILL**
SEQUENCE Look for the order in which events of the water cycle occur.

[ ] → [ ] → [ ]

The Water Cycle

As you are on the way home from school, it suddenly starts raining. Where does rain come from? When rain reaches the ground, where does it go?

Water is constantly moving through the environment. Water moves from the surface of Earth to the air and then back to Earth's surface again in a never-ending process called the **water cycle**.

Energy from the sun drives the water cycle. When the sun's energy warms water on Earth's surface, the water changes from a liquid to a gas.

The gas form of water, called water vapor, goes into the air. If the water vapor cools, it becomes liquid water again and falls back to Earth. Water that falls back to Earth is called **precipitation** (pree•sip•uh•TAY•shuhn). Precipitation can be rain, snow, sleet, or hail. Rain is liquid water. Snow, sleet, and hail are frozen water. Energy from the sun changes precipitation to water vapor once again. This continues the water cycle.

Focus Skill **SEQUENCE** What steps must take place in order for ocean water to become rain?

When the sun warms the surface of water, the water changes to water vapor, a gas. The gas then becomes part of the air.

A cloud forms when water vapor cools. The water vapor becomes liquid again in a process known as condensation. The liquid water in clouds is in the form of tiny droplets that can stay up in the air.

In the clouds, water droplets can bump into each other and join to make larger droplets. Soon the droplets become heavy and fall to Earth as precipitation.

Some precipitation soaks into the ground. Precipitation can also run over the ground and flow into streams, rivers, lakes, and eventually the ocean.

Parts of the Water Cycle

It's a hot day. To cool off, you take a swim. When you get out of the water, you dry yourself with a towel. You leave the towel in the sunlight while you play with your friends. When you come back, the towel is dry. Where did the water in the towel go?

The water evaporated. **Evaporation** (ee•vap•uh•RAY•shuhn) is the process by which a liquid changes into a gas. A large amount of water evaporates from Earth's oceans, lakes, and rivers every day. But water also evaporates from the soil, from puddles, and even from your skin as you sweat.

Water vapor mixes with other gases in the air. When the wind blows, air moves. The water vapor moves with the air. Sometimes the water vapor can move very long distances. The water vapor can also move high up into the air.

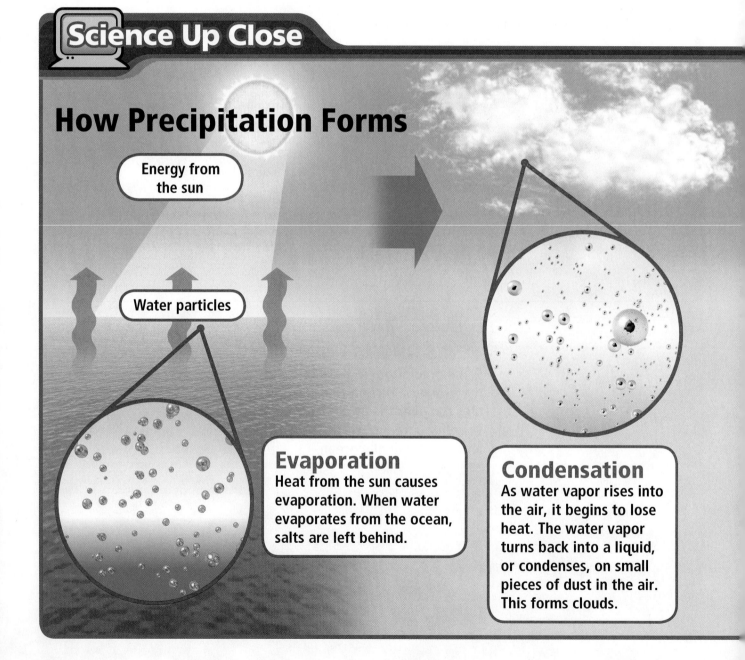

Science Up Close

How Precipitation Forms

Energy from the sun

Water particles

Evaporation
Heat from the sun causes evaporation. When water evaporates from the ocean, salts are left behind.

Condensation
As water vapor rises into the air, it begins to lose heat. The water vapor turns back into a liquid, or condenses, on small pieces of dust in the air. This forms clouds.

When the water vapor moves up in the air, it becomes cooler. If the water vapor cools enough, condensation (kahn•duhn•SAY•shuhn) happens. **Condensation** is the process by which a gas changes into a liquid. Have you ever seen water dripping from an air conditioner? The dripping water is from water vapor that condensed as it cooled.

Air has many small bits of dust in it. When water vapor cools, it condenses on the dust particles. The condensed water and dust particles form clouds. Inside clouds, tiny droplets of water can join to make larger droplets. These droplets can join to make even larger, heavier droplets. When the droplets become too heavy to stay in the air, they fall to Earth as precipitation. The type of precipitation that falls depends on the temperature of the air around it.

 SEQUENCE Heat causes a piece of ice to melt. What will happen next?

For more links and activities, go to www.hspscience.com

Precipitation

Inside clouds, small water droplets join to form larger droplets. In time, these larger droplets become raindrops that fall to Earth. The water in raindrops is fresh water.

Forms of Water

Fill a glass with ice. Fill another glass with room temperature water. Observe the glasses for at least five minutes. Describe any changes you see. What property of the glasses was different? What process occurred on the outside of one glass? Why did this process occur? Can you control the process? Try it.

Groundwater and Runoff

When rain falls on land, some of it soaks into the soil. Plants use much of this water. Also, some of the water in the soil evaporates back into the air. But not all of the water in soil evaporates or is used by plants.

Some of the water that goes into soil moves deeper into the ground. The water in the ground moves down until it gets to solid rock. Because the water cannot move through the rock, it begins to collect there. After a while, a lot of collected water forms a body of groundwater.

Many people rely on groundwater for their drinking water. They dig wells to reach the groundwater. Then they pump the water up to the surface.

Rain that is not soaked up by the soil becomes runoff. The runoff flows into creeks and streams, which flow into rivers. Large rivers, such as the Mississippi River and the Columbia River, flow into larger bodies of water.

SEQUENCE **In what sequence of events does groundwater form?**

Some precipitation that falls on the land becomes either groundwater or runoff. ▼

Runoff

Groundwater

Focus Skill

1. SEQUENCE Draw and complete each graphic organizer.

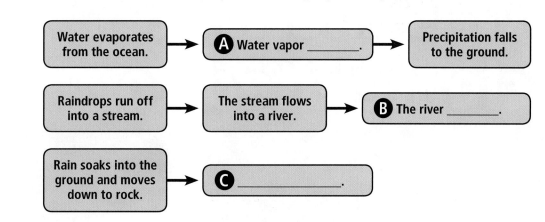

Water evaporates from the ocean. → **A** Water vapor _____. → Precipitation falls to the ground.

Raindrops run off into a stream. → The stream flows into a river. → **B** The river _____.

Rain soaks into the ground and moves down to rock. → **C** _____.

2. SUMMARIZE Draw a diagram that summarizes this lesson.

3. DRAW CONCLUSIONS Will pond water evaporate faster on a warm, sunny day or on a warm, cloudy day? Explain.

4. VOCABULARY Write one sentence that uses all the vocabulary terms for the lesson.

Test Prep

5. Critical Thinking Most rainwater comes from the ocean, but rainwater is not salty. Why not?

6. Which of the following happens when water vapor cools?

A. condensation   **C.** heating

B. evaporation   **D.** vaporization

Links

Writing

Persuasive Writing
Less than 3 percent of Earth's water is fresh. Write a **speech** that explains to people why it's important to protect Earth's freshwater resources. Present your speech to the class.

Math 9÷3

Make a Circle Graph
Earth is known as "the water planet." Find out how much of Earth's surface is covered by water. Make a circle graph that shows this information.

Social Studies

Where Is Water?
Find a world map. Make a list of all the major bodies of water you see. Research one of the bodies of water, and report on it. Include information such as how the body of water formed.

For more links and activities, go to www.hspscience.com

How Is the Water Cycle Related to Weather?

Fast Fact

When It Rains, It Pours Floods cause billions of dollars of damage to property every year. It takes only 60 cm (2 ft) of moving floodwater to sweep away a car. Higher waters sweep away trees, bridges, and even buildings! In the Investigate activity, you will model a flood.

Modeling a Flood

Materials
- aluminum baking pan
- plastic bag
- plastic gloves
- soil
- water
- toothpick
- beaker

Procedure

Step 1

1. Half-fill the aluminum baking pan with soil. Make a path in the soil to form a "river channel" that runs through the center of the pan. Build up some small hills around the river channel. Press the soil in place.

2. Use the toothpick to poke several holes in the bottom of the plastic bag.

3. Measure 150 mL of water in the beaker. One partner should hold the plastic bag over the pan while the other partner slowly pours the water into the bag. Let the water drip over the pan to model a rainy day. Record what you observe.

Step 3

4. Repeat Step 3 several times until the pan becomes three-fourths full of water.

Draw Conclusions

1. What happened to the soil in the pan after the first "rainy day"? What happened after the last "rainy day"?

2. **Inquiry Skill** Scientists often gather, record, and interpret data to understand how things work. Interpret what you observed and recorded using your model. What do you think causes floods?

Investigate Further

Would the results be the same if there were several days between each rainfall? Plan and conduct a simple investigation to find out.

SCIENCE CONCEPTS

▶ what some kinds of precipitation are

▶ what causes different kinds of weather

READING FOCUS SKILL

CAUSE AND EFFECT Look for the causes of certain types of weather.

| cause | → | effect |

Kinds of Precipitation

You may think of precipitation as bad weather. After all, rain keeps you from playing outdoors. It can also cause floods. Hail can damage cars and homes. Sleet can make roads dangerous. Snow can pile up on driveways and on sidewalks. However, all of these kinds of precipitation are simply part of the water cycle.

What causes different kinds of precipitation? Most water on Earth, such as ocean water, is liquid. You learned in Lesson 1 that if water is heated enough, it becomes water vapor, a gas. If water is cooled enough, it freezes.

Rain, the most common kind of precipitation, is liquid water. Rain falls if the temperature is higher than 0°C (32°F). **Sleet** is frozen rain. Sleet is

Kinds of Precipitation

Types	Causes
Rain	Water vapor condenses in air.
Snow	Water vapor turns into ice crystals instead of a liquid.
Sleet	Falling rain passes through a layer of freezing-cold air and turns into ice.
Hail	Rain freezes and then falls to a warmer pocket of air. The frozen rain is coated with liquid water and then carried back up to a cold pocket of air, where the liquid coating also freezes.

RAIN
Rain is liquid precipitation. Tiny raindrops are called drizzle. Heavy rain can cause floods.

caused when rain falls through a layer of freezing-cold air. This turns the rain into ice pellets. **Snow** is made of ice crystals. Snow is caused when the air temperature is so cold that water vapor turns directly into ice. **Hail** is round pieces of ice. Hail is caused when rain freezes and then falls to a warmer part of the air. Raindrops coat the frozen rain before it is carried back up to a colder part of the air by wind. The new liquid coating then freezes also. This happens over and over until the hail is too heavy and it falls to the ground.

 CAUSE AND EFFECT What causes rain to become sleet?

SNOW
Snow is made of ice crystals. The crystals, which come in many different shapes, form high in the air.

▲ **SLEET**
Sleet is made of frozen raindrops. Sleet forms when rain falls through a pocket of cold air.

▲ **HAIL**
Hail can be as small as a pea or as large as a grapefruit. The size of a piece of hail depends on how many times it is carried up and down in a storm cloud.

Severe Storms

Heat from the sun powers the water cycle. This same energy causes severe storms.

One type of severe storm is a thunderstorm. Thunderstorms are storms with lightning, strong winds, and heavy rain. Sometimes tornadoes form during thunderstorms. A **tornado** is a fast-spinning spiral of wind that stretches from the clouds of a thunderstorm to the ground. Tornadoes can have wind speeds greater than 400 kilometers (250 mi) per hour! Every year, there are about 800–1000 tornadoes in the United States.

Another kind of severe storm is a hurricane. **Hurricanes** are large tropical storms with wind speeds of 119 kilometers (74 mi) per hour or

▲ The United States has more tornadoes per year than any other country in the world.

Blizzards are severe snowstorms that can last for hours. Blizzards have strong winds, blowing snow, and very low air temperatures. ▼

Hurricanes are categorized by their wind speed. Does a hurricane's wind speed relate to the amount of damage it causes?

Hurricane Strength

Category/ Wind Speed	Hurricanes	Cost of damage in dollars
5 (>155 mph)	Hurricane Andrew, 1992	$34.1 billion
4 (131–155 mph)	Hurricane Charley, 2004	$14 billion
3 (111–130 mph)	Hurricane Betsy, 1965	$9 billion
2 (96–110 mph)	Hurricane Floyd, 1999	$4.9 billion
1 (74–95 mph)	Hurricane Agnes, 1972	$9.1 billion

Three pictures of Hurricane Andrew

more. Hurricanes form over warm water in the tropical oceans. These storms can last for weeks out at sea. But when a hurricane reaches land, it no longer gets energy from warm water. It soon becomes weaker.

The winds of a hurricane spin around the calm center of the storm, called the "eye." Rain, waves, and "storm surge," a huge bulge of water pushed onto the land by the storm, can cause flooding.

CAUSE AND EFFECT What causes flooding during a hurricane?

Insta-Lab

Tornado in a Bottle
Fill a clear, plastic bottle three-fourths full of water. Tape a washer over the mouth of the bottle. Tape a second clear, plastic bottle upside down on top of the first bottle. Turn the bottles over and swirl the top bottle around quickly. What do you observe?

Weather Safety

Severe storms are dangerous. Injuries can be caused by downed power lines and trees. Floods can occur. It's important to keep yourself safe during severe weather. One way to stay safe is to follow safety rules in your community. Local radio or TV stations will tell you if there is a severe storm in your area.

There are other ways to warn people about severe weather. For example, some areas have weather sirens that are turned on when a severe storm is detected. Some sirens can even detect nearby tornadoes on their own and warn people in the area.

When there is a severe storm, stay inside a building unless officials tell you to leave. Sometimes people are asked to leave an area before a storm strikes. If that happens, people will follow a safe route away from the area.

Focus Skill **CAUSE AND EFFECT How might a severe storm affect you?**

Weather siren ▶

▲ Watch TV during severe weather to get directions about what to do.

◀ These flags warn that a hurricane is coming.

Follow signs like these if you are asked to leave an area when a hurricane is coming. ▶

1. CAUSE AND EFFECT Draw and complete each graphic organizer.

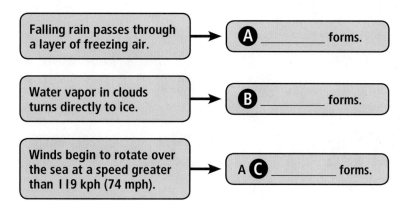

Falling rain passes through a layer of freezing air. → **A** _____ forms.

Water vapor in clouds turns directly to ice. → **B** _____ forms.

Winds begin to rotate over the sea at a speed greater than 119 kph (74 mph). → A **C** _____ forms.

2. SUMMARIZE Summarize this lesson by describing what causes these different kinds of weather: rain, snow, sleet, hail, tornado, hurricane.

3. DRAW CONCLUSIONS What affects the kind of precipitation that will fall?

4. VOCABULARY Write a weather report that uses at least four vocabulary terms from this lesson.

Test Prep

5. Critical Thinking Explain how weather is related to the water cycle.

6. Which of the following is **not** a kind of precipitation?

A. air   **C.** rain

B. hail   **D.** sleet

Links

Writing

Narrative Writing

Suppose that you're a drop of water in a cloud. Write a **story** that describes what you experience as you continue your travel through the water cycle.

Math

Measure Temperature

Measure the outdoor temperature. Based on the temperature you found, what kind of precipitation is most likely to fall now in your area?

Health

Weather and Health

Make a booklet that shows what to do to stay safe during severe weather, such as tornadoes, thunderstorms, and hurricanes.

For more links and activities, go to **www.hspscience.com**

How Do Land Features Affect the Water Cycle?

Thunderstorms in a Row When cold air over the ocean meets warm air over the land, squall lines can form. A squall line is a long line of moving thunderstorms. Squall lines can stretch across the land for hundreds of kilometers! In the Investigate, you will observe how land and water heat up.

Heating Land and Water

Materials
- 2 small plastic or foam cups
- water
- 2 thermometers
- stopwatch
- dark soil or sand
- light source with 100-W bulb or greater

Procedure

1. Fill one cup with dark soil or sand. Fill the second cup with water. Place a thermometer upright in each cup.

2. Time one minute, using the stopwatch. Then measure and record the temperatures of the two cups.

3. Remove the thermometer after every measurement. Place the cups under the light. Make sure that both cups get an equal amount of light.

4. After the cups have been under the light for 5 minutes, measure and record their temperatures. Repeat this step 3 times.

5. Turn the lamp off. Time 5 minutes, and then measure and record the temperatures of the cups. Repeat this step twice.

Draw Conclusions

1. Describe how the soil and water heated differently. How did they cool differently?

2. **Inquiry Skill** Scientists use what they observe to form a hypothesis. Use your observations from this investigation to hypothesize how the weather on Earth would be different if Earth's surface were mostly land instead of mostly water.

Step 3

Step 4

Investigate Further

Does wet soil heat differently from dry soil? Conduct an experiment to find out.

Reading in Science

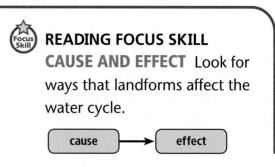

VOCABULARY
sea breeze p. 284
land breeze p. 284
rain shadow p. 286

SCIENCE CONCEPTS
▶ how temperature affects the water cycle
▶ how landforms affect the water cycle

READING FOCUS SKILL
CAUSE AND EFFECT Look for ways that landforms affect the water cycle.

Sea Breezes and Land Breezes

Have you ever been to the beach on a hot day? It might be so hot that your feet burn when you walk on the sand. But when you go into the water, you quickly cool off. That's because the water is cooler than the sand.

Land heats up much more quickly than water. Land also cools down more quickly than water. Because of this, the temperature of the air over land is almost always different from the temperature of air over nearby water. During the day, the air over water is cooler than the air over land. The hot air over a beach is pushed upward by the cool air moving in from over the water. This causes a sea breeze. A **sea breeze** is a breeze moving from the water to the land. During the night, the land becomes cooler than the water. This causes a land breeze. A **land breeze** is a breeze moving from the land to the water.

CAUSE AND EFFECT What causes a land breeze?

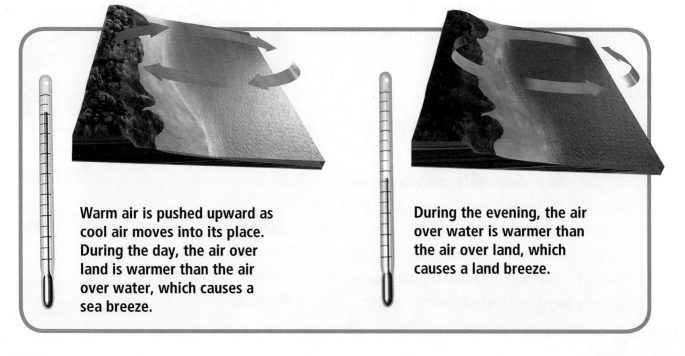

Warm air is pushed upward as cool air moves into its place. During the day, the air over land is warmer than the air over water, which causes a sea breeze.

During the evening, the air over water is warmer than the air over land, which causes a land breeze.

Over the Florida peninsula, sea breezes can blow from many different directions.

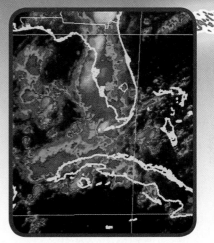

Doppler radar can be used to track sea breeze storms. ▶

Sea Breeze Storms

You learned in Lesson 1 that when water vapor cools, it condenses to form precipitation. Sometimes, cool sea breezes push clouds toward the shore. The clouds can then produce storms over the land. These storms are called sea breeze storms.

A peninsula is a piece of land that is surrounded by water on three sides. Over a peninsula like Florida, sea breezes can come in from the east and from the west. The collision of the two sea breezes causes the air to become unstable. If the two bodies of air have a lot of water vapor, a very strong sea breeze storm could form over the center of the peninsula. This type of sea breeze storm happens often in Florida during the summer.

 CAUSE AND EFFECT What causes a sea breeze storm?

Rain Shadows

Shorelines are not the only landform that affects the water cycle. Mountains do, too. Suppose a moving body of air hits the side of a mountain range. What happens? The air can't move through the mountains. Instead, the air is pushed up the side of the mountains and then over them. As the air moves up, it cools. The water vapor in the cooler air condenses and brings rain to that side of the mountains. By the time the air reaches the other side, the air is dry. So, it doesn't rain on the other side. This causes a rain shadow. A **rain shadow** is the area on the far side of a mountain range that gets little or no rain or cloud cover.

CAUSE AND EFFECT What is the effect of a rain shadow?

Insta-Lab

Lightning and Thunder

The next time a thunderstorm is in your area, watch for lightning. When you see the lightning, start counting, "One-Mississippi, two-Mississippi, ..." and so on. When you hear the thunder, stop counting. For every three seconds you count, the thunderstorm is about one kilometer from you. How far away is the thunderstorm?

Focus Skill

1. CAUSE AND EFFECT Copy and complete this graphic organizers.

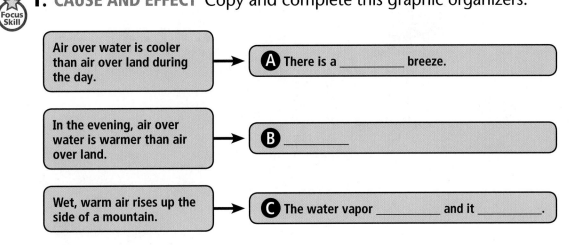

Air over water is cooler than air over land during the day. → **A** There is a _____ breeze.

In the evening, air over water is warmer than air over land. → **B** _____

Wet, warm air rises up the side of a mountain. → **C** The water vapor _____ and it _____.

2. SUMMARIZE Write a paragraph summarizing the lesson. Start with this sentence: The water cycle is affected by landforms.

3. DRAW CONCLUSIONS Will sea breeze storms happen more often in warm places or cool places? Explain.

4. VOCABULARY Explain the difference between a land breeze and a sea breeze.

Test Prep

5. Critical Thinking Explain why a mountain may be green on one side and desertlike on the other.

6. How does warm air move?
   A. It falls.   **C.** It spins.
   B. It is pushed   **D.** It stays still.
        upward.

Links

Writing

Expository Writing
Suppose that you are an early explorer of a mountain range that experiences the rain shadow effect. Write a **journal** describing your explorations of the range.

Math

Solve Problems
A sea breeze storm is moving across Florida from the northeast to the southwest at 23 km/hr. How long does the storm take to reach Tampa if it started above Orlando, which is 137 km away?

Physical Education

Water Sports
Many water sports, such as sailing, make use of sea breezes. Choose a sport that uses sea breezes, and write a simple how-to guide for this sport.

For more links and activities, go to **www.hspscience.com**

How Can Weather Be Predicted?

Fast Fact

A Winter Wonderland Ice storms deposit massive amounts of ice over everything. In fact, during a severe ice storm about 45,000 kilograms (99,000 lb) of ice can pile up on a 15-meter (50-ft) pine tree! In the Investigate, you will make and use a weather instrument used to help predict weather.

Making a Barometer

Materials
- plastic jar
- safety goggles
- wooden craft stick
- scissors
- large rubber band
- large index card
- large round balloon
- tape
- ruler

Procedure

1. **CAUTION: Wear safety goggles.** Be careful when using scissors. Use the scissors to cut the neck off the balloon.

2. Have your partner hold the jar while you stretch the balloon over the open end. Secure the balloon with the rubber band.

3. Tape the craft stick to the top of the balloon. More than half of the craft stick should extend beyond the jar's edge.

4. On the blank side of an index card, draw a line and label it *Day 1.* Tape the card to a wall. The line should be at the same height as the stick on your barometer. Next to it, record the current weather.

5. Air pressure is the force of air pressing down on Earth. Measure air pressure by marking the position of the wooden stick on the index card for the next four days. Label the marks *Days 2–5.* Record the pressure and weather each day.

Draw Conclusions

1. How did the air pressure change? What might cause changes in air pressure?

2. **Inquiry Skill** Scientists use instruments to measure weather data. Infer how a barometer works.

Step 3

Step 4

Investigate Further

Track changes in air pressure and weather for five more days. What can you infer is the relationship between air pressure and type of weather?

SCIENCE CONCEPTS

▶ what makes an air mass
▶ how to read a weather map

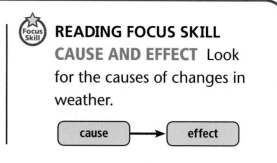

READING FOCUS SKILL
CAUSE AND EFFECT Look for the causes of changes in weather.

cause ➞ effect

Air Masses

Have you ever wondered why the weather can be sunny one day and rainy the next? Movements of air masses cause weather changes. An **air mass** is a large body of air. All of the air in an air mass has a similar temperature and moisture level. Moisture level means the amount of water that is in air.

The map shows where the air masses that affect North America form. Cool air masses are in blue. Warm air masses are in red. ▼

The temperature and moisture level of an air mass depend on where the air mass formed. Air masses that form over land are dry. Air masses that form over water have a lot of moisture in them. In the United States, cold air masses come from the north. Warm air masses come from the south.

The temperature and moisture level of an air mass affect the kind of weather the air mass brings. Cold, wet air masses can bring snow to an area. But cold, dry air masses can bring cool weather

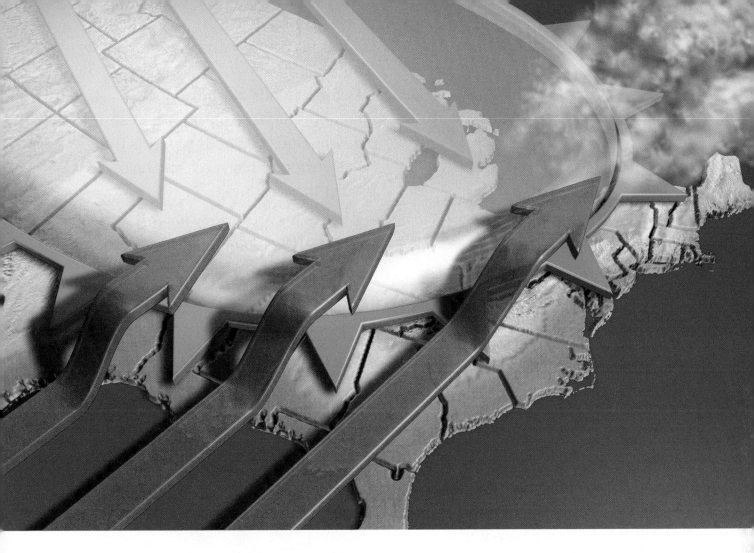

▲ Air masses do not mix very much with each other. Instead, they stay separate as they move.

with little or no precipitation. Warm air masses with a lot of moisture usually bring precipitation. But warm, dry masses can bring warm weather with little or no precipitation.

As air masses move, they tend to stay separate from each other. That's because warm air is lighter than cold air. When they come in contact with each other, warm air masses are pushed upward and cold air masses sink.

CAUSE AND EFFECT What causes the weather to change?

Insta-Lab

Making an Air Mass

Fill a cup halfway with ice cubes. Wait five minutes. With one hand, pour chilled water into the cup. Hold the other hand over the cup as you pour the water. What do you feel? If the air you felt were an air mass, how would you describe it? In a cold front, the air is colder behind the front than ahead of it.

Fronts

When air masses move, they come into contact with other air masses. The border between one air mass and another is called a front. Most storms happen at fronts.

There are two main types of fronts: cold fronts and warm fronts. A **cold front** forms where a cold air mass moves under a warm air mass. This causes the warm air mass to move upward. As the warm air mass moves up, it begins to cool. Remember that water vapor condenses when it cools. The condensing water vapor in the upward-moving air mass forms clouds. It might begin to rain along the front. Thunderstorms will often develop. Also, the air temperature will become cooler as the cold air mass moves forward.

A **warm front** forms where warm air moves over cold air. The warm air slides up over the cold air as it moves forward. Warm fronts generally move slowly. Because of this, warm fronts bring steady rain instead of thunderstorms. Warm fronts are then followed by clear, warm weather as the warm air mass moves over the area.

Fronts do not always move. A front that stays in one place for many days is called a stationary front. Stationary fronts happen when the two air masses along a front do not have enough energy to move. The weather along a stationary front is often cloudy and wet. This kind of front can leave many inches of snow or cause flooding rains.

For this reason, stationary fronts can be dangerous.

Different kinds of fronts move differently. Because of this, they cause different kinds of clouds to form. The types of clouds in an area can help you predict the weather.

 CAUSE AND EFFECT What are the effects of a cold front?

▲ In a warm front, the air is warmer behind the front than ahead of it.

In a cold front, the air is colder behind the front than ahead of it. ▼

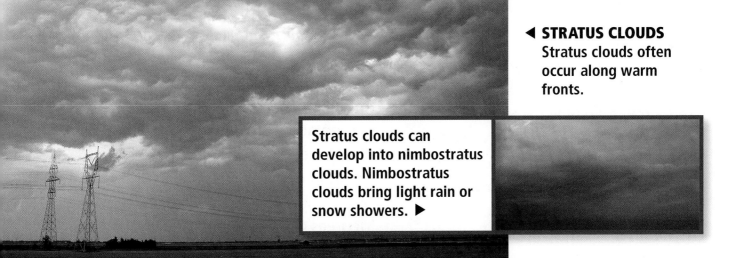

◀ STRATUS CLOUDS
Stratus clouds often occur along warm fronts.

Stratus clouds can develop into nimbostratus clouds. Nimbostratus clouds bring light rain or snow showers. ▶

◀ CUMULUS CLOUDS
Cumulus (KYOO•myuh•luhs) clouds are common on clear, warm days.

Cumulus clouds can develop into cumulonimbus, or thunderstorm, clouds. ▶

CIRRUS CLOUDS
Cirrus (SIR•uhs) clouds usually indicate cool, fair weather.

Weather Maps

Have you ever used a street map to find a friend's house? Have you ever used a trail map while hiking? Another kind of map you can use is a weather map. A weather map helps you know what the weather is like in an area.

Weather maps use symbols to show the weather. A sun symbol means it is sunny in the area. A symbol of a cloud with rain means it is raining in the area.

Fronts are also shown on weather maps. The symbol for a warm front is a red line with half circles along it. A blue line with triangles shows a cold front.

Many weather maps show temperature. Sometimes the temperature is written on the map. In the United States, the temperature is given in degrees Fahrenheit. Almost all other countries give the temperature in degrees Celsius. When the temperature is not written on the weather map, it may be shown using colors. When an area is warm, it will be colored red (very hot), orange (warm), or yellow (mild).

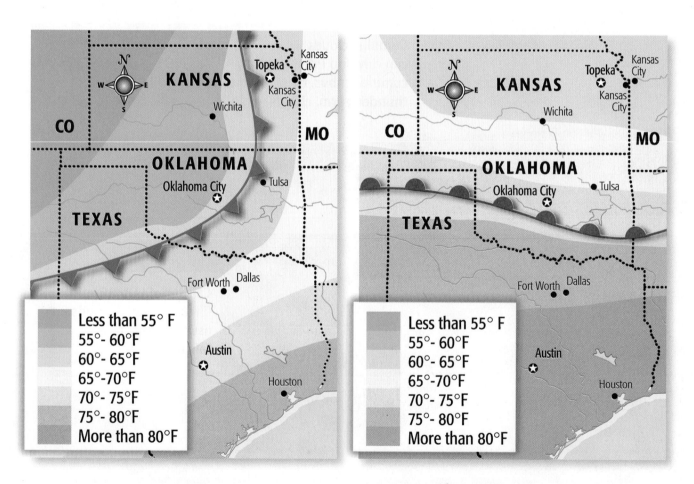

▲ A line with triangles is the symbol for a cold front. The triangles point in the direction of movement.

▲ A line with half circles is the symbol for a warm front. The half circles point in the direction the front is moving.

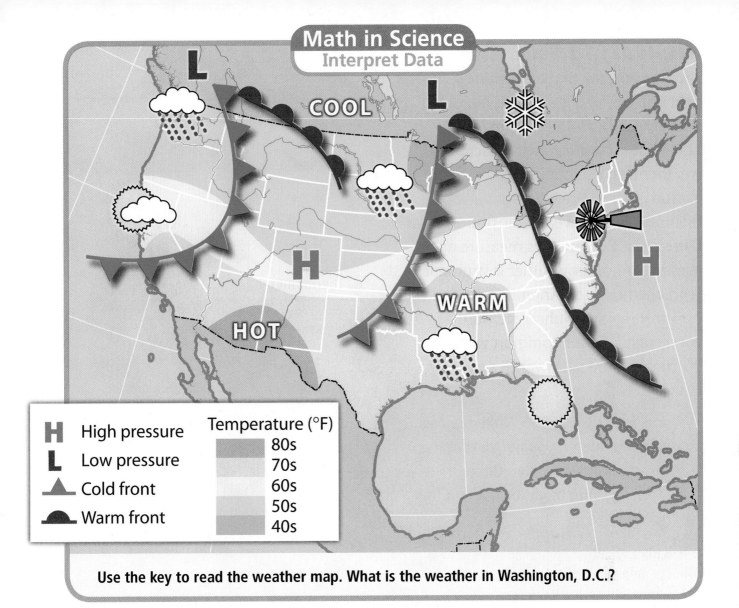

L L

COOL

L

H

WARM

HOT

H

H	High pressure	Temperature (°F)
L	Low pressure	80s
▲	Cold front	70s
●	Warm front	60s
		50s
		40s

Use the key to read the weather map. What is the weather in Washington, D.C.?

When an area is cold, it will be colored green (cool) or blue (very cold).

Other information you may see on a weather map includes wind speed and direction, air pressure, and the highest and lowest temperature in an area for that day.

Where does all the information on a weather map come from? Weather information is collected at thousands of weather stations across the country. A weather station is a place that has

many different instruments that measure weather. The information from the weather stations is reported to the National Weather Service (NWS). The NWS then studies the weather data from all the weather stations. Each day, the NWS makes weather maps based on the information collected at all the weather stations.

CAUSE AND EFFECT How would the weather map above look if a warm front were moving through Florida?

Measuring Weather

When you say that it is hot or cold outside, you are describing one part of weather—the temperature. The most accurate way to describe weather is to use data from weather instruments. In the Investigate, you built one kind of weather instrument—a barometer. **Barometers** measure air pressure. Another weather instrument is an anemometer. **Anemometers** (an•uh•MAHM•uht•uhrz) measure wind speed. Other common weather instruments are wind vanes and rain gauges.

⭐ **Focus Skill** **CAUSE AND EFFECT** While reading a thermometer, you notice that the temperature has fallen throughout the day. What might be causing this?

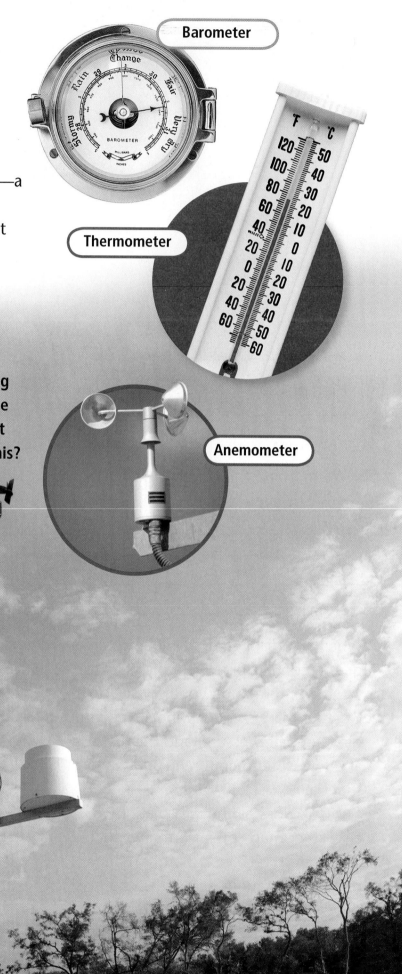

Barometer

Thermometer

Anemometer

This school weather station collects data for students. The data is shared with other schools. ▶

1. CAUSE AND EFFECT Copy and complete the following graphic organizer.

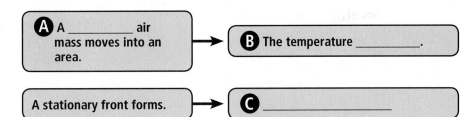

A A _____ air mass moves into an area. → **B** The temperature _____.

A stationary front forms. → **C** _____

2. SUMMARIZE Write a paragraph explaining how air masses, fronts, and the water cycle are related.

3. DRAW CONCLUSIONS Why might it have been more difficult to predict weather years ago?

4. VOCABULARY Use each vocabulary term in the lesson in a sentence.

Test Prep

5. Critical Thinking You hear on the radio that a cold front is headed toward your town. What type of weather can you expect?

6. Which of the following instruments measures wind speed?

   A. anemometer   **C.** rain gauge

   B. barometer   **D.** thermometer

Links

Writing

Narrative Writing

Use what you have learned in this chapter to write a short **poem** about weather and the water cycle. Use these words in your poem: air mass, front, rain, clouds.

Math 9÷3

Subtract Decimals

Suppose you record a rainfall of 0.3 cm in the gauge in the morning. You don't empty the gauge. In the afternoon, the gauge reads 1.5 cm. How much new rain fell?

Language Arts

Be a Weather Forecaster

Make up a weather map of your state. Present your forecast to the class. Be sure to use the correct vocabulary for the weather you are describing.

For more links and activities, go to **www.hspscience.com**

INTO THE EYE OF THE STORM

Hurricane Charley occurred in August 2004. Normally, during such a deadly storm, many people run, drive, or fly away as fast and as far as possible. One flight crew working for the National Weather Service, however, flew into (yes, into) the storm. Called Hurricane Hunters, they actually flew a plane into the center of Charley.

Hurricanes are powerful, whirling storms that form over warm oceans and cause torrential rains and heavy winds. The eye of a hurricane is the calm center of the storm. The eye has little wind and few clouds. Swirling around the eye are heavy winds.

Hurricane Hunters fly directly into the eye of a hurricane—not above it. The reason is that a hurricane can be more than 15,000 meters (50,000 ft) high, and the planes can fly only as high as 9000 meters (30,000 ft).

Hurricanes are rated on a scale of 1 to 5. The ratings are based on a storm's wind speed and potential for destruction.

CATEGORY 1	74 to 95 miles per hour (mph) Minor damage to trees and shrubs; minor flooding
CATEGORY 2	96 to 110 mph Some trees and signs blown down; some flooding; no major damage to buildings; some evacuations
CATEGORY 3	111 to 130 mph Some large trees and signs destroyed; some damage to small buildings; some evacuations
CATEGORY 4	131 to 155 mph Extreme damage to buildings; major beach erosion; evacuations up to 2 miles from shore
CATEGORY 5	Greater than 155 mph Severe damage to buildings; some small buildings knocked down; evacuations up to 10 miles from shore

A Hurricane Hunter drops a tube into the eye of a storm.

As the plane "punched through" the eye wall of Charley, crew members experienced a rocky ride. The eye wall is a solid ring of thunderstorms around the eye. The strongest winds and heaviest rains are located here.

The plane contains equipment that records weather. In the eye of the storm, Hurricane Hunters released small tubes attached to parachutes. Each tube was about the size of a can of tennis balls. The tubes sent information about wind speed, power, and moisture back to the crew.

Accurate Forecasting

As part of their job, Hurricane Hunters help forecasters rate storms. Hurricanes are rated on a scale of 1 to 5.

A storm's rating is based on wind speed and potential for damage. Before hitting land, Charley was a Category 4 storm.

Charley packed winds of up to 230 kilometers (145 mi) per hour by the time it hit land. The storm first walloped Jamaica and Cuba before slamming into Florida.

Hurricane Charley left about a million Florida households without electricity. The storm destroyed or severely damaged at least 16,000 homes and left thousands of residents without running water.

THINK ABOUT IT

1. Why is it important that forecasters accurately predict the path of a hurricane?
2. How do you think hurricanes can cause flooding on land?

Find out more! Log on to
www.hspscience.com

Saving the Earth

Earth Day encourages kids around the world to take action. From cleaning up local parks to testing local water, kids help the Earth on Earth Day, which is held on April 22.

But eleven-year-old Michaela Piersanti from New Haven, Connecticut, thinks the environment needs to be protected all year long, not just on Earth Day.

Although the event is important to millions of kids like Michaela, more needs to be done. "We need to keep the Earth clean," Michaela said. "If we pollute, it can make animals sick and possibly kill them."

Water for Life

A big part of Earth Day is making people aware of water pollution. In fact, the theme of a recent Earth Day was "Water for Life."

That theme was chosen because more than 1 billion people around the world do not have clean drinking water. Water gets polluted from sewage, factories, and chemicals. Pollution harms the plants and animals that live in the water. It also makes drinking water unsafe.

You Can Do It!

Make a Rain Gauge

Materials
- 1-L clear plastic bottle
- scissors
- plastic ruler
- masking tape

Procedure

1. CAUTION: **Be careful when using scissors. Remove the cap from the bottle, and have an adult cut the top off the bottle.**

2. Tape the ruler to the outside of the bottle. The zero mark should be at the bottom of the bottle.

3. Turn the bottle top over so that it will act like a funnel, and put it inside the bottle bottom.

4. Put the rain gauge out in the open, but away from any roof edges or trees.

5. After it rains, measure the rainfall, and empty the bottle.

Draw Conclusions

How much rainfall did you measure? How did measuring rainfall help you describe weather?

Weather and the Seasons

How does weather in your area change from season to season? Design an investigation in which you use various weather instruments to measure weather over the course of a year. Record data regularly. Use your data to compare measurements such as average daily temperature, wind speed and direction, and amount of precipitation among the different seasons. Then draw graphs that show how weather in your area changes over the year.

Review and Test Preparation

Vocabulary Review

Use the terms below to complete the sentences. The page numbers tell you where to look in the chapter if you need help.

precipitation p. 268

water cycle p. 268

evaporation p. 270

condensation p. 271

hurricane p. 278

land breeze p. 284

air mass p. 290

warm front p. 292

barometer p. 296

anemometer p. 296

1. A breeze moving from the land to the sea is a _____.

2. A large tropical storm with high wind speeds is called a _____.

3. Air pressure is measured with a _____.

4. A gas changes to a liquid during the process of _____.

5. A large body of air is called an _____.

6. Water that falls to Earth from the air is known as _____.

7. A liquid changes to a gas during the process of _____.

8. Warm air pushes forward and moves over cold air along a _____.

9. Wind speed is measured with an _____.

10. The movement of water through the environment is known as the _____.

Check Understanding

Write the letter of the best choice.

11. In the water cycle, what happens before water condenses in clouds?
    A. Water dissolves salt.
    B. Water evaporates.
    C. Water falls as precipitation.
    D. Water vapor changes to a gas.

12. Look at the diagram below. What is shown?
    F. evaporation
    G. groundwater formation
    H. cirrus clouds
    J. sea breeze

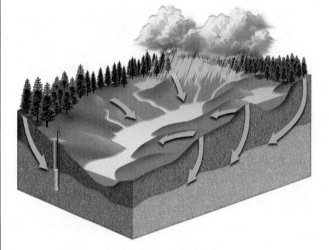

13. What type of precipitation is shown in the picture?

   A. hail   **C.** sleet

   B. rain   **D.** snow

14. Landforms such as mountains affect the water cycle.

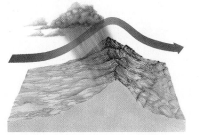

What is it called when one side of a mountain is dry?

   F. a land breeze   **H.** a sea breeze

   G. a rain shadow   **J.** a tornado

15. There is a stationary front over Centerville. What kind of weather is Centerville most likely having?

   A. a few hours of drizzly rain

   B. a few hours of thunderstorms

   C. clear weather

   D. several days of rain or snow

16. How would an air mass that forms over the Gulf of Mexico most likely be described?

   F. cold and dry

   G. cold and moist

   H. warm and dry

   J. warm and moist

Inquiry Skills

17. You **observe** clouds forming on a warm, sunny day. What can you **infer** is happening in the atmosphere? What may happen later in the day?

18. Suppose you plan to **measure** weather conditions over the next week. What will you measure, and what equipment will help you?

Critical Thinking

19. Look at the weather map below. Describe the weather in Miami.

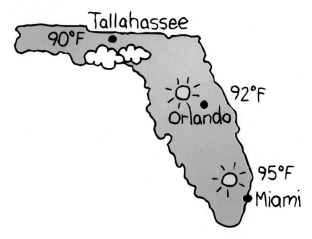

20. Tonya watches the weather report every day for a week. Each day, the average temperature is the same, and the air pressure doesn't change.
Part A Explain what might be happening to cause the weather in Tonya's town.
Part B How would the weather change if a warm front came through the area?

Planets and Other Objects in Space

Vocabulary

axis	sun
orbit	constellation
moon	galaxy
phases	universe
solar system	
planet	
comet	
star	

What do YOU wonder?

On a clear night away from city lights, about 3,000 stars are visible. Why can we see these objects only at night? What other objects can be seen in the night sky?

How Do Earth and Its Moon Move?

Sun, Moon, and Myths To the ancient Romans, Diana was the goddess of the moon. They honored Apollo as the sun god. The ancient Romans believed that their gods caused day and night and brought about changes in weather and seasons. In the Investigate, you will learn more about what really causes the seasons on Earth.

Seasons and Sunlight

Materials
- small 60-watt table lamp
- ruler
- graph paper
- black construction paper
- thermometer

Procedure

1. Work with a partner. Shine the lamp straight down from a height of 30 cm onto a sheet of graph paper. Draw an outline of the lit area, and label it Step 1.

2. Repeat Step 1 with a new sheet of graph paper, this time placing the lamp at an angle. Label this outline Step 2.

3. Shine the lamp straight onto a sheet of black paper. After 15 minutes, measure the temperature of the paper in the lit area. Record the temperature on the sheet of graph paper labeled Step 1.

4. Now use another sheet of black paper, and angle the light as you did in Step 2. Again, measure the temperature of the lit area after 15 minutes. Record the temperature on the sheet of graph paper labeled Step 2.

Draw Conclusions

1. How did the area covered by the light change? How did the temperature in that area change? Explain why these changes occurred.

2. **Inquiry Skill** How could scientists measure the effect that the sun has on seasons?

Step 1

Step 4

Investigate Further

Try your experiment on the real thing! Choose a sunny spot outdoors, and measure and record its temperature throughout the day. Why do you think it changes?

VOCABULARY
axis p. 308
orbit p. 308
moon p. 310
phases p. 310

SCIENCE CONCEPTS
▶ why there are seasons on Earth
▶ why the moon appears to change shape

READING FOCUS SKILL
SEQUENCE Events in a sequence happen in a certain order.

Earth's Tilt and the Seasons

Night follows day. Spring follows winter. The changes of night and day, as well as the seasons, occur because of the ways Earth moves.

Earth moves in two ways. Earth rotates, or spins, on its axis. An **axis** is an imaginary line through both poles. It takes about 24 hours for Earth to completely rotate on its axis. The second way Earth moves is by orbiting, or revolving around, the sun. The path of one object in space around another object is its **orbit**.

As Earth orbits the sun, part of it is tilted toward the sun. That part of Earth takes in more energy from the sun. This energy is in the form of heat. The part of Earth that is tilted away from the sun takes in less energy from the sun.

In this illustration, Earth's tilt is causing the sun's rays to shine more directly on the Northern Hemisphere than on the Southern Hemisphere. So the Northern Hemisphere has summer.

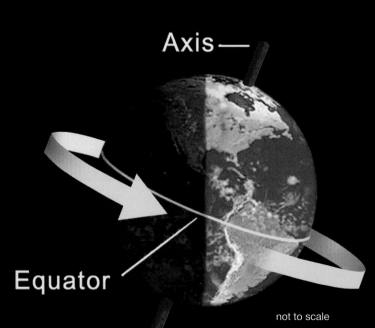

Axis—

Equator

not to scale

1 The summer *solstice* (SAHL•stis), about June 21 in the Northern Hemisphere, is the day of the year that has the most hours of daylight. **3** The winter solstice, about December 21, is the day that has the most hours of darkness.

2 On the autumn *equinox* (EE•kwih•nahks), about September 21, and the **4** spring equinox, about March 21, the hours of daylight and darkness are the same. These dates mark the beginning of autumn and of spring.

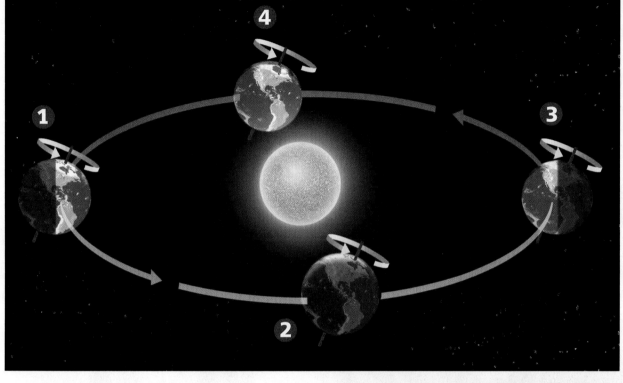

During June, July, and August, the Northern Hemisphere of Earth is tilted toward the sun and the Southern Hemisphere is tilted away. The sun's rays shine more directly on the Northern Hemisphere, which has summer, than on the Southern Hemisphere, which has winter. As Earth continues its orbit, the Northern Hemisphere is tilted away from the sun, causing winter. The Southern Hemisphere is tilted toward it, causing summer. This cycle continues as Earth orbits the sun.

 SEQUENCE What happens next after the Northern Hemisphere has been tilted away from the sun?

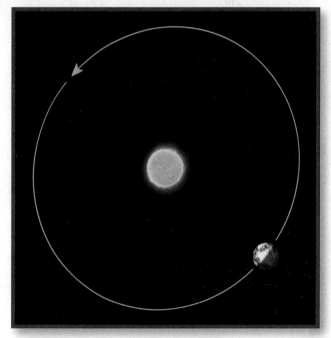

▲ Earth's orbit around the sun is almost a perfect circle.

Moon Phases

The **moon** is a small planetlike body that orbits Earth, rather than the sun. As Earth orbits the sun, the moon orbits Earth.

The moon appears to shine, but the light you see is actually reflected light from the sun. As the moon orbits Earth, different amounts of its lit surface can be seen. That's why the moon seems to have different shapes, or **phases**.

The phases of the moon follow the same pattern about every $29\frac{1}{2}$ days. On one of those days, all of the lit side of the moon can be seen from Earth. When this happens, we say there is a full moon. Then, as the days pass and the position of the moon changes, from Earth we see less of the lit side. Finally, we see none of the lit side at all. On that night, the moon is called a new moon.

Focus Skill

SEQUENCE What phase of the moon happens after we see less and less of the moon at night?

During the first half of the moon's cycle, the amount of the lit side of the moon seen from Earth *waxes*, or increases.

New moon

First quarter

Full moon

Waxing

During the second half of the moon's cycle, the amount of the lit side of the moon seen from Earth *wanes*, or decreases. Then the cycle begins again.

Full moon

Third quarter

New moon

Waning

One half of the moon is always being lit by the sun. Whether people can see all, some, or none of the lit side depends on the positions of the moon and Earth.

During the new moon phase, the lit side of the moon can't be seen from Earth.

The full moon phase occurs about 15 days after the new moon phase.

New Moon To Full Moon

When the moon's orbit brings it between Earth and the sun, its lit side can't be seen from Earth. This phase is called the new moon. Later in the month, when Earth is between the moon and the sun, we see the sun's light reflected from one whole side of the moon. When this happens, we see a full moon.

Insta-Lab

Sun, Moon, and Earth

Model the moon phases in a dark room. Use a flashlight for your "sun" and two balls for your "moon" and "Earth." Shine the sun toward Earth, and move the moon around Earth. What causes changes in how much of the moon's lit side can be seen from Earth?

For more links and activities, go to www.hspscience.com

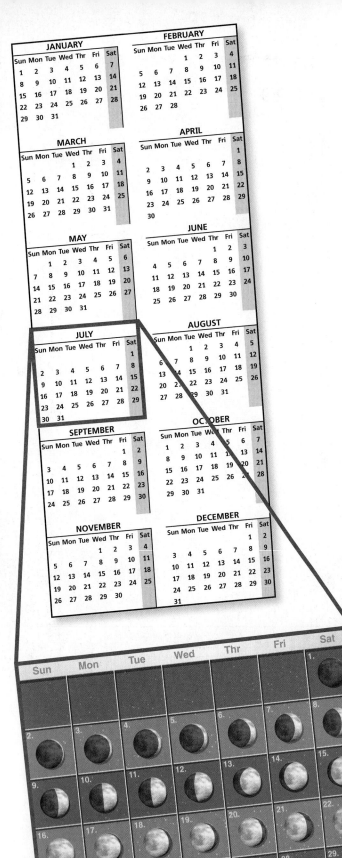

Calendars

We use calendars to divide time into days, months, and years. All of these units of time are based on the movements of Earth.

A solar year is 365 days, 5 hours, 48 minutes, and $45\frac{1}{2}$ seconds long. This is based on the amount of time it takes Earth to make one complete orbit around the sun. Today's calendars have only 365 days in a year. So every four years, an extra day is added in February to make up for the extra hours and minutes in a solar year. Years with an extra day are called leap years.

Some ancient people based months on the movements of the moon. They knew that the moon completes a cycle of phases in about $29\frac{1}{2}$ days. Each cycle was considered a month, and 12 months made a lunar year. However, a lunar year is $11\frac{1}{2}$ days shorter than a solar year. Some cultures that use lunar calendars add a month to their calendar every few years to make up for the shorter lunar year.

SEQUENCE What occurs after three years have 365 days each?

◄ Most calendars are based on the solar year. Many also show the phases of the moon, which don't happen on the same day each month.

312

1. SEQUENCE Copy and complete this graphic organizer.

| winter solstice | → | spring (A) _____ | → | (B) _____ | → | fall equinox |

2. SUMMARIZE Explain how the position and movement of Earth cause the seasons.

3. DRAW CONCLUSIONS If Earth took 500 days instead of 365 to orbit the sun, how would the seasons be different? Why?

4. VOCABULARY Use *axis* in a sentence that explains its meaning.

Test Prep

5. Critical Thinking How would day and night be different if Earth's axis were not tilted?

6. If you live in the Southern Hemisphere, what season do you have in August?

A. spring   **C.** fall

B. summer   **D.** winter

Links

Writing

Expository Writing

Suppose a friend from the Southern Hemisphere plans to visit you in December. Write a **letter** explaining what kind of clothes to pack and why.

Math

Use Data

A normal year has 365 days. In a normal year, on average, how many days are in a month? How many days, on average, are there in each season?

Social Studies

Different Calendars

Research and report on a calendar other than the one you use. It can be an ancient calendar or one that is used today in a different part of the world.

For more links and activities, go to www.hspscience.com

313

How Do Objects Move in the Solar System?

Rings Around a Planet Saturn's rings have fascinated sky gazers since the astronomer Galileo (gal•uh•LAY•oh) first saw them in 1610. We've learned that the rings are made of rock, gas, and ice. Saturn is millions of kilometers from Earth. In the Investigate, you will make a model to help you understand that distance.

Distances Between Planets

Materials • 4-m length of string • tape measure
• 9 markers of different colors

Procedure

1. Copy the table.

2. At one end of the string, make a large knot. This knot will stand for the sun as you make your model.

3. An AU (astronomical unit) is Earth's average distance from the sun. In your model, 10 cm will represent 1 AU. Use the tape measure to measure Earth's distance from the knot that represents the sun. Use a marker to mark this point on the string. Record on the table which color you used for Earth by placing a small dot with the marker next to the planet name.

4. Complete the Scale Distance column of the table. Repeat Step 3 for each planet. Use a different color for each planet.

Planet Data

Planet	Average Distance from the Sun (km)	Average Distance from the Sun (AU)	Scale (cm)	Planet's Diameter (km)
Mercury	58 million	$\frac{4}{10}$	4	4876
Venus	108 million	$\frac{7}{10}$	7	12,104
Earth	150 million	1		12,756
Mars	228 million	2		6794
Jupiter	778 million	5		142,984
Saturn	1429 million	10		120,536
Uranus	2871 million	19		51,118
Neptune	4500 million	30		49,532
Pluto*	5900 million	39		2274

*In 2006, scientists classified Pluto as a "dwarf planet."

Draw Conclusions

1. In your model, how far away from the sun is Mercury? How far away is Pluto?

2. Why do scientists use AUs to measure distances in the solar system?

3. **Inquiry Skill** How does it help to use numbers instead of using real distances?

Step 3

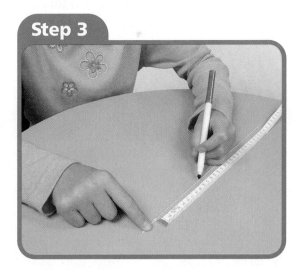

Investigate Further

Use a calculator to make a model of planet diameters. Use 1 cm to represent Earth's diameter. Then divide the other planets' diameters by Earth's. Make a scale drawing.

Reading in Science

VOCABULARY
solar system p. 316
planet p. 316
comet p. 320

SCIENCE CONCEPTS
▶ what makes up our solar system
▶ what the inner and outer planets are

 READING FOCUS SKILL

COMPARE AND CONTRAST
Look for phrases such as *by contrast* and *in common*.

alike	—	different

Our Solar System

A **solar system** is a group of objects in space that orbit a star in the center, plus the star itself. The sun is the star in the center of our solar system. Everything else in the solar system is small compared to the sun.

Our solar system contains a variety of objects. These include planets and moons as well as asteroids, which are small and rocky. A **planet** is a large object that orbits a star. A moon is a smaller object that orbits a planet.

In our solar system, there are eight planets. Often, scientists group them as the inner planets, which are closer to the sun, and the outer planets, which are farther from the sun. These groups of planets are separated by a ring of asteroids that orbit the sun between Mars and Jupiter.

 COMPARE AND CONTRAST How are moons and planets similar and different?

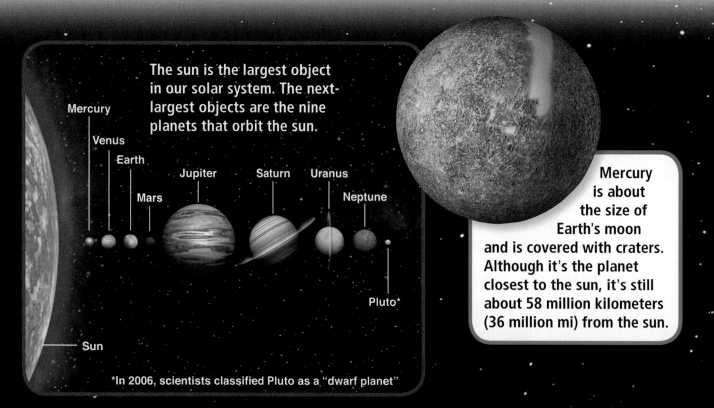

The sun is the largest object in our solar system. The next-largest objects are the nine planets that orbit the sun.

Mercury
Venus
Earth
Mars
Jupiter
Saturn
Uranus
Neptune
Pluto*
Sun

Mercury is about the size of Earth's moon and is covered with craters. Although it's the planet closest to the sun, it's still about 58 million kilometers (36 million mi) from the sun.

*In 2006, scientists classified Pluto as a "dwarf planet"

The Inner Planets

The inner planets are those closest to the sun. They are Mercury, Venus, Earth, and Mars. These planets are alike in many ways. They all have rocky surfaces and are smaller than most of the outer planets. Also, none of the inner planets has more than two moons.

There are also differences among the inner planets. For example, it can be 450°C on Mercury—hot enough to melt lead—while Mars's temperature never gets higher than 20°C.

Earth is the most unusual inner planet. Only Earth has liquid water on its surface and a large amount of oxygen in the atmosphere. This water and oxygen help support life on Earth.

 COMPARE AND CONTRAST How are the inner planets similar?

Mars is called the Red Planet because it looks fiery red from Earth. Mars is small—its diameter is only half of Earth's. It has huge dust storms that can last for months. Scientists think that at one time, Mars may have had liquid surface water.

Venus is about the same size as Earth. Venus is the third-brightest object in Earth's sky—only the sun and the moon appear brighter. Clouds of sulfuric (suhl•FYUR•ik) acid make the planet difficult to study from Earth. This radar image shows a surface made up of volcanoes, mountain ranges, highland regions, craters, and lava plains.

Earth is the largest of the inner planets. It's the only planet known to have life and the only one whose surface is mostly water. Earth's distance from the sun helps the planet maintain a temperature that supports life.

The Outer Planets and Pluto

Beyond Mars, on the far side of the asteroid belt, are the outer planets. They are Jupiter, Saturn, Uranus, and Neptune.

The outer planets have many similarities. These four planets are huge and made mostly of gases. These planets are often called the gas giants. They all have many moons, and they all are surrounded by rings that are made of dust, ice, or rock.

Pluto is unlike the outer planets. For almost 80 years Pluto was listed as the ninth planet in the solar system. In 2006, scientists met to form a new definition of a planet. They decided that a planet is a large round object in a clear orbit around a star. Because Pluto is not in a clear orbit, scientists removed it from the list of planets. They classified it as a "dwarf planet." The large asteroid Ceres, and the newly discovered object Eris, which orbits beyond Pluto, are also classified as "dwarf planets."

Focus Skill **COMPARE AND CONTRAST** **How is Uranus different from the other outer planets?**

Jupiter—the largest planet in our solar system—has a diameter that's more than 11 times the diameter of Earth. Jupiter has at least 63 moons. For more than 300 years, a gigantic hurricane-like storm called the Great Red Spot has raged on Jupiter.

Saturn has rings that are visible from Earth through a telescope. Saturn has at least 31 moons. Its atmosphere is mostly hydrogen and helium. Like the other gas giants, Saturn has no known solid surface.

Length of a Year

On any planet, a year is the length of time it takes that planet to orbit the sun. Here is a list of how long a year is on some planets in our solar system, compared to a year on Earth.

Planet Years

Planet	Length of Year (in Earth years)
Mars	1.9
Jupiter	11.9
Saturn	29.5
Neptune	165
Pluto*	249

*In 2006, scientists classified Pluto as a "dwarf planet."

If a person has just turned 60 on Earth, about how old is he or she in Saturn years?

Pluto, a "dwarf planet," has a rocky core covered with nitrogen ice and small amounts of methane and carbon dioxide ices. Its atmosphere is mostly nitrogen. Pluto's largest moon is almost as large as Pluto itself. From the surface of Pluto, the sun looks like any other bright star in the sky.

Neptune's atmosphere is mainly hydrogen and helium. It is one of the windiest places in the solar system. Winds can reach 2000 kilometers per hour (1200 mi/hr). Neptune has at least 13 moons.

Uranus is another gas giant. Uranus rotates on its side as it orbits the sun. Scientists think this may be the result of a collision with an object the size of Earth. Uranus has at least 27 moons.

Insta-Lab

Planet Sizes

Compare the approximate sizes of planets. Use a marble to represent Pluto, a table tennis ball to represent Earth, and a basketball to represent Jupiter. Which of the three balls would best represent the size of Venus?

Other Objects in the Solar System

There are objects besides planets orbiting the sun. Two types of such objects are asteroids and comets. Although both orbit the sun, comets and asteroids are very different.

Asteroids are bits of rock and metal. Most are less than 1 kilometer (0.6 mi) across. The largest known asteroid is about 1000 kilometers (620 mi) in diameter. Most asteroids orbit the sun in a belt between Mars and Jupiter.

By contrast, a **comet** is a ball of rock, ice, and frozen gases. Most comets are less than 10 kilometers (6 mi) across, but the tails can be as much as 100,000 kilometers (62,000 mi) long. As a comet's orbit brings it close to the sun, the sun's heat may turn some of the frozen matter into gas. That gas, and dust that rises with it, then looks like a fiery tail and may be visible from Earth.

Focus Skill **COMPARE AND CONTRAST** **What do comets and asteroids have in common?**

Some comets, like Halley's comet, become well known because their orbits bring them close to Earth.

◀ This is the asteroid Gaspra. Asteroids are harder to see from Earth than comets. A 1991 space probe took the first close-up pictures of an asteroid.

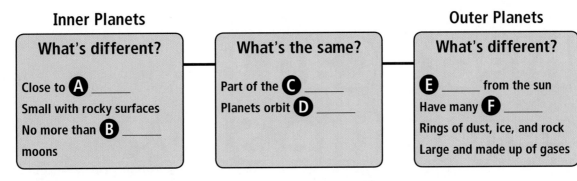

1. COMPARE AND CONTRAST Copy and complete this graphic organizer. Write differences and similarities of the inner planets and the gas giants.

Inner Planets

What's different?

Close to **A** _____
Small with rocky surfaces
No more than **B** _____ moons

What's the same?

Part of the **C** _____
Planets orbit **D** _____

Outer Planets

What's different?

E _____ from the sun
Have many **F** _____
Rings of dust, ice, and rock
Large and made up of gases

2. SUMMARIZE Write two sentences that tell the most important information in this lesson.

3. DRAW CONCLUSIONS Why do you think life hasn't been found on any of the other planets in the solar system?

4. VOCABULARY Write a definition for *solar system*.

Test Prep

5. Critical Thinking Suppose you look into the sky and see a comet. What can you conclude about the comet?

6. What separates the inner planets from the outer planets?

   A. asteroid belt   **C.** Earth
   B. comets   **D.** Venus

Links

Writing

Narrative Writing
Research a planet other than Earth. Write a travel guide that could be used by people who might visit that planet. Tell about the sights they would see or what a typical day might be like.

Math

Make a Bar Graph
Use the table in the Investigate to find the diameters of the planets in our solar system. Make a bar graph that compares their diameters.

Literature

Planet Fiction
Read a short story about life on another planet or about space travel. Decide whether the story could really happen. Report to the class on what you read.

For more links and activities, go to
www.hspscience.com

What Other Objects Can Be Seen in the Sky?

Fast Fact

Deep Space Images from the Hubble Space Telescope show distant objects in detail. They show space objects, such as the Omega Nebula, that are very far from Earth. In the Investigate, you will make your own telescope.

Make a Telescope

Materials
- modeling clay
- I thin (eyepiece) lens
- small-diameter cardboard tube
- I thick (objective) lens
- large-diameter cardboard tube

Procedure

1. Use the clay to fasten the thin lens in one end of the small tube. Set the lens as straight as possible, taking care not to smear the middle of the lens with clay.

2. Repeat Step 1, using the thick lens and the large tube. Slide the open end of the small tube into the large tube. You have just made a telescope.

3. Hold your telescope up, and look through each lens. **CAUTION: Never look directly at the sun.** Slide the small tube into and out of the large tube until what you see is in focus. How do objects appear through each lens? Record your observations.

Draw Conclusions

1. What did you observe as you looked through each lens?

2. **Inquiry Skill** Astronomers are scientists who study objects in space. Astronomers use telescopes to observe objects that are far away. How would you plan and conduct a simple investigation to observe Earth's moon?

Step 1

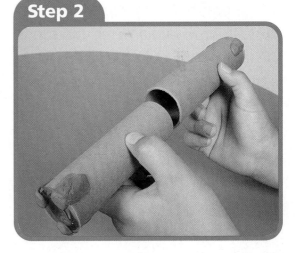

Step 2

Investigate Further

Use your telescope to observe the moon at night. List details you can see by using your telescope that you can't see by using only your eyes.

Reading in Science

VOCABULARY

star p. 324
sun p. 324
constellation p. 326
galaxy p. 326
universe p. 326

SCIENCE CONCEPTS

▶ what stars and galaxies are
▶ what constellations are

READING FOCUS SKILL

MAIN IDEA AND DETAILS

Look for the details that support each main idea.

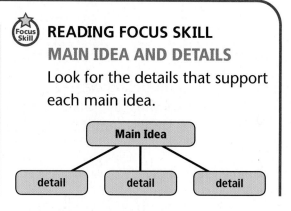

The Sun and Other Stars

You have probably looked up at the stars in the night sky and noticed their different sizes and colors. You may know that a **star** is a huge ball of superheated gases. The **sun** is a star that is at the center of our solar system.

At more than 1 million kilometers (621,000 mi) in diameter, the sun is the largest object in the solar system. It is the source of most of the energy on Earth—without it life could not exist.

From Earth, the sun looks like a ball of light. Like other stars, it is made up of gases, mostly hydrogen and helium.

The sun sometimes has dark spots called sunspots on its surface. They do not give off as much light and heat energy as the rest of the sun's surface. The red streams and loops are solar flares, gases that shoot out from the sun. These hot fountains of gas often begin near a sunspot and extend tens of

▼ Although they appear fiery, the loops of gases shooting from the sun's surface are cooler than the rest of the sun.

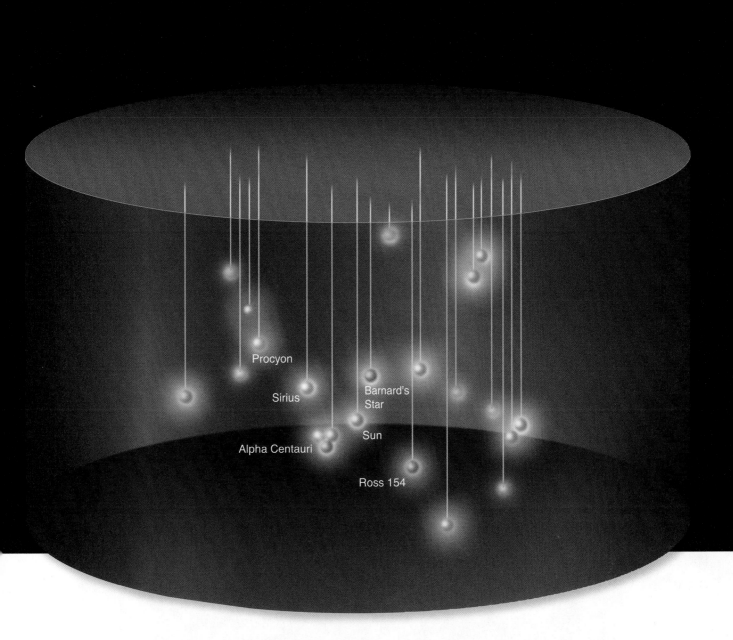

▲ This map shows the positions of the 20 nearest stars. The three closest to our solar system make up Alpha Centauri (AL•fuh sen•TAW•ry). From Earth, Alpha Centauri looks like one star.

thousands of kilometers into space. Both sunspots and solar flares last only a few days.

Stars' colors tell us about the stars' temperatures. Red stars are the coolest and blue the hottest. The sun, a medium-size yellow star, is between the hottest and the coolest.

Stars go through stages. They form from clouds of spinning dust and gas, which gravity squeezes. When the mass is squeezed enough, changes take place that form a star. The mass of the star then begins to change into light and heat. Over billions of years, most of the mass of the star is converted to light and heat.

MAIN IDEA AND DETAILS What does a star's color tell about the star?

Groups of Stars

Have you ever seen the Big Dipper in the night sky? The Big Dipper belongs to a group of stars called Ursa Major. These stars form a **constellation**, a group of stars that form an imaginary picture in the sky. In ancient times, people often gave names to these imaginary star pictures. Constellations are helpful to people because their patterns serve as landmarks in the night sky. For hundreds of years, sailors have used them to find their way.

Have you seen a bright band of stars on a clear summer night? If so, you were looking at the Milky Way, the galaxy in which our solar system lies. A **galaxy** is a huge system of gases, dust, and stars.

Galaxies contain billions of stars. Our sun is on the edge of the Milky Way galaxy. Constellations are made up of stars in our own galaxy. The Milky Way is only one of the millions of galaxies in the universe. The **universe** is everything that exists in space.

There are many galaxy shapes. The Milky Way is a spiral (SPY•ruhl) galaxy. A barred spiral galaxy has two main arms. Some galaxies look like balls or eggs. Other galaxies have no regular shape.

MAIN IDEA AND DETAILS **What are two ways in which people classify groups of stars?**

▲ This is a drawing of Orion, a hunter in Greek myths.

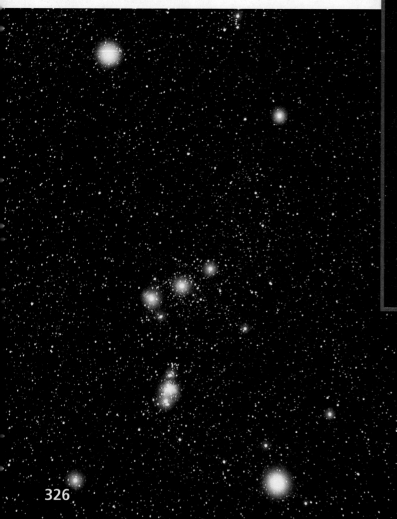

◀ This is how the constellation Orion appears in the night sky.

This barred spiral galaxy has two main arms branching out from it.

This photo, taken by the Hubble Space Telescope, shows some of the many galaxies in the universe.

Insta-Lab

Make a Constellation Model

Use a pencil point or toothpick to poke a "constellation" in a piece of aluminum foil. Use a rubber band to fasten the foil to the end of a paper towel tube. Look through the tube to see your constellation. Turn the tube while you look through it. What planetary motion are you modeling when you turn the tube?

327

Seasonal Star Positions

Each day, the sun appears to rise in the east, move across the sky, and set in the west. The same is true for stars at night. However, what is actually moving is Earth.

The positions of the stars appear to change with the seasons, too. In winter, you may see Orion clearly in the night sky. A few months later, Orion may no longer be visible.

This, too, is due to Earth's movement. As Earth revolves around the sun, we see different parts of space at different times of the year.

To see Orion in the same place you saw it last winter, you must wait until next winter. It will be visible again when Earth reaches that part of its orbit of the sun.

Where you live determines the constellations you will see. In the Northern Hemisphere, people see different sets of constellations from those people see in the Southern Hemisphere. People who live near the equator can see some constellations of both hemispheres.

MAIN IDEA AND DETAILS Explain why constellations seem to change their locations.

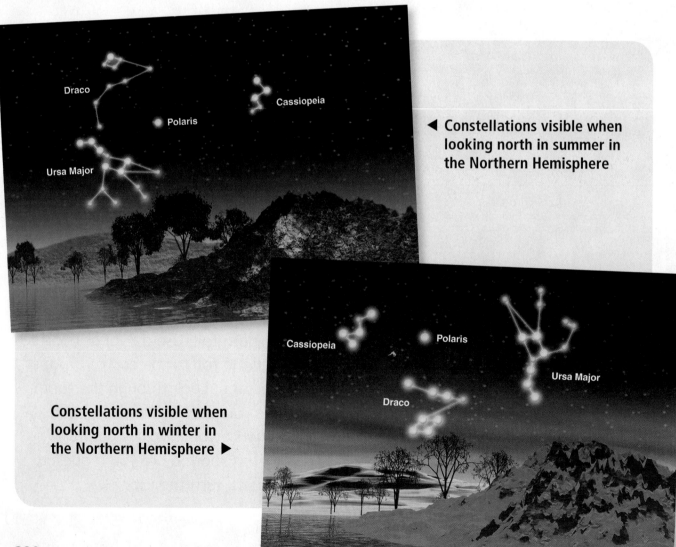

◀ **Constellations visible when looking north in summer in the Northern Hemisphere**

Constellations visible when looking north in winter in the Northern Hemisphere ▶

Focus Skill

1. MAIN IDEA AND DETAILS Copy and complete this graphic organizer. Write two supporting details for each main idea about stars.

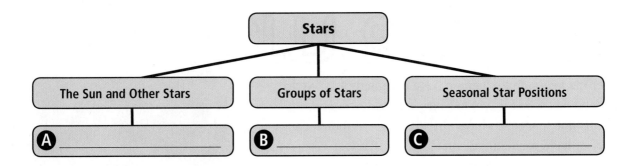

Stars

- The Sun and Other Stars
  - **A** _____
- Groups of Stars
  - **B** _____
- Seasonal Star Positions
  - **C** _____

2. SUMMARIZE Write a sentence or two to tell the important facts you learned about stars.

3. DRAW CONCLUSIONS If the sun were a red star or a blue star, how would it be different?

4. VOCABULARY Use the terms *star, galaxy,* and *universe* in a sentence about objects in space.

Test Prep

5. Critical Thinking How were constellations useful to sailors long ago? When might they be useful to sailors today?

6. Which **best** describes the sun?

A. small star **C.** large star

B. medium-size star **D.** very large star

Writing

Expository Writing
Choose a constellation in the illustration of the winter sky. Write a **paragraph** explaining how to find it on a winter night.

Math 9÷3

Multiply AUs
Earth is 150 million km from the sun. Scientists refer to this distance as 1 AU, or 1 astronomical unit. Neptune is 30 AUs from the sun. How many km is that?

Social Studies

Careers in Space
The United States began to explore space in the 1960s. Research space-related careers, and report to the class.

For more links and activities, go to www.hspscience.com

WATER WORLD

Over the years, many people have dreamed of going to Mars. The day when travel to Mars is possible is coming closer. Robot spacecraft have already traveled there. Those spacecraft have made many amazing discoveries.

One of the most recent spacecraft to journey to the fourth rock from the sun is *Mars Odyssey*. Photos taken by *Mars Odyssey* show that Mars has water. Because it is very cold on Mars, the water is frozen. Most of the water is frozen under the surface of Mars.

Lots of Lakes

Even though lots of ice crystals are mixed in with the Martian soil, Mars doesn't have as much water as Earth. Mars has buried lakes of water, not buried oceans of water. In fact, some scientists think that if you could collect all the water on Mars, it would fill a lake about twice the size of Lake Michigan.

There is evidence that some of the frozen water locked under the surface of Mars might melt every once in a while. Some of the water is only 46 centimeters (18 in.) below the surface. Molten rock deep beneath the surface of Mars might heat the ice. The water may then flow onto the surface.

A Grand Canyon?

Photos taken by *Mars Odyssey* show long, dark streaks on the walls of some canyons. The streaks might indicate areas where water recently flowed down the canyon walls.

Not all scientists agree, however. Many scientists say wind blowing across Mars caused the streaks. Scientists have long known about powerful wind storms on Mars. Some of those storms blow across the surface for months at a time.

Even if liquid water and life do not exist on Mars today, many scientists still want to explore the red planet. "I'm interested in Mars because it's probably the most fascinating planet in the solar system besides Earth, and probably the only one that could have ever supported other forms of life," said one NASA scientist.

THINK ABOUT IT

1. What would life on Earth be like if Earth had as little water as there is on Mars?
2. How have satellites helped us learn about other planets?

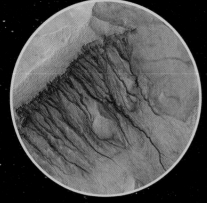

Some scientists say these dark lines were caused by streams of water flowing down a canyon wall.

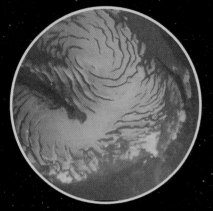

Frozen carbon dioxide covers the North Pole of Mars.

The *Mars Odyssey* spacecraft studies Mars. Photos by the spacecraft show that ice exists on Mars.

Find out more! Log on to
www.hspscience.com

Moonstruck

Recently, Christopher Ray Clark carried his telescope into his backyard. He set it up and pointed it skyward. Then, he saw an amazing sight.

As Christopher looked at the nighttime sky, he saw a total lunar eclipse. Christopher saw a shadow slowly move across the moon. The moon had a red color when the shadow completely covered it. The eclipse lasted for a few hours.

A total lunar eclipse occurs when the moon passes through Earth's inner shadow, called the **umbra**. As the moon passes through the umbra, Earth blocks all direct sunlight from reaching the moon. A small amount of red light makes it through Earth's atmosphere, making the moon appear red or orange.

SCIENCE Projects
for Home or School
You Can Do It!

Materials
- small ball of clay
- pencil, ruler
- 15-cm x 20-cm cardboard

Tell Time by Using the Sun

Procedure

1. On the cardboard, draw a half circle with a 7-cm radius. Put the clay in the center of the straight side.

2. Stand the pencil in the clay with the point up. You have made a sundial.

3. Put your sundial on a sunny windowsill, with the straight side along the window. Every hour, mark the pencil's shadow on the cardboard. Write the time at the mark.

4. On the next sunny day, use your sundial to tell time.

Draw Conclusions
How does your sundial work? Would it work in any sunny window? Why or why not?

Design Your Own Investigation

Make a Spiral Galaxy

A spiral galaxy gets its shape from many orbiting stars. Use a paper punch to punch out many "stars" from construction paper. Fill a large bowl halfway with water. Pour the stars into the water. How can you make them form a "spiral galaxy"? How does what you do show what happens in space?

Review and Test Preparation

Vocabulary Review

Use the terms below to complete the sentences. The page numbers tell you where to look in the chapter if you need help.

axis p. 308   **comet** p. 320

orbit p. 308   **star** p. 324

moon p. 310   **sun** p. 324

solar system p. 316   **galaxy** p. 326

planet p. 316   **universe** p. 326

1. The star at the center of our solar system is the _____.

2. The path an object takes around another object is its _____.

3. A star and a group of objects that orbit it make up a _____.

4. The imaginary line through both poles of a planet is its _____.

5. A small mass of rock, ice, and frozen gases that orbits the sun is a _____.

6. A large object that orbits a star is a _____.

7. An enormous ball of superheated gases in space is a _____.

8. Everything that exists in space is part of the _____.

9. A large system of stars, dust, and gas is a _____.

10. A natural object that orbits a planet is a _____.

Check Understanding

Write the letter of the best choice.

11. **MAIN IDEA AND DETAILS** Which detail is true of the sun?
   - **A.** It's a ball of hydrogen and helium.
   - **B.** It's a ball of oxygen and hydrogen.
   - **C.** It's a ball of helium and phosphorus.
   - **D.** It's a ball of carbon dioxide and oxygen.

12. **COMPARE AND CONTRAST** How are asteroids and comets different?
   - **F.** Asteroids are much smaller than comets.
   - **G.** Comets orbit the sun, while asteroids orbit Earth.
   - **H.** Comets are made up of rock, ice, and frozen gases, while asteroids are made up of rock and metals.
   - **J.** Asteroids are pieces of Earth, while comets are pieces of the sun.

13. Which **best** describes the sun's location in the universe?

    A. near the barred spiral galaxy

    B. at the edge of the solar system

    C. at the edge of a galaxy called the Milky Way

    D. in the center of a galaxy called Alpha Centauri

14. Samantha must label this diagram of the sun.

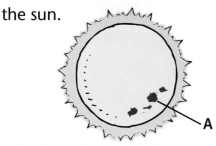

    Which label should she use to identify area A?

    F. bits of rock   **H.** spinning dust

    G. oxygen   **J.** sunspot

15. What are the gas giants?

    A. comets

    B. stars in the Milky Way

    C. the four outer planets

    D. the sun and Alpha Centauri

16. What does this illustration **best** show?

    F. why Earth rotates

    G. why planets orbit the sun

    H. why the moon has phases

    J. why Earth has seasons

Inquiry Skills

17. You **used numbers** to understand distances in space. What other ideas in this chapter did using numbers help you understand?

18. How could **measuring** the orbit of a comet help scientists understand when it will next be visible from Earth?

Critical Thinking

19. Why are there phases of the moon?

20. Suppose that you have been asked to do a presentation about our solar system. You are to present information about the planets and show where they are located in space.

    Part A Make a labeled drawing of the solar system. Include the nine planets and the sun.

    Part B Write a paragraph that explains how the inner planets and the outer planets are different.

Matter and Energy

PHYSICAL SCIENCE

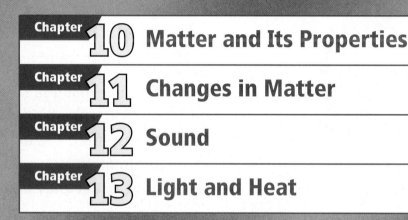

Speedwell Ironworks

TO: richard@hspscience.com

FROM: faye@hspscience.com

RE: Morristown, New Jersey

Dear Richard,

Imagine how long it took for you to get this e-mail. Do you think it took less than a second? Well, just think about what life was like before the telegraph. People got their news by listening to the town crier or by getting mail delivered by the Pony Express! That's a long way from e-mail! Who knew that a "dot, dash, dot, dot, dash" would change the world?

Your friend,

Faye

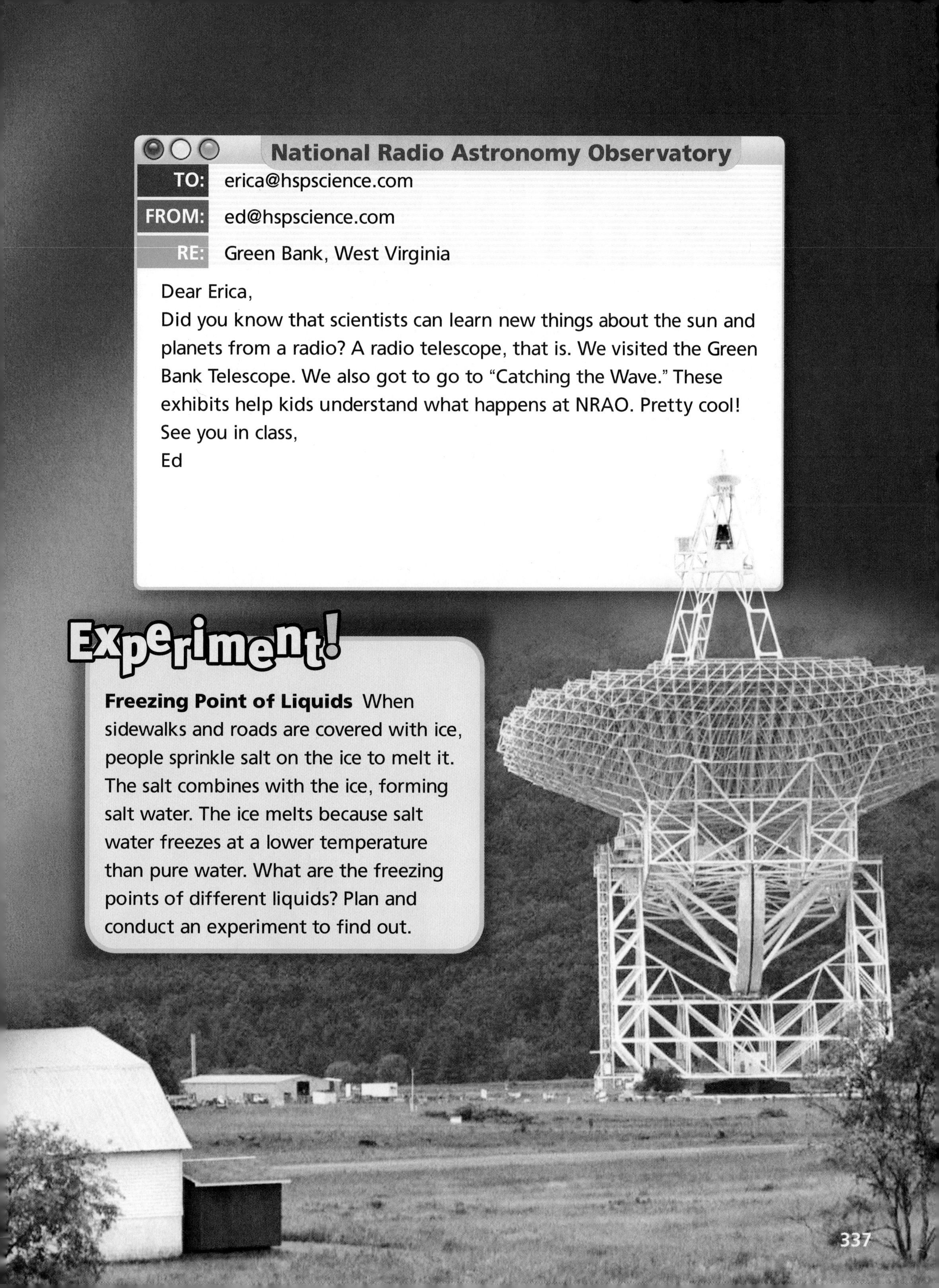

National Radio Astronomy Observatory

TO: erica@hspscience.com

FROM: ed@hspscience.com

RE: Green Bank, West Virginia

Dear Erica,

Did you know that scientists can learn new things about the sun and planets from a radio? A radio telescope, that is. We visited the Green Bank Telescope. We also got to go to "Catching the Wave." These exhibits help kids understand what happens at NRAO. Pretty cool!

See you in class,

Ed

Experiment!

Freezing Point of Liquids When sidewalks and roads are covered with ice, people sprinkle salt on the ice to melt it. The salt combines with the ice, forming salt water. The ice melts because salt water freezes at a lower temperature than pure water. What are the freezing points of different liquids? Plan and conduct an experiment to find out.

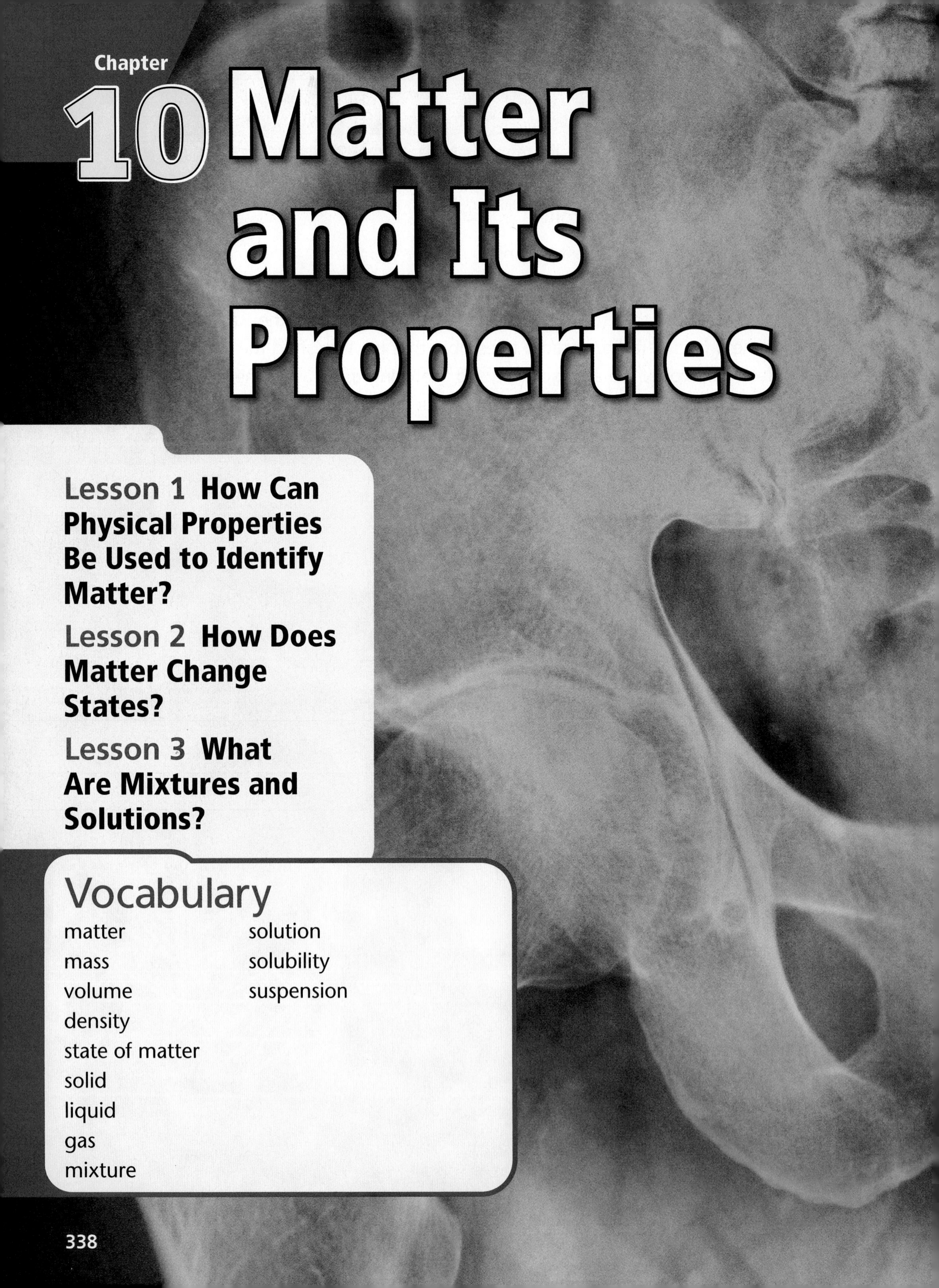

Chapter

10 Matter and Its Properties

Lesson 1 How Can Physical Properties Be Used to Identify Matter?

Lesson 2 How Does Matter Change States?

Lesson 3 What Are Mixtures and Solutions?

Vocabulary

matter
mass
volume
density
state of matter
solid
liquid
gas
mixture
solution
solubility
suspension

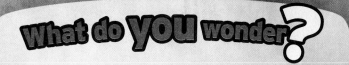

What do YOU wonder?

Doctors use plastic and metal to replace hip joints. Think about a material that could replace bone. What might it be like?

How Can Physical Properties Be Used to Identify Matter?

Fast Fact

Amazing Water Density affects the floating of liquids and solids. Water is unusual. It's less dense when it is solid ice than when it is liquid water. That's why ice floats on water. No other common material has this property of being denser as a liquid than as a solid. In the Investigate, you will find the densities of three liquids. Amazing water is one of them.

Measuring the Densities of Liquids

Materials
- graduate
- vegetable oil
- balance
- corn syrup
- water

Procedure

1. Make sure the graduate is empty, clean, and dry. Then use the balance to find its mass. Record the mass.

2. Add 10 mL of water to the graduate. Measure and record the mass of the graduate again. Empty the graduate and dry it.

3. Repeat Step 2, using 10 mL of vegetable oil.

4. Repeat Step 2, using 10 mL of corn syrup.

5. Subtract the mass of the empty graduate from each of the masses you measured in Steps 2, 3, and 4. Record each result.

6. To find the densities, divide the mass of each liquid by its volume, 10 mL. Record and compare the densities.

Draw Conclusions

1. Which liquid has the greatest density? Which has the least? Compare the amount of matter in each liquid sample.

2. **Inquiry Skill** Display data by making a bar graph that shows the density of each liquid you measured.

Step 1

Step 2

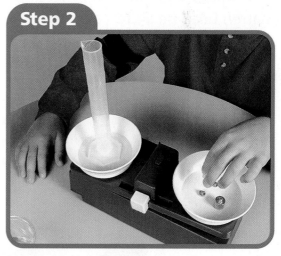

Investigate Further

Tint 10 mL of water red. Pour it into the graduate. Then add 10 mL of corn syrup. Observe what happens. How do you explain your observation?

341

Reading in Science

VOCABULARY

matter p. 342
mass p. 343
volume p. 344
density p. 344

SCIENCE CONCEPTS

▶ how physical properties can be used to identify substances

▶ how density can be determined

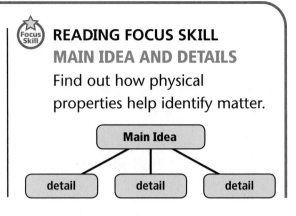

READING FOCUS SKILL

MAIN IDEA AND DETAILS

Find out how physical properties help identify matter.

Matter

What is matter? Just about everything! Everything that takes up space is **matter**. This includes you, your skateboard, the clothes you're wearing, and the sidewalk under you. Breakfast cereal is matter. Your bowl, your spoon, and the milk you pour on the cereal are all matter, too.

If you can taste, smell, or touch something, it's matter. Even a breeze is matter, because air takes up space. You prove that when you blow up a balloon. The air you blow into the balloon pushes out its sides. The air inside the balloon takes up space.

Some things exist without taking up space, so they are not matter. What is not matter? Heat, light, and ideas are examples of things that are *not* matter. Even though they exist, they don't take up any space.

MAIN IDEA AND DETAILS Define *matter*, and name three examples.

◀ What do you have in common with a skateboard?

▲ Mass is measured with a balance. The mass of this orange is about 360 grams.

Mass

Matter not only takes up space but also has mass. **Mass** is the amount of matter something contains. A heavy object has more mass than a light object. Finding mass is a way of measuring matter.

All matter is made of tiny particles. You can see them only under the strongest microscopes. In general, the more particles an object has, the more mass it has. The more mass it has, the heavier it is.

A golf ball and a table tennis ball both are made of matter. The balls are about the same size. However, the golf ball is heavier because it has more mass.

The mass of an object is one of its physical properties. A physical property is something you can observe or measure. You can measure mass. Other physical properties include an object's appearance and texture.

⭐ Focus Skill **MAIN IDEA AND DETAILS** Define *mass.* Name one object with a lot of mass and one with little mass.

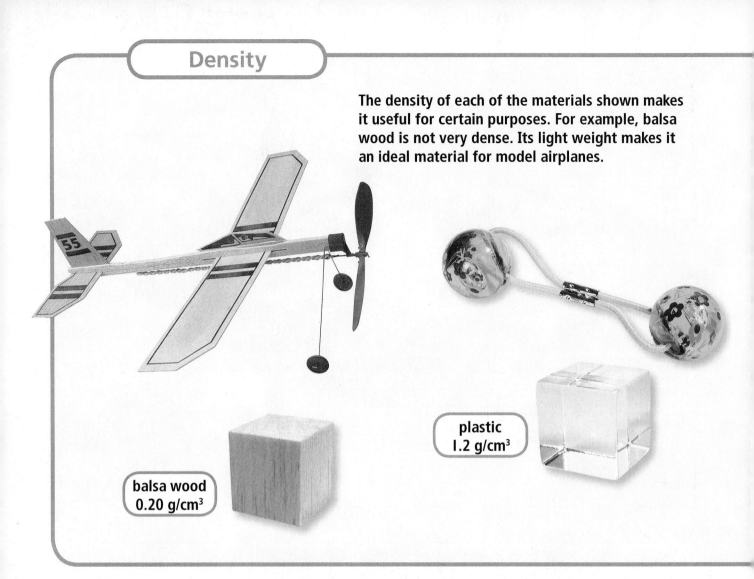

The density of each of the materials shown makes it useful for certain purposes. For example, balsa wood is not very dense. Its light weight makes it an ideal material for model airplanes.

plastic
1.2 g/cm³

balsa wood
0.20 g/cm³

Volume and Density

Volume is the amount of space that matter takes up. Some objects, such as a blown-up balloon, have little mass (few particles). Yet a balloon takes up a lot of space. A marble has more mass but takes up little space. How can we show this relationship between mass and space?

The answer is density. **Density** is the amount of matter in an object compared to the space it takes up. In the Investigate, you measured density. You divided the masses of three liquids by their volumes. Each liquid had the

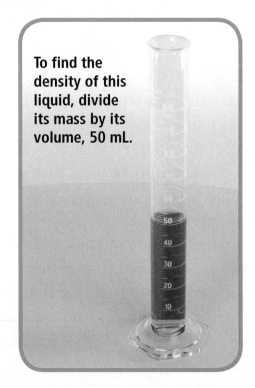

To find the density of this liquid, divide its mass by its volume, 50 mL.

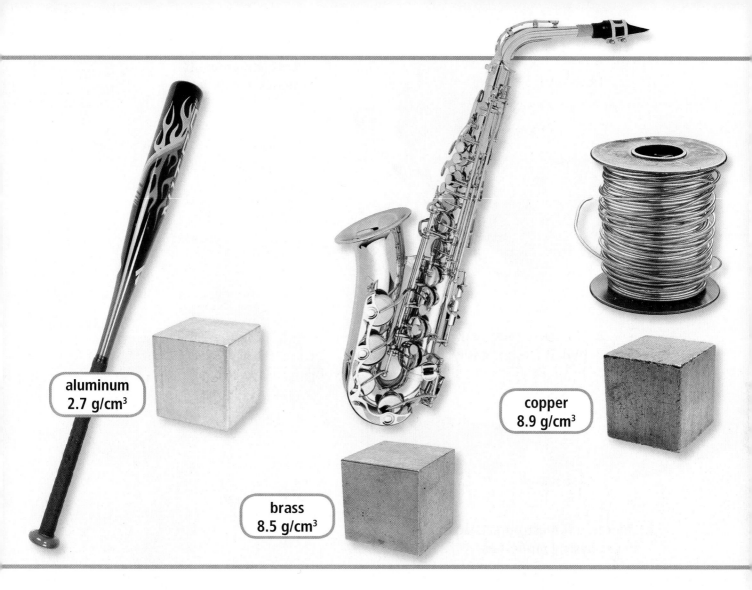

aluminum
2.7 g/cm³

copper
8.9 g/cm³

brass
8.5 g/cm³

same volume but a slightly different mass. This showed that each liquid had a different density.

You can find the density of a solid object by dividing its mass by its volume. For example, a certain wooden block has a mass of 20 grams. Its volume is 10 cubic centimeters (cm³). When you divide its mass by its volume, the answer is 2 grams per cubic centimeter—2 g/cm³. So, the block has a density of 2 grams per cubic centimeter.

 MAIN IDEA AND DETAILS How are mass and density different?

Insta-Lab

Wet Test
Which has more density, 50 drops of water or 10 mL of water? Add 50 drops to a graduate. Use a balance to find the mass of the water. Divide the mass of the water by the volume in mL. What did you find out?

The foam tube is soft and green. It bends easily. ▶

▲ The foil is shiny and thin. It crushes easily.

The glass is clear. It breaks easily. ▶

▲ You can tell these objects apart by their physical properties.

Other Properties of Matter

Suppose two marbles have the same mass, volume, and density. How can you tell them apart? By their colors, of course! You can tell one object from another by their physical properties. You have learned that physical properties include mass, volume, and density.

Color is another physical property. Shape and texture are two more physical properties. You use your senses to detect physical properties.

In the next lesson, you will learn that another physical property of matter is state. Matter might be a liquid, a solid, or a gas.

The ability to transfer heat and electricity is another physical property. Some substances, such as copper, transfer heat and electricity easily. Others, such as plastic, do not.

You use physical properties to identify objects and substances every day.

MAIN IDEA AND DETAILS What physical properties could you use to describe a rock?

Focus Skill

1. MAIN IDEA AND DETAILS Draw and complete this graphic organizer.

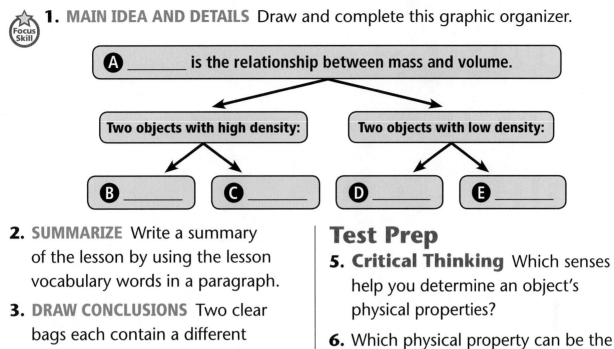

A _____ is the relationship between mass and volume.

Two objects with high density:

Two objects with low density:

B _____

C _____

D _____

E _____

2. SUMMARIZE Write a summary of the lesson by using the lesson vocabulary words in a paragraph.

3. DRAW CONCLUSIONS Two clear bags each contain a different unknown object. What physical properties can you use to tell the objects apart?

4. VOCABULARY In a sentence or two, explain why you must measure mass before you can determine density.

Test Prep

5. Critical Thinking Which senses help you determine an object's physical properties?

6. Which physical property can be the same for both a large marble and a small one?

A. color **C.** volume

B. mass **D.** weight

Links

Writing

Informative Writing

Suppose you are a scientist who has discovered a new substance. Write a **report** to describe its physical properties.

Math 9÷3

Find the Density

A green ball has a mass of 100 grams and a volume of 200 cubic centimeters. A yellow ball has a mass of 50 grams and a volume of 10 cubic centimeters. Which ball has the greater density?

Physical Education

Catch This!

You can use an air pump to change the density of air inside a soccer ball or basketball. What happens when you pump more air into an inflated ball?

For more links and activities, go to www.hspscience.com

How Does Matter Change States?

Fast Fact

Frozen Art Every March, ice artists like this one gather at the World Ice Art Championships in Fairbanks, Alaska. The artists depend on changing states of matter to shape and polish the giant sculptures. In the Investigate, you will have a chance to observe changes of state.

07-19

Melt, Boil, Evaporate

Materials
- 4 ice cubes
- hot plate
- safety goggles
- oven mitts
- pan
- graduate

Procedure

1. Draw the ice cubes and describe their physical properties. Be sure to tell how they look and feel.

2. **CAUTION: Put on safety goggles.** Put the ice in the pan. Your teacher will carefully heat the pan. If you must touch the handle, use oven mitts. Predict the changes you expect to see in the ice cubes.

3. When the ice cubes melt, your teacher will pour the hot water into the graduate. Record its volume.

4. Use oven mitts as you pour the water back into the pan. Your teacher will put it on the hot plate again. Let the water boil. Predict what will happen this time.

   CAUTION: Remember to turn off your hotplate. Remove the pan from the heat before it is dry. Place the pan on a burn-proof surface.

Draw Conclusions

1. What caused the water to change?

2. **Inquiry Skill** Infer where the water is now. When it evaporated, what did the liquid water become?

Step 2

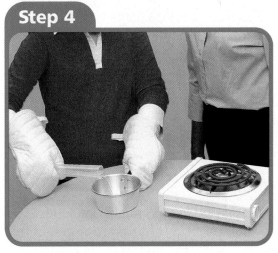

Step 4

Investigate Further

Using oven mitts, pick up an ice cube in each hand. Push the cubes together without touching them with your hands. Explain what you observe.

Reading in Science

VOCABULARY
state of matter p. 350
solid p. 350
liquid p. 350
gas p. 351

SCIENCE CONCEPTS
▶ what three states of matter are
▶ how temperature can change the state of a substance without matter being lost or gained

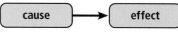 **READING FOCUS SKILL**
CAUSE AND EFFECT Look for things that cause changes in a state of matter.

cause ⟶ effect

States of Matter

Every day, you see and touch three **states of matter**: solid, liquid, and gas. But why is an apple solid, while milk is liquid? What makes the air you breathe a gas? The answer lies in the particles that you read about earlier.

All matter is made of particles. The way those particles are arranged determines whether the matter is a solid, a liquid, or a gas.

In a **solid**, the particles are packed together in a tight pattern. This pattern gives solids an exact shape, so the solid takes up a certain amount of space. When you roll a bowling ball, the particles stay tightly packed. As a result, the ball does not change its shape.

You learned that the particles in matter are always moving. Particles in solids are packed too tightly to move around. They vibrate in place instead.

Particles in **liquids** have more movement. They slide around, taking

Solids

Gems and bowling balls are solids. Their particles are packed together in tight patterns that give the objects their shape.

Liquids

Liquids take the shape of their containers and have definite volume.

Gases

Gases take the shape of their containers but have no definite volume.

the shape of their container. A liquid also takes up a certain amount of space. However, if you spill a liquid, its shape changes as its particles slide around.

A **gas** has no definite shape or volume. Particles move fastest in a gas. When you open a container and release a gas into the air, its particles move away quickly. That's why you smell perfume after it is sprayed. Then the scent gets weaker because its gas particles move away and spread out.

 CAUSE AND EFFECT What causes solids to keep their shape?

Insta-Lab

Spaces and Places

Fill a glass with water until the water bulges above the top. Next, slowly sprinkle 2 teaspoons of salt into the glass. The glass is full of water, so where does the salt go?

351

Changes in the State of Water

Water clearly shows how heating and cooling change the state of matter. Heat makes particles in matter move faster. If ice gains energy, its particles move faster. They begin to slide around each other. The solid loses its shape and becomes a liquid.

Particles in the liquid move around and take the shape of the container. If you pour the liquid into another container, the liquid particles take its shape. The volume of the water stays the same.

If you keep adding heat to the water, its particles move even faster. They evaporate into a gas—water vapor. The gas particles bounce into each other and spread out in all directions.

Cooling the gas particles slows their movement. The particles condense into a liquid. If the liquid gets cold enough, the particles freeze into solid ice again.

Although heat changes the state of matter, it does not change the amount of matter.

CAUSE AND EFFECT How does heat change the state of water?

Heat Makes the Difference

Ice is water in its solid state. The particles in a solid are arranged in a tight, evenly spaced pattern. The particles still vibrate.

As ice warms, it melts into a liquid—water. As the particles warm up, they move and slide around one another. The even spaces between the particles become different-size spaces.

As the water is heated, the particles move faster and faster. The liquid boils and becomes a gas. The particles bounce off one another and fly out of the spout. If this water vapor cools, it will condense back into tiny drops of water.

For more links and activities, go to www.hspscience.com

Other Materials Change States

Water is not the only material that changes state. Some materials change state in different ways. For example, dry ice is the solid form of carbon dioxide. Carbon dioxide changes directly from a solid into a gas.

Some gases change directly into solids. One example of a solid that forms this way is frost. Solid crystals of frost form from water vapor in the air.

⭐ **CAUSE AND EFFECT** What causes dry ice to change state?

Dry ice changes from a solid directly into a gas.

Math in Science
Interpret Data

Freezing and Boiling Points

Almost anything will melt or boil if its temperature gets high enough or low enough. Which of these substances would be useful in an industry in which resistance to heat is important?

Substance	Melting Point	Boiling Point
Iron	1538°C (2800°F)	2862°C (5184°F)
Mercury	−39°C (−38°F)	357°C (675°F)
Nitrogen	−209°C (−344°F)	−196°C (−321°F)
Oxygen	−218°C (−360°F)	−183°C (−297°F)

Metals become liquid at very high temperatures. After a metal is cooled in a mold, it becomes a solid again. Now it has a new shape.

354

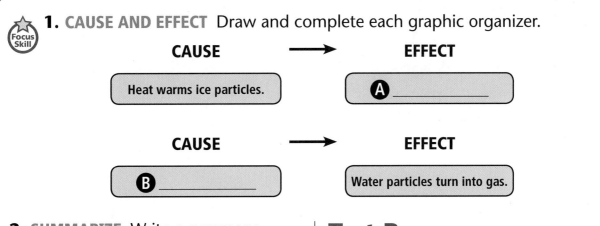

1. CAUSE AND EFFECT Draw and complete each graphic organizer.

CAUSE → EFFECT

| Heat warms ice particles. | | Ⓐ _____ |

CAUSE → EFFECT

| Ⓑ _____ | | Water particles turn into gas. |

2. SUMMARIZE Write a summary of this lesson. Begin with this sentence: There are three common states of matter on Earth.

3. DRAW CONCLUSIONS What do you think happens when gas particles cool off?

4. VOCABULARY Make a crossword puzzle that has the vocabulary terms as answers. Write clear clues for the words.

Test Prep

5. Critical Thinking How can you change the state of water?

6. In which state of water are the particles the most organized?

A. ice   **C.** liquid

B. gas   **D.** water vapor

Links

Writing

Narrative Writing

Suppose you are a drop of water. Write a **story** about how you experience all three states of matter in one day.

Math 9÷3

Using Numbers

The metal mercury melts at about –40°C and boils at about 360°C. In which state is mercury at room temperature? How do you know?

Language Arts

Name Origins

We use two temperature scales: Celsius and Fahrenheit. Find out when and how these scales were created and named.

For more links and activities, go to www.hspscience.com

What Are Mixtures and Solutions?

Fast Fact

Salty, Salty Seas Most lakes have fresh water, but some lakes are saltier than the ocean. Mono Lake, in California, has salts and minerals dissolved in it. In warm weather, its water evaporates, leaving behind some of the salts and minerals. When the lake's water level drops, a crust of minerals forms along its shore. In the Investigate, you will find out how salt and other solids dissolve in water.

Which Solids Will Dissolve?

Materials
- water
- teaspoon
- sand
- 4 clear containers
- stirrer
- salt
- sugar
- baking soda

Procedure

1. Half-fill each container with water.

2. Put 1 spoonful of sand into one container. Observe and record what happens.

3. Stir the mixture for 1 minute, and then record what you see.

4. Repeat Steps 2 and 3, using salt, sugar, and baking soda. Observe and record all the results.

Draw Conclusions

1. Which solid dissolved the most? Which did not dissolve at all?

2. **Inquiry Skill** Scientists often plan a simple investigation to test an idea quickly. What idea did this activity test? What is another simple investigation you could do with these materials?

Step 2

Step 3

Investigate Further

Dissolve table sugar and powdered sugar in separate containers of water. Compare how quickly the two kinds of sugar dissolve. Explain your results.

Reading in Science

VOCABULARY
mixture p. 358
solution p. 360
solubility p. 361
suspension p. 362

SCIENCE CONCEPTS
▶ how a mixture, a solution, and a suspension differ
▶ differences in how substances dissolve

Focus Skill **READING FOCUS SKILL**
MAIN IDEA AND DETAILS
Look for details about mixtures.

Main Idea		
detail	detail	detail

Mixtures

Do you like salad? Salad is a mixture. A **mixture** is two or more substances that are combined without being changed. These substances can be separated from each other again. For example, if you don't like onions, you can take them out of your salad.

Mixtures can contain different amounts of the substances. Your salad might have a lot of lettuce and just a little bit of onion.

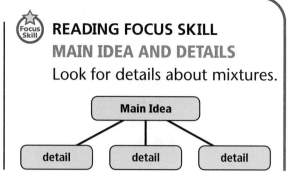

oatmeal flakes

raisins

nuts

dried cranberries

This spoonful of granola is a mixture of good things to eat. ▶

Not all mixtures are made of solids. Salt water is a mixture of a solid and a liquid. Fog is a mixture of water drops and air. Air itself is a mixture of nitrogen, oxygen, carbon dioxide, and other gases.

The pictures show how one mixture can be separated. The mixture begins as a pile of rocks, dust, salt, and bits of iron. First, larger rocks and particles are strained from the mixture. Only the smaller particles can pass through the holes in the strainer.

Next, a magnet draws out the iron bits. Then, water is added to the remaining mixture. The wet dust and salt are poured through a filter. Water and dissolved salt pass through. The dust is left behind.

Finally, the salty water is heated. The water boils away, leaving the salt behind.

All the substances in the original mixture are separated. Being in the mixture did not change them.

MAIN IDEA AND DETAILS Define the term *mixture,* and name three examples.

▲ The mixture begins as a pile of rocks, dust, dirt, salt, and bits of iron. The rocks are screened out first.

◄ A magnet takes away bits of iron.

◄ Water is added. Then the filter removes dust and dirt.

The salt water is heated. ▼

◄ The water is boiled away. Only salt is left behind.

Solutions

A solution is a kind of mixture. In a **solution**, different kinds of matter are mixed completely with each other. Salt water is a solution. The salt and the water are so evenly mixed that you can't see the salt. You can tell it is there by tasting the water. The air you breathe is also a solution.

On the other hand, a bowl of salad is not a solution. You can always tell the ingredients apart. The tomatoes might all be on top. Most of the lettuce might be on the bottom.

When a solid forms a solution with a liquid, the solid dissolves in the liquid. In the Investigate, you found that salt dissolves easily in water. The water particles pull the salt particles away from one another. All the particles are moving, so the salt particles spread evenly through the water.

However, sand doesn't dissolve in water. Water can't pull sand particles apart. Instead, they fall to the bottom. Sand in water is not a solution.

MAIN IDEA AND DETAILS Why is pizza a mixture but not a solution?

Sugar crystals are added to water.

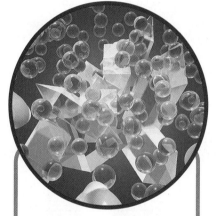

Water particles start pulling the sugar crystals apart.

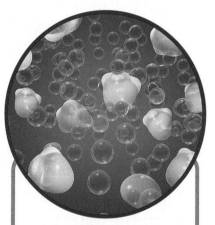

The water has dissolved the sugar. The sugar bits are now too small to see, but you can taste them.

What would happen if sand dissolved in water as easily as salt does?

This salt was once dissolved in ocean water. After the water evaporated, particles of solid salt were left.

Solubility

You found in the Investigate that substances dissolve differently. **Solubility** (sahl•yoo•BIL•uh•tee) is a measure of how much of one material will dissolve in another. For example, 204 grams (7.2 oz) of sugar will dissolve in 100 milliliters (3.4 oz) of water at room temperature. So, sugar has a solubility of 204 g/100 mL. However, no sand will dissolve in water. Sand has a solubility of zero.

 MAIN IDEA AND DETAILS Name two things besides sand that are not soluble in water.

Insta-Lab

Cool, Warm, or Hot?

Pour 10 mL of cold water into one cup. Into another, pour 10 mL of lukewarm water, and into a third, pour 10 mL of hot water. Add a small spoonful of sugar to each cup, and stir. In which cup of water does the most sugar dissolve?

Other Mixtures

In some mixtures, the ingredients are not spread out evenly. When these mixtures sit, some of the ingredients settle to the bottom. Other ingredients rise to the top. This kind of mixture is called a **suspension**. Particles of one ingredient are suspended, or floating, in another ingredient. Some suspensions you can eat are shown here.

If you have taken a walk on a foggy day, you have walked through a suspension. Drops of water are suspended in the air. If you dip water out of a muddy creek, you will see a suspension. Bits of soil are suspended in the water.

⭐ **Focus Skill** **MAIN IDEA AND DETAILS** How can you tell whether a mixture is a suspension?

You must shake the orange juice container because the pulp settles out of the juice. ▶

You must also shake most salad dressings. Otherwise, you might have just oil on your salad! ▶

Fog is a suspension of water droplets in air.

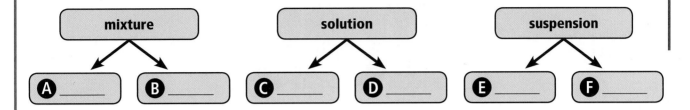

Focus Skill

1. MAIN IDEA AND DETAILS Draw and complete this graphic organizer. List two details about each main idea.

mixture	solution	suspension

A _____ **B** _____ **C** _____ **D** _____ **E** _____ **F** _____

2. SUMMARIZE Use your completed graphic organizer to write a lesson summary.

3. DRAW CONCLUSIONS Why is lemonade made from a powdered mix a solution and not a suspension?

4. VOCABULARY Write two sentences. Use all four vocabulary words.

Test Prep

5. Critical Thinking Name two mixtures you have eaten in the past week. Explain whether each is a simple mixture, a solution, or a suspension.

6. Which of these is a mixture?

   A. apple   **C.** carrot stick

   B. broccoli   **D.** ham sandwich

Links

Writing

Narrative Writing

Suppose you are out walking on a rainy day. Write a **description** of what you see, and mention at least four mixtures. Include one solution and one suspension in your description.

Math

Make a Bar Graph

Use a graph to show the solubility of each of these substances in 100 mL of water at room temperature: sugar, 204 g; salt, 36 g; baking soda, 7 g; and sand, 0 g.

Social Studies

The Bronze Age

Bronze is a mixture of the metals tin and copper. Find out why people mix these two metals. Then research the Bronze Age. Find out what years it covered, and name an important event from that time.

For more links and activities, go to **www.hspscience.com**

FIGHTING FIRES WITH DIAPERS

Firefighters usually use water and chemicals to fight wildfires. But firefighters battling a wildfire near Jackson, Wyoming, fought a fire with a new weapon: disposable diapers.

Well, actually it is the chemical found in disposable diapers that is used. The chemical is now being used across the country as an effective weapon against fire.

Firefighting Gel

Inside a disposable diaper is a chemical called *polyacrylate* (pah•lee•AK•rih•layt). This chemical draws moisture away from babies' bottoms. Scientists have been able to use the chemical, in a gel form, as a fire retardant.

What happens is that when a fire breaks out near a house, firefighters can spray the gel, nicknamed "green slime," wherever they need it. The gel stays put for hours and can be rinsed off with a hose once danger has passed.

During the Jackson, Wyoming, fires, the gel was sprayed on nearly 200 houses. Because the green slime doesn't burn, it protected the houses from the fire. And as one fire department official said, "It is well worth being slimed to save your house."

THINK ABOUT IT

1. Why is it important that homeowners be able to wash the green slime away with water?
2. Why would putting the chemicals into a gel form help fight fires?

Find out more! Log on to
www.hspscience.com

MARIE CURIE
Scientific Pioneer

Marie Curie (1867–1934) was a French scientist. She changed science forever and was the first woman to win the Nobel Prize.

Curie worked with her husband, Pierre. Together, they discovered the element radium. They also explored the idea of radiation. Now, doctors use radiation to find and treat diseases.

Marie Curie was born in Warsaw, Poland, on November 7, 1867. Her father inspired her to study science. He taught high school physics. Later, Curie moved to France. That's where she met and married Pierre Curie.

A Nobel Prize medal

Career Nuclear Medicine Technologist

A nuclear medicine technologist uses radiation to take pictures inside a medical patient. First, the patient swallows a liquid that has a safe dose of radioactive material in it. The technologist then uses special cameras to take 3-D pictures. By looking at how the liquid moves through the patient, a doctor can learn if there are any problems.

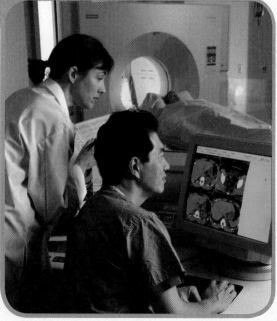

SCIENCE Projects
for Home or School

You Can Do It!

Quick and Easy Project

Materials
- deep container of water
- 2 identical marbles
- 2 balloons

Don't Be Dense!

Procedure

1. Find the mass of each marble to make sure they are identical.
2. Put a marble inside each balloon.
3. Knot one balloon close to the marble.
4. Blow some air into the other balloon, and knot the balloon close to its mouth.
5. Put both balloons in the water, and observe what happens.

Draw Conclusions
Which balloon has more mass? Which has more volume? Which has more density? Which balloon floats? Explain.

Design Your Own Investigation

Cooling Off
You have learned that particles move more slowly as their temperature drops. How could you use a round balloon, a tape measure, and a freezer to prove that air particles move closer together as they get colder? Write the steps for a procedure and the results you expect—your prediction. Then carry out the experiment to test your prediction.

367

Vocabulary Review

Use the terms below to complete the sentences. The page numbers tell you where to look in the chapter if you need help.

mass p. 343   **solid** p. 350
volume p. 344   **liquid** p. 350
density p. 344   **solubility** p. 361
state of matter p. 350   **suspension** p. 362

1. When some solids get warm enough, they become a _____.

2. When a liquid gets cool enough, it becomes a _____.

3. Mass divided by volume is _____.

4. The amount of a substance that can be dissolved in another substance is the measure of its_____.

5. Gas is one _____.

6. If particles settle out of a mixture, the mixture is a _____.

7. The amount of space an object takes up is its _____.

8. _____ is the measure of the amount of matter an object has.

Check Understanding

Write the letter of the best choice.

9. Which of these is made of matter?
   A. a dream   **C.** happiness
   B. a book   **D.** an idea

10. Which of these is a mixture?
    F. pail of sand and soil
    G. copper wire
    H. ring of pure gold
    J. pinch of salt

11. **MAIN IDEA AND DETAILS** Which of these is an example of a solution?
    A. granola   **C.** pizza
    B. iced tea   **D.** salad

12. Which of these has no definite volume?
    F. gas   **H.** matter
    G. liquid   **J.** solid

13. **CAUSE AND EFFECT** Which of these probably has the **most** mass?
    A. apple   **C.** brick
    B. balloon   **D.** golf ball

14. Which term best describes the contents of this glass?

    F. density   **H.** suspension
    G. mass   **J.** volume

15. Which is a measure of how closely particles are packed together?

A. density   **C.** solubility

B. matter   **D.** volume

16. Which has mass and takes up space?

F. height   **H.** volume

G. matter   **J.** weight

Inquiry Skills

17. Compare the arrangement of particles in a solid with the arrangement of particles in a gas.

18. Two boxes are the same size and have the same density. What can you **infer** about their masses?

Critical Thinking

19. You have a red box and a black box that are exactly the same size. The red box is heavier than the black one. What does this tell you about the physical properties of the boxes?

20. The air around us is a mixture of nitrogen, oxygen, carbon dioxide, and other gases. This morning, the air outside looked like Picture A below. Right now, the air outside looks like Picture B.

Part A Use the terms *solution* and *suspension* to describe the air this morning and the air right now.

Part B Explain how air can be a mixture, a solution, and a suspension.

Picture B

Picture A

Chapter 11 Changes in Matter

Lesson 1 What Is Matter Made Of?

Lesson 2 What Are Physical Changes in Matter?

Lesson 3 How Does Matter React Chemically?

Vocabulary

atom
element
change of state
physical change
physical property
chemical property
chemical change
chemical reaction
compound

What do YOU wonder?

The shrinking of a sea left this ship behind. What happened to the sea floor? What is happening to the outside of the ship?

What Is Matter Made Of?

Tiny Circles Each of the little peaks on the oval marks an iron atom. Iron atoms are very tiny. It would take more than 40 million iron atoms to make a 1-cm-long line. In the Investigate, you will observe a way that matter can change.

A Solution to the Problem

Materials
- iodized salt
- kosher salt
- sea salt
- granulated sugar
- powdered sugar
- brown sugar
- 6 spoons
- 6 paper plates
- 6 plastic cups
- water

Procedure

1. Place a small amount of each kind of salt and each kind of sugar on its own plate.

2. **Compare** each sample's color and texture. **Record** your observations.

3. **Compare** the grain sizes of the samples. **Record** your observations.

4. Place the same amount of water in each of the six cups. Use a clean spoon to place the same amount of each sample in its own cup. Stir. **Record** your observations.

Step 1

Step 4

Draw Conclusions

1. Which samples—the light-colored ones or the darker-colored ones—mixed into the water more quickly?

2. Which samples—the ones with larger grains or the ones with smaller grains—mixed into water more quickly?

3. **Inquiry Skill** Scientists interpret data to draw conclusions. What can you conclude about how color and grain size affect the speed with which a sample mixed into water?

Investigate Further

Sequence the samples by how quickly they mixed into water. Predict where sugar cubes will fit in your list. Test your prediction.

Reading in Science

VOCABULARY
atom p. 376
element p. 378

SCIENCE CONCEPTS
▶ that matter is made up of atoms
▶ that an element is a substance made up of just one kind of atom

READING FOCUS SKILL
MAIN IDEA AND DETAILS
Look for details about atoms.

```
        Main Idea
     /      |      \
 detail   detail   detail
```

Basic Properties of Matter

What do your bed, the water in the ocean, and the air in your classroom all have in common? Not much, really. In fact, they have only one thing in common—they are all examples of matter. As you learned earlier, matter is anything that has mass and takes up space.

Sunlight is not matter. A light room does not have more mass than a dark room has. An idea also is not made of matter. Your brain doesn't take up more space when you think hard.

What is matter made of, though? You know that it has different properties. How does it come together to make the things you see and touch?

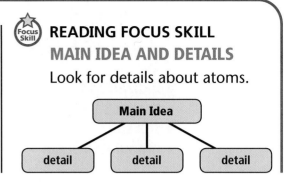

Like matter, these toy pieces can be put together to form objects of many shapes and sizes. Each object has mass and takes up space. ▶

The soccer ball at the right has more mass than the one at the left. Where does the extra mass come from? ▶

Air is something around you every day. You need it to breathe. You know it is matter. The two balls on this page show that you can squeeze different amounts of it into a container.

The fact that you can squeeze more and more air into a container is evidence. It hints at the size of the particles of matter. You can't see the particles. With an air pump you can pack more and more of them into the same space. They must be very small.

Other properties of matter are also hints. Substances have properties such as solubility, mass, and hardness. As you learned in the Investigate, some materials act differently when mixed with water. You also know that metal knives are heavier and harder than

plastic ones. So, some particles must be heavier or hold together more tightly. These differences are because the tiny particles that make up each substance are different. In the rest of this lesson, you'll learn more about these particles.

 MAIN IDEA AND DETAILS How do you define *matter*?

Insta-Lab

Diving Bell

Hold a cup upside down in a bowl of water, and then remove it. Is it wet inside? (If you can't tell, tape a wadded-up tissue inside the bottom of the cup and try again.) What do you think happened?

Particles of Matter

More than 2000 years ago, a Greek thinker named Democritus (dih•MAHK•ruh•tuhs) had an idea about matter. Democritus said that all matter is made up of tiny particles, or bits. He said that different kinds of matter are made up of different kinds of particles. And he thought that these particles could not be split endlessly into smaller parts.

Democritus didn't experiment or test his ideas in any way. Still, it turns out that he was partly right. We now know that matter can be broken down only so far. If you divide something into smaller and smaller particles, you end up with an atom. An **atom** is the smallest possible particle of a substance.

Science Up Close

1 How small can something get? Start with a bag of charcoal briquets. It is about $\frac{1}{2}$ m long, and it has a fair amount of mass.

2 It's easy to break down the contents of the bag into smaller parts. This is one briquet. It is about 5 cm square, and it has a small mass.

3 Can you break the briquet into smaller pieces? Yes. Each of the large chunks is 1 or 2 cm across and has a smaller mass than a whole briquet.

As you might guess, an atom is very small. It's really, really small. In fact, it's so small that you can't see it. Even with a regular microscope you couldn't see an atom. Why not? Because single atoms are too small to reflect light! So there's no way you can see a single atom at all unless you use a special microscope.

Democritus made up the word *atom.* It comes from a word that means "cannot be divided." Think about a tank of oxygen. You can divide all the oxygen inside into smaller and smaller parts. But when you get to an oxygen atom, you have to stop. If you break it up further, it won't be oxygen anymore.

MAIN IDEA AND DETAILS What is an atom?

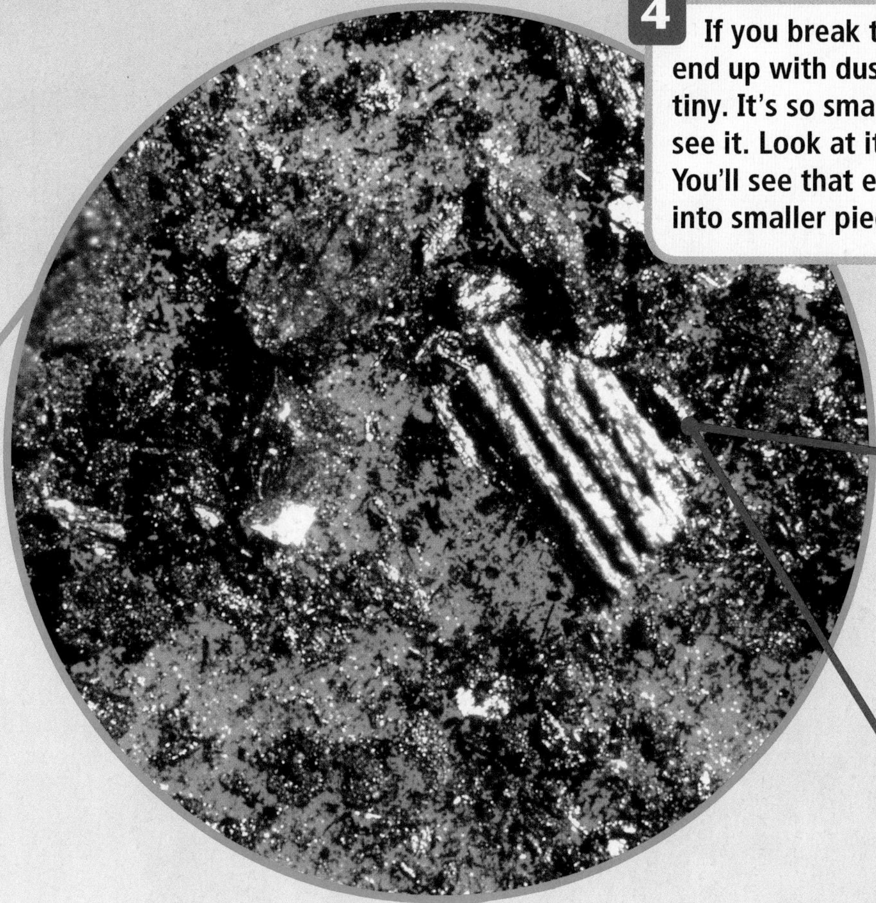

4 If you break the chunks further, you end up with dust. A dust grain is very tiny. It's so small that you can barely see it. Look at it under a microscope. You'll see that even it can be broken into smaller pieces.

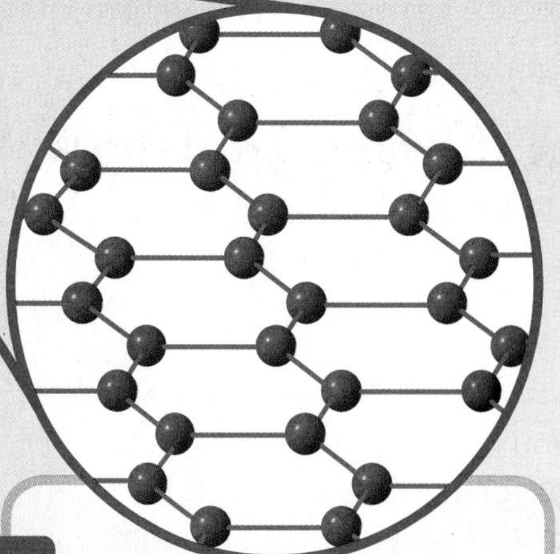

5 This diagram shows how atoms make up the dust grain. This is as far as you can go and still have charcoal.

For more links and activities, go to www.hspscience.com

Elements

You just read that if you were to break all the oxygen inside a tank into smaller and smaller parts, you would end up with an oxygen atom. What if you did the same thing with a drop of water? Would you end up with a single water atom? No, because there is no such thing as an atom of water. The smallest possible particle of water is made up of two different kinds of atoms—two hydrogen atoms and one oxygen atom.

Hydrogen and oxygen are elements. An **element** is a substance that is made up of just one kind of atom. A sample of oxygen is made up of many billions of only oxygen atoms. But a sample of water is made up of many billions of oxygen atoms and hydrogen atoms joined together. So, water is not an element.

Some elements are very common, and you probably know about them. You can see some of these elements on these two pages.

⭐ **Focus Skill** **MAIN IDEA AND DETAILS**
What is an element?

Remember the atoms in charcoal? They were carbon atoms. The pile of dark powder is pure carbon. Carbon is also the element that makes up most of the point of a pencil.

You've already read that oxygen is an element. It is one of several elements that people must have in order to live. Climbers sometimes must carry extra oxygen with them to help them breathe.

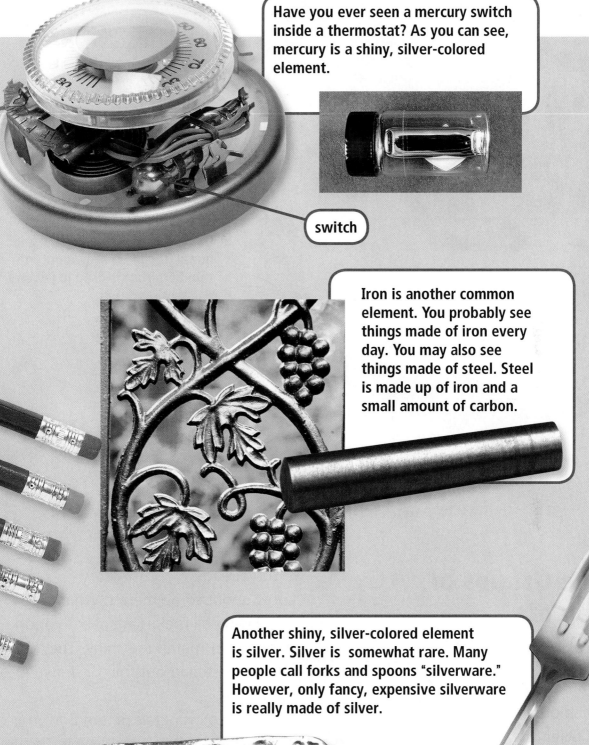

Have you ever seen a mercury switch inside a thermostat? As you can see, mercury is a shiny, silver-colored element.

switch

Iron is another common element. You probably see things made of iron every day. You may also see things made of steel. Steel is made up of iron and a small amount of carbon.

Another shiny, silver-colored element is silver. Silver is somewhat rare. Many people call forks and spoons "silverware." However, only fancy, expensive silverware is really made of silver.

5.0 OZ .999 SILVER

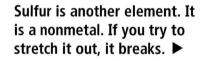

◀ Gold is an element. It is also a metal. It can be drawn out into thin wire that is used in jewelry and in electronics.

Sulfur is another element. It is a nonmetal. If you try to stretch it out, it breaks. ▶

Some Groups of Elements

You've probably noticed that scientists classify things into groups. Forming groups helps people see how things are like each other and different from each other. Scientists have classified elements into several groups. Two of these groups are metals and nonmetals.

Many metals, such as iron, gold, and silver, are elements. However, not all metals are elements. Steel, for example, is made up of at least two elements, iron and carbon.

You already know about some metals. What are some ways all metals are alike? For one thing, most metals are shiny. They can also be stretched out thin or drawn into long wires.

How are nonmetals different from metals? Nonmetals aren't shiny. They're dull. They can't be stretched out thin. Most nonmetals are brittle. They break instead of stretching. Some nonmetals, such as oxygen, aren't even solids.

 MAIN IDEA AND DETAILS Name two groups of elements.

Focus Skill

1. MAIN IDEA AND DETAILS Draw and complete this graphic organizer.

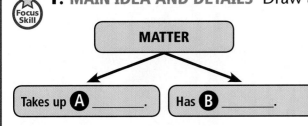

MATTER

Takes up **A** _____.   Has **B** _____.

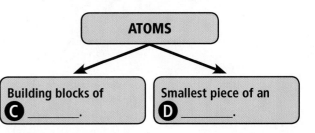

ATOMS

Building blocks of **C** _____.   Smallest piece of an **D** _____.

2. SUMMARIZE Write a summary of this lesson by using each of the lesson vocabulary words in a sentence.

3. DRAW CONCLUSIONS The scientific name for table salt is sodium chloride. Why do you think it has this name?

4. VOCABULARY Make a word puzzle by using the lesson vocabulary words. Be sure to write a clue for each word.

Test Prep

5. Critical Thinking Why is "anything you can touch and pick up" not a good definition of *matter*?

6. Which is the smallest particle of an element?
A. atom   **C.** chunk
B. bit   **D.** grain

Links

Writing

Narrative Writing
Imagine that you have been shrunk down to the size of an atom. Write a short **story** about what you see and do.

Math 9÷3

Identify Place Value
You have read that you would have to line up more than 40 million iron atoms to get a line of them 1 cm long. How do you write the numeral for 40 million?

Social Studies

Explore the History of Science
Did everyone accept Democritus's ideas about atoms 2000 years ago? Do some research. Then write a paragraph about people's reactions to Democritus's ideas.

For more links and activities, go to www.hspscience.com

What Are Physical Changes in Matter?

Fast Fact

Bubble Life Span A scientist once kept a bubble in a jar for three months! It never popped, but it eventually shrank down until the air in the bubble was gone. The shape of the bubble changed, but the substance didn't. In the Investigate, you will observe changes in three liquids over time.

Drop by Drop

Materials • **3 droppers** • **rubbing alcohol** • **safety goggles**
• **water** • **3 plates**
• **vegetable oil**

Procedure

1. CAUTION: **Wear safety goggles.** Place 3 drops of water on one plate, 3 drops of vegetable oil on the second plate, and 3 drops of rubbing alcohol on the third plate. Be sure to use a different dropper for each liquid.

2. Record your observations of each liquid.

3. Repeat Step 2 every half hour for the rest of the school day.

Step 1

Draw Conclusions

1. What did you observe at the end of the day?

2. **Inquiry Skill** When scientists give a possible explanation for what they observe, we say they are making a hypothesis. Then the scientists test the hypothesis. What hypothesis can you make from your observations?

Step 2

Investigate Further

What could you do to test your hypothesis? Plan and carry out an investigation to find out.

Reading in Science

VOCABULARY
change of state, p. 384
physical change,
   p. 386

SCIENCE CONCEPTS
► that solid, liquid, gas are three states of matter
► that physical changes do not make new substances

READING FOCUS SKILL
COMPARE AND CONTRAST
Look for similarities and differences in states of matter.

alike	—	different

States of Matter

Have you ever seen ice cubes melt in a glass? The ice becomes water. Or maybe you've seen water boil away on a stove. It seems to disappear. Whatever you've experienced, you probably figured out long ago that water, ice, and steam are all the same thing.

But this fact isn't as easily known as you might think. After all, ice is cold and hard, and water is wet and soft. Steam is water, too, but you can't see it. And you wouldn't want to feel steam—it's very, very hot.

So, how is it that water can have three forms that are so different? Actually, every substance on Earth can exist as a solid, as a liquid, or as a gas. These are called the *three states of matter.*

A **change of state** occurs when a substance changes from one state to another. Each change of state has its

Liquid
The particles of water in this glass are close to each other. They move quickly and slide past each other easily.

These monkeys get warm by sitting in a hot spring. They are surrounded by water in all three of its states. ▶

own name. If a solid is heated enough, it will eventually turn into a liquid. This is called *melting.* If a liquid is cooled enough, it will turn into a solid. This is called *freezing.*

If a liquid is heated enough, it will turn into a gas. This is called *boiling.* If a gas cools, it will turn into a liquid. This is called *condensing.*

You know that all matter is made up of tiny particles. These particles are always moving. Since ice, water, and steam are all the same substance, they are made up of the same kind of particles.

The difference between them is in the way the particles move. Ice particles don't move around at all; they just vibrate in place. Water particles move easily. Steam particles very quickly fly all over the place.

COMPARE AND CONTRAST **How are the particles of ice, water, and steam different? How are they the same?**

Solid
The particles of ice are locked in place, although they're still vibrating.

Gas
The particles of air in this balloon are far apart and are moving very quickly.

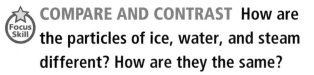

Physical Changes

Look at the pictures of the icicles melting and the water boiling. What do they have in common? They both show changes of state.

Now look at the pictures on the next page. One sheet of paper is being shredded, another sheet of paper is being cut, and wood is being carved with a chain saw. Those pictures have something in common with the pictures on this page. Do you know what it is?

The paper and wood are being changed, but none of these changes is a change of state. All the pictures on these two pages show physical changes. A **physical change** is a change that does not result in a new substance. Changes of state are examples of physical changes. So are shredding, cutting, and carving.

▲ The icicles are melting and becoming water. Ice and water are two forms of the same thing.

Both of these pictures show physical changes taking place.

The water is boiling into steam, a gas you cannot see. Water and steam are two forms of the same thing. ▼

The shredder is changing paper into many, many thin strips of paper. ▼

The scissors are changing a large sheet of paper into two smaller pieces of paper. ▶

This artist is using a chain saw to change a log into a deer statue and wood chips. ▼

How do you know that a change of state is a physical change? Well, you know that ice, water, and steam are all different forms of the same thing. If ice changes to water or water changes to steam, no new substance is made. So, that change is a physical change.

After you shred a sheet of paper, what do you get? You get shreds of paper. And when you cut a sheet of paper in two, you get two smaller pieces of paper. The size and shape are different, but they are all still paper.

The chain saw makes lots and lots of wood chips. They're small, but they're still wood. Since wood is not being changed into another substance, the change is a physical change.

COMPARE AND CONTRAST What do all physical changes have in common?

Insta-Lab

Change It

Take an everyday object, such as a piece of chalk or a sheet of paper. Describe its physical properties—is it smooth or rough, hard or soft, shiny or dull? Now break it or tear it. What are the physical properties of the pieces?

Dissolving

You know that a change of state is a kind of physical change. This picture shows another kind of physical change—*dissolving*. The sugar dissolves in, or becomes evenly mixed into, the hot water in the jar.

How can you tell that dissolving is a physical change? You can let the water in the jar *evaporate*, which is another physical change. After the water evaporates, the sugar is left behind in the beaker. The sugar doesn't change into another substance. It's still there.

Focus Skill **COMPARE AND CONTRAST How is dissolving like evaporating?**

The sugar dissolves in the hot water.

After the water evaporates, the sugar is left behind.

1. **COMPARE AND CONTRAST** Copy and complete the graphic organizer.

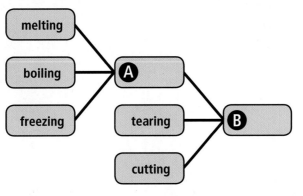

2. **SUMMARIZE** Write a summary of this lesson. Begin with this sentence: *Matter can be in one of three states.*

3. **DRAW CONCLUSIONS** A glass falls to the floor and smashes into hundreds of tiny pieces. Is this a physical change? Why or why not?

4. **VOCABULARY** Write a fill-in-the-blank sentence for each vocabulary term. Show the right answers.

Test Prep

5. **Critical Thinking** A cook adds oil to vinegar and then mixes it to make salad dressing. Is this a physical change? Why or why not?

6. Which might occur if you heat a substance?
   A. boiling   **C.** shredding
   B. freezing   **D.** none of these

Links

Writing

Expository Writing
Imagine that you are helping a younger student learn about science. Write a short **explanation** of the changes that occur when a substance goes through a change of state.

Math 9÷3

Estimate Measurements
Nancy combines 950 mL of vinegar with 800 mL of oil. About how many liters is that in all?

Health

Food Changes
When you eat, your body changes food so that you can digest it. Make a diagram that shows two places in the body in which food undergoes a physical change. (Hint: Read about digestion.)

For more links and activities, go to www.hspscience.com

How Does Matter React Chemically?

Fast Fact

Bang! Zoom! The energy made by two chemical reactions is enough to lift the space shuttle into orbit. Believe it or not, the substance that is made by one reaction is water. In the Investigate, you will find out about another reaction that involves water.

Wet Wool

Materials • 3 pieces of steel wool
• water
• 2 paper plates
• bowl

Procedure

1. Put one piece of steel wool on a plate.

2. Soak another piece of steel wool in water. Then put it on the other plate.

3. Fill the bowl with water, and put the third piece of steel wool in the water. Make sure none of it sticks out above the water.

4. Place all three samples in the same area, away from direct sunlight. Examine them every day for a week. Record your observations.

Draw Conclusions

1. How do the three samples compare?

2. **Inquiry Skill** Scientists can draw conclusions from the results of their experiments. What two things can you conclude caused the changes?

Step 2

Step 3

Investigate Further

What do you predict will happen if you place the three samples in direct sunlight? Carry out a test to find out.

Reading in Science

VOCABULARY
physical property, p. 393
chemical property, p. 393
chemical change, p. 394
chemical reaction, p. 394
compound, p. 394

SCIENCE CONCEPT
▶ that one or more new substances are produced during a chemical change

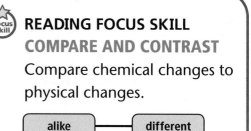 **READING FOCUS SKILL**
COMPARE AND CONTRAST
Compare chemical changes to physical changes.

alike — different

Chemical and Physical Properties

How would you describe a pencil? You might say that it's yellow, that it's long and thin, and that it has six sides. You might say that you use it to write, and that the tip breaks easily.

All of these descriptions have something in common—they all describe the pencil by itself.

Can you also describe something in relation to another substance? Yes, you can. You can describe something by the way it interacts with other substances.

Think about the wood in the pencil. If there is oxygen near the wood and the temperature is hot enough, the wood will burn. So, another description of the pencil might be "It burns if there is oxygen near it and the temperature is very high."

	Physical Properties	
Water	• colorless • odorless • liquid at room temperature	• boils at 100°C • melts at 0°C
Silver	• shiny • soft • silver in color	• boils at 2163°C • melts at 962°C
Iron	• shiny • hard • grayish silver in color	• boils at 2861°C • melts at 1538°C
Sulfur	• dull • brittle • yellow	• boils at 445°C • melts at 115°C

So, now you know two different ways to describe a substance. One way is to tell about its physical properties. **Physical properties** are traits that involve a substance by itself.

Another way to describe a substance is to tell about its chemical properties. **Chemical properties** are properties that involve how a substance interacts with other substances.

Look at the table. You're probably familiar with most of these substances. You're probably also familiar with some of these changes. Have you ever seen rusted iron or tarnished silver?

 COMPARE AND CONTRAST How are physical properties different from chemical properties?

Boiling Mad

Which substance in the graph has the highest boiling point? Which has the lowest boiling point?

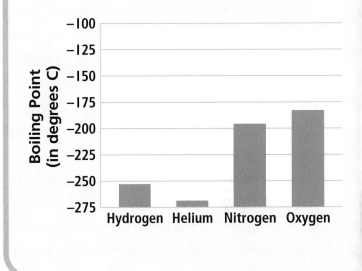

Chemical Properties
• reacts with calcium metal to release hydrogen gas • many substances dissolve easily in it
• does not react with many other substances • does not react with air • reacts with ozone or sulfur to form tarnish
• reacts easily with many other substances • reacts with oxygen to form the minerals hematite and magnetite • reacts with oxygen in presence of water to form rust
• reacts with any liquid element • reacts with any solid element except gold and platinum • reacts with oxygen to form sulfur dioxide, a form of air pollution

◀ Notice that in the table, one particular word is used in nearly every line. That word is *react* or *reacts.* What does that word mean in science? Well, it's a big topic, and you'll start reading about it on the next page.

393

Chemical Changes

You know that hydrogen and oxygen are usually gases. Do you know what happens when hydrogen burns? It combines with oxygen to form water.

This change results in a new substance—water. Clearly the formation of water is not a physical change. A physical change does not result in a new substance. This change is a chemical change. A **chemical change** is a change that results in one or more new substances. Another word for a chemical change is a **chemical reaction**. Now you know what the word *react* or *reacts* means in the table on the previous page. It means "goes through a chemical change."

You know that an element is something made up of only one kind of atom. Since water is made up of hydrogen and oxygen atoms, it is not an element. It's a compound. A **compound** is made up of two or more different elements that have chemically combined.

 COMPARE AND CONTRAST How is a chemical change different from a physical change?

Sulfur in the match head is what helps the match light quickly.

Iron reacts with oxygen in the presence of water to form rust.

Insta-Lab

Bubble, Bubble, Bubble!

Use a funnel to pour some water into a balloon. Then put half of a foaming antacid tablet inside, and tie the balloon closed. What happens inside the balloon? How can you tell?

Silver reacts with sulfur to form tarnish. This helps you know that either sulfur or compounds that contain sulfur were in the air.

Sulfur reacts with oxygen to form sulfur dioxide. Often *reacts with oxygen* means that the substance burns.

Recognizing Chemical Changes

Water is made up of two gases—oxygen and hydrogen. They react to form a liquid. It's easy to understand that a chemical reaction took place. Water is a liquid, not a gas!

There are clues that help you know that chemical changes are probably taking place. You can read about some of them in the table below. But remember that none of these clues is perfect. When water freezes, it becomes solid—a new physical property. But freezing is a physical change, not a chemical change.

 COMPARE AND CONTRAST
Suppose you bake bread. Suppose you draw with a marker on paper. How are the changes in color that occur different from one another?

Before bread dough is baked, it's white or very pale tan.

After the bread is baked, its crust is dark brown. That's because baking causes a chemical change.

The smell of eggs frying tells you that a chemical change is taking place. So does seeing the egg yolk change from a runny liquid to a solid. ▶

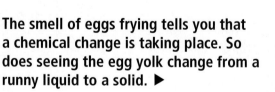

Clues to Chemical Changes		
Clue	**Example**	**Description**
Color Change	Bread dough baking	Changes from white to brown
Smell	Eggs rotting	Gives off a terrible smell
New Physical Property	Iron rusting	Changes from hard and silvery to brittle and reddish brown
Substance Given Off	Wood burning	Smoke is released into the air
Heat Given Off	Sulfur burning	Fire is hot

Focus Skill

1. COMPARE AND CONTRAST Copy and complete the graphic organizer.

	PHYSICAL	BOTH	CHEMICAL
Properties	deal with a substance by itself	describe a **A**_____	deal with how a substance **B** _____ with other substances
Changes	**C** _____ in a new substance	involve a change in appearance	**D** _____ in a new substance

2. SUMMARIZE Write a summary of this lesson by using the lesson vocabulary terms in a paragraph.

3. DRAW CONCLUSIONS A car engine uses gasoline and oxygen. The exhaust given off has water and the gas carbon dioxide. Was this a chemical reaction? Explain.

4. VOCABULARY Use each of the lesson vocabulary terms in a sentence.

Test Prep

5. Critical Thinking Explain why the burning of wood is a chemical change. List as many clues as you can.

6. Which is a chemical property of a substance?

A. what color it is

B. whether it floats

C. whether it burns when oxygen is present

D. what its melting temperature is

Links

Writing

Expository Writing

It is often easier to remember something you've learned if you describe it to someone else. Write a **friendly letter** telling a relative what you learned in this lesson.

Math 9÷3

Estimate Sums

A lab has 22 grams of iron, 14 g of sulfur, 31 g of sodium, and 29 g of potassium. Estimate the total mass of these four chemicals.

Art

Illustrate a Reaction

Choose one of the chemical reactions described in this lesson. Draw or paint a picture illustrating this reaction.

Dear Aunt Suzie,
Today we did a fun science lab.

For more links and activities, go to www.hspscience.com

WHAT A Taste Test

What do you get when you cross blueberries with meat? Sometimes you get a blueberry hamburger! Some scientists hope that blueberry burgers will soon be on your school cafeteria's menu.

Food scientist Al Bushway told *Weekly Reader* (*WR*) that his lab has experimented with adding blueberry powder and blueberry puree (pyoo•RAY) to beef, chicken, and turkey. Puree is a thick paste. It's made when fruit is mashed in a blender.

Why the odd food combination? Bushway says it's a way to increase the nutrition in meat and to make school lunches more healthful. Blueberries are rich in special chemicals that help fight diseases, such as cancer. A serving of blueberries can give kids plenty of calcium, magnesium, vitamin C, and vitamin A. The combination of the vitamins and minerals in the meat and the fruit makes for a healthier meal than just meat alone.

A Colorful Combo?

Do blueberries turn the meat blue? "In beef, you can't see the difference," Bushway told *WR*. "However, ground turkey turns a grayish blue color."

So far, many adult taste tasters have been giving the food the thumbs up. But will it be a hit with kids? One 8-year-old from Illinois said she would love to try a blueberry burger. Her 11-year-old sister didn't feel the same. "I like my hamburger with ketchup," she said.

At Home Taste Test

With an adult's help, kids can try this fruit-and-meat combo at home. Allow about one half to one ounce of frozen blueberries to come to room temperature. Then, with an adult's help, use a blender to puree them. Finally, add the puree to ground hamburger meat. Be sure the mix is well cooked. Then taste it.

THINK ABOUT IT

1. What other foods can help you stay healthy?
2. What are some food combinations that you like to eat?

Spin-In

Find out more! Log on to
www.hspscience.com

HIGH-FLYING SCIENTIST

In 1991, the United States government sent chemist Peter Daum to the Middle East. Daum was not there to fight in the first Persian Gulf War, however. He was sent there to study the environmental effects of the oil fires set by the retreating Iraqi Army during the war.

Daum works for the U.S. Department of Energy's Brookhaven Laboratory. He studies pollution that is in Earth's atmosphere.

When Daum is at home in the United States, he and other scientists spend a lot of time flying in a plane that is an airborne laboratory. The plane's equipment can measure the levels of pollutants in the air.

Career   Food Manufacturer

This is a job to sink your teeth into. People who make, or manufacture, food work with raw fruits, vegetables, grains, meats, and dairy products. They change the raw materials into finished, packaged goods to sell to grocery stores or restaurants.

Quick and Easy Project

Practicing Changes

Materials
- 3 ordinary disposable objects

Procedure

1. Gather three ordinary objects—for example, a sheet of paper, an old button, and a tissue.
2. List at least four physical properties of each object.
3. For each object, try to change each of the properties you listed without changing the substance itself. In other words, put the object through physical changes but not chemical changes.

Draw Conclusions

Which physical properties could be altered by physical changes? Which physical properties could not be altered by physical changes?

Design Your Own Investigation

Demonstrate Basic Properties

Imagine that you are teaching a science class. Some students are having trouble understanding that air has mass and takes up space. Design an investigation that will demonstrate this in a way that is different from the two procedures from Lesson 1. Gather the materials, and carry out the investigation.

11 Review and Test Preparation

Vocabulary Review

Write the term that fits each definition or description. Some terms may be used twice. The page numbers tell you where to look in the chapter if you need help.

atom p. 376
element p. 378
change of state p. 384
physical change p. 386
physical property p. 393
chemical property p. 393
chemical change p. 394
chemical reaction p. 394
compound p. 394

1. A substance having atoms of more than one element that are combined chemically.

2. Describes a substance by itself.

3. Results in a new substance.

4. Describes how a substance reacts with other substances.

5. Process of melting or freezing.

6. Another name for *chemical change.*

7. Process of boiling.

8. Substance having just one kind of atom.

9. The smallest possible particle of an element.

10. Does not result in a new substance.

Check Understanding

Write the letter of the best choice.

11. What is all matter made of?
   A. atoms   **C.** water
   B. oxygen   **D.** wood

12. Which statement about atoms is true?
   F. They are all the same.
   G. All substances are made of just one kind.
   H. You can see them with your eyes.
   J. They are too small to be seen with an ordinary microscope.

13. The diagrams show iron, oxygen, carbon dioxide, and hydrogen.

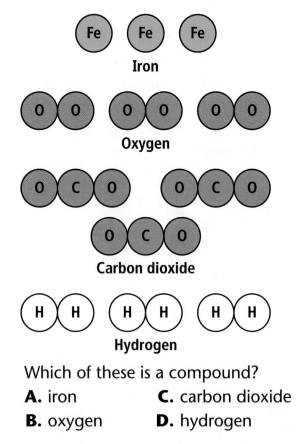

Iron

Oxygen

Carbon dioxide

Hydrogen

Which of these is a compound?
   A. iron   **C.** carbon dioxide
   B. oxygen   **D.** hydrogen

14. An element is made up of how many kinds of atoms?

    F. none

    G. one

    H. two

    J. two or more

15. **MAIN IDEA AND DETAILS** Which always happens during a chemical change?

    A. Matter disappears.

    B. A smell is produced.

    C. A gas is formed.

    D. A new substance is produced.

16. **COMPARE AND CONTRAST** How are physical properties and chemical properties similar?

    F. They both describe how one substance reacts with another.

    G. They both describe a substance.

    H. They both describe the size of a substance.

    J. They both describe a substance by itself.

Inquiry Skills

17. You're watching a chemist work. She mixes a green powder with a blue liquid and then heats the mixture. A yellow gas rises out of the beaker. When she is done, all that remains in the beaker is a crumbly orange solid. Do you think a chemical reaction took place? Explain your **conclusion.**

18. Next, the chemist places a whitish solid in a beaker and heats it. Before long, the solid has turned into a clear liquid. **Hypothesize** what might happen if she continues to heat the beaker.

Critical Thinking

19. Do you think butter can have a change of state? Why or why not?

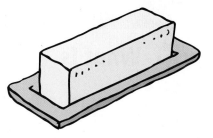

20. Suppose you leave a metal hand tool in a garden for a few weeks. Your area gets rain several times. When you finally pick up the tool, you see orange-brown spots on it.

Part A What are the spots?

Part B Explain what caused the orange-brown spots on the tool.

14 Making and Using Electricity

Vocabulary

static electricity	magnetic field	geothermal energy
current electricity	electromagnet	solar energy
series circuit	generator	chemical energy
parallel circuit	electric motor	mechanical energy
conductor	potential energy	
insulator	kinetic energy	
magnet	hydroelectric power	
magnetic pole		

What do YOU wonder?

These huge machines are turbines and generators. Where might you find them? What do you think they do?

What Is Electricity?

Fast Fact

Ceramic Insulators Insulators are made of a ceramic material through which electricity can't flow. Sparks heat the air around the insulators to 3,000°C (5,400°F) or more! In the Investigate, you'll see what kinds of paths let electricity flow.

Light a Bulb

Materials   • **D-cell battery**   • **flashlight bulb**   • **masking tape**
• **insulated electric wire, about 30 cm with ends stripped**

Procedure

CAUTION: Don't touch the sharp ends of the wire!

1 Using these materials, how can you make the bulb light? Predict the kind of setup that will make the bulb light.

2 Draw a picture of your prediction.

3 Test your prediction. Put the materials together the way your drawing shows.

4 Record your results. Beside your drawing, write *yes* if the bulb lit. Write *no* if it didn't.

5 Make more predictions and drawings. Test them all. Record the results of each try.

Draw Conclusions

1. How must the materials be put together to make the bulb light?

2. **Inquiry Skill** Look at your drawings and notes. How did you record data? Scientists publish their results so that others can check them. Could someone use your records to double-check your tests? Explain.

Step 2

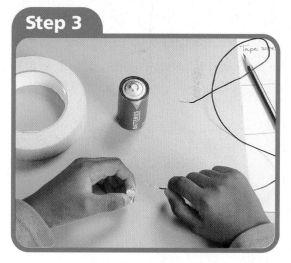

Step 3

Investigate Further

Predict the kind of setup that will light two bulbs at the same time. Test your prediction.

SCIENCE CONCEPTS

▶ what electricity is
▶ how electricity moves

(Focus Skill) **READING FOCUS SKILL**

SEQUENCE Look for the steps by which electricity is generated and the ways it moves.

Static Electricity

Have you ever pulled your sweater out of the clothes dryer and found your socks stuck to it? If so, you have seen static electricity in action. **Static electricity** is an electrical charge that builds up on an object. Static electricity results from changes in matter.

Most of the time, matter is electrically neutral. It has the same number of positive charges and negative charges. The charges cancel each other out, so the matter has no electrical charge.

In the dryer, your socks rub against other clothes. Some clothes gain negative charges. These clothes end up with a negative electrical charge. Other clothes lose negative charges and end up with a positive electrical charge.

Objects with opposite charges attract, or pull, each other. That's why your socks stick to your sweater. Objects with the same charge repel, or push away, each other.

Static electricity stays in an object until something happens to remove it.

◀ **What electric charges make this girl's hair stand on end?**

Objects with the same charges move away from each other. What happens if their charges are different? ▼

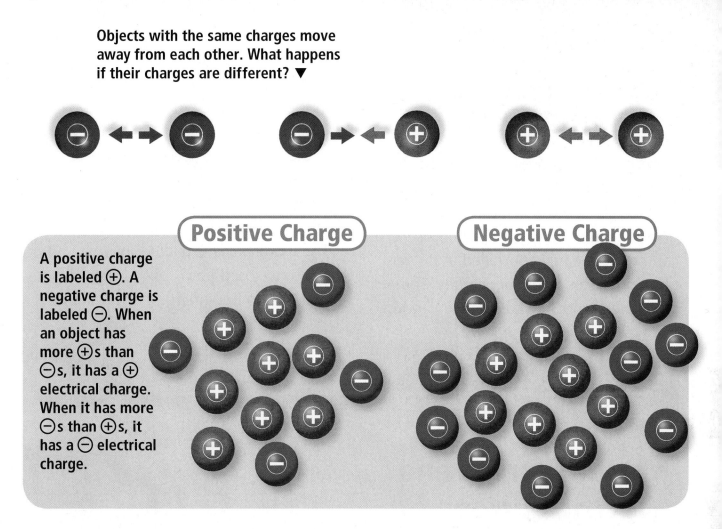

Positive Charge

Negative Charge

A positive charge is labeled ⊕. A negative charge is labeled ⊖. When an object has more ⊕s than ⊖s, it has a ⊕ electrical charge. When it has more ⊖s than ⊕s, it has a ⊖ electrical charge.

Pulling your socks off your sweater forces charges to move. You hear a crackle of sparks as extra negative charges move between the sweater and the socks. Then the socks aren't charged anymore.

Lightning is caused by static electricity. During a storm, ice crystals in clouds rub together and gain negative charges. The ground loses negative charges, so it has a positive charge. Soon the difference in charges becomes large. Negative charges move from the clouds to the ground as a giant spark. Flash! You see lightning.

 SEQUENCE Explain the sequence of events that leads to a flash of lightning.

Insta-Lab

Pull Together or Push Apart?

Blow up two balloons. Rub one with wool. Hold it up to a wall. What happens? Tie a string to each balloon. Rub the balloons together. Hold them by their strings. Put them close together. What happens? Why?

Current Electricity

Static electricity is one form of electricity. Another form is **current electricity**, or a steady stream of charges. In current electricity, an electric current moves through a material such as a copper wire.

Current electricity is more useful to people than static electricity because it can be more easily controlled. A power plant produces a flow of charges. The plant then sends the current along wires to homes and businesses, where people use it to provide light and heat and to run machines.

In the Investigate, you lit a bulb by using an electric current. The battery was the source of the current. The current moved along a path that linked the battery and bulb. The path that an electric current follows is a circuit.

The word *circuit* is related to *circle* and refers to a closed path. Like a circle, a circuit has no beginning or end. Charges

Science Up Close

Water Current and Electric Current

The water in this fountain follows an unbroken path, or circuit. The pump lifts the water, which then falls down through the fountain. ▶

Pump

flow around a circuit without starting or stopping. For any electrical machine to work, the circuit must be complete, or closed.

In the Investigate, the bulb lit only when the path of wire connecting it to the battery was closed. You needed a circuit with no gaps in it. Unhooking a wire at any point broke the circuit, leaving it incomplete, or open. Then the bulb stayed dark because no electric current flowed through it.

Light bulbs aren't the only things that work when they are part of a closed circuit. Turning the key in a car's ignition closes a circuit. The closed circuit starts the car's engine. Pushing the power button on a computer closes a circuit and starts the computer. Closing an electrical circuit can make a doorbell ring or the beaters of an electric mixer spin.

SEQUENCE What happens when a driver presses on the steering wheel to honk the horn of a car?

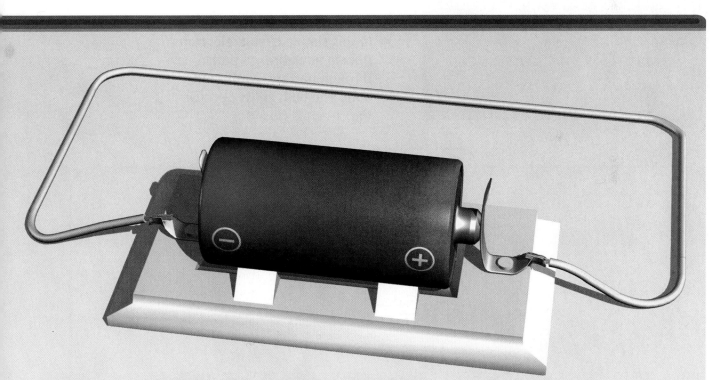

▲ An electric current follows a circuit. Like the pump, the battery provides energy to the circuit.

 For more links and activities, go to **www.hspscience.com**

477

Electrical Circuits

Electrical circuits are not all laid out in the same way. A circuit that has only one path for the current to follow is a **series circuit**.

A simple example has two bulbs, one battery, and wires. The current flows in a path from the battery, through the first bulb, through the second bulb, and back to the battery. While both bulbs are in place and undamaged, they glow. But the flow of charges stops if either bulb burns out or is unscrewed. If one part of a series circuit fails, the whole circuit fails.

A **parallel circuit** has more than one path for the electric current to follow. If something stops charges from moving along one path, they can take another.

In the pictures of a parallel circuit, you can see two circular paths. The current can travel through both bulbs and light them both. If one bulb is missing or damaged, however, the current can still travel through the other bulb. Breaking

◀ In this simple circuit, electrons flow in an unbroken path through battery, wires, and bulb. The bulb lights because the circuit is closed.

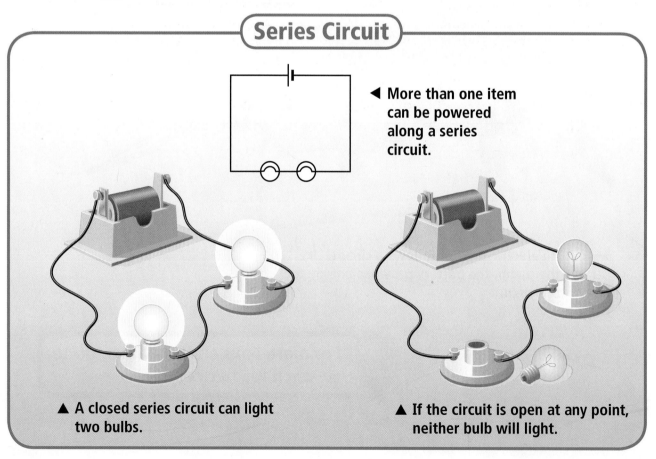

Series Circuit

◀ More than one item can be powered along a series circuit.

▲ A closed series circuit can light two bulbs.

▲ If the circuit is open at any point, neither bulb will light.

Parallel Circuit

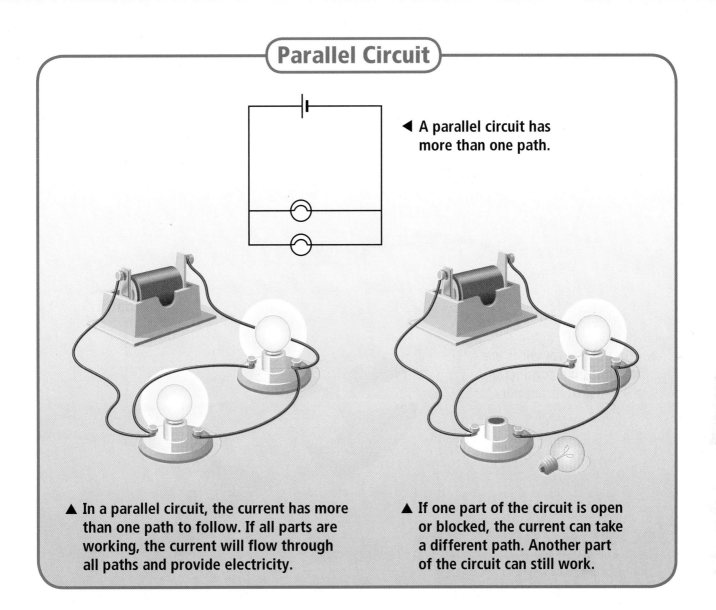

◄ A parallel circuit has more than one path.

▲ In a parallel circuit, the current has more than one path to follow. If all parts are working, the current will flow through all paths and provide electricity.

▲ If one part of the circuit is open or blocked, the current can take a different path. Another part of the circuit can still work.

one path doesn't stop the current. When one part of a parallel circuit fails, other parts of the circuit continue to work. The electric current still has a path along which it can travel.

Think of electrical circuits as streets in a city. A series circuit is like a single street that goes around in a circle. If the street is blocked at any point, all traffic stops. A parallel circuit is more like several streets that cross one another. If traffic backs up on one street, cars and buses can turn and take a different route.

Series and parallel circuits make many devices work. In a flashlight, a series circuit lets current flow between the batteries and the bulb. Homes and schools have many lights. These lights are wired in parallel circuits. Any of these lights can work alone, or many can work at the same time. If one light burns out or is turned off, the others can still work because the electric current travels through parallel circuits.

SEQUENCE Describe the path of current in a two-bulb series circuit.

Insulators

The plastic coating on the wires and the rubber handles on the pliers are insulators. They stop currents. ▼

Conductors

Insulator

▲ **Most electrical wires are made from a conducting metal, such as copper.**

Electrical Conductors and Insulators

It's no secret that electricity is dangerous. It can cause painful shocks, burns, injuries, or even death. Parents often put plastic covers over wall outlets. The covers stop small children from poking their fingers into the outlets. Yet it's safe to touch the electrical cord of a lamp or an appliance. Have you ever wondered why?

The answer is connected with the properties of materials. Some materials, called **conductors**, let electric charges move through them easily. Other materials, called **insulators**, do not.

Most metals are good conductors of electricity. That's why the working parts of an electrical outlet are metal. Most electrical wires are metal, too—usually copper. You should never touch any bare metal electrical wires at home. The electrical cords of appliances have a coating of plastic or rubber around the metal wire to protect you when you handle them. Plastic and rubber are good insulators.

Many everyday things do their jobs safely and well because of the way insulators and conductors work together. If you look at the bottom of a light bulb,

480

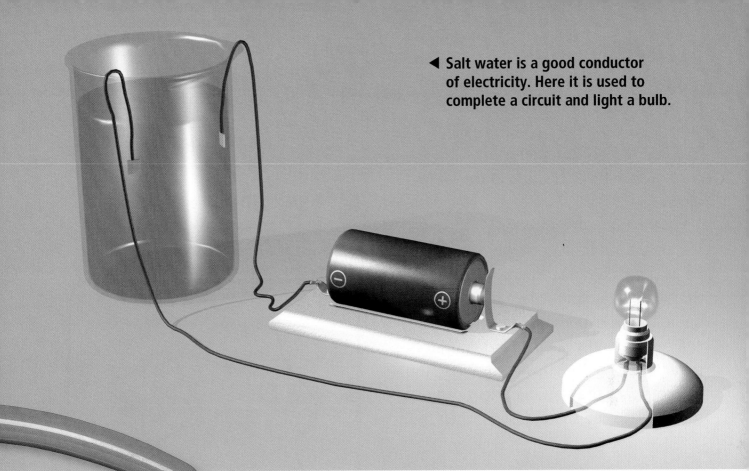

◄ Salt water is a good conductor of electricity. Here it is used to complete a circuit and light a bulb.

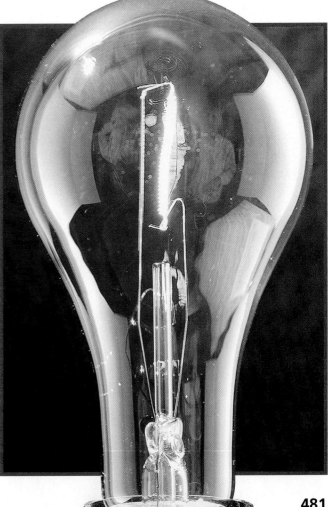

Light comes from a bulb because an electric current makes a thin wire inside it glow. ▶

you will see the small metal tip that conducts the current from the socket into the bulb. Just above the tip, you will see a black band. This band is an insulator. It does not allow the current to flow from the metal tip to the metal screw threads above it.

 SEQUENCE What happens when a current reaches a conductor? What happens when it reaches an insulator?

481

Switches

A switch is a device that opens or closes a circuit. When you switch on a lamp, you close the circuit. You allow two conductors to touch so that the current can flow. The bulb in the lamp glows.

When you switch off a lamp, you open the circuit. An insulator—which may be as simple as an air space—separates the two conductors. When the circuit is open, the bulb doesn't glow.

A switch works like the kind of bridge that can be raised or lowered. When the switch opens the circuit, current can't travel across the space, just as when the bridge is up, traffic can't travel across the river. When the bridge is lowered, traffic can continue across the river. In the same way, when the switch closes the circuit, current can travel through it once again.

SEQUENCE Describe the flow of current through an electric heater when the heater is switched on.

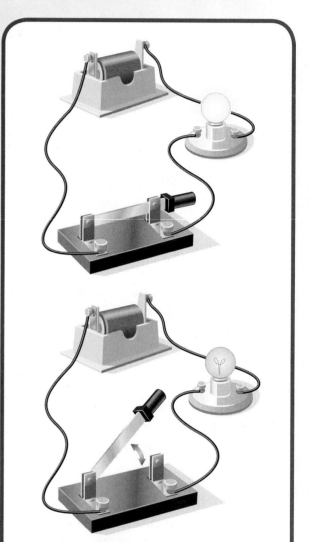

Find the switches in these pictures. Why is the bulb glowing in one circuit but not the other?

Some switches are levers that you flip. Some are buttons that you push. ▼

1. SEQUENCE Copy and complete the graphic organizer. Write these terms in the boxes to describe a working series circuit.

wire   switch   more wire   bulb   battery or wall outlet

2. SUMMARIZE Use the graphic organizer to tell what a circuit is and how it works.

3. DRAW CONCLUSIONS Suppose you want to decorate a room for a party. You plan to buy strings of lights. Which type of circuit would it be better to get? Why?

4. VOCABULARY How are insulators and conductors different? Why are both important?

Test Prep

5. Critical Thinking How are static electricity and current electricity alike? How are they different?

6. What does a switch bring together?
A. circuits   C. currents
B. conductors   D. charges

Links

Writing

Expository Writing
Write a **report** about a charge that travels through a circuit. Tell how it moves from a power plant, where electricity is generated, to the lights in your home and back to the power plant.

Math

Compare Whole Numbers
Electrical power is measured in units called watts. Which light bulb do you think would burn brighter—a 100-watt bulb or a 60-watt bulb? Explain.

Music

Compose a Tune
Connect some bells and buzzers in series and parallel circuits with switches. Use the switches to make the bells and buzzers play a rhythm or a tune.

For more links and activities, go to www.hspscience.com

How Are Electricity and Magnetism Related?

Fast Fact

Mighty Magnets! The world's strongest magnets are made from iron, boron, and neodymium, a metal. A tiny 50-mm (2-in.) magnet made of these materials can lift up to 30 kg (66 lb)! This sculpture uses pairs of these strong magnets. In the Investigate, you'll learn how to make a different kind of magnet.

Can Electricity Make a Magnet?

Materials
- bar magnet
- small compass
- sheet of cardboard
- tape
- D-cell battery
- 30-cm length of insulated wire with stripped ends

Procedure

1. Move a bar magnet around a compass. Observe what the compass needle does. Put the magnet away.

2. Tape the battery to the cardboard. Tape one end of the wire to the flat end of the battery. Leave the other end loose.

3. Tape the wire to the cardboard in a loop, as shown in the picture.

4. Place the compass on top of the loop. Observe the direction in which the compass needle points.

5. Touch the loose end of the wire to the pointed end of the battery. Observe what the compass needle does. Record your observations.

Draw Conclusions

1. How does a magnet affect a compass needle?

2. How does an electric current affect a compass needle?

3. **Inquiry Skill** Compare electricity and magnetism. How are they alike?

Step 3

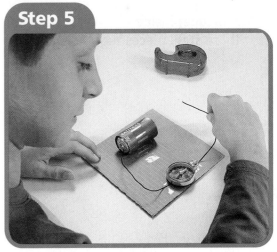

Step 5

Investigate Further

Repeat steps 4 and 5, with the compass *under* the loop. Compare your observations.

SCIENCE CONCEPTS
▶ how electric currents are like magnets
▶ how generators and motors work

READING FOCUS SKILL
COMPARE AND CONTRAST
Look for ways in which magnets and electric currents are alike and different.

| alike | — | different |

Magnets

Have you ever played with a magnet? If you haven't, you may want to now! As you move a magnet around and bring it close to objects, you can discover what a magnet does.

A **magnet** is an object that attracts iron and a few (not all) other metals. Magnets attract steel because it contains iron. When you bring an iron object or a steel object close to a magnet, the object moves toward the magnet. Try this for yourself. Place a steel paper clip near a magnet. What happens? Try the same thing with a plastic paper clip. How do your results compare?

All magnets attract iron, but they may not look alike. Some magnets are shaped like bars. Others are U-shaped. Some magnets that stick to refrigerator doors are thin, flat shapes.

A magnet inside the plastic base holds these steel pieces together. ▼

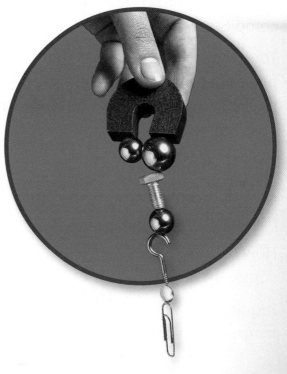

▲ The horseshoe magnet attracts these metal objects. What metal do the objects contain?

Some magnets are shaped like bars.

N S

Why do these plastic letters stick to this refrigerator door? ▶

Distance affects the strength of a magnet's attraction. A small steel object that is close to a magnet moves toward it. However, if the same object is farther away, it will not move toward the magnet.

Other forces can overcome the force of a magnet. Refrigerator magnets stick well to the door, but you can easily pull them off.

Barriers can interfere with a magnet's pull, too. A refrigerator magnet may hold one or two sheets of paper to the door, but if you put too many sheets under it, the magnet will fall.

Magnets can make some other objects magnetic. For example, if you rub a needle over a magnet several times in the same direction, the needle will become magnetic enough to pick up other needles.

 COMPARE AND CONTRAST How are all magnets alike? How are they different?

Magnetic Poles and Magnetic Fields

A magnet has two places at which its force is the strongest. Each of these is called a **magnetic pole**, or *pole* for short. If you tie a string around the middle of a bar magnet and let it swing, one end will point north. That end is the magnet's north-seeking pole. It is often marked with an *N.* The end that points south is often marked *S.*

Forces between magnetic poles act like forces between electrical charges. Opposite poles attract, and like poles repel. If you hold two S poles or two N poles near each other, they push apart. If you hold an N pole and an S pole near each other, they attract.

Magnets of every shape have N and S poles. Try holding two round refrigerator magnets close together. If you turn them in one direction, they attract each other. If you turn them in the other direction, they repel each other.

Magnets keep their poles even if you change their shape. If you cut a bar magnet into pieces, each piece would be a magnet with both an N pole and an S pole.

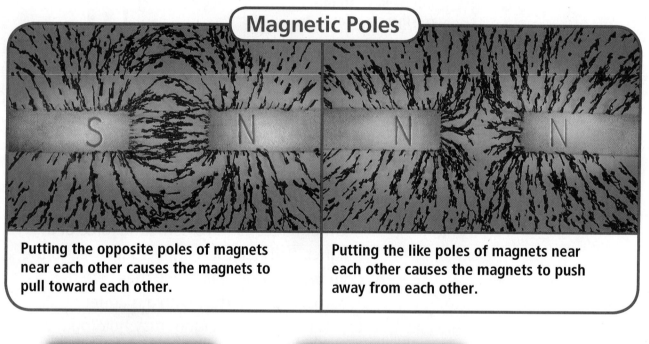

Magnetic Poles

Putting the opposite poles of magnets near each other causes the magnets to pull toward each other.

Putting the like poles of magnets near each other causes the magnets to push away from each other.

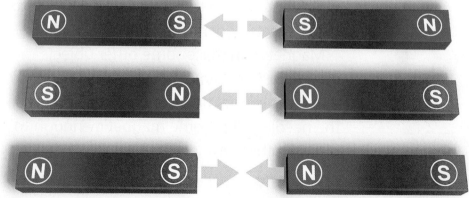

◄ All magnets have N and S poles. Poles that are the same repel, or push apart. Poles that are opposite attract, or pull together.

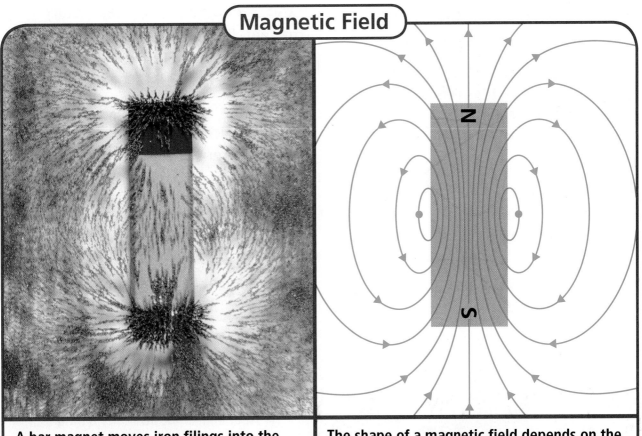

Magnetic Field

A bar magnet moves iron filings into the shape of the magnet's field.

The shape of a magnetic field depends on the shape of the magnet. A magnetic field forms loops all around this bar magnet.

You can use a compass to see a magnet's force. If you put a compass close to a bar magnet, the needle will point toward the magnet's N pole and away from the magnet's S pole.

A **magnetic field** is the space around a magnet in which the force of the magnet acts. If you put iron filings around the magnet, you will be able to see the shape of the magnet's field. The filings will form circles that start and end at the poles, where the magnet's pull is the strongest.

COMPARE AND CONTRAST How are a magnet's magnetic force and magnetic field different?

Insta-Lab

Needle Dance

Place a compass near one pole of a magnet. Then move it all around the magnet. What does the needle do in each position? What does this tell you?

Electromagnets

In the Investigate, you saw that a current of electricity causes a magnetic force. You showed that electricity and magnetism are related.

Actually, an electric current produces a magnetic field around a wire. You can't see the field, but it circles the wire. The field around a single wire is weak. The field around many wires close together is strong. When coils wrap around an iron core, such as a nail, the core becomes an **electromagnet**.

An electromagnet is a temporary magnet. It has a magnetic force only when an electric current moves through the wire. The electromagnet does not work if the current is switched off.

With many coils of wire and a strong current, electromagnets can be made very strong. In junkyards, such electromagnets lift many tons of scrap iron and steel.

COMPARE AND CONTRAST How are a magnet and an electromagnet alike? How are they different?

A steel nail is not normally a magnet, but it becomes one when an electric current runs around it. How can you tell that this nail is now a magnet? What would happen if you took one of the wire ends off the battery?

Math in Science
Interpret Data

In one experiment, a student built and tested an electromagnet. This graph shows the results. What hypothesis was the student testing? How did the student measure the magnet's strength? What conclusion can you draw from this graph?

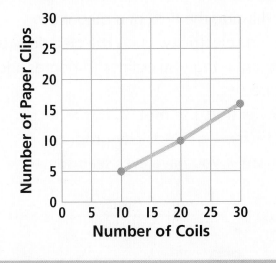

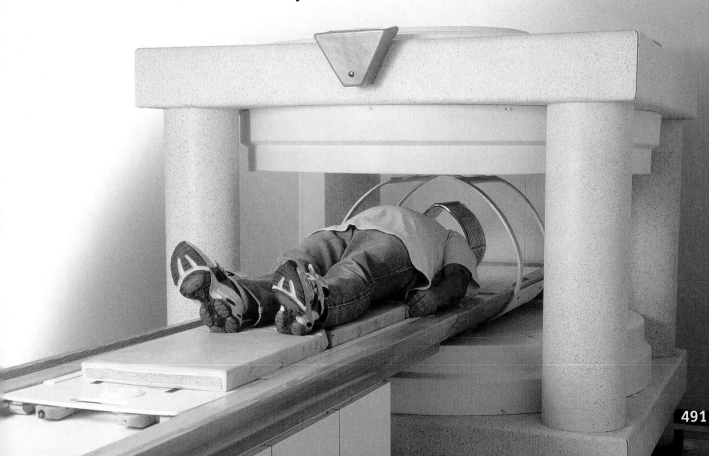

▲ This powerful electromagnet is being used to move scrap iron in a junkyard.

▼ This is an MRI (magnetic resonance imaging) machine in a hospital. It uses a magnetic field to take pictures of the brain, the muscles, and other soft tissues inside the body.

491

Generators and Motors

Electricity can produce a magnetic field. Luckily for us, the reverse is also true—a magnetic field can produce electricity. If you move a coil of wire near a magnet, current electricity flows in the wire. That is how a **generator**, a device that produces an electric current, works.

Any source of energy that can turn a coil of wire in a magnetic field can produce electricity. Hand-cranked generators use human power to turn the coil. During a power failure, you might use a gasoline-powered generator to produce electricity for lights.

Power plants in large cities use many huge generators to produce enough electricity to meet people's needs. Most power plants burn coal, oil, or natural gas. The fuel heats water until it turns to steam. The steam's pressure turns a turbine. A turbine is a machine that produces electricity. The turbine spins a coil inside the field of a magnet to produce electricity. Then the electricity is sent out along power lines to homes and businesses.

Generators use motion to produce electricity. Can electricity produce motion? If you have ever seen someone

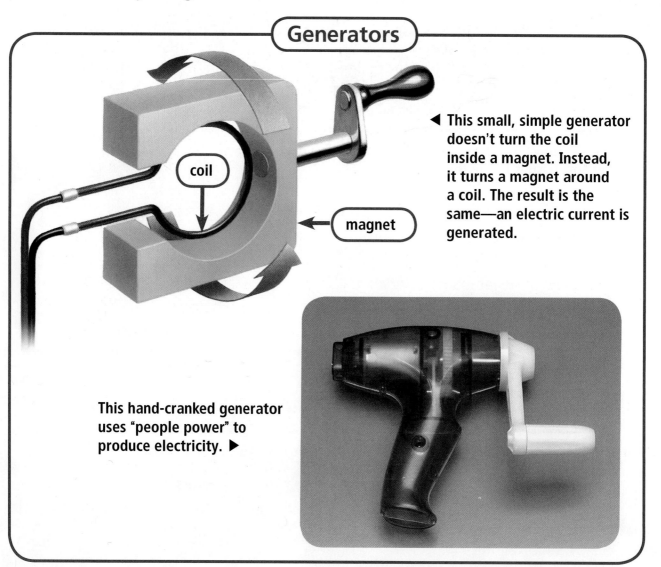

Generators

coil

magnet

◄ This small, simple generator doesn't turn the coil inside a magnet. Instead, it turns a magnet around a coil. The result is the same—an electric current is generated.

This hand-cranked generator uses "people power" to produce electricity. ▶

Motors

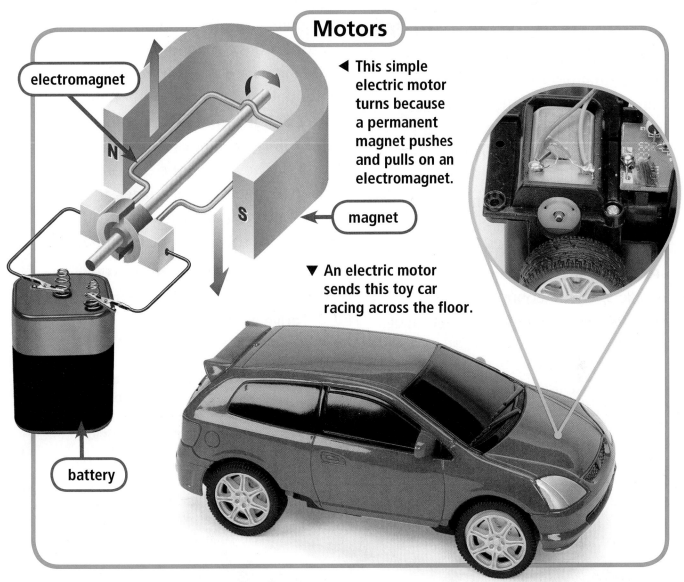

electromagnet

N

S

◀ This simple electric motor turns because a permanent magnet pushes and pulls on an electromagnet.

magnet

▼ An electric motor sends this toy car racing across the floor.

battery

use a mixer or an electric drill, you know that the answer is yes. Such tools have an electric motor in them. An **electric motor** is a device that changes electrical energy into mechanical energy.

In some motors, an electromagnet lies between the poles of a permanent magnet. Like all magnets, the electromagnet has an N pole and an S pole. The poles are pushed away from the like poles of the permanent magnet. They are pulled toward the opposite poles of the permanent magnet.

The motor's shaft turns until the poles of the electromagnet are near

the opposite poles of the permanent magnet. Then the current of the electromagnet reverses. Its N pole becomes its S pole, and its S pole becomes its N pole. The shaft turns again. The current keeps reversing, and the shaft keeps spinning.

Electric motors do many useful things. They start cars. They run CD players. The next time you turn on a fan, thank the inventors of motors!

⭐ Focus Skill **COMPARE AND CONTRAST** How are a generator and a motor alike? How are they different?

Other Uses of Magnets

Generators and motors aren't the only devices that work because of magnets. Compasses point north because they respond to Earth's natural magnetic field. This helps people find their way on land and at sea.

Magnets are used in computers, compact disc players, and magnetic recording devices, such as VCRs. They are also inside headphones, stereo speakers, and telephone receivers. Doorbells and phones ring because of magnets. Even the strip on the back of a credit card is a magnet.

Magnets are used for recording information. On a computer hard drive or floppy disk, for example, electromagnets move across the disk's surface. They make one disk area more magnetic than another. Later, the disk spins under a part called the head. The head reads the magnetic information.

 COMPARE AND CONTRAST How are a videotape and a computer hard drive alike?

When the head inside the VCR records, an electromagnet "writes" a magnetic field on the videotape. When the tape is played back, the magnetic field on the tape produces an electrical signal. ▼

◀ On this computer hard drive, information is stored as a pattern of magnetic fields.

Computers have magnets inside. ▼

▲ A VCR (video cassette recorder) uses electricity and magnetism to record sounds and pictures.

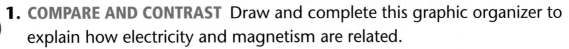

1. COMPARE AND CONTRAST Draw and complete this graphic organizer to explain how electricity and magnetism are related.

Alike	Different
Opposite types **A** _____.	Magnetic **B** _____ interact.
Like types repel.	Electrical charges interact.
	Moving magnets make **C** _____.
	Moving charges make an electromagnet.

2. SUMMARIZE Use the completed graphic organizer to write a lesson summary.

3. DRAW CONCLUSIONS Tell why the relationship between electricity and magnetism is important to people.

4. VOCABULARY Use the terms *electricity* and *magnet* in a sentence to explain how a generator works.

Test Prep

5. Critical Thinking Why is an electromagnet not a permanent magnet?

6. If you turn the N poles of two magnets toward each other, what will they do?

A. attract   **C.** repel

B. produce electricity   **D.** spin

Links

Writing

Expository Writing
Write a **paragraph** for a friend. Tell your friend how an electric motor works.

Math 9÷3

Make a Bar Graph
Test the strength of one magnet by measuring how many paper clips it can pick up. Then test two, three, and four magnets stuck together. Does it matter how the magnets are put together? Make a bar graph of your results.

Social Studies

History of Names
Electricity is measured in amperes, coulombs, ohms, watts, and volts. Find out more about the famous scientists whose names are used for these units of measurement. Share what you learn with the class.

For more links and activities, go to **www.hspscience.com**

What Are Some Sources of Electricity?

Where Does It Come From? Wind farms provide the energy to produce only a small fraction of the electricity used in the United States. In the Investigate, you'll see two kinds of energy.

The Ups and Downs of Energy

Materials
- piece of lightweight poster board, about 30 cm x 70 cm
- ballpoint pen
- masking tape
- books
- marble
- ruler

Procedure

1. Build a "roller coaster" for the marble. Using the ruler, draw a line along both long edges of the piece of poster board, about 1 cm in from each edge. Press hard with a ballpoint pen. Fold up along the marked lines to make walls to keep the marble from rolling off the edges.

2. Place the poster board between two stacks of books so that it forms a valley. Tape the two ends of it to the books.

3. Hold a marble at the top on one side. Let it go, and observe what happens. Does it go past the bottom and all the way up the other side? Hypothesize about what affects the marble's path.

4. Change your setup as necessary so that the marble goes all the way up the hill the way a roller coaster car does.

Draw Conclusions

1. What was the source of energy for the marble?

2. **Inquiry Skill** To make a roller coaster that worked, you had to change a variable. Which variable did you change? Explain.

Step 1

Step 2

Investigate Further

Plan and conduct an investigation. **Determine whether the weight of a marble affects how it behaves on the ramp.**

VOCABULARY

potential energy p. 499
kinetic energy p. 499
hydroelectric power
  p. 500
geothermal energy p. 501
solar energy p. 502

SCIENCE CONCEPTS

▶ how energy changes form

▶ how people produce electricity from other forms of energy

🟊 READING FOCUS SKILL
MAIN IDEA AND DETAILS

Look for forms and sources of energy.

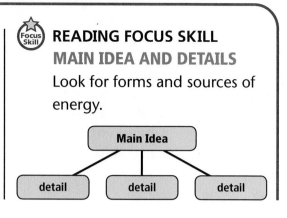

Potential and Kinetic Energy

You can't always see energy, but you know it's there. A pot of water boils on the stove. An egg fries in a pan. Cooking takes a lot of energy. So does moving around. Jet airplanes speeding between cities use energy. So do birds soaring through the sky.

Anytime something gets warmer, gets cooler, or moves, energy is being changed from one form to another. Often you can see or feel the effects of released energy. For example, your body gets energy from food. This energy keeps you alive and provides power for all you do. The energy stored in the food is released in your body. The gasoline used in a car also has stored energy. Burning the fuel releases the energy.

Objects can also have energy because of their position or because of what is done to them. A roller coaster car at the top of a hill has energy. A rubber band has energy when it is stretched. These

◀ The bicycle's position at the top of the hill gives it potential energy. It can coast down the hill.

Kinetic energy is the energy of motion. This bicycle and rider have some kinetic energy. They are moving slowly. ▶

This bicycle and rider have greater kinetic energy. They are moving faster. ▶

are both examples of **potential energy**, or energy due to an object's position or condition. You can't always see evidence of it, but you can guess that it exists when an object is in a high place or in a stretched condition. When an object moves, it has **kinetic energy**, or the energy of motion. You can see evidence of kinetic energy.

How are potential and kinetic energy related? Suppose you push a bicycle up a hill. At the top, the bicycle has

potential energy because of its position. It can coast down the hill. If it does, its potential energy will change to kinetic energy as it rolls downhill.

You can measure kinetic energy. The faster an object moves, the more kinetic energy it has. For example, if you pedal a bicycle slowly, your kinetic energy is less than if you race it at top speed.

⭐ **MAIN IDEA AND DETAILS** What are two main differences between potential and kinetic energy?

Hydroelectric Power

Another good example of potential and kinetic energy is a waterfall. At the top of a waterfall, the water has potential energy. When it falls, it gains kinetic energy. People use dams to change the kinetic energy of falling water into electrical energy called **hydroelectric power**.

Many hydroelectric power plants are on rivers. A dam blocks the flow of the river. A reservoir (REZ•er•vwar), or human-made lake, forms behind the dam. To produce electricity, water is released. The falling water flows through and turns a large, fanlike turbine. The turning turbine causes a generator to spin.

Another kind of dam stores energy by pumping water from a lower reservoir to a higher one. When electricity is needed, the water is released.

A huge dam can produce enough electricity to supply a big city. A small dam can produce enough for a farm or ranch.

MAIN IDEA AND DETAILS What is hydroelectric power?

▼ Dams change the kinetic energy of falling water into electricity.

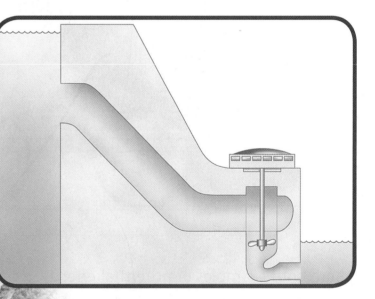

▲ As water flows down from the reservoir, it turns the turbine. The turbine turns the generator, which produces an electric current.

Inside a geothermal plant, heat from below ground is used to make steam that turns turbines.

▲ The Geysers Power Plant in Calistoga, California, is the world's largest producer of geothermal power.

Geothermal Power

It might surprise you to learn that people can use the heat inside Earth. You know that Earth is hot deep underground. Heat from inside Earth is called **geothermal energy**.

In some places, reservoirs of hot water lie 3 kilometers (2 mi) or more below Earth's surface. A deep well can reach the hot water. Then people can pump up the water and use it to heat buildings.

Not all geothermal heat pumps must go so deep. In winter, the upper 3 meters (10 ft) of the ground is warmer than the air. In summer, it is cooler than the air. Pipes can move heat between the ground and a building to warm or cool the building.

Geothermal energy can be used to produce electricity. Most power plants burn coal, oil, or natural gas to produce heat to turn water to steam. The steam turns turbines, and the turbines spin generators. Geothermal power plants don't need to burn fuel for heat. The heat is ready to use right from the ground.

MAIN IDEA AND DETAILS What is geothermal power?

501

Solar Power

You feel heat and see light—two forms of energy—when you go outside on a sunny day. People can use **solar energy**, or the energy of sunlight, to meet some of their energy needs.

Solar energy can heat buildings without any special equipment. The south side of a building gets more sunlight than the other sides. Big windows on the south side can let in sunlight to heat the building.

Solar energy can also heat water. A flat solar panel, or collector, on a roof stores water in clear tubes. The sun shines on this water and heats it. Then the hot water is pumped inside the building for people to use.

Solar energy can also be used to produce electricity. Solar cells use sunlight to produce electricity. This solar power is used to run many devices, including watches, calculators, and outdoor garden lights.

MAIN IDEA AND DETAILS What is solar power?

◀ Solar cells change the sun's energy to electrical energy to power this highway emergency phone.

Insta-Lab

Solar Heating

Take two empty soft drink cans. Put a thermometer into each can, and seal the opening around it with clay. Tape white paper around one can and black paper around the other. Leave the cans on their sides in the sun. What happens? Why?

Focus Skill **1. MAIN IDEA AND DETAILS** Draw and complete this graphic organizer. List details about kinds and sources of energy.

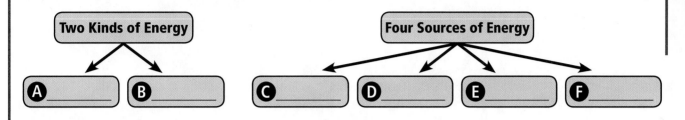

Two Kinds of Energy

A _____ B _____

Four Sources of Energy

C _____ D _____ E _____ F _____

2. SUMMARIZE Use the completed graphic organizer to write a lesson summary.

3. DRAW CONCLUSIONS What energy source do you think people will use most in the future? Explain.

4. VOCABULARY Write a sentence to explain the difference between potential energy and kinetic energy.

Test Prep

5. Critical Thinking Tell how a dam is used to make electricity.

6. Which energy source can provide both direct heat and electricity?
  A. a turbine   **C.** sun
  B. falling water **D.** wind

Links

Writing

Expository Writing

Write a **paragraph** about ways to classify energy. Give examples of different forms of energy. Tell why they are important and how people use them.

Math

Using Angles

Earth's surface absorbs the most solar energy when the sun's rays shine straight down. It absorbs less when the rays strike the surface at a slant. Draw pictures of two solar water heaters on roofs. Show one that would work well and one that wouldn't.

Health

Sun Safety

The sun is a good source of energy, but it also causes risks to human health. Research the dangers of too much exposure to sunlight. Make a list of "Sun Safety Rules" to post in the classroom.

For more links and activities, go to www.hspscience.com

How Do People Use Energy Resources?

Fast Fact

Think Trillions! Energy is measured in kilowatt-hours (kWh). A 100-watt light bulb burning for 10 hours on this Ferris wheel uses 1 kilowatt-hour of electricity. Power plants in the United States generate nearly 4 trillion kilowatt-hours of electricity every year! In the activity, you'll examine some sources of energy.

Energy Sources and Uses

Materials
- 10 index cards (5 yellow and 5 blue)
- pens, pencils, drawing materials

Procedure

1. On each blue card, write *Uses of Energy.* On each yellow card, write *Sources of Energy.*

2. With your classmates, brainstorm ways you use energy every day. Choose five of these ways, and draw a picture of each way on a separate blue card. Label each picture with a word or two.

3. Determine the source of energy for each use you named. Draw and label the sources on the yellow cards.

4. Match your energy source cards with your energy use cards.

5. Exchange sets of cards with classmates, and work to match up their sources and uses.

Draw Conclusions

1. In what ways do you and your classmates use energy? What are the sources of the energy you use?

2. **Inquiry Skill** Sort your cards to classify the uses and sources of energy you listed. Give reasons for the way you sorted the cards.

Step 1

Step 2

Investigate Further

Make cards that show how energy moves and changes from a source through one use of it. Communicate this sequence to your classmates.

VOCABULARY
chemical energy p. 508
mechanical energy p. 509

SCIENCE CONCEPTS
▶ ways people use energy
▶ ways people can save energy

READING FOCUS SKILL
MAIN IDEA AND DETAILS
Look for details about ways people use energy.

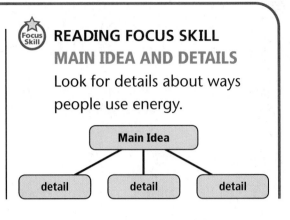

Main Idea
detail	detail	detail

Uses of Electricity

Can you imagine a world without electricity? Strange as it may seem, people have been using electricity for only a short time. Thomas Edison made his first successful electric light bulb in 1879. The first electric power plant opened that same year. That may seem like a long time ago to you, but it's a short time in human history.

The refrigerator was invented in 1913. Microwave ovens were invented in the 1950s, but few people had them before 1970. The first wind farm for making electricity started working in 1980.

Today, we often take electricity for granted. We use it in our homes and in businesses. About one-third of the electricity used in the United States is used in homes. It warms and cools

◀ We use electricity to light our homes, schools, and businesses. Can you imagine living without electric lights?

The heater uses electricity to heat a room. In what other ways do we use electricity for heat? ▼

In computer speakers, electricity is changed to sound energy.

rooms. It heats water for showers. It cooks food, and it keeps food cold to preserve it.

Businesses such as stores and offices use another one-third of our energy. Like homes, these businesses use electricity for heating, cooling, and light. They also use it to run machines, such as computers and photocopiers. Businesses use electricity to keep offices clean and to provide services to their customers.

Another one-third of our electricity is used in manufacturing businesses.

Workers in factories use electricity to make or prepare many of the products we buy. For example, in food processing factories, electricity runs the canning and freezing equipment.

Electricity is used to mine metals and to drill for and refine oil. It is used to make cars, trains, and airplanes. It's hard to imagine what life was like before people learned to use electricity!

 MAIN IDEA AND DETAILS How is electricity used in homes and businesses?

Uses of Chemical Energy

Electricity is an important form of energy. However, it is not the only one we use. We use the energy stored in gasoline to move the cars and airplanes that take people from one place to another. Gasoline also fuels trucks, ships, and trains that carry goods.

Chemical energy is energy stored in the arrangement of particles of matter. Gasoline, which is made from oil, has chemical energy. So do coal and natural gas. Coal, oil, and natural gas all formed inside Earth from the remains of ancient plants and animals. The remains decayed under great pressure millions of years ago.

Because they come from ancient living things, these fuels are called fossil fuels. Fossil fuels remained underground for centuries. Then, people started mining coal and drilling for oil. Today, we burn huge amounts of fossil fuels.

Chemical energy can be changed into other forms of energy. Many power plants burn fossil fuels to change their stored chemical energy into heat. The heat is used to produce steam to turn

This toothbrush moves because a chemical change in its batteries produces an electrical current. ▶

▲ Batteries contain stored chemical energy that can be changed to heat, light, sound, or mechanical energy.

When it is finished, this combustion turbine will work like a jet engine. It will burn natural gas to generate electricity. ▶

◀ This portable generator uses gasoline, which has stored chemical energy. Burning it releases the energy.

the turbines that generate electricity. Car engines burn gasoline to change its chemical energy into mechanical energy. **Mechanical energy** makes machine parts move.

Chemical energy is what makes batteries work. A chemical change inside the battery releases charges from atoms. The current causes CD players to make sound or battery-operated toys to move.

 MAIN IDEA AND DETAILS Explain two ways people use chemical energy.

Insta-Lab

Chemical Energy

Wrap a dry pad of steel wool around the base of a thermometer. Put them together into a clear jar, and close it. Wait 5 minutes. Read the temperature. Remove the pad and thermometer from the jar. Soak the pad in vinegar for 1 minute. Squeeze out the extra vinegar, and wrap the pad around the base of the thermometer again. Put them back in the jar and close it. Wait 5 minutes. Read the temperature again. What happens? How can you explain it?

509

Energy Conservation

Most of the energy you use comes from burning fossil fuels. Today, people are using Earth's stores of energy faster than ever. Fossil fuels were formed millions of years ago. When they have been used up, it will take millions of years for more to form.

When fossil fuels are gone, we will need other energy sources to take their place. It will take time to develop new energy sources, so we must make the fossil fuels last as long as possible. We can do this by conserving, or using less of them.

How can you help with this? You can turn off the TV when you aren't watching it. You can take shorter showers or use cooler water. Talk about ways you can save energy at school. See what you and your classmates can do to conserve energy.

Focus Skill **MAIN IDEA AND DETAILS** **Tell why people should conserve energy.**

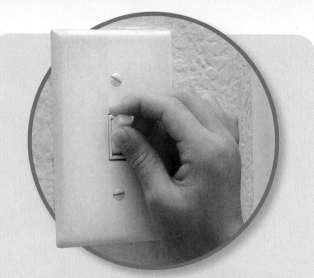

▲ Turning off lights that you are not using is a good way to conserve energy.

▲ Insulation in attics and walls helps save energy. Insulated buildings lose less heat in winter and stay cooler in summer than uninsulated ones.

◀ This car may look ordinary, but it isn't. It's a "hybrid" car. A hybrid car's engine uses both gasoline and electricity.

Focus Skill

1. MAIN IDEA AND DETAILS Draw and complete this graphic organizer. Give details about forms and uses of energy.

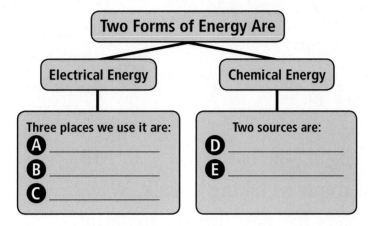

Two Forms of Energy Are

Electrical Energy

Chemical Energy

Three places we use it are:
Ⓐ _____
Ⓑ _____
Ⓒ _____

Two sources are:
Ⓓ _____
Ⓔ _____

2. SUMMARIZE Use the completed graphic organizer to write a lesson summary.

3. DRAW CONCLUSIONS Which kind of energy is most important? Why?

4. VOCABULARY Use the terms *chemical energy* and *mechanical energy* to explain how a battery-operated toy works.

Test Prep

5. Critical Thinking List some things you can do to conserve energy.

6. In which form is energy stored inside a battery?
A. chemical   C. kinetic
B. electrical   D. mechanical

Links

Writing

Persuasive Writing
Write a **letter** someone might send to the editor of your local newspaper. Explain why you think people in your community should work harder to conserve energy.

Math

9÷3

Solve a Problem
Energy use is measured in kilowatt-hours (kWh). *Kilo-* means "one thousand," so 1 kWh equals 1,000 watts used for 1 hour. How long would five 100-watt bulbs need to burn to use 1 kWh?

Literature

Write a Poem
Use a thesaurus to find words related to energy. Use them to write a rhyming poem about ways people can save energy. Trade poems with a partner, and read them aloud. Display your poems on a bulletin board.

For more links and activities, go to **www.hspscience.com**

These BOOTS Were Made for WALKING

In the future, recharging the battery in your MP3 player may be as simple as taking a walk. Why? A California company has developed a material that can be placed in a pair of boots. It changes the mechanical energy of walking into electrical energy that can charge batteries and other devices.

Charge It!

The material is an electroactive polymer that's called "artificial muscle." When a person walks, the electroactive polymer in the boots' soles compresses and releases.

The polymer is a very thin film of rubbery material. It bends when an electric current flows through it. This is why the polymer is called *artificial muscle*. The polymer also works in reverse. When it is bent or squeezed, it makes a weak electric current. A wire connected to the boot can then store the energy in a battery or use it to power a device, such as a cell phone.

Used in the Field

A team of scientists worked for 15 years to develop the artificial muscle. Some of the first people to make use of the material might be U.S. soldiers in the field. By going on a march, soldiers could power up hand-held gear such as computers.

Scientists working on the project believe that the artificial muscle material could also be used by recreational hikers and walkers to power such things as a radio or a CD player.

THINK ABOUT IT

1. What other inventions can you think of that might help U.S. soldiers in the field?
2. How might artificial muscles in your shoes help you?

Spin-In

Find out more! Log on to
www.hspscience.com

LIGHTING THE WAY

Without the help of Lewis Latimer (1848–1929), you would have to read at night by candlelight. Latimer helped to design the electric light bulb.

In the early 1880s, Thomas Edison invented an electric lamp. Electricity passed through a thin thread of carbon to make light. The thread was inside a glass bulb. The thin thread burned out after only a few days.

Latimer worked to design a light bulb that would last longer. In 1882, he succeeded. He later was awarded patents for the new design.

Career   Power Plant Technician

Electricity plays a huge role in our daily lives. The people who make electricity possible are the power plant operators. These technicians control and monitor the machines that generate the electricity to power homes, schools, and businesses. The plant operators also control the complex network of circuits that carries the electricity.

Quick and Easy Project

Insulators and Conductors

Procedure

1. Build a series circuit, but leave two wire ends open. Touch them together to make sure the circuit works.

2. Touch the ends to a test material to see if it will complete the circuit. Does the bulb light? Record your results.

3. Repeat Step 2 for each test material.

Materials

- three 30-cm pieces of wire, with insulation trimmed from the ends
- D-cell battery
- flashlight bulb
- test materials of your choice

Draw Conclusions

Which materials are conductors? Which are insulators? How do you know?

Design Your Own Investigation

Generate Electricity

Does moving a bar magnet inside a coil of wire generate an electric current? You can use a compass to find out. Use wire, a bar magnet, and a compass to build and test a simple generator. Record and explain your findings. How can you make sure that it's an electric current, and not the magnet, that's affecting your compass? How can you make your generator stronger? Test your ideas.

Vocabulary Review

Use the terms below to complete the sentences. The page numbers tell you where to look in the chapter if you need help.

static electricity
p. 474

magnet
p. 486

current electricity
p. 476

electromagnet
p. 490

series circuit
p. 478

generator
p. 492

parallel circuit
p. 478

potential energy
p. 499

conductor
p. 480

kinetic energy
p. 499

1. An object that attracts iron is a
_____.

2. The charge that builds up on an object is _____.

3. A circuit that has only one path for electricity to follow is a _____.

4. The energy of motion is _____.

5. A device that produces an electric current is a _____.

6. A material that electricity can flow through easily is a _____.

7. An _____ is a temporary magnet.

8. Electricity that flows along a wire is _____.

9. The energy an object has because of its position is _____.

10. A circuit that has two or more paths that electricity can follow is a
_____.

Check Understanding

Write the letter of the best choice.

11. **COMPARE AND CONTRAST** What is one way in which all magnets are alike?

   A. They stick to aluminum cans.
   B. They attract iron.
   C. They need a current to work.
   D. They have one or two poles.

12. **MAIN IDEA AND DETAILS** What kind of energy does water at the top of a dam have?

   F. chemical
   G. kinetic
   H. mechanical
   J. potential

13. How do charges move in a circuit?

   A. along two or more paths
   B. along a loop with no beginning and no end
   C. through an insulator
   D. up and down

14. What energy source is used to produce most of the electricity we use today?

  F. fossil fuels

  G. geothermal energy

  H. falling water

  J. wind

15. Which pair is made up of two things that work in opposite ways?

  A. bar magnet and horseshoe magnet

  B. chemical energy and mechanical energy

  C. generator and motor

  D. solar energy and geothermal energy

16. What does an electromagnet have that a bar magnet does not have?

  F. attraction for iron

  G. magnetic field

  H. two poles

  J. wire coil

Inquiry Skills

17. The needle of a compass moves when you put a bar of metal close to it. What can you **infer** from this observation?

18. A student team builds two electromagnets. The students use 20 coils of wire in one. They use 40 coils in the other. Everything else is the same. **Compare** the strengths of the two electromagnets.

Critical Thinking

19. Suggest a practical use for an electromagnet. Explain why it would be a good use for it.

20. Suppose you woke up one morning and one use of electricity had disappeared.

  Part A How would your life change?

  Part B How would your community change?

References

Contents

Health Handbook

Reading in Science Handbook

Math in Science Handbook R28

Your Skin

Your skin is your body's largest organ. It provides your body with a tough protective covering. It protects you from disease. It provides your sense of touch, which allows you to feel pressure, textures, temperature, and pain. Your skin also produces sweat to help control your body temperature. When you play hard or exercise, your body produces sweat, which cools you as it evaporates. The sweat from your skin also helps your body get rid of extra salt and other wastes.

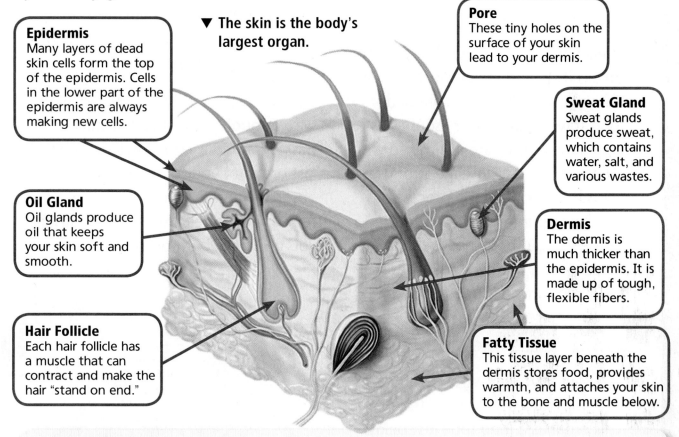

▼ The skin is the body's largest organ.

Epidermis
Many layers of dead skin cells form the top of the epidermis. Cells in the lower part of the epidermis are always making new cells.

Oil Gland
Oil glands produce oil that keeps your skin soft and smooth.

Hair Follicle
Each hair follicle has a muscle that can contract and make the hair "stand on end."

Pore
These tiny holes on the surface of your skin lead to your dermis.

Sweat Gland
Sweat glands produce sweat, which contains water, salt, and various wastes.

Dermis
The dermis is much thicker than the epidermis. It is made up of tough, flexible fibers.

Fatty Tissue
This tissue layer beneath the dermis stores food, provides warmth, and attaches your skin to the bone and muscle below.

Caring for Your Skin

- To protect your skin and to keep it healthy, you should wash your body, including your hair and your nails, every day. This helps remove germs, excess oils and sweat, and dead cells from the epidermis, the outer layer of your skin. Because you touch many things during the day, you should wash your hands with soap and water frequently.

- If you get a cut or scratch, you should wash it right away and cover it with a sterile bandage to prevent infection and promote healing.

- Protect your skin from cuts and scrapes by wearing proper safety equipment when you play sports or skate, or when you're riding your bike or scooter.

Your digestive system is made up of connected organs. It breaks down the food you eat and disposes of the leftover wastes your body does not need.

Mouth to Stomach

Digestion begins when you chew your food. Chewing your food breaks it up and mixes it with saliva. When you swallow, the softened food travels down your esophagus to your stomach, where it is mixed with digestive juices. These are strong acids that continue the process of breaking your food down into the nutrients your body needs to stay healthy. Your stomach squeezes your food and turns it into a thick liquid.

Small Intestine and Liver

Your food leaves your stomach and goes into your small intestine. This organ is a long tube just below your stomach. Your liver is an organ that sends bile into your small intestine to continue the process of digesting fats in the food. The walls of the small intestine are lined with millions of small, finger-shaped bumps called villi. Tiny blood vessels in these bumps absorb nutrients from the food as it moves through the small intestine.

Large Intestine

When the food has traveled all the way through your small intestine, it passes into your large intestine. This last organ of your digestive system absorbs water from the food. The remaining wastes are held there until you go to the bathroom.

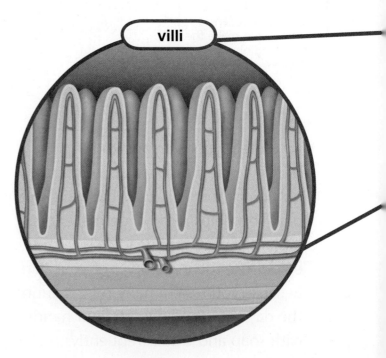

villi

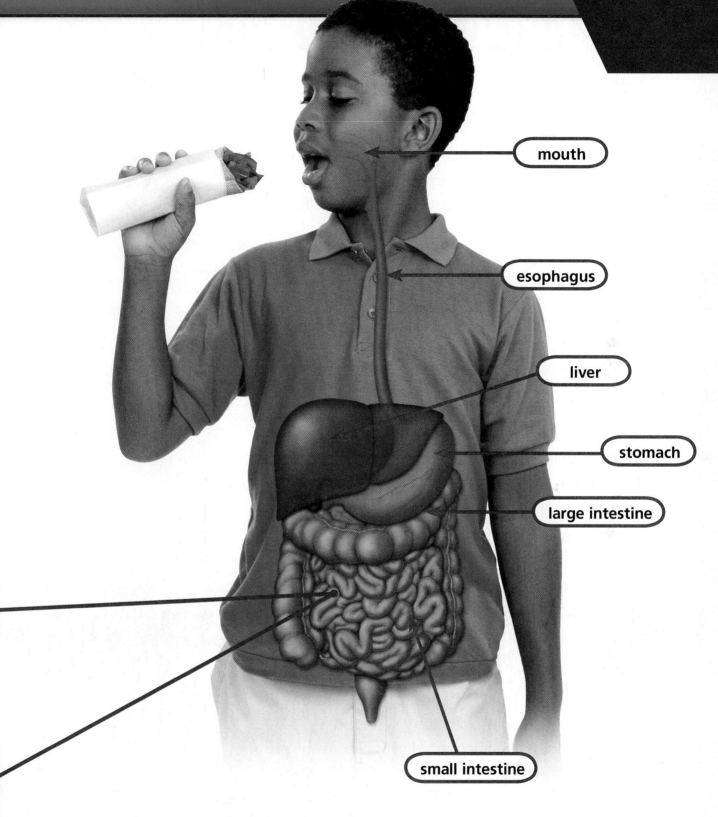

mouth

esophagus

liver

stomach

large intestine

small intestine

Your Circulatory System

Your circulatory system carries to every cell in your body the nutrients your digestive system takes from food and the oxygen your lungs take from the air you breathe. As your blood moves throughout your body, it also helps your body fight infections, control your temperature, and remove wastes from your cells.

Your Heart and Blood Vessels

Your heart is the organ that pumps your blood through your circulatory system. Your heart is a strong muscle that beats continuously. As you exercise, your heart adjusts itself to beat faster to deliver the energy and oxygen your muscles need to work harder.

Blood from your heart is pumped through veins into your lungs, where it releases carbon dioxide and picks up oxygen. Your blood then travels back to your heart to be pumped through your arteries to every part of your body.

Your Blood

The blood in your circulatory system is a mixture of fluids and specialized cells. The watery liquid part of your blood is called plasma. Plasma allows the cells in your blood to move through your blood vessels to every part of your body. It also plays an important role in helping your body control your temperature.

vein

heart

artery

Blood Cells

There are three main types of cells in your blood. Each type of cell in your circulatory system plays a special part in keeping your body healthy and fit.

Red Blood Cells are the most numerous cells in your blood. They carry oxygen from your lungs throughout your body. They also carry carbon dioxide back to your lungs from your cells, so you can breathe it out.

White Blood Cells help your body fight infections when you become ill.

Platelets help your body stop bleeding when you get a cut or other wound. Platelets clump together as soon as you start to bleed. The sticky clump of platelets traps red blood cells and forms a blood clot. The blood clot hardens to make a scab that seals the cut and lets your body begin healing the wound.

blood cells

Caring for Your Circulatory System

- Eat foods that are low in fat and high in fiber. Fiber helps take away substances that can lead to fatty buildup in your blood vessels.

- Eat foods high in iron to help your red blood cells carry oxygen.

- Drink plenty of water to help your body replenish your blood.

- Avoid contact with another person's blood.

- Exercise regularly to keep your heart strong.

- Never smoke or use tobacco.

Your skeletal system includes all of the bones in your body. These strong, hard parts of your body protect your internal organs, help you move, and allow you to sit and to stand up straight.

Your skeletal system works with your muscular system to hold your body up and to give it shape.

Your skeletal system includes more than 200 bones. These bones come in many different shapes and sizes.

Your Skull

The wide flat bones of your skull fit tightly together to protect your brain. The bones in the front of your skull give your face its shape and allow the muscles in your face to express your thoughts and feelings.

Your Spine

Your spine, or backbone, is made up of nearly two dozen small, round bones. These bones fit together and connect your head to your pelvis. Each of these bones, or vertebrae (VUHR•tuh•bree), is shaped like a doughnut with a small round hole in the center. Your spinal cord is a bundle of nerves that carries information to and from your brain and the rest of your body. Your spinal cord runs from your brain down your back to your hips through the holes in your vertebrae. There are soft, flexible disks of cartilage between your vertebrae. This allows you to bend and twist your spine. Your spine, pelvis, and leg bones work together to allow you to stand, sit, or move.

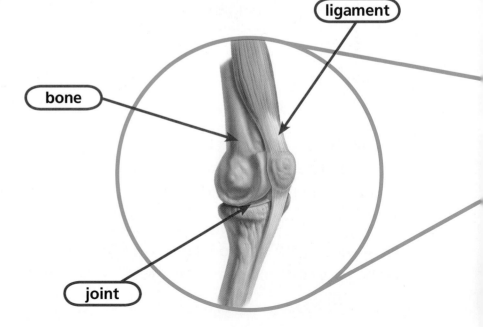

ligament

bone

joint

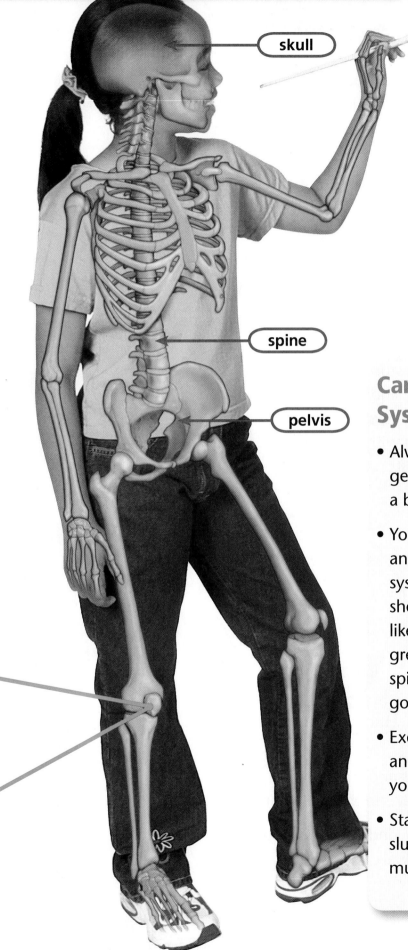

skull

spine

pelvis

Caring for Your Skeletal System

- Always wear a helmet and proper safety gear when you play sports, skate, or ride a bike or a scooter.

- Your bones are made mostly of calcium and other minerals. To keep your skeletal system strong and to help it grow, you should eat foods that are high in calcium like milk, cheese, and yogurt. Dark green, leafy vegetables like broccoli, spinach, and collard greens are also good sources of calcium.

- Exercise to help your bones stay strong and healthy. Get plenty of rest to help your bones grow.

- Stand and sit with good posture. Sitting slumped over puts strain on your muscles and on your bones.

Your Muscular System

A muscle is a body part that produces movement by contracting and relaxing. All of the muscles in your body make up the muscular system.

Voluntary and Involuntary Muscles

Voluntary Muscles are the muscles you use to move your arms and legs, your face, head, and fingers. You can make these muscles contract or relax to control the way your body moves.

Involuntary Muscles are responsible for movements you usually don't see or control. These muscles make up your heart, your stomach and digestive system, your diaphragm, and the muscles that control your eyelids. Your heart beats and your diaphragm powers your breathing without your thinking about them. You cannot stop the action of these muscles.

How Muscles Help You Move

All muscles pull when they contract. Moving your body in more than one direction takes more than one muscle. To reach out with your arm or to pull it back, you use a pair of muscles. As one muscle contracts to extend your arm, the other relaxes and stretches. As you pull your arm back, the muscles reverse their functions.

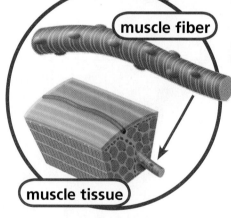

muscle fiber

muscle tissue

Your muscles let you do many kinds of things. The large muscles in your legs allow you to walk and run. Tiny muscles in your face allow you to smile.

arm muscle

Your Muscles and Your Bones

The muscles that allow you to move your body work with your skeletal system. Muscles in your legs that allow you to kick a ball or ride a bicycle pull on the bones and joints of your legs and lower body. Your muscles are connected to your skeletal system by strong, cordlike tissues called tendons.

Your Achilles tendon just above your heel connects your calf muscles to your heel bone. When you contract those muscles, the tendon pulls on the heel bone and allows you to stand on your toes, jump, or push hard on your bicycle's pedals.

Caring for Your Muscular System

- Always stretch and warm your muscles up before exercising or playing sports. Do this by jogging or walking for at least ten minutes. This brings fresh blood and oxygen into your muscles and helps prevent injury or pain.

- Eat a balanced diet of foods to be sure your muscles have the nutrients they need to grow and remain strong.

- Drink plenty of water when you exercise or play sports. This helps your blood remove wastes from your muscles and helps you build endurance.

- Always cool down after you exercise. Walk or jog slowly for five or ten minutes to let your heartbeat slow and your breathing return to normal. This helps you avoid pain and stiffness after your muscles work hard.

- Stop exercising if you feel pain in your muscles.

- Get plenty of rest before and after you work your muscles hard. They need time to repair themselves and recover from working hard.

Your Eyes and Vision

Your eyes allow you to see light reflected by the things around you. This diagram shows how an eye works. Light enters through the clear outer surface called the cornea. It passes through the pupil. The lens bends the incoming light to focus it on the retina. The retina sends nerve signals along the optic nerve. Your brain uses the signals to form an image. This is what you "see."

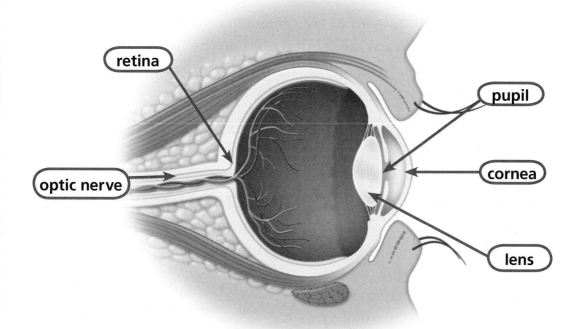

Caring for Your Eyes

- You should have a doctor check your eyesight every year. Tell your parents or your doctor if your vision becomes blurry or if you are having headaches or pain in your eyes.

- Never touch or rub your eyes.

- Protect your eyes by wearing safety goggles when you use tools or play sports.

- Wear swim goggles to protect your eyes from chlorine or other substances in the water.

- Wear sunglasses to protect your eyes from very bright light. Looking directly at bright light or at the sun can damage your eyes permanently.

Your Ears and Hearing

Sounds travel through the air in waves. When some of those waves enter your ear you hear a sound. This diagram shows the inside of your ear.

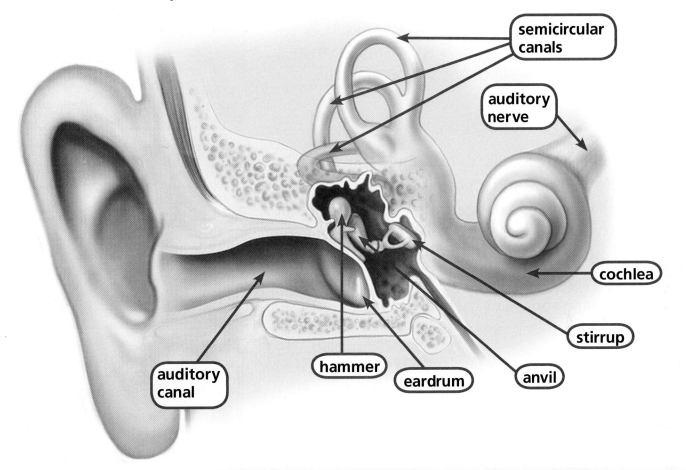

semicircular canals

auditory nerve

cochlea

stirrup

anvil

eardrum

hammer

auditory canal

Caring for Your Ears

- Never put anything in your ears.

- Wear a helmet that covers your ears when you play sports.

- Keep your ears warm in winter.

- Avoid loud sounds and listening to loud music.

- Have your ears checked by a doctor if they hurt or leak fluid or if you have any loss of hearing.

- Wear earplugs when you swim. Water in your ears can lead to infection.

Your Immune System

Pathogens and Illness

You may know someone who had a cold or the flu this year. These illnesses are caused by germs called pathogens. Illnesses spread when pathogens move from one person to another.

Types of Pathogens

There are four kinds of pathogens—viruses, bacteria, fungi, and protozoans. Viruses are the smallest kind of pathogen. They are so small that they can be seen only with very powerful electron microscopes. Viruses cause many types of illness, including colds, the flu, and chicken pox. Viruses cannot reproduce by themselves. They must use living cells to reproduce.

Bacteria are tiny single-cell organisms that live in water, in the soil, and on almost all surfaces. Most bacteria can be seen only with a microscope. Not all bacteria cause illness. Your body needs some types of bacteria to work well.

The most common type of fungus infection is athlete's foot. This is a burning, itchy infection of the skin between your toes. Ringworm is another skin infection caused by a fungus. It causes itchy round patches to develop on the skin.

Protozoans are the fourth type of pathogen. They are single-cell organisms that are slightly larger than bacteria. They can cause disease when they grow in food or drinking water.

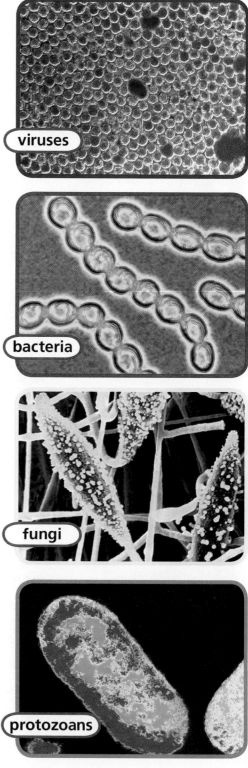

viruses

bacteria

fungi

protozoans

Fighting Illness

Pathogens that can make you ill are everywhere. When you become ill, a doctor may be able to treat you. You also can practice healthful habits to protect yourself and others from the spread of pathogens and the illnesses they can cause.

The best way to avoid spreading pathogens is to wash your hands with warm water and soap. This floats germs off of your skin. You should wash your hands often. Always wash them before and after eating, after handling animals, and after using the bathroom. Avoid touching your mouth, eyes, and nose. Never share hats, combs, cups, or drinking straws. If you get a cut or scrape, pathogens can enter your body. It is important to wash cuts and scrapes carefully with soap and water. Then cover the injury with a sterile bandage.

When you are ill, you should avoid spreading pathogens to others. Cover your nose and mouth when you sneeze or cough.

Don't share anything that has touched your mouth or nose. Stay home from school until an adult or your doctor tells you that you are well enough to go back.

Even though pathogens are all around, most people become ill only once in a while because the body has systems that protect it from pathogens. These defenses keep pathogens from entering your body.

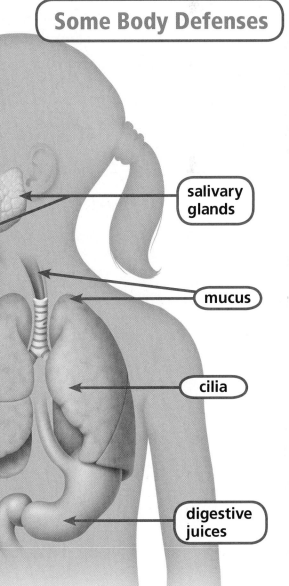

Some Body Defenses

salivary glands

mucus

cilia

digestive juices

Eat a Balanced Diet

Eating the foods that your body needs to grow and fight illness is the most important thing you can do to stay healthy. A balanced diet of healthful foods gives your body energy. Your body's systems need nutrients to function properly and work together.

Choosing unhealthful foods can cause you to gain excess weight and to lack energy. Inactivity and poor food choices can lead to your becoming ill more frequently. Unhealthful foods can also cause you to develop noncommunicable diseases. Unlike communicable diseases, which are caused by germs, these illnesses occur because your body systems are not working right.

Exercise Regularly

Exercise keeps your body healthy. Regular exercise helps your heart, lungs, and muscles stay strong. It helps your body digest food. It also helps your body fight disease. Exercising to keep your body strong also helps prevent injury when you play sports.

Exercise allows your body to rest more effectively. Getting enough sleep prepares your body for the next day. It allows your muscles and bones to grow and recover from exercise. Resting also helps keep your mind alert so you can learn and play well.

Identify the Main Idea and Details

Many of the lessons in this science book are written so that you can understand main ideas and the details that support them. You can use a graphic organizer like this one to show a main idea and details.

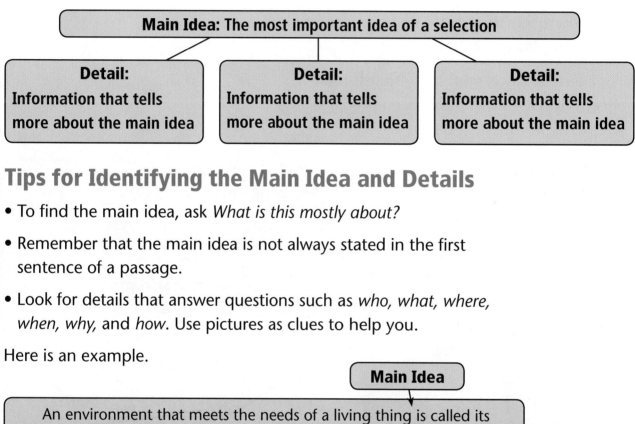

Main Idea: The most important idea of a selection

Detail: Information that tells more about the main idea

Detail: Information that tells more about the main idea

Detail: Information that tells more about the main idea

Tips for Identifying the Main Idea and Details

- To find the main idea, ask *What is this mostly about?*

- Remember that the main idea is not always stated in the first sentence of a passage.

- Look for details that answer questions such as *who, what, where, when, why,* and *how*. Use pictures as clues to help you.

Here is an example.

Main Idea

An environment that meets the needs of a living thing is called its habitat. Some habitats are as big as a whole forest. This is often true for birds that fly from place to place. Some habitats are very small. For example, fungi might grow only in certain places on a forest floor.

Detail

Here is what you could record in the graphic organizer.

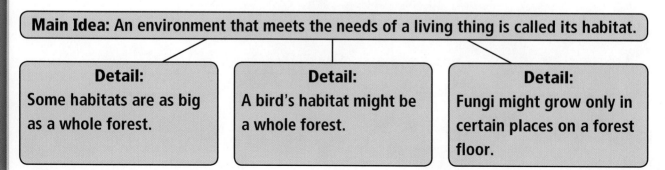

Main Idea: An environment that meets the needs of a living thing is called its habitat.

Detail: Some habitats are as big as a whole forest.

Detail: A bird's habitat might be a whole forest.

Detail: Fungi might grow only in certain places on a forest floor.

More About Main Idea and Details

Sometimes the main idea is not at the beginning of a passage. If the main idea is not stated, it can be understood from the details. Look at the graphic organizer. What do you think the main idea is?

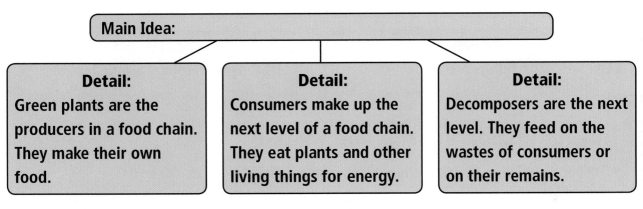

Main Idea:

Detail:
Green plants are the producers in a food chain. They make their own food.

Detail:
Consumers make up the next level of a food chain. They eat plants and other living things for energy.

Detail:
Decomposers are the next level. They feed on the wastes of consumers or on their remains.

A paragraph's main idea may be supported by details of different types. In this paragraph, identify whether the details give reasons, examples, facts, steps, or descriptions.

A group of the same species living in the same place at the same time is called a population. A forest may have populations of several different kinds of trees. Trout may be one of several populations of fish in a stream. Deer may be one population among many in a meadow.

Skill Practice

Read the following paragraph. Use the Tips for Identifying the Main Idea and Details to answer the questions.

Animals do not get their energy directly from the sun. Many eat plants. The plants use sunlight to make food. Animals that don't eat plants still depend on the energy of sunlight. They eat animals that eat plants. The sun is the main source of energy for all living things.

1. What is the main idea of the paragraph?

2. What supporting details give more information about the main idea?

3. What details answer any of the questions *who, what, where, when, why,* and *how?*

Compare and Contrast

Focus Skill

Some lessons are written to help you see how things are alike or different. You can use a graphic organizer like this one to compare and contrast.

Topic: Name the two things you are comparing and contrasting.	
Alike **List ways the things are alike.**	**Different** **List ways the things are different.**

Tips for Comparing and Contrasting

- To compare, ask *How are the people, places, objects, ideas, or events alike?*
- To contrast, ask *How are the people, places, objects, ideas, or events different?*
- When you compare, look for signal words and phrases such as *similar, alike, both, the same as, too,* and *also.*
- When you contrast, look for signal words and phrases such as *unlike, different, however, yet,* and *but.*

Here is an example.

Compare

Mars and Venus are the two planets closest to Earth. They are known as inner planets. Venus and Earth are about the same size, but Mars is a little smaller. Venus does not have any moons. However, Mars has two moons.

Contrast

Here is what you could record in the graphic organizer.

Topic: Mars and Venus	
Alike **Both are inner planets.** **Are the planets closest to Earth.**	**Different** **Mars is smaller than Venus.** **Mars has two moons.**

More About Compare and Contrast

You can better understand new information about things when you know how they are alike and how they are different. Use the graphic organizer from page R18 to sort the following items of information about Mars and Venus.

Mars	Venus
Mars is the fourth planet from the sun.	Venus is the second planet from the sun.
A year on Mars is 687 Earth days.	A year on Venus is 225 Earth days.
Mars has a diameter of 6794 kilometers.	Venus has a diameter of 12,104 kilometers.
The soil on Mars is a dark reddish brown.	Venus is dry and has a thick atmosphere.

Sometimes a paragraph compares and contrasts more than one topic. In the following paragraph, one topic being compared and contrasted is underlined. Find the second topic being compared and contrasted.

Radio telescopes and optical telescopes are two types of telescopes that are used to observe objects in space. A radio telescope collects radio waves with a large, bowl-shaped antenna. Optical telescopes use light. There are two types of optical telescopes. A refracting telescope uses lenses to magnify an object and a reflecting telescope uses a curved mirror to magnify an object.

Skill Practice

Read the following paragraph. Use the Tips for Comparing and Contrasting to answer the questions.

Radio telescopes and optical telescopes work in the same way. However, optical telescopes collect and focus light, while radio telescopes collect and focus invisible radio waves. Radio waves are not affected by clouds and poor weather. Computers can make pictures from data collected by radio telescopes.

1. How are radio and optical telescopes alike? Different?

2. What are two compare and contrast signal words in the paragraph?

 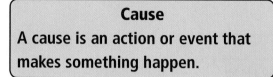

Some of the lessons in this science book are written to help you understand why things happen. You can use a graphic organizer like this one to show cause and effect.

Cause	**Effect**
A cause is an action or event that makes something happen.	An effect is what happens as a result of an action or event.

Tips for Identifying Cause and Effect

- To find an effect, ask *What happened?*

- To find a cause, ask *Why did this happen?*

- Remember that actions and events can have more than one cause or effect.

- Look for signal words and phrases such as *because* and *as a result* to help you identify causes and effects.

Here is an example.

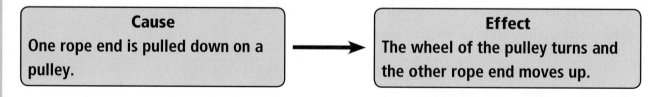

Cause
Effect

A pulley is a simple machine. It helps us do work. It is made up of a rope or chain and a wheel around which the rope fits. When you pull down on one rope end, the wheel turns and the other rope end moves up.

Here is what you could record in the graphic organizer.

Cause	**Effect**
One rope end is pulled down on a pulley.	The wheel of the pulley turns and the other rope end moves up.

More About Cause and Effect

Actions and events can have more than one cause or effect. For example, suppose the paragraph on page R20 included a sentence that said *The pulley can be used to raise or lower something that is light in weight.* You could then identify two effects of operating a pulley.

| **Cause**
One rope end is pulled down on a pulley. | → | **Effect**
The wheel of the pulley turns and the other rope end moves up. |
| | → | **Effect**
Something light in weight is raised or lowered. |

Some paragraphs contain more than one cause and effect. In the following paragraph, one cause and its effect are underlined. Find the second cause and its effect.

> A fixed pulley and a movable pulley can be put together to make a compound machine. The movable pulley increases your force. As more movable pulleys are added to a system, the force is increased. The fixed pulley changes the direction of your force.

Skill Practice

Read the following paragraph. Use the Tips for Identifying Cause and Effect to help you answer the questions.

> A lever can be used to open a paint can. The outer rim of the can is used as the fulcrum. Your hand supplies the effort force. The force put out by the end under the lid is greater than the effort force. As a result, the can is opened.

1. What causes the paint can to open?

2. What is the effect when an effort force is applied?

3. What signal phrase helped you identify the cause and effect in this paragraph?

Sequence

Some lessons in this science book are written to help you understand the order in which things happen. You can use a graphic organizer like this one to show a sequence.

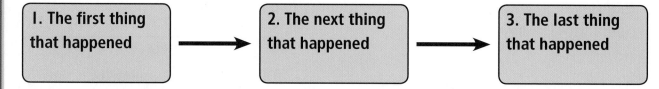

| I. The first thing that happened | → | 2. The next thing that happened | → | 3. The last thing that happened |

Tips for Understanding a Sequence

- Pay attention to the order in which events happen.

- Recall dates and times to help you understand the sequence.

- Look for signal words such as *first, next, then, last,* and *finally.*

- Sometimes it is helpful to add your own time-order words to help you understand a sequence.

Here is an example.

Time-order words

Thermal energy is transferred from an electric stove burner to water in a metal pot by conduction. First, the burner gets hot and the particles in it move faster. Next, the particles in the burner bump into particles in the bottom of the pot. The bumping causes the particles in the pot to move faster, and the pot becomes hotter. Then, the particles in the pot bump into the nearby particles of water. The bumping makes the water particles move faster, and the water gets hotter.

Here is what you could record in the graphic organizer.

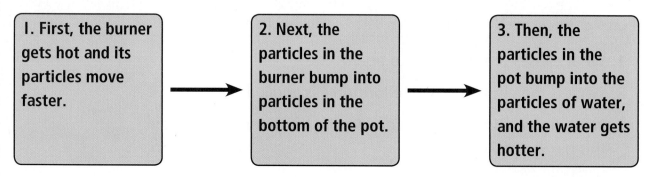

| I. First, the burner gets hot and its particles move faster. | → | 2. Next, the particles in the burner bump into particles in the bottom of the pot. | → | 3. Then, the particles in the pot bump into the particles of water, and the water gets hotter. |

More About Sequence

Sometimes information is sequenced by time. For example, an experiment might be done to measure temperature change over time. Use the graphic organizer to sequence the experiment.

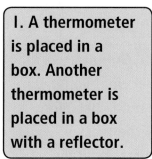 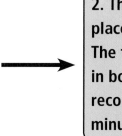 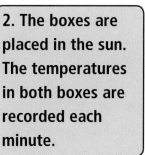 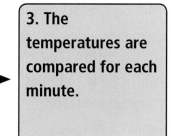

I. A thermometer is placed in a box. Another thermometer is placed in a box with a reflector.

2. The boxes are placed in the sun. The temperatures in both boxes are recorded each minute.

3. The temperatures are compared for each minute.

When time-order words are not given, add your own words to help you understand the sequence. In the paragraph below, one time-order word has been included and underlined. How many more time-order words can you add to understand the paragraph's sequence?

Convection is the transfer of thermal energy in a fluid, a liquid or gas. As the fluid near a hot object gets hot, it expands. The hot fluid is forced up by the cooler, denser fluid around it. As the hot fluid is forced up, it warms the fluid around it. <u>Then</u>, as it slowly cools, it sinks.

Skill Practice

Read the following paragraph. Use the Tips for Understanding a Sequence to answer the questions.

Solar energy can be used to heat water in a home. First, solar panels are placed on the roof of a house. Next, the panels absorb infrared radiation from the sun. Then, the radiation heats the water as it flows through the panels.

1. What is the first thing that happens in the sequence?

2. How many steps are involved in the process?

3. What three signal words helped you identify the sequence in this paragraph?

At the end of every lesson in this science book, you are asked to summarize. When you summarize, you use your own words to tell what something is about. In the lesson, you will find ideas for writing your summary. You can also use a graphic organizer like this one to summarize.

Main Idea: Tell about the most important information you have read.	+	**Details:** Add details that answer important questions such as *who, what, where, when, why,* **and** *how.*	=	**Summary:** Retell what you have just read, including only the most important details.

Tips for Summarizing

- To write a summary, first ask *What is the most important idea of the paragraph?*

- To add details, ask *who, what, when, where, why,* and *how.*

- Remember to use fewer words than the original.

- Tell the information in your own words.

Here and on the next page is an example.

Main Idea

Details

The water cycle is the constant recycling of water. As the sun warms the ocean, water particles leave the water and enter the air as water vapor. This is evaporation, the process of a liquid changing to a gas. Clouds form when water vapor condenses high in the atmosphere. Condensation occurs when the water vapor rises, cools, and changes from a gas to liquid. When the drops of water are too large to stay up in the air, precipitation occurs.

Here is what you could record in the graphic organizer.

Main Idea:		**Details:**		**Summary:**
The water cycle is the constant recycling of water.	+	Evaporation is the change from a liquid to a gas. Condensation is the change from a gas to a liquid. Precipitation is water that falls to Earth.	=	The constant recycling of water is the water cycle. It includes evaporation, condensation, and precipitation.

More About Summarizing

Sometimes a paragraph has details that are not important enough to be included in a summary. The graphic organizer remains the same because those details are not important to understanding the paragraph's main idea.

Skill Practice

Read the following paragraph. Use the Tips for Summarizing to answer the questions.

> Tides are the changes in the ocean's water level each day. At high tide, much of the beach is covered with water. At low tide, waves break farther away from the shore and less of the beach is under water. Every day most shorelines have two high tides and two low tides. High tides and low tides occur at regular times and are usually a little more than 6 hours apart.

1. If a friend asked you what this paragraph was about, what information would you include? What would you leave out?

2. What is the main idea of the paragraph?

3. Which two details would you include in a summary of the paragraph?

Draw Conclusions

At the end of each lesson in this science book, you are asked to draw conclusions. To draw conclusions, use the information that you have read and what you already know. Drawing conclusions can help you understand what you read. You can use a graphic organizer like this.

| **What I Read** Use facts from the text to help you understand. | + | **What I Know** Use your own experience to help you understand. | = | **Conclusion:** Combine facts and details in the text with personal knowledge or experience. |

Tips for Drawing Conclusions

• To draw conclusions, first ask *What information from the text do I need to think about?*

• Then ask *What do I know from my own experience that could help me draw a conclusion?*

• Ask yourself whether the conclusion you have drawn is valid, or makes sense.

Here is an example.

Plants need air, nutrients, water, and light to live. A plant makes its own food by a process called photosynthesis. Photosynthesis takes place in the plant's leaves. In an experiment, a plant is placed in a dark room without any light. It is watered every day.

Text information

Here is what you could record in the graphic organizer.

| **What I Read** A plant needs air, nutrients, water, and light to live. | + | **What I Know** Plants use light to make the food they need to live and grow. | = | **Conclusion:** The plant will die since it is not getting any light. |

More About Drawing Conclusions

Sensible conclusions based on your experience and the facts you read are valid. For example, suppose the paragraph on page R26 included a sentence that said *After a day, the plant is removed from the dark room and placed in the sunlight.* You could then draw a different conclusion about the life of the plant.

What I Read		**What I Know**		**Conclusion:**
A plant needs air, nutrients, water, and light to live.	+	Plants use light to make the food they need to live and grow.	=	The plant will live.

Sometimes a paragraph might not contain enough information to draw a valid conclusion. Read the following paragraph. Think of one valid conclusion you could draw. Then think of one conclusion that would be invalid or wouldn't make sense.

> Cacti are plants that are found in the desert. Sometimes it does not rain in the desert for months or even years. Cacti have thick stems. The roots of cactus plants grow just below the surface of the ground.

Skill Practice

Read the following paragraph. Use the Tips for Drawing Conclusions to answer the questions.

> Animals behave in ways that help them meet their needs. Some animal behaviors are instincts, and some are learned. Tiger cubs learn to hunt by watching their mothers hunt and by playing with other tiger cubs. They are not born knowing exactly how to hunt.

1. What conclusion can you draw about a tiger cub that is separated from its mother?

2. What information from your own experience helped you draw the conclusion?

3. What text information did you use to draw the conclusion?

Using Tables, Charts, and Graphs

As you do investigations in science, you collect, organize, display, and interpret data. Tables, charts, and graphs are good ways to organize and display data so that others can understand and interpret your data.

The tables, charts, and graphs in this Handbook will help you read and understand data. The Handbook will also help you choose the best ways to display data so that you can draw conclusions and make predictions.

Reading a Table

A scientist is studying the rainfall in Bangladesh. She wants to know when the monsoon season is, or the months in which the area receives the greatest amounts of rainfall. The table shows the data she has collected.

Monthly Rainfall in Chittagong, Bangladesh	
Month	Rainfall (inches)
January	1
February	2
March	3
April	6
May	10
June	21
July	23
August	10
September	13
October	7
November	2
December	1

Title
Headings
Data

How to Read a Table

1. **Read the title** to find out what the table is about.

2. **Read the headings** to find out what information is given.

3. **Study** the data. Look for patterns.

4. **Draw conclusions.** If you display the data in a graph, you might be able to see patterns easily.

By studying the table, you can see how much rain fell during each month. If the scientist wanted to look for patterns, she might display the data in a graph.

Reading a Bar Graph

The data in this bar graph is the same as that in the table. A bar graph can be used to compare the data about different events or groups.

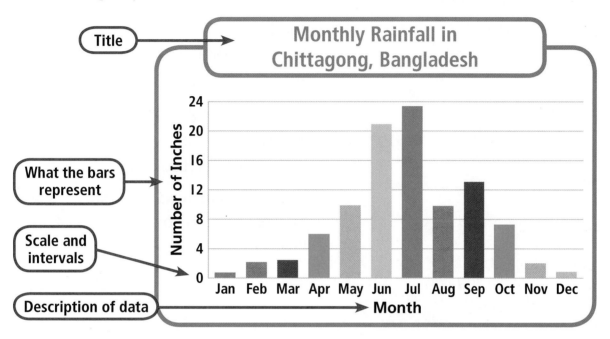

Title → **Monthly Rainfall in Chittagong, Bangladesh**

What the bars represent

Scale and intervals

Description of data

How to Read a Bar Graph

1. **Look** at the graph to determine what kind of graph it is.

2. **Read** the graph. Use the numbers and labels to guide you.

3. **Analyze** the data. Study the bars to compare the measurements. Look for patterns.

4. **Draw conclusions.** Ask yourself questions like the ones under Skills Practice.

Skills Practice

1. In which two months does Chittagong receive the most rainfall?

2. Which months have the same amounts of rainfall?

3. **Predict** During which months are the roads likely to be flooded?

4. How does the bar graph help you identify the monsoon season and the rainfall amounts?

5. Was the bar graph a good choice for displaying this data?

Reading a Line Graph

A scientist collected this data about temperatures in Pittsburgh, Pennsylvania.

Average Temperatures in Pittsburgh	
Month	Temperature (degrees Fahrenheit)
January	28
February	29
March	39
April	50
May	60
June	68
July	74
August	72
September	63
October	52
November	43
December	32

How to Read a Line Graph

1. **Look** at the graph to determine what kind of graph it is.

2. **Read** the graph. Use the numbers and labels to guide you.

3. **Analyze** the data. Study the points along the lines. Look for patterns.

4. **Draw conclusions.** Ask yourself questions like the ones under Skills Practice.

Here is the same data displayed in a line graph. A line graph is used to show changes over time.

- Title
- What the points represent
- Scale and intervals
- Description of data

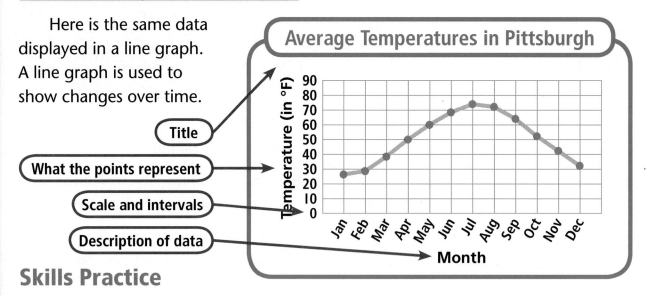

Average Temperatures in Pittsburgh

Skills Practice

1. In which three months are the temperatures the warmest in Pittsburgh?

2. **Predict** During which months are ponds in Pittsburgh likely to freeze?

3. Was the line graph a good choice for displaying this data? Explain why.

Reading a Circle Graph

Some scientists counted 100 animals at a park. The scientists wanted to know which animal group had the most animals. They classified the animals by making a table. Here is their data.

Animal Groups at the Park	
Animal Group	**Number Observed**
Mammals	7
Insects	63
Birds	22
Reptiles	5
Amphibians	3

The circle graph shows the same data as the table. A circle graph can be used to show data as a whole made up of parts.

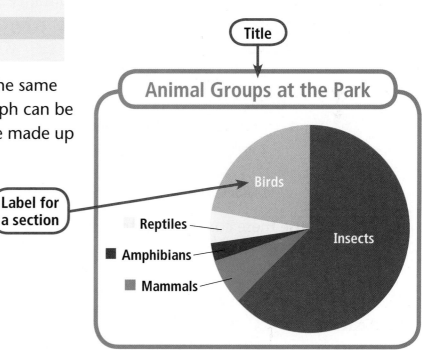

Title

Animal Groups at the Park

Label for a section

Birds

Reptiles

Amphibians

Mammals

Insects

How to Read a Circle Graph

1. **Look** at the title of the graph to learn what kind of information is shown.

2. **Read** the graph. Look at the label of each section to find out what information is shown.

3. **Analyze** the data. Compare the sizes of the sections to determine how they are related.

4. **Draw conclusions.** Ask yourself questions like the ones under Skills Practice.

Skills Practice

1. Which animal group had the most members? Which one had the fewest?

2. **Predict** If you visited a nearby park, would you expect to see more reptiles or more insects?

3. Was the circle graph a good choice for displaying this data? Explain.

Measurements

When you measure, you compare an object to a standard unit of measure. Scientists almost always use the units of the metric system.

Measuring Length and Capacity in Metric Units

When you measure length, you find the distance between two points. The table shows the metric units of **length** and how they are related.

Equivalent Measures
1 centimeter (cm) = 10 millimeters (mm)
1 decimeter (dm) = 10 centimeters (cm)
1 meter (m) = 1000 millimeters
1 meter = 10 decimeters
1 kilometer (km) = 1000 meters

You can use these comparisons to help you learn the size of each metric unit of length:

A **millimeter (mm)** is about the thickness of a dime.	A **centimeter (cm)** is about the width of your index finger.	A **decimeter (dm)** is about the width of an adult's hand.	A **meter (m)** is about the width of a door.
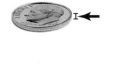	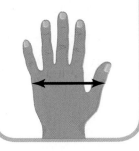		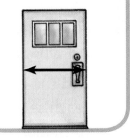

The following diagram shows how to multiply and divide to change to larger and smaller units.

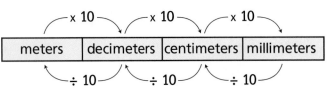

When you measure capacity, you find the amount a container can hold when it is filled. The images show the metric units of **capacity** and how they are related.

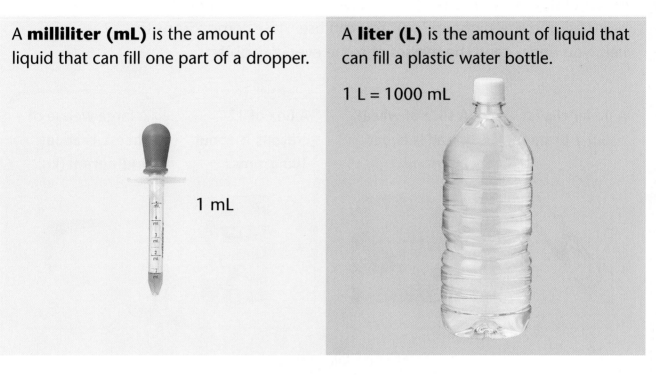

A **milliliter (mL)** is the amount of liquid that can fill one part of a dropper.

1 mL

A **liter (L)** is the amount of liquid that can fill a plastic water bottle.

1 L = 1000 mL

You can use multiplication to change liters to milliliters.

You can use division to change milliliters to liters.

2 L = _____ mL	4000 mL = _____ L
Think: There are 1000 mL in 1 L.	Think: There are 1000 mL in 1 L.
2 L = 2 x 1000 = 2000 mL	4000 ÷ 1000 = 4
So, 2 L = 2000 mL.	So, 4000 mL = 4 L.

Skills Practice

Complete. Tell whether you multiply or divide.

1. 3 L = _____ mL

2. 5000 mL = _____ L

3. 7000 mL = _____ L

4. 6 L = _____ mL

5. 500 dm = _____ cm

6. 4 m = _____ mm

7. 8 _____ = 80 cm

8. _____ m = 1400 cm

Measuring Mass

Matter is what all objects are made of. **Mass** is the amount of matter that is in an object. The metric units of mass are the gram (g) and the kilogram (kg). You can use these comparisons to help you understand the masses of some everyday objects:

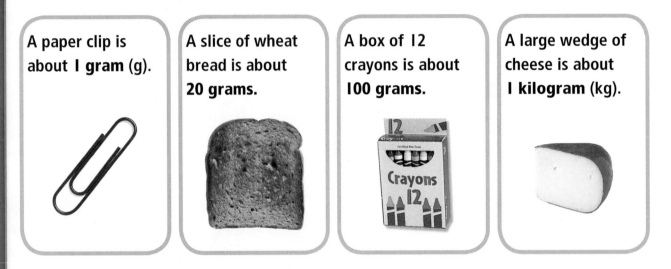

A paper clip is about **1 gram** (g).

A slice of wheat bread is about **20 grams.**

A box of 12 crayons is about **100 grams.**

A large wedge of cheese is about **1 kilogram** (kg).

You can use multiplication to change kilograms to grams.

You can use division to change grams to kilograms.

2 kg = _____ g	4000 g = _____ kg
Think: There are 1000 g in 1 kg.	Think: There are 1000 g in 1 kg.
2 kg = 2 x 1000 = 2000 g	4000 ÷ 1000 = 4
So, 2 kg = 2000 g.	So, 4000 g = 4 kg.

Skills Practice

Complete. Tell whether you multiply or divide by 1000.

1. 5000 g = _____ kg

2. 3000 g = _____ kg

3. 4 kg = _____ g

4. 7 kg = _____ g

Measurement Systems

SI Measures (Metric)

Temperature
Ice melts at 0 degrees Celsius (°C).
Water freezes at 0°C.
Water boils at 100°C.

Length and Distance
1000 meters (m) =
                1 kilometer (km)
100 centimeters (cm) = 1 m
10 millimeters (mm) = 1 cm

Force
1 newton (N) = 1 kilogram x
   1 meter/second/second (kg-m/s^2)

Volume
1 cubic meter (m^3) =
                1 m x 1 m x 1 m
1 cubic centimeter (cm^3) =
                1 cm x 1 cm x 1 cm
1 liter (L) = 1000 millimeters (mL)
1 cm^3 = 1 mL

Area
1 square kilometer (km^2) =
                1 km x 1 km
1 hectare = 10,000 m^2

Mass
1000 grams (g) = 1 kilogram (kg)
1000 milligrams (mg) = 1 g
1000 kilograms = 1 metric ton

Rates
km/hr = kilometers per hour
m/sec = meters per second

Customary Measures

Temperature
Ice melts at 32 degrees
   Fahrenheit (°F).
Water freezes at 32°F.
Water boils at 212°F.

Length and Distance
12 inches (in.) = 1 foot (ft)
3 ft = 1 yard (yd)
5280 ft = 1 mile (mi)

Force
16 ounces (oz) = 1 pound (lb)
2000 pounds = 1 ton (T)

Volume of Fluids
2 cups (c) = 1 pint (pt)
2 pt = 1 quart (qt)
4 qt = 1 gallon (gal)

Area
1 square mile (mi^2) = 1 mi x 1 mi
1 acre = 4840 sq ft

Rates
mph = miles per hour
ft/sec = feet per second

Safety in Science

Doing investigations in science can be fun, but you need to be sure you do them safely. Here are some rules to follow.

1. **Think ahead.** Study the steps of the investigation so you know what to expect. If you have any questions, ask your teacher. Be sure you understand any caution statements or safety reminders.

2. **Be neat.** Keep your work area clean. If you have long hair, pull it back so it doesn't get in the way. Roll or push up long sleeves to keep them away from your activity.

3. **Oops!** If you should spill or break something, or get cut, tell your teacher right away.

4. **Watch your eyes.** Wear safety goggles anytime you are directed to do so. If you get anything in your eyes, tell your teacher right away.

5. **Yuck!** Never eat or drink anything during a science activity.

6. **Don't get shocked.** Be especially careful if an electric appliance is used. Be sure that electric cords are in a safe place where you can't trip over them. Don't ever pull a plug out of an outlet by pulling on the cord.

7. **Keep it clean.** Always clean up when you have finished. Put everything away and wipe your work area. Wash your hands.

Glossary

As you read your science book, you will notice that new or unfamiliar terms have been respelled to help you pronounce them while you are reading. Those respellings are called *phonetic respellings.* In this Glossary you will see the same kind of respellings.

In phonetic respellings, syllables are separated by a bullet (•). Small uppercase letters show stressed syllables.

The boldfaced letters in the examples in the Pronunciation Key below show which letters and combinations of letters are pronounced in the respellings.

The page number (in parentheses) at the end of a definition tells you where to find the term, defined in context, in your book. Depending on the context in which it is used, a term may have more than one definition.

Pronunciation Key

Sound	As in	Phonetic Respelling	Sound	As in	Phonetic Respelling
a	b**a**t	(BAT)	oh	**o**ver	(OH•ver)
ah	l**o**ck	(LAHK)	oo	p**oo**l	(POOL)
air	r**a**re	(RAIR)	ow	**ou**t	(OWT)
ar	**ar**gue	(AR•gyoo)	oy	f**oi**l	(FOYL)
aw	l**aw**	(LAW)	s	**c**ell	(SEL)
ay	fa**c**e	(FAYS)		**s**it	(SIT)
ch	**ch**apel	(CHAP•uhl)	sh	**sh**eep	(SHEEP)
e	t**e**st	(TEST)	th	**th**at	(THAT)
	m**e**tric	(MEH•trik)		**th**in	(THIN)
ee	**ea**t	(EET)	u	p**u**ll	(PUL)
	f**ee**t	(FEET)	uh	m**e**dal	(MED•uhl)
	sk**i**	(SKEE)		tal**e**nt	(TAL•uhnt)
er	pap**er**	(PAY•per)		penc**i**l	(PEN•suhl)
	f**er**n	(FERN)		**o**nion	(UHN•yuhn)
eye	**i**dea	(eye•DEE•uh)		playf**u**l	(PLAY•fuhl)
i	b**i**t	(BIT)		d**u**ll	(DUHL)
ing	go**ing**	(GOH•ing)	y	**y**es	(YES)
k	**c**ard	(KARD)		r**i**pe	(RYP)
	kite	(KYT)	z	bag**s**	(BAGZ)
ngk	ba**nk**	(BANGK)	zh	trea**s**ure	(TREZH•er)

A

abiotic [ay•by•AHT•ik] Describes a nonliving part of an ecosystem **(142)**

absorption [ab•ZAWRP•shuhn] The taking in of light or sound energy by an object **(427)**

acceleration [ak•sel•er•AY•shuhn] Any change in the speed or direction of an object's motion **(531)**

adaptation [ad•uhp•TAY•shuhn] A body part or behavior that helps an organism survive **(100)**

air mass [AIR MAS] A large body of air that has a similar temperature and moisture level **(290)**

amplitude [AM•pluh•tood] A measure of the amount of energy in a wave **(417)**

anemometer [an•uh•MAHM•uht•er] A weather instrument that measures wind speed **(296)**

atom [AT•uhm] The smallest unit of an element that has all the properties of that element **(376)**

axis [AK•sis] The imaginary line around which Earth spins as it rotates **(308)**

B

bacteria [bak•TIR•ee•uh] Members of the kingdom of one-celled living things that lack nuclei **(33)**

barometer [buh•RAHM•uh•ter] A weather instrument used to measure air pressure **(296)**

basic needs [BAY•sik NEEDZ] Food, water, air, and shelter that an organism needs to survive **(98)**

bedrock [BED•rahk] The solid rock that forms Earth's surface **(217)**

biotic [by•AHT•ik] Describes a living part of an ecosystem **(140)**

C

carnivore [KAHR•nuh•vawr] An animal that eats only other animals **(168)**

change of state [CHAYNJ uhv STAYT] A physical change that occurs when matter changes from one state to another, such as from a liquid to a gas **(384)**

chemical change [KEM•ih•kuhl CHAYNJ] A reaction or change in a substance, produced by chemical means, that results in a different substance **(394)**

chemical energy [KEM•ih•kuhl EN•er•jee] Energy that can be released by a chemical reaction **(508)**

chemical property [KEM•ih•kuhl PRAHP•er•tee] A property that involves how a substance interacts with other substances **(393)**

chemical reaction [KEM•ih•kuhl ree•AK•shuhn] A chemical change **(394)**

clay [KLAY] The smallest particles that make up soil **(218)**

cold front [KOHLD FRUHNT] The boundary where a cold air mass moves under a warm air mass **(292)**

comet [KAHM•it] A ball of rock, ice, and frozen gases in space **(320)**

community [kuh•MYOO•nuh•tee] All the populations of organisms living together in an environment **(136)**

compound [KAHM•pownd] A substance made of two or more different elements that have combined chemically **(394)**

condensation [kahn•duhn•SAY•shuhn] The process by which a gas changes into a liquid **(271)**

conduction [kuhn•DUK•shuhn] The movement of heat between two materials that are touching **(450)**

conductor [kuhn•DUK•ter] Materials that let electric charges travel through them easily **(485)**

constellation [kahn•stuh•LAY•shuhn] A pattern of stars that form an imaginary picture or design in the sky **(326)**

consumer [kuhn•SOOM•er] A living thing that can't make its own food and must eat other living things **(166)**

convection [kuhn•VEK•shuhn] The movement of heat in liquids and gases from a warmer area to a cooler area **(451)**

current electricity [KER•uhnt ee•lek•TRIS•uh•tee] A steady movement of charges through certain materials **(476)**

decomposer [dee•kuhm•POHZ•er] A living thing that feeds on the wastes and remains of plants and animals **(170)**

density [DEN•suh•tee] The amount of matter in an object compared to the space it takes up **(344)**

deposition [dep•uh•ZISH•uhn] The dropping of bits of rock and soil by a river as it flows **(244)**

direct development [duh•REKT dih•VEL•uhp•muhnt] A kind of growth in which an organism gets larger but doesn't go through other changes **(84)**

diversity [duh•VER•suh•tee] A great variety of living things **(146)**

earthquake [ERTH•kwayk] The shaking of Earth's surface caused by movement of rock in the crust **(242)**

ecosystem [EE•koh•sis•tuhm] A community and its physical environment together **(132)**

electric motor [uh•LEK•trik MOHT•er] A device that changes electrical energy to energy of motion **(490)**

electromagnet [ee•lek•troh•MAG•nit] A temporary magnet caused by an electric current **(490)**

element [EL•uh•muhnt] A substance made up of only one kind of atom **(378)**

energy pyramid [EN•er•jee PIR•uh•mid] A diagram showing how much energy is passed from one organism to the next in a food chain **(180)**

energy transfer [EN•er•jee TRANS•fer] A change of energy from one form to another **(457)**

environment [en•VY•ruhn•muhnt] All of the living and nonliving things surrounding an organism. **(132)**

erosion [uh•ROH•zhuhn] The process of moving sediment from one place to another **(212)**

evaporation [ee•vap•uh•RAY•shuhn] The process by which a liquid changes into a gas **(270)**

experiment [ek•SPAIR•uh•muhnt] A test of a hypothesis **(15)**

extinction [ek•STINGK•shuhn] The death of all the members of a certain group of organisms **(118)**

food chain [FOOD CHAYN] A series of organisms that depend on one another for food **(176)**

food web [FOOD WEB] A group of food chains that overlap **(178)**

force [FAWRS] A pull or push of any kind **(532)**

fossil [FAHS•uhl] The remains or traces of a plant or an animal that lived long ago **(114, 250)**

fossil record [FAHS•uhl REK•erd] The information about Earth's history that is contained in fossils **(252)**

frequency [FREE•kwuhn•see] A measure of the number of waves that pass in a second **(417)**

friction [FRIK•shuhn] A force that resists motion between objects that are touching **(541)**

fulcrum [FUL•kruhm] The fixed point on a lever **(556)**

fungi [FUHN•jy] Organisms that can't make food and can't move about **(46)**

galaxy [GAL•uhk•see] A huge system of many stars, gases, and dust **(326)**

gas [GAS] The state of matter that does not have a definite shape or volume **(351)**

gene [JEEN] The basic unit of heredity **(67)**

generator [JEN•er•ayt•er] A device that produces an electric current **(492)**

geothermal energy [jee•oh•THER•muhl EN•er•jee] Heat that comes from the inside of Earth **(501)**

glacier [GLAY•sher] A large, moving mass of ice **(245)**

gravitation [grav•ih•TAY•shuhn] A force that acts between any two objects and pulls them together **(539)**

gravity [GRAV•ih•tee] The force of attraction between Earth and other objects, the expression of gravitation **(539)**

habitat [HAB•ih•tat] An environment that meets the needs of an organism **(174)**

habitat restoration [HAB•ih•tat res•tuh•RAY•shuhn] Returning a natural environment to its original condition **(153)**

hail [HAYL] Round pieces of ice formed when frozen rain is coated with water and refreezes **(277)**

herbivore [HER•buh•vawr] An animal that eats only plants, or producers **(168)**

heredity [huh•RED•ih•tee] The process by which traits are passed from parents to offspring **(66)**

hibernation [hy•ber•NAY•shuhn] A dormant, inactive state in which normal body activities slow **(107)**

horizon [huh•RY•zuhn] A layer in the soil **(217)**

humus [HYOO•muhs] The remains of decayed plants or animals in the soil **(216)**

hurricane [HER•ih•kayn] A large tropical storm with wind speeds of at least 74 miles per hour **(278)**

hydroelectric power [hy•droh•ee•LEK•trik POW•er] Electrical energy made by using the kinetic energy of falling water **(500)**

hypothesis [hy•PAHTH•uh•sis] A statement of what you think will happen and why **(15)**

igneous rock [IG•nee•uhs RAHK] A type of rock that forms from melted rock that cools and hardens **(196)**

inclined plane [in•KLYND PLAYN] A simple machine that is a slanted surface **(570)**

inertia [in•ER•shuh] The property of matter that keeps an object at rest or keeps it moving in a straight line **(534)**

inference [IN•fer•uhns] An untested conclusion based on your observations **(12)**

instinct [IN•stinkt] A behavior that an animal begins life with and that helps it meet its needs **(106)**

insulator [IN•suh•layt•er] A material that does not let current electricity move through it easily **(480)**

intensity [in•TEN•suh•tee] A measure of how loud or soft a sound is **(411)**

invertebrates [in•VER•tuh•brits] The group of animals without backbones **(52)**

kinetic energy [kih•NET•ik EN•er•jee] The energy of motion **(499)**

land breeze [LAND BREEZ] A breeze that moves from the land to the water **(284)**

landform [LAND•fawrm] A natural feature on Earth's surface **(232)**

learned behavior [LERND bee•HAYV•yer] A behavior that an organism doesn't begin life with **(110)**

lever [LEV•er] A simple machine made of a bar that pivots on a fixed point **(556)**

life cycle [LYF CY•kuhl] All the stages a living thing goes through **(74)**

light [LYT] A form of energy that can travel through space and lies partly within the visible range **(440)**

liquid [LIK•wid] The state of matter that has a definite volume but no definite shape **(350)**

magnet [MAG•nit] An object that attracts iron and a few other (but not all) metals **(486)**

magnetic field [mag•NET•ik FEELD] The space around a magnet in which the force of the magnet acts **(489)**

magnetic poles [mag•NET•ik POHLZ] The parts of a magnet at which its force is strongest **(488)**

mass [MAS] The amount of matter in an object **(343)**

matter [MAT•er] Anything that has mass and takes up space (342)

mechanical energy [muh•KAN•ih•kuhl EN•er•jee] The total potential and kinetic energy of an object (509)

metamorphic rock [met•uh•MAWR•fik RAHK] A type of rock that forms when heat or pressure change an existing rock (198)

metamorphosis [met•uh•MAWR•fuh•sis] Major changes in the body form of an animal during its life cycle (86)

microscope [MY•kruh•skohp] A tool that makes an object look several times bigger than it is (6)

microscopic [my•kruh•SKAHP•ik] Too small to be seen with the eyes alone (33)

migration [my•GRAY•shuhn] The movement of animals from one region to another and back (108)

mineral [MIN•er•uhl] A solid nonliving substance that occurs naturally in rocks or in the ground (194)

mixture [MIKS•cher] A blending of two types of matter that are not chemically combined (358)

moon [MOON] A natural body that revolves around a planet (310)

motion [MOH•shuhn] A change of position of an object (522)

mountain [MOUNT•uhn] An area that is much higher than the land around it (232)

niche [NICH] The role of an organism in its habitat (175)

nonvascular [nahn•VAS•kyuh•ler] Without tubes or channels (44)

observation [ahb•zer•VAY•shuhn] Information from your senses (12)

omnivore [AHM•nih•vawr] An animal that eats both plants and other animals (168)

orbit [AWR•bit] The path of one object in space around another object (308)

organism [AWR•guh•niz•uhm] A living thing (32)

pan balance [PAN BAL•uhns] A tool that measures mass (8)

parallel circuit [PAIR•uh•lel SER•kit] A circuit that has more than one path for an electric current to follow (478)

phases [FAYZ•uhz] The different shapes that Earth's moon seems to have (310)

physical change [FIZ•ih•kuhl CHAYNJ] A change in matter from one form to another that doesn't result in a different substance (386)

physical property [FIZ•ih•kuhl PRAHP•er•tee] A trait that involves a substance by itself (393)

pitch [PICH] A measure of how high or low a sound is (410)

planet [PLAN•it] A large object that moves around a star (316)

pollution [puh•LOO•shuhn] Waste products that damage an ecosystem (152)

Multimedia Science Glossary: www.hspscience.com

population [pahp•yuh•LAY•shuhn] All the individuals of the same kind living in the same ecosystem **(134)**

position [puh•ZISH•uhn] The location of an object **(522)**

potential energy [poh•TEN•shuhl EN•er•jee] Energy that an object has because of its position or its condition **(499)**

precipitation [pree•sip•uh•TAY•shuhn] Water that falls to Earth **(268)**

predator [PRED•uh•ter] A consumer that eats prey **(176)**

prey [PRAY] Consumers that are eaten by predators **(176)**

producer [pruh•DOOS•er] A living thing, such as a plant, that can make its own food **(166)**

protist [PROHT•ist] One of the kingdoms of living things that are one-celled **(33)**

pulley [PUHL•ee] A simple machine made of a wheel with a line around it **(562)**

radiation [ray•dee•AY•shuhn] The movement of heat without matter to carry it **(452)**

rain [RAYN] Precipitation that is liquid water **(276)**

rain shadow [RAYN SHAD•oh] The area on the side of a mountain range that gets little or no rain or cloud cover **(286)**

reflection [rih•FLEK•shuhn] The bouncing of light, sound, or heat off an object **(426, 441)**

refraction [rih•FRAK•shuhn] The bending of light when it moves from one kind of matter to another **(443)**

rock [RAHK] A solid substance made of one or more minerals **(194)**

rock cycle [RAHK SY•kuhl] The sequence of processes that change rocks from one type to another over long periods **(202)**

sand [SAND] The largest particles that make up soil **(218)**

scientific method [sy•uhn•TIF•ik METH•uhd] A way that scientists find out how things work and affect each other **(20)**

screw [SKROO] A simple machine made of a post with an inclined plane wrapped around it **(572)**

sea breeze [SEE BREEZ] A breeze that moves from the water to the land **(284)**

sedimentary rock [sed•uh•MEN•ter•ee RAHK] A type of rock that forms when layers of sediment are pressed together **(197)**

series circuit [SIR•eez SER•kit] A circuit that has only one path for an electric current to follow **(478)**

simple machine [SIM•puhl muh•SHEEN] A machine with few or no moving parts that you apply just one force to **(555)**

sleet [SLEET] Precipitation made when rain falls through freezing-cold air and turns to ice **(276)**

snow [SNOH] Precipitation made when water vapor turns directly into ice and forms ice crystals **(277)**

solar energy [SOH•ler EN•er•jee] The power of the sun **(502)**

solar system [SOH•ler SIS•tuhm] A group of objects in space that revolve around a central star **(316)**

solid [SAHL•id] The state of matter that has a definite shape and a definite volume **(350)**

solubility [sahl•yoo•BIL•uh•tee] A measure of how much of a material will dissolve in another material **(361)**

solution [suh•LOO•shuhn] A mixture in which two or more substances are mixed completely **(360)**

speed [SPEED] The measure of an object's change in position during a unit of time **(524)**

spring scale [SPRING SKAYL] A tool that measures forces, such as weight **(8)**

standard measure [STAN•derd MEZH•er] An accepted measurement **(4)**

star [STAR] A huge ball of superheated gases **(324)**

state of matter [STAYT uhv MAT•er] One of three forms (solid, liquid, and gas) that matter can exist in **(350)**

static electricity [STAT•ik ee•lek•TRIS•uh•tee] An electrical charge that builds up on an object **(474)**

sun [SUHN] The star at the center of our solar system **(324)**

suspension [suh•SPEN•shuhn] A kind of mixture in which particles of one ingredient are floating in another ingredient **(362)**

topography [tuh•PAHG•ruh•fee] The shape of landforms in an area **(234)**

tornado [tawr•NAY•doh] A fast-spinning spiral of wind that touches the ground **(278)**

trait [TRAYT] A characteristic that makes one organism different from another **(66)**

transmission [tranz•MISH•uhn] The passing of light or sound waves through a material **(428)**

universe [YOO•nuh•vers] Everything that exists in space **(326)**

vascular [VAS•kyuh•ler] Having tubes or channels **(42)**

velocity [vuh•LAHS•uh•tee] The measure of the speed and direction of motion of an object **(530)**

vertebrates [VER•tuh•brits] The group of animals with backbones **(50)**

vibration [vy•BRAY•shuhn] A quick back-and-forth motion **(408)**

volcano [vahl•KAY•noh] A mountain that forms as lava flows through a crack onto Earth's surface **(242)**

volume [VAHL•yoom] The amount of space an object takes up **(344)**

warm front [WAWRM FRUHNT] The boundary where a warm air mass moves over a cold air mass **(292)**

waste heat [WAYST HEET] Heat that can't be used to do useful work **(460)**

water cycle [WAW•ter SY•kuhl] The movement of water from the surface of Earth into the air and back again **(268)**

wavelength [WAYV•length] The distance between a point on one wave and the identical point on the next wave **(417)**

weathering [WETH•er•ing] The breaking down of rocks on Earth's surface into smaller pieces **(208)**

wedge [WEJ] A simple machine made of two inclined planes placed back to back **(574)**

weight [WAYT] A measure of the gravitational force acting on an object **(540)**

wheel-and-axle [weel•and•AK•suhl] A simple machine made of a wheel and an axle that turn together **(564)**

work [WERK] The use of a force to move an object over a distance **(554)**

Index

MRI (magnetic resonance imaging), 491
Mudstone, 198
Mullets, 176
Multicelled organisms, 34
Munsell, Albert H., 224
Muscle, artificial, 512–513
Muscular system, R8–R9
in vertebrates, 50
Mushrooms, 46
Musical instruments, 408, 410, 418
Mussels, 52

National Weather Service (NWS), 295
Natural fertilizers, 220
Natural forces, 538
Natural gas, 508
Natural resources
in ecosystems, 150
humans' uses of, 151
Neodymium, 484
Neptune, 318, 319
Nerves, hearing and, 425
Nervous system (vertebrates), 50
New moon, 310, 311
Niche, 175
Nickerson, Dorothy, 224
Niezrecki, Chris, 464
Nimbostratus clouds, 293
Nitrogen, melting/boiling points of, 354
Nonliving things (in ecosystems), 132, 142–143
Nonmetals, 380
Nonrenewable resources, 150
Nonvascular plants, 44–45
Northern Hemisphere
constellations visible in, 328
seasons in, 309
solstices and equinoxes in, 309
Nuclear medicine technologists,

366
Nucleus (one-celled organisms), 36
Number skills. *See* Using numbers
Nurse logs, 102
Nurture, 68
Nutrients in soil, 220
Nutrition, R14
NWS (National Weather Service), 295
Nyberg, Michael, 432
Nymphs, 86

Observation, 12
animal tracks, 249
backbones, 49
heating of land/water, 283
landform models, 231
making telescopes, 323
plant stems, 41
rubber bands, 553
in scientific method, 20
tools for, 6–7
Oceans
food web in, 178–179
fossil record and changes in, 252
invertebrates in, 52
new crust in, 241
plates and, 241
water in, 266
Offspring, inherited traits of, 66–67
Omega Nebula, 322
Omnivores, 168, 169
One-celled organisms, 33, 34, 36
bacteria, 37
in Precambrian Era, 254
protists, 38
sponges, 52
Opaque materials, 442
Orbits
of Earth, 308, 309

gravitation and, 539
of moon, 310
Orb-weaver spiders, 106
Ordering, 81. *See also* Classification
Oregon coast, 238
Organisms
classification of, 32–33
definition of, 32
multicelled, 34
one-celled, 33, 34. *See also* One-celled organisms
See also Living things
Organs, human. *See also specific organs, for example:* Stomach
Orion, 326, 328
Oscilloscope, 420
Outer core (Earth), 240
Outer ear, 425
Outer planets, 316, 318–319
Oxygen, 378
melting/boiling points of, 354
Oyster mushrooms, 46

Pacific Ocean, coral islands in, 236
Pacific yew tree, 151
Pahoehoe lava, 200
Paleontologists, 184
Paleozoic Era, 254
Palo Duro Canyon (Texas) 233
Pan balances, 8
Paper cutter, 558
Paradise tree snakes, 120–121
Parallel circuits, 478–479
Parents, inherited traits from, 66–67
Particles (matter), 350–352, 376–377
Pathogens, R12–R13
Peninsulas, 285
Petrified Forest (Arizona), 251
Petrified wood, 116, 251
Phases (of moon), 310–311

Photo Credits

KEY: (*t*) top, (*b*) bottom, (*l*) left, (*r*) right, (*c*) center, (*bg*) background, (*fg*) foreground

Cover

(front) Alaska Stock Images; (back) Art Wolfe/The Image Bank/Getty Images; (back) (*bg*) Tom Walker/Visuals Unlimited

Front End Sheets

Page 1 Bruce Lichtenberger/Peter Arnold, Inc.; **Page 2** (*t*) Bruce Lichtenberger/Peter Arnold, Inc.; (*b*) Ray Coleman/Visuals Unlimited; (*bg*) Jim Steinberg.Photo Researchers; **Page 3** (*t*) Tom Brakefield/The Image Works/Getty Images; (*b*) Gerard Lacz/Peter Arnold

Title Page

Alaska Stock Images

Copyright Page

(*bg*) Tom Walker/Visuals Unlimited; (inset) Alaska Stock Images

Back End Sheets

Page 1 Yva Momatiuk/John Eastcott/Minden Pictures; (*b*) Tom Walker/Visuals Unlimited; (*bg*) Jim Steinberg.Photo Researchers; **Page 2** (*t*) T. Kitchin/V. Hurst/Photo Researchers; (*c*) Jim Brandenburg/Minden Pictures; (*b*) Frieder Blickle/Peter Arnold, Inc.; (*bg*) Jim Steinberg.Photo Researchers; **Page 3** (*l*) Klein/Peter Arnold, Inc.; (*r*) Tim Fitzharris/Minden Pictures; (*bg*) Jim Steinberg.Photo Researchers

Table of Contents

v Stuart Westmoreland/CORBIS; **vii** David Muench/Corbis; **ix** Ted Kinsman/Photo Researchers

Introduction

x–1 (*c*) S Frink/Masterfile; **2** (*c*) AP Photo/NASA; **7** (inset) Sinclair Stammers/Science Photo Library; **10** (*c*) AP Photo/David J.Phillip; **18** (*c*) National Research Council Canada; **20** (inset) Mark Gibson/Index Stock Imagery, Inc.; **20** (*bc*) Robert Llewellyn/CORBIS;

Unit A

26 Reuters/CORBIS; **27** Mark Newman/Bruce Coleman, Inc.; **28–29** Stuart Westmoreland/CORBIS; **30** (*c*) Robert Winslow/Animals Animals; **32** (*r*) BSIP Agency/Index Stock Imagery; (*l*) Eric V. Grave/Photo Researchers; (*bg*) Garry Black/Masterfile; **33** (*r*) Bill Beatty/Visuals Unlimited; (*c*) Wally Eberhart/Visuals Unlimited; (*b*) Adam Jones/Visuals Unlimited; **34** (*l*) Biophoto Associates/Photo Researchers; **35** (*r*) LSHTM/Photo Researchers; **36** (*tl*) Jan Hinsch/Photo Researchers; (*cl*) Biophoto Associates/Photo Researchers; (*bg*) Astrid & Hanns-Frieder Michler/Photo Researchers; **37** (*cl*) Tom Adams/Visuals Unlimited; (*cr*) Science Photo Library/Photo Researchers; (*bl*) Dr. Kari Lounatmaa/Photo Researchers; **38** (*tr*) M.I. Walker/Photo Researchers; (*cl*) Microfield Scientific LTD/Photo Researchers; **40** (*bg*) Freeman Patterson/Masterfile; (*c*) Dan Suzio/Photo Researchers; **42** (*br*) Steve Satushek/Getty Images; **44** (inset) Norman Owen Tomalin/Bruce Coleman; (*bg*) David Noton/Masterfile; **45** (*tr*) James Richardson/Visuals Unlimited; (*tl*) Henry Robison/Visuals Unlimited; **46** (*tr*) Robert Pickett/CORBIS; (*tcr*) SciMAT/Photo Researchers; (*cr*) Carolina Biological/Visuals Unlimited; (*bc*) Jacqui Hurst/CORBIS; (*br*) E. R. Degginger/Color-Pic; (*bg*) CORBIS; **48** Roger Archibald/Animals Animals; **50** (*bl*) Frans Lanting/Minden Pictures; (*br*) Ken Lucas/Ardea London; **51** (*tl*) Michael & Patricia Fogden/Minden Pictures; **52** (*tl*) OSF/Mantis W.F./Animals Animals; (*cl*) Paul Sutherland/Inedependent Photography Network; (*cl*) Alex Fradkin/Images.com/Independent Photography Network; **53** (*tl*) Lightwave Photography/Animals Animals; (*cl*) Roger de la Harpe/Animals Animals; **54** (*r*) Pascal Goetgheluck/Ardea; **56** (*t*) James H Robinson/Photo Researchers; (*b*) Getty Images; **57** (*t*) Getty Images; (inset) Getty; **58** (*t*) JamesRobinson/Photo Researchers; (*b*) Roy Morsch/Corbis; **59** (*bg*) CORBIS; **62–63** Bill Curtsinger/Getty Images; **64** John Daniels/Ardea; **66** (*b*) Getty Images; **67** (*t*) Rob Lewine/CORBIS; (*cr*) Getty Images; **68** (*tl*) Ray Kachatorian/Getty Images; (*tr*) Gio Barto/Getty Images; (*bl*) AGE Fotostock; (*bc*) H. & D. Zielske/Peter Arnold, Inc.; (*br*) Jonathan Nourok/PhotoEdit; **69** (*tl*) Phil Degginger/Animals Animlas; (*tcl*) Klein/Hubert/Peter Arnold; (*tc*) Burke/Triolo Productions/Getty Images; (*tcr*) Jack Milchanowski/Visuals Unlimited; (*tr*) Frans Lanting/Minden Pictures; (*cr*) Arthur Morris/Visuals Unlimited; **70** (*tr*) E. A. Janes/AGE Fotostock; (*cr*) Bruce Coleman, Inc.; (*bl*) John Anderson/Animals Animals; (*br*) Cheryl Ertlet/Visuals Unlimited; **72** Dwight Kuhn; **74** (*bl*) Brent Bergherm/AGE Fotostock; (*bc*) Rachel Weill/Getty Images; (*br*) Carltons/Getty Images; **76** (*cl*) Michael Gadomski/Photo Researchers; (*br*), (*cr*) Dwight Kuhn; **77** (*br*) Steve Satushek/AGE Fotostock; **78** (*l*) Santiago Fernandez/AGE Fotostock; (*r*), (*cl*) Alamy Images; (*cr*) Dwight Kuhn; (*bg*) Bernard Photo Productions/Animals Animals; **80** Ray Coleman/Visuals Unlimited; **82** (*tr*) SuperStock; (*bl*) Georgette Douwma/Getty Images; (*br*) Zigmund Leszczynski/Animals Animals; **83** (*l*) Curtis Richter/Alamy Images; (*r*) Morales/AGE Fotostock; **84** (*r*) Cosmos Blank/Photo Researchers; (*cl*) Norbert Rosing/Getty Images; (*bl*) Tom Brakefield/CORBIS; **85** (*tl*) Susan Solie Patterson/CORBIS; (*tr*) David Zelick/Getty Images; (*cl*) Photodisc/Getty Images; (*c*) Photodisc/Getty Images; (*cr*) Hans-George Gaul/Getty Images; **86** (*cl*), (*cr*) & (*bl*) Dwight Kuhn; (*br*) Patti Murray/Animals Animals; **91** (*bg*) USDA/Science Source/Photo Researchers; **94–95** Dave Watts/Nature Picture Library; **96** Luiz C. Marigo/Peter Arnold; **98** Peter Arnold/Peter Arnold, Inc.; **99** (*cr*) E & P Bauer/Bruce Coleman, Inc.; (*br*) Gil Lopez Espina/Visuals Unlimited; **99** (*cl*) Masa Ushioda/Bruce Coleman, Inc.; **100** (*cl*) Jean Paul Ferrero/Ardea London; (*cr*) Lynn Stone/Animals Animals; (*bl*) Michael & Patricia Fogden/Minden Pictures; (*br*) David Moore/Alamy Images; **101** (*t*) Chase Swift/CORBIS; (*tcr*) Alan G. Nelson/Animals Animals; **102** (*cl*) Brad Mitchell/Alamy Images; (*b*) Robert W. Domm/Visuals Unlimted; **104** Francois Gohier/Ardea; **106** (*bl*) Bernard Castelein/Nature Picture Library; (*bcr*) Hanne & Jens Eriksen/Nature Picture Library; **107** (*tr*) Patti Murray/Animals Animals; (*tcr*) Georgette Douwma/Nature Picture Library; (*cr*) Dietmar Nill/Nature Picture Library; (*bl*) Jennifer Loomis/Animals Animals; (*br*) Doug Wechsler/Animals Animals; **108** (*tr*) Nigel Bean/Nature Picture Library; (*br*) Bob Cranston/Animals Animals; **109** (*tr*) Staffan Widstrand/Nature Picture Library; (*bcr*) Arthur Morris/CORBIS; **110** (*tr*) Ray Richardson/Animals Animals; (*c*) Michael Habicht/Animals Animals; (*bl*) M. Watson/Ardea; **112** Tammy L. Johnson/Florida Museum of Natural History; **114** (*bg*) Mitsuaki Iwago/Minden Images; (*cr*) Paul A. Souders/CORBIS; (*br*) Roger Harris/Science Photo Library; **115** (*t*)(*bg*) SuperStock; (*tl*) Jeff Gage/Florida Museum of Natural History; (*cr*) Peter Scoones/Science Photo Library; (*br*) Dr. Schwimmer/Bruce Coleman, Inc.; **116** (*bg*) Carol Havens/Corbis; (*br*) Kevin Schafer/CORBIS; **117** (*tl*) E.R. Degginger/Bruce Coleman, Inc.; (*tc*) Barry Runk/Stan/Grant Heilman Photography; (*tr*) Ken Lucas/Visuals Unlimited; (*bl*) Patti Murray/Animals Animals; (*bcl*) D. Robert & Lorri Franz/CORBIS; (*br*) David Cavagnaro/Visuals Unlimited; **118** (*cl*) Gianni Dagli Orti/CORBIS; (*cr*) Hulton Archive/Getty Images; (*b*) Ron Testa/The Field Museum; **121** (*tr*) Luiz C. Marigo/Peter Arnold; **122** (*t*) Whitehead Institute for Biomedical Research; (*b*) Photo Researchers; **123** (*bg*) Dwight Kuhn; **125** (*tl*) Hal Brindley/VWPICS/Alamy Images.

Unit B

126–127 Joann Whitmore; **127** AP/Wide World Photos; **128–129** Fritz Polking/Visuals Unlimited; **130** Bob Thomas/Getty Images; **132** (*cr*) Bob & Clara Calhoun/Bruce Coleman; (*br*) Beth Davidow/Visuals Unlimited; **132** (*b*) Cathy Melloan/PhotoEdit; **133** (*t*) E. R. Degginger/Bruce Coleman, Inc.; (*cl*) George Sanker/Bruce Coleman, Inc.; **134** (*t*) Dennis MacDonald/PhotoEdit; (*tl*) Dennis MacDonald/PhotoEdit; **135** (*bl*) Steve Maslowski/Visuals Unlimited; (*b*) Kenneth Fink/Bruce Coleman, Inc.; **136** (*cl*) Jeremy Woodhous/Getty Images; **138** Karl Kummels/SuperStock; **140** (*c*) Jerome Wexler/Visuals Unlimited; (*bl*) Adam Jones/Visuals Unlimited; (*br*) Rob Simpson/Visuals Unlimited; **141** David L. Shirk/Animals Animals; **145** (*tr*) Greg Neise/Visuals Unlimited; (*tl*) Julie Eggers/Bruce Coleman, Inc.; (*cl*) Adam Jones/Visuals Unlimited; (*cr*) Richard Thom/Visuals Unlimited; (*bl*) Patrick Endres/Visuals Unlimited; (*br*) Eastcott-Momatiuk/The Image Works; **148** Jim Richardson/CORBIS; **150** (*bl*) Dennis Brack/IPN; (*b*) Joel Sartore/Getty Images; (*tl*) Micheal Rose/Photo Researchers; (*tr*) Stuart Westmorland/CORBIS; (*cl*) CORBIS; (*cr*) Masterfile; **152** (*tcr*) Susan Van Etten/Photo Edit; (*r*) Mark Richards/PhotoEdit; (*bcr*) Steve Maslowski/Visuals Unlimited; (*br*) Rick Poley/Visuals Unlimited; **153** (*tl*) Cary Wolinsky/IPN; (*tr*) Nancy Richmond/The Image Works; **154** (*cr*) Frank Ordonez/Syracuse Newspapers/The Image Works; (*bl*) CORBIS; **156–157** All Photos NOAA; **158** (*bg*)Index Stock; (inset) Courtesy Mutual of Omaha; **159** (*bg*) Dennis MacDonald/Alamy Images; **161** (*b*) Eastcott-Momatiuk/The Image Works; **162–163** Tom and Pat Leeson; **164** Kim Taylor/Bruce Coleman, Inc.; (*tl*) Darrell Gulin/CORBIS; (*tr*) Lynn Stone/Animals Animals; (*br*) D. Robert & Lorri Franz/CORBIS; **169** (*tc*) Lynn Stone/Animals Animals; (*cl*) Kevin Schafer/CORBIS; (*cr*) Bob Barber/Barber Nature Photography; (*bl*) Michael Fogden/Animals Animals; **170** (*cr*) Wolfgang Kaehler/CORBIS; (*cl*) Ken Lucas/Visuals Unlimited; (*b*) Jim Brandenburg/Minden Picures; **171** (*br*) D.Hurst/Alamy Images; **172** CDC/PHIL/CORBIS; **174** (*cr*) Gerry Ellis/Minden Pictures; (*b*) Royalty-Free/CORBIS; (*br*) Darrell Gulin/CORBIS; **174** (*tr*) ZSSD/MINDEN PICTURES; **175** (*tl*) CORBIS; (*tr*) Dale Sanders/Masterfile; (*c*) Andrew J. Martinez/Photo Researchers; (*br*) Dale Sanders/Masterfile; **176** (*bl*) M. Timothy O'Keefe/Bruce Coleman, Inc.; (*br*) Doug Perrine/SeaPics.com; (*bg*) Wolfgang Kaehler/CORBIS; **177** (*tl*) Jim Zipp/Photo Researchers; (*tc*) Bill Brooks/Masterfile; (*cr*) Barry Runk/Stan/Grant Heilman Photography; (*bl*) Joe McDonald/CORBIS; **182** (*bl*) Animals Animals; **183** (*t*) Wildlife Conservation Society; (*br*) Animals Animals; **184** (*t*) Assign Nature Conservation Foundation; (*b*) Corbis; **185** (*bg*) Mark Mattock/Getty Images

Unit C

188–189 Larry Crumpler/New Mexico Museum of Natural History and Science; **189** John Elk III; **190–191** Keren Su/CORBIS; **192** Kerrick James/Getty Images; **194** (*bl*) Herve Berthoule/JACANA/Science Photo Library; (*bc*) Mark A. Schneider/Visuals Unlimited; (*br*) Bildagentur/Alamy Images; **195** (*tl*) Arnold Fisher/Science Photo Library; (*cl*) Marli Miller/Visuals Unlimited; **195** (*tr*) Marli Miller/Visuals Unlimited; (*cr*) Michael Barnett/Science Photo Library; **196** (*cl*), (*tcr*), (*cr*), & (*bl*) Wally Eberhart/Visuals Unlimited; (*br*) Sciencephotos/Alamy Images; **197** (*tl*) Glenn Oliver/Visuals Unlimited; (*tr*) E. R. Degginger/Color-Pic; (*cl*) Joyce Photographics/Photo Researchers; (*cr*) Wally Eberhart/Visuals Unlimited; **198** (*tcr*) A. J. Copley/Visuals Unlimited; (*bcr*) & (*bl*) Wally Eberhart/Visuals Unlimited; (*br*) Joyce Photographics/Photo Researchers; **200** Ronen Zilberman/AP Photo; **204** (*tr*) Ed Degginger/Color-Pic; (*bl*) Albert J. Copley/Visuals Unlimited; **206–207** (*tr*) John Lawrence/Getty Images; **208** (*bcr*) Peter Kubal/Pan Photo; (*b*) Claire Selby/Animals Animals; **209** (*bg*) AP PHOTO; **210** (*cl*) Freeman Patterson/Masterfile; (*b*) George and Monserrate Schwartz/Alamy Images; **211** (*t*) Masterfile; (*cr*) John Kieffer/Peter Arnold, Inc.; **212** (*r*) Jim Wark/Airphoto; (*bl*) Greg Probst; **214** Louie Psihoyos/IPN; **218** (*b*) Wally Eberhart/Visuals Unlimited; **219** (*tc*) Roland Liptak/Alamy Images(*tr*) Peter Griffith/Masterfile; **219** (*tl*) Jim Craigmyle/CORBIS; (*fg*) Diane Hirsch/Fundamental Photographs; **220** (*bl*) Nigel Cattlin/Alamy Images; (*br*) Jeff Morgan/Alamy Images; **221** (*br*) Dorothea Lange/Library of Congress; **222** Roger Wood/Corbis; **222–223** Stone/Getty Images; **224** (*t*) Photographer's Choice/Getty Images; (*b*) AP/Wide World Photos; **225** (*bg*) Tom Vezo/Peter Arnold, Inc.; **228–229** Mediacolor's/Alamy Images; **230** G. Alan Nelson Outdoor Photography; **232** (*bl*) Paul A. Souders/Corbis; (*br*) Darrell Gulin/Corbis; **233** (inset) Gary Yeowell/Getty Images; (*bg*) Josef Beck/Getty Images; **234** (*bg*) James Strachan/Getty Images; (inset) AirphotoNA.com; **235** (*t*) NASA/Corbis, **235** (*b*) David Muench/Corbis; **236** (*cr*) Photri/Topham/The Image Works; (*b*) Douglas Peebles; **238** Jean-Paul Ferrero/Ardea; **241** (*bg*) David Paterson/Getty Images; **242** (*bg*) Bernhard Edmaier/Science Photo Library; **243** (*tr*) David Butow/Corbis SABA; (*br*) David Hume Kennerly/Getty Images; **244** (*tr*) Ernest Manewal/Index Stock Imagery; (*br*) Pat O'Hara/CORBIS; **245** (*tr*) Arnulf Husmo/Getty Images; (*tl*) Harvey Lloyd/Getty Images; **246** (*bg*) M. T. O'Keefe/Robertstock.com; (inset) Mark Gibson/Index Stock Imagery; **248** James L. Amos/Corbis; **250** (*bg*) Runk/Schoenberger/Grant Heilman Photography, Inc.; **251** (*tl*) Francois Gohier/Photo Researchers; (*tr*) Eberhard Grames/Bilderberg/Peter Arnold, Inc.; (*c*) Imagenes de Nuestro Mundo; **252** (inset) Indiana Dept. of Natural Resources/Falls of the Ohio State Park; (*b*) Indiana Dept. of Natural Resources/Falls of the Ohio River; **253** (*cr*) Sinclair Stammers/Photo Researchers; **259** (*bg*) James King-Holmes/Science Photo Library; **261** (*bl*) Martin Siepmann/AGE footstock

Unit D

262 The Daily Journal, International Falls, MN.; **262–263** Eddie Brady/Lonely Planet Images; **264–265** SuperStock; **266** Jeff Greenberg/The Image Works; **274** David Sailors/CORBIS; **276** (*b*) Royalty-Free/CORBIS; (*tr*) Oote Boe/Alamy Images; (*cr*) Layne Kennedy/Dembinksy Photo Assoc.; (*b*) Rob Atkins/Getty Images; **278** (*tr*) Royalty-Free/CORBIS; (*bl*) Alaska Stock Images; **279** (*bg*) Royalty-Free/CORBIS; **280** (*cl*) Gene Rhoden; (*cr*) Micheal Heller/911 Pictures; (*bl*) Silver Image; (*br*) Richard Cummins/CORBIS; **282** Alan R. Moller/Getty Images; **285** (*cr*) NOAA/AP Photo; **288** Gene Rhoden/Peter Arnold, Inc.; **293** (*tl*) Eastcott/Momatiuk/The Image Works; (*tr*) Tom Dietrich/Getty Images; (*cl*) John Eastcott & Yva Momatiuk/Getty Images; (*cr*) George Post/Photo Researchers; (*b*) Getty Images; (*tc*) Paul Seheult; (*tcr*) Burke/Triolo Productions/Getty Images; (*c*) David Young-Wolff/Photo Edit; (*bg*) Eye Ubiquitous/CORBIS; **301** (*bg*) Robert Carr/Bruce Coleman, Inc.; **303** (*tl*) Layne Kennedy/Dembinsky Photo Associates; **304–305** David Nunuk/Photo Researchers; **306** Warren Flagler/Index Stock Imagery; **313** (*bl*) Gianni Dagli Orti/CORBIS; **314** NASA/JPL/Space Science Institute; **316** (*bg*) StockTrek/Getty Images; (*bcr*) USGS /Photo Researchers; **317** (*tr*) US Geological Survey/Photo Researchers; (*bcr*) Getty Images; **318** (*bg*) Getty Images; (*br*) & (*cl*) NASA; **319** (*tr*) NASA; (*c*) Getty Images; (*bl*) STScl/NASA/Photo Researchers; **320** (*c*) Jerry Lodriguss/Photo Researchers; (*bl*) Reuters/CORBIS; **322** Reuters/CORBIS; **324** (*bl*) GoodShoot/SuperStock; **326** (*bl*) John Chumack/Photo Researchers; **327** (*bg*) Celestial Image Co./Photo Researchers; (*bl*) NASA; **330–331** All photos NASA; **332** (*t*) Photo Researchers; (*b*) Tony Freeman/Photo Researchers; (inset) Peter Falkner; **333** (*bg*) Frank Zullo/Photo Researchers

BEHAVIOR Playing helps wolf cubs develop strength and hunting skills.

HOWLING Wolves howl to communicate with other wolves or sometimes just for fun.

BEHAVIOR Wolves bare their teeth when they are angry.

SPEED Wolves can run up to 56 kilometers per hour.

SENSES Wolves can hear prey up to 12 km away, can smell prey up to 3 km away, and have excellent eyesight.